D0400907

Saracens

Saracens

Islam in the Medieval European Imagination

John V. Tolan

LCCC LIBRARY

Columbia University Press

New York

Columbia University Press
Publishers Since 1893
New York   Chichester, West Sussex

© 2002 Columbia University Press
All rights reserved

Library of Congress Cataloging-in-Publication Data
Tolan, John Victor, 1959–
Saracens : Islam in the medieval European imagination / John V. Tolan.
p.   cm.
Includes bibliographical references and index.
ISBN 0-231-12332-9 (cloth: alk. paper)—ISBN 0-231-12333-7 (pbk.: alk. paper)
1. Christianity and other religions—Islam.   2. Islam—Relations—Christianity.
3. Islam—Historiography.   4. Middle Ages—Historiography.   I. Title.
BP172 .T62 2002
261.2'7—dc21   2001047706

∞

Columbia University Press books are
printed on permanent and durable acid-free paper.

Printed in the United States of America

c 10 9 8 7 6 5 4 3 2 1
p 10 9 8 7 6 5 4 3 2 1

This book is dedicated to the memory of my father, Larry Tolan

22,50
3-0-0220

Contents

ఴఞఴ

Acknowledgments

I WOULD HAVE BEEN unable to complete this book without the generous support I received from the American Historical Association, the
University of North Carolina at Greensboro, the National Endowment for
the Humanities, the American University in Cairo, the University of Wisconsin Institute for Research in the Humanities, and the American Council
of Learned Societies.

Portions of this book have been presented at the following seminars
and colloquia: the Annual Congress of Medieval Studies, Kalamazoo, Michigan; the Medieval Studies Program, University of Wisconsin; the University of Wisconsin Institute for Research in the Humanities; the Medieval
Academy of America; the Instytut Historii, Łódź, Poland; the Centre d'Études
Supérieures de Civilisation Médiévale, Université de Poitiers; Casa de Velázquez, Madrid; the Centre de Recherches Historiques, École des Hautes
Études en Sciences Sociales, Paris; the Collège d'Espagne, Paris; the bi-
annual congress of the New Chaucer Society; the American University of
Cairo; the American Historical Association; the Medieval Association of
the Pacific; UC-Riverside Medieval Studies Colloquium; and the Midwest
Medieval History Association. My thanks to those who invited me to these
events and to those who provided comments and corrections, in particu-
lar: Charles Amiel, Jacques Berlioz, Jodi Bilinkoff, David Blanks, Stéphane
Boisselier, Paul Boyer, Thomas Burman, Michael Chamberlain, Malgorzata
Dąbrowska, Robert Durand, Ana Echevarria, Alberto Ferreiro, Jean Flori,
Piotr Gorecki, Sidney Griffith, Philippe Josserand, Christopher Kleinhenz,
Kathryn Miller, David Nirenberg, Marie-Anne Polo de Beaulieu, Amy Rem-
ensnyder, Adeline Rucquoi, Jean-Claude Schmitt, Philippe Sénac, Michael
Shank, Larry Simon. Thanks to Edward Colbert for sending me a copy of
his *Martyrs of Córdoba.*

A number of people have read drafts of this book and have offered invaluable suggestions, questions, and corrections: special thanks to Lamis Andoni, Robert Bartlett, Thomas Burman, Adnan Husain, Jean-Claude Schmitt, Larry Simon, and Sandy Tolan.

I also thank my graduate students for sharing my interest in medieval ideologies and for deepening my understanding of these issues as they researched their own projects. I particularly thank Nicolas Boyer, Mickaël Guichaoua, Laurence Lechappe, and Arzhela Rouxel.

And finally, my thanks to Michelle, who has heard and read much of what follows in various forms and has frequently contributed enthusiastic support and critical good sense. And thanks to Paraska and Marie, who have worked hard at keeping the author of this book from becoming completely obsessed with this project and from taking himself too seriously.

Abbreviations

✣

Listed below are abbreviations for works cited most frequently in this study. They appear in the notes and in the select bibliography.

AASS   *Acta Sanctorum*

CCCM   *Corpus Christianorum continuatio medieaevalis*. Turnhout: Brepols.

CSM   Juan Gil, ed. *Corpus Scriptorum Muzarabicorum*. 2 vols. Madrid: Consejo Superior de Investigaciones Científicas, 1973.

DHGE   *Dictionnaire d'Histoire et de Géographie Ecclésiastiques*

DS   *Dictionnaire de la Spiritualité*

EI²   *Encyclopaedia of Islam*. 2d edition. Leiden, 1960–.

MGH   Monumenta Germaniae Historica

MGH AA   Monumenta Germaniae Historica, Auctores

MGH SS   Monumenta Germaniae Historica, *Scriptores*

MOFPH   *Monumenta Ordinis Fratrum Praedicatorum Historica* (Rome and Stuttgart)

PG   J. P. Migne, ed. *Patrologiae graecae cursus completus*. 162 vols. Paris, 1857–86.

PL   J. P. Migne, ed. *Patrologiae latinae cursus completus*. 217 vols. Paris, 1844–64.

RHC occ   *Recueil des Historiens des Croisades: Historiens Occidentaux*. 5 vols. Paris, 1841–1906.

Typologie   L. Genicot, dir., *Typologie des sources du moyen âge occidental* Turnhout: Brepols, 1972–.

Introduction:
Riccoldo's Predicament, or How to Explain Away the Successes of a Flourishing Rival Civilization

ᰔᖇᖙ

And so it came to pass that I was in Baghdad, "among the captives by the river of Chebar" [Ezek. 1:1], the Tigris. This garden of delights in which I found myself enthralled me, for it was like a paradise in its abundance of trees, its fertility, its many fruits. This garden was watered by the rivers of Paradise, and the inhabitants built gilt houses all around it. Yet I was saddened by the massacre and capture of the Christian people. I wept over the loss of Acre, seeing the Saracens joyous and prospering, the Christians squalid and consternated: little children, young girls, old people, whimpering, threatened to be led as captives and slaves into the remotest countries of the East, among barbarous nations.

Suddenly, in this sadness, swept up into an unaccustomed astonishment, I began, stupefied, to ponder God's judgment concerning the government of the world, especially concerning the Saracens and the Christians. What could be the cause of such massacre and such degradation of the Christian people? Of so much worldly prosperity for the perfidious Saracen people? Since I could not simply be amazed, nor could I find a solution to this problem, I decided to write to God and his celestial court, to express the cause of my astonishment, to open my desire through prayer, so that God might confirm me in the truth and sincerity of the Faith, that he quickly put an end to the law, or rather the perfidy, of the Saracens, and more than anything else that he liberate the Christian captives from the hands of the enemies.

—Riccoldo da Montecroce, *Epistolae V de perditione Acconis* (1291)

R ICCOLDO DA MONTECROCE expresses all the ambivalence, the attraction and repulsion, that medieval Latin Christendom felt for the world of Islam. Having come to Baghdad to preach Christianity, he finds himself in awe and admiration of the beauty, the wealth, and (as he says elsewhere) the learning of Baghdad—even though the city is only a shadow of the grandeur it once enjoyed as the capital of the 'Abbasid caliphate. His admiration does not extend to Islam, which he describes as "perfidy." By 1291 he had spent three years in the Muslim East, trying (with little success) to convert Muslims to Christianity. On May 18, al-Ashraf Khalîl, Mamluk Sultan of Egypt, captured Acre, the last crusader outpost on the mainland. Riccoldo contemplates in distress as the booty from Acre fills the markets of Baghdad: liturgical books, slaves. How could God allow this to happen?

For God is the moving force behind history, for the Christian (or Muslim, or Jew) of the Middle Ages. God picks the winners and losers, and his judgments are always righteous. The Muslims (or "Saracens," as Riccoldo calls them) seem smugly satisfied with their victory, yet another proof that God is on their side. How can a Christian explain such a setback? Can it be that God indeed prefers the religion of the victors? Riccoldo prays that God help him combat his doubt: "confirm me in the truth and sincerity of the Faith." If Riccoldo is to remain Christian, he needs to answer this perplexing question: how and why should God allow his Christians to be defeated by Muslims? Riccoldo feels the attraction of Muslim civilization—its wealth, culture, learning; indeed, this attraction makes it all the more necessary for him to affirm his Christian identity, to argue for the superiority of Christianity over the "Saracen perfidy." Christendom is in peril, and Riccoldo needs to reassure his reader (and himself) that God is still on the Christians' side. To do so, he has to explain Islam's role in Christian history and to define it theologically.

Countless Christians, throughout the Middle Ages and beyond, found themselves in Riccoldo's predicament: confronted by an expanding, dynamic Muslim civilization, they needed to make sense of it. In the first century of Islam, most of the former Christian Roman Empire, from Syria to Spain, was brought under Muslim control in a conquest of unprecedented proportions. How was God's apparent abandonment of his Christian Empire to be explained? True, over the course of the Middle Ages Christian states conquered (or "reconquered") many of the islands of the Mediterranean, all of the Iberian peninsula, and even, for a fleeting eighty-eight years, Jerusalem, Holy City to three religions. Yet at the same time, Islam was expanding across Asia and Africa and (with the rise of the Ottomans in the late fourteenth century) into the heart of Europe. How were Christians to respond? The simplest and obvious choice, for many, was to accept the logic of Muslim expansion; God must indeed prefer Islam; historical destiny and social pressure offered strong arguments in favor of conversion to Islam.

Those Christians who rejected conversion, who chose to remain Christian, needed to come up with another explanation. This was to be sought, naturally, in authoritative books: the Bible and the writings of church fathers. These were indeed a rich source of explanation: the Hebrew prophets, Gospel, and the book of Revelation spoke of the tribulations that God's people were to suffer at the hands of infidel oppressors. These passages were redeployed and reinterpreted to make sense of the Muslim victories.

We live in an age where ecumenism, dialogue, and tolerance are often evoked (if not as often practiced) in relations between mainstream religious groups. We define Islam and Christianity as two distinct and valid "religions" among many. In many countries, the choice of religion is (at least in theory) a matter of personal choice, with different religions considered equal before a lay state. Such a perspective was not possible in the Middle Ages. For Muslims, Christians, and Jews of the Middle Ages, there could be only one true "religion," just as there was only one God. Rival faiths were at best imperfect expressions of the true religion, at worst diabolically inspired error. There was no "lay" state; as each ruler claimed to uphold God's law, each saw God as the source of his authority over his subjects. One was born into a religious community, and one's community determined one's legal status: Jews, Christians, and Muslims had separate, segregated legal and judicial systems, whether they lived in Baghdad or Barcelona. Ecumenism was not available to the medieval Christian: confronted with the astounding successes of Islam, many Christians embraced the faith of the prophet Muhammad. Among those who did not, a number assigned to Islam a place in the pantheon of God's enemies in order to discourage fellow Christians from converting to Islam or to justify military action against Muslims. It is the anti-Muslim works of these Christian authors from the seventh to the thirteenth century that constitute the subject of this book.

"Islam" in Arabic means submission, submission to God's will; a "Muslim" is one who has submitted to God's will. Yet medieval Christian writers did not speak of "Islam" or "Muslims," words unknown (with very few exceptions) in Western languages before the sixteenth century.[1] Instead, Christian writers referred to Muslims by using ethnic terms: Arabs, Turks, Moors, Saracens. Often they call them "Ishmaelites," descendants of the biblical Ishmael, or Hagarenes (from Hagar, Ishmael's mother). Their religion is referred to as the "law of Muhammad" or the "law of the Saracens."

The major and still-dominant book about medieval Christian polemical portrayals of Islam is Norman Daniel's *Islam and the West: The Making of an Image* (1960, republished in a slightly revised version in 1993); it was followed by Richard Southern's brief *Western Views of Islam in the Middle Ages* (1962). Since these two books, there have been numerous detailed studies on particular aspects of Christian-Muslim relations in the Middle Ages, but no general study on medieval Christian images of Islam.[2]

This lacuna is all the more striking when compared with the plethora of studies on medieval Christendom's portrayals of Jews and heretics. Robert Moore's *Formation of a Persecuting Society: Power and Deviance in Western Europe, 950-1250* (1987), explores the links between clerical ideologies of power and the identification and persecution of various groups of "deviants": Jews, heretics, lepers, homosexuals—but not Muslims. Since 1945 many books have been written—in Europe, North America, and Israel—exploring and debating what are often called the "medieval roots of anti-Semitism." Others have examined medieval strategies of caricaturing and demonizing "heretics," often a convenient label pinned on dissenters from prevailing ruling or clerical ideologies. Yet others have exposed the medieval European image of the geographical other: Africa and the Far East. But no book has attempted on a broad scale to examine Christian images of Islam from this perspective; none has attempted to elucidate the medieval roots of modern Western attitudes toward Islam and toward Arabs.

This book is an attempt to fill this gap: to examine how and why medieval Christians portrayed Islam—or rather, portrayed what they preferred to call the "law of the Saracens." I hope to complement, rather than replace, the work done by Norman Daniel forty years ago. Daniel was first and foremost a scholar of Islam: he cataloged in great detail what many medieval Christians wrote about Muhammad, the Koran, and Muslim ritual. He was also a Catholic devoted to finding new, less adversarial strategies for creating dialogue with Muslims in hopes of eventually converting them to Christianity; indeed his basic outlook was not so far removed from that of the more irenic of the thirteenth-century authors he discussed.[3] Daniel was shocked by the inaccuracy and hostility of what he found in many of the medieval texts he analyzed, and understandably so. Medieval Christian writings about Islam contain much that is appalling to the twentieth-century reader: crude insults to the Prophet, gross caricatures of Muslim ritual, deliberate deformation of passages of the Koran, degrading portrayals of Muslims as libidinous, gluttonous, semihuman barbarians. Daniel's reaction to his own catalog of such hostile caricature is to shake his head in sad consternation. Yet there is little in his book to suggest *why* Christian writers presented Islam in this way or what ideological interests these portrayals might have served. This is all the more unfortunate because Daniel's work has become *the* reference in its field: Edward Said, in his *Orientalism,* bases most of his short passage about the Middle Ages on Daniel's book.

There is no need to stress the importance of the history of relations between Muslims and Christians ever since the *Hijra:* anyone familiar with Western news media can see that Western attitudes toward Muslims and toward Arabs (terms that are often poorly distinguished) are still problematic, still tinged with condescension and mistrust, still rife with contradictions.[4] One could retort that the same is true about Muslim attitudes toward Christianity or about Arab attitudes toward the West. True enough, but that is not the subject of this book. A sentiment of Western superiority over Muslims and over Arabs runs deep in European and North American culture: this sentiment has its roots in the Middle Ages. "Roots" is a deliberately vague term: I do not mean to suggest that twentieth-century Europeans and North Americans have passively inherited a prejudice that has remained unchanged since the thirteenth century. Thirteenth-century Europeans defined their perceived "superiority" primarily as religious (though cultural and other concerns were inseparable from religion); their twentieth-century counterparts tend to see themselves as culturally or intellectually superior: more "enlightened," more technologically advanced, and so on. Feelings of rivalry, contempt, and superiority have existed on both sides all through the intervening centuries, tinged or tempered at times with feelings of doubt, inferiority, curiosity, or admiration.

At the turn of the twenty-first century, drawing such connections between medieval and modern attitudes toward Muslims may seem farfetched. Not so for René Grousset, writing the history of the crusades in 1934; he cites a passage in which the Muslim traveler Ibn Jubayr affirms that the Christian rulers of the crusading states often treat their subjects as well or better than Muslim rulers. Ibn Jubayr meant this comment to be more a criticism of incompetent and greedy petty lords in Muslim Syria than anything else, but for Grousset this represents "the finest praise of French colonization."[5] As France and England carved out empires in the Arab world, Grousset and others looked to the Crusades as a glorious precursor. The accolades of a Muslim writer of the twelfth century could be used to justify conquest and colonization in the nineteenth or twentieth. It is no accident that the Hall of the Crusades in Versailles, whose murals dramatize the exploits of the medieval crusaders, was painted in the 1830s, as France was conquering Algeria. Various twentieth-century Arab writers have in their turn portrayed French and British colonists as heirs to the greed and fanaticism of the medieval crusaders.[6] The Middle Ages are of more than academic interest for those concerned with relations between Europe and the Muslim world.

This book is also meant to complement Edward Said's *Orientalism*, which has inspired much debate and much emulation since its publication in 1978. Said describes convincingly (if polemically) the ideological implications of representations of the Orient in nineteenth- and twentieth-century British and French culture. "Orientalism," for Said, is "Western style for dominating, restructuring, and having authority over the Orient."[7] Orientalism as discourse, for Said, is the ideological counterpart to the political and military realities of British and French empires in the Near East: orientalism provides justification for empire. In the same way, from the seventh century to the thirteenth, anti-Muslim discourse by Christian authors is used to authorize and justify military action, legal segregation, and social repression of Muslims. This is not to say that Said's schema can be unproblematically transferred back six or ten centuries: during much of the Middle Ages, Europe was in a position of military, economic, and intellectual inferiority to the Muslim world; nineteenth-century Europeans were convinced of their superiority. A careful look at the relations in the Middle Ages will shed light on both sides of this equation.

WHY CONCLUDE this study with the thirteenth century? Because in the twelfth and thirteenth centuries Latin Europe first came to terms with and tried to confront the world of Islam. That confrontation was in part military: crusade and Spanish *reconquista*. But it was also intellectual: European scholars studied philosophy and science in Arabic treatises, many of which they translated into Latin. Theologians attempted to prove, through preaching and rational argumentation, Christian truth to Muslims (as well as to Jews and heretics); this movement was a dismal failure, as writers of the thirteenth and fourteenth centuries increasingly admitted. At the same time, Christian authors tried to define and limit the place of Muslims in Christian society (through legislation) and in Christian history (through chronicles and theological tracts). If the Muslim "other" could not be eliminated through war or conversion, at least he could be intellectually and socially circumscribed.

The following centuries showed little innovation in approaches to what was considered the "problem" of Islam. The solutions of the thirteenth century were recycled: Popes and publicists urged princes to crusade against the "Turk" in much the same language as their thirteenth-century counterparts (albeit at times in humanistic Latin style); polemicists compiled the anti-Muslim arguments of their thirteenth-century forbears, rather than creating their own. When Martin Luther sought to combat the religion of the "Turk," he did so by approving the printing of Latin texts from the twelfth century (including the earliest translation of the Koran) and by translating Riccoldo da Montecroce into German. The thirteenth century saw the crystallization of European images of Islam that were to endure (with minor variations) into the seventeenth century—and in some respects into the twentieth. Not that these variations are not in themselves worth studying: the arsenal of polemical images were reused in different ways and with different purposes in the varying contexts of Iberian colonization of Africa and America, expulsion of Muslims and Moriscos from the Iberian Peninsula, attempts to rally European opinion against the "Turk," European wars of religion—and straight through to the colonial program derided by Said. From the fourteenth century to the twentieth, Western authors writing about Muslims, Arabs, Turks, or Orientals, referred to the fundamental texts and images created from the seventh century to the thirteenth.

PART 1 of this book examines the mutual images of Christians and Muslims in the seventh and eighth centuries. "Arabs" or "Saracens" (the terms are often used interchangeably by medieval authors) are mentioned in the Bible, and they appear in the writings of church fathers such as Jerome and Isidore. The Christian writers of the seventh and eighth centuries, confronted with "Saracen" invasions, looked to the Bible and church fathers for information about who these Saracens were. The construction of a polemical image of Saracens started *before* the rise of Islam. For this reason, my first chapter presents the Christian worldview (and the Saracens' place in it) before Muhammad.

Chapter 2 examines how Muslims viewed Christianity and how their sacred texts (the Koran and the Hadîth, or traditions) present proper relations between Muslims and Christians. The Muslim conquests inspire in Muslim writers a triumphalist view of Muslim history. The goal in this chapter is to better understand the challenge that Islam represented to Christianity and to perceive the original meaning of the Muslim sources that were subsequently distorted under the hostile pens of Christian polemicists.

When, in 634, the caliph 'Umar entered Jerusalem as a conqueror, clad in a dirty camel-hair garment, it was a sweet victory for Muslims, a victory of the pious and humble, given by God's grace. It looked quite different, of course, to Sophronios, patriarch of Jerusalem, who proclaimed: "Verily, this is the abomination of desolation standing in a holy place, as has been spoken through the prophet Daniel."[8] Muslim victories were punishments of Christians' sins but in no way reflected God's approval of Islam. Chapter 3 examines the earliest Christian texts about Islam. Christian churchmen, thrust into the role of minority, struggled to discourage their flocks from converting to Islam: since the material advantages of conversion were clear, these authors needed to portray Islam as spiritually inferior to Christianity at the same time that they explained why God should allow the Muslims' stunning successes. Many of these authors presented Islam as a heresy, a debased version of the true religion, a creed devoted primarily to the worldly delights of sex, wealth, and power; Christianity, by contrast, was a religion of the next world and involved voluntary rejection of worldly pleasures. Some authors fabricated comforting prophecies of the imminent demise of Islam and the triumphant return of Christian Empire.

Part 2 considers Western Europe from the eighth to the twelfth centuries. Chapter 4 examines the first reactions of Latin writers as the Muslim invasions swept westward across North Africa and northward into Spain, Gaul, and Italy. Chroniclers such as Bede made little effort to distinguish these Saracens from the other "barbarian" invaders ravaging Europe; what little curiosity they exhibited was easily satisfied by cataloging what the Bible, Isidore, and other "authorities" had said about the Saracens. The situation was of course different in Spain, which had come under Muslim dominion. Ninth-century Spanish Christian writers offered a picture of Islam quite similar to that proffered by their eighth-century Eastern brethren: Islam as a worldly, debauched heresy, doomed to a swift demise.

These Spanish and Eastern Christians were hostile to Islam but relatively knowledgeable about it. Such is not the case with many medieval European writers, who (as I show in chapter 5) portray the Saracens as idolaters, praying and sacrificing to the statues of a colorful pantheon: Apollo, Tervagant, Jupiter, and especially Mahoumet (or various other garbled versions of the name Muhammad). Ecclesiastical writers schooled in the Latin classics had a vivid image of pagan worship, an image they transposed to create a portrait of the religious error of the "pagan" Saracens. The chroniclers of the first Crusade used this image to glorify and justify the crusaders' exploits. Epic poets developed the same images in the *Chansons de Geste;* fourteenth-century dramatists worked them into their passion plays. For many medieval authors, the Saracens were pagan idolaters.

Through increased contact with Muslims, many Christians realized how erroneous this image of Saracen paganism was. In the twelfth century, as contacts between the Latin West and the Muslim world multiplied (through trade, crusade, and intellectual exchange), some Latin writers learned more about Islam and attempted to incorporate that knowledge into their Christian worldview (as discussed in chapter 6). Peter the Venerable, abbot of Cluny, had the Koran translated into Latin. He and other authors studied the works of earlier Spanish Christian polemicists against Islam. These twelfth-century authors wrote theological refutations of Islam, trying to prove the superiority of Christianity. They viewed Islam as a heresy, an illegitimate deviation of the true religion. The culprit was Muhammad, portrayed as a scoundrel and trickster.

The thirteenth century saw a flourishing of different strategies to grapple with the "problem" of Islam: crusade, theological refutation, mission, martyrdom. Part 3 is devoted to exploring the complex and varied approaches to Islam in the thirteenth-century Latin West; the focus is on the development of the polemical images of Islam analyzed in part 2 and their deployment for specific ideological purposes: justification of conquest and subjugation of Muslims, elaboration of strategies to convert Muslims, and so on. Chapter 7 examines the use of anti-Muslim images in some of the chronicles and legal texts of thirteenth-century Spain. These polemical ideas, in particular the hostile biography of Muhammad, were used to deny any political legitimacy to Muslim rule in Spain and to justify the social and political subjugation of Muslim subjects of Spanish Christian rulers.

Chapter 8 examines how various chroniclers struggled to make sense of the Crusades, from the loss of Jerusalem in 1187 to the fall of Acre in 1291. Like their counterparts in earlier centuries, these chroniclers needed to explain the place of these events in the divine plan. Pope Innocent III identified Islam with the beast of the Apocalypse and hoped that new Crusades could bring about its demise. The chroniclers of these Crusades described the hopes raised by their initial successes and by rumors of a grand anti-Muslim alliance with the Mongols, and how these hopes were progressively dashed.

For many thirteenth-century Latin writers, one of the bright lights of their age was Francis of Assisi. Francis and his followers, the Friars Minor, or Franciscans, sought to rekindle the "apostolic life," a life of poverty, ascesis, and preaching modeled on that of the apostles. Mission to the infidel (in particular, to Muslims) played a significant role in this apostolic life; Francis himself preached to the Egyptian Sultan al-Kâmil in 1219, and in the following centuries many Franciscan missionaries followed in his footsteps. Their goal (the topic of chapter 9) was not merely to live the apostolic life but to die the apostolic death: the apostles, after all, found martyrdom at the hands of infidels, and thirteenth-century Franciscans found that when sufficiently provoked (through public insults to Muhammad and the Koran, for example), many Muslim rulers obligingly conferred the crown of martyrdom upon them.

The other great mendicant order of the thirteenth century, the Dominicans, took a different approach to mission to the Saracens (the subject of chapter 10). Formed in order to preach to Cathar heretics and devoted to a life of ascesis, the Dominicans soon expanded their missionary efforts to include Jews and Muslims. The Dominicans often preferred to preach to "captive" audiences of non-Christian subjects of Christian rulers. They also staged theological debates with prominent Muslim and Jewish leaders. To further their strategies, Dominican missionaries founded language schools (in particular, Arabic) and wrote polemical texts meant to provide "refutations" of Islam (and Judaism) ready to be deployed by Dominican missionaries. These missionaries traveled far and wide (Riccoldo da Montecroce reached Baghdad), yet met little success outside of Christian-controlled Spain.

Chapter 11 is devoted to the work of one man, Ramon Llull, a harsh critic of Franciscans and Dominicans, who formed his own idiosyncratic missionary strategy. The other missionaries were intellectually ill-equipped to convert infidels: ignorant of their languages and of the finer points of philosophy. Worse, he claims, there were some who knew enough philosophy to disprove Islam but not enough to prove the truth of Christianity: he accuses Dominican Ramon Martí of destroying the faith of the King of Tunis without providing him with a new faith, leaving him adrift. The starting point for religious dialogue should not be an attack on the rival religion but a search for a common ground of belief. On this common ground, positive philosophical argument can prove, Llull claimed, the Christian doctrines of the Trinity, Incarnation, and so on, without the need to resort to attacks on Muhammad and the Koran. Real Muslims (or Jews), however, showed little inclination to be converted by his arguments, and Llull gradually adopted a less irenic and more hostile depiction of Islam.

What is the point of this portrait gallery of Christian images of the Muslim other, images often (though not always) deformed, hostile, ugly? How is the reader meant to react? Not simply by wringing one's hands in regret at how awful "we" Westerners were to the Muslim other (or for the

Muslim reader, how awful the Christian "other" was to "us"). Nor should we feel smugly satisfied that we "moderns" are more tolerant and intelligent than our benighted medieval ancestors: the events of the twentieth century disprove this several times over. The point is to further our understanding of (or at least our reflection on) two problems, one specific and one more general. The first issue is to understand, in context, the development and expression of a variety of European images (most of them hostile) of the Muslim world, a civilization seen as a rival and a threat through the Middle Ages and beyond. The second issue involves how cultures define themselves over and against outside groups depicted as "enemies." The writers and works analyzed in these pages were not written in vacuums; they were written for specific audiences and for specific (and various) purposes. They provide concrete examples of how one perceived as other can be pinned down through discourse, made explicable, rendered inert, made useful (or at least harmless) to one's own ideological agenda. These examples of the social and ideological uses of contempt can be of interest to historians, anthropologists, and others who are not specifically interested in the Middle Ages. They show how the denigration of the other can be used to defend one's own intellectual construction of the world.

Saracens

Be courteous when you argue with the People of the Book, except with those among them who do evil. Say: "We believe in that which is revealed to us and which was revealed to you. Our God and your God is one. To Him we surrender ourselves."

Koran 29:46

Upon the Muslims, too, the Church looks with esteem. They adore one God, living and enduring, merciful and all-powerful, Maker of heaven and earth and Speaker to men. They strive to submit wholeheartedly even to His inscrutable decrees, just as did Abraham, with whom the Islamic faith is pleased to associate itself. Though they do not acknowledge Jesus as God, they revere him as a prophet. They also honor Mary, His virgin mother; at times they call on her, too, with devotion. In addition they await the day of judgment when God will give each man his due after raising him up. Consequently, they prize the moral life, and give worship to God especially through prayer, almsgiving, and fasting.

Although in the course of the centuries many quarrels and hostilities have arisen between Christians and Muslims, this most sacred Synod urges all to forget the past and to strive sincerely for mutual understanding. On behalf of all mankind, let them make common cause of safeguarding and fostering social justice, moral values, peace, and freedom.

Vatican II, "Declaration on the Relationship of the Church
to Non-Christian Religions"

Part One

FOUNDATIONS
(SEVENTH–EIGHTH CENTURIES)

Chapter 1
❧❦❧

GOD AND HISTORY IN THE CHRISTIAN WEST C. 600

It seems that whatever we perceive is organized into patterns for which we, the perceivers, are largely responsible. Perceiving is not a matter of passively allowing an organ—say of sight or hearing—to receive a ready-made impression from without, like a palette receiving a spot of paint. . . . It is generally agreed that all our impressions are schematically determined from the start. As perceivers we select from all the stimuli falling on our senses only those which interest us, and our interests are governed by a pattern-making tendency, sometimes called a schema. In a chaos of shifting impressions, each of us constructs a stable world in which objects have recognizable shapes, are located in depth, and have permanence. . . . Uncomfortable facts which refuse to be fitted in, we find ourselves ignoring or distorting so that they do not disturb these established assumptions. By and large anything we take note of is preselected and organized in the very act of perceiving. We share with other animals a kind of filtering mechanism which at first only lets in sensations we know how to use.

Mary Douglas, *Purity and Danger*

THESE OBSERVATIONS by anthropologist Mary Douglas aptly describe Christian attitudes toward Islam in the Middle Ages. Before the rise of Islam, Christians had established categories for the religious other: Jew, pagan, and heretic. When Christians encountered Muslims, they tried to fit them into one of those categories, "ignoring or distorting" those "uncomfortable facts" that did not fit the preestablished schema so as not to disturb these assumptions. Out of the chaos of the first centuries of Christian history, bedeviled by persecution, heresy, and the crumbling of much of the old Roman empire, Christian writers had labored to construct "a stable world in which objects have recognizable shapes." This Christian "filtering

3

mechanism" involved a belief that God is the moving force behind history: that everything in the natural world and every event in human history is part of God's grand scheme, a scheme that reflects his reason and justice.

Medieval Christians who attempted to understand, define, and characterize Islam were anything but detached, objective observers. Their perceptions of Muslims are based less on Islam than on their own Christian preconceptions of divine history and divine geography. The patristic writers of the first Christian centuries forged a vision of the world—its peoples, its religions, its history—that the advent of Islam would not change. In other words, when medieval Christians looked at Islam, they did so through the filter of the Bible and of writers such as Eusebius, Jerome, Augustine, and Isidore.

This is why I begin this survey of Christian perceptions of Islam *before* the rise of Islam. The point is to show how key Latin Christian authors of the seventh century viewed their world: in particular, how they defined the differences between Christian and non-Christians (Jews, pagans, and heretics) and what they saw as their place in history. For when they first meet Muslims they will try to understand their military successes and their religion in terms familiar to them, to fit Islam into already existing Christian categories by portraying them, variously, as a divinely sent punishment, as pagan idolaters, as Christian heretics, as followers of Satan, or as devotees of Antichrist. When these Christian authors wish to understand Islam, they will turn only rarely to Muslims themselves, normally preferring those time-honored authorities, the Bible and the church fathers. Medieval Christians, with very few exceptions, did not use the words "Muslim" or "Islam"; instead they used ethnic terms such as "Arab," "Saracen," "Ishmaelite." Information about these peoples could be found in the venerable books of old.

Few medieval authors embody the search for truth via dependence on authority better than Isidore of Seville, contemporary of Muhammad. Isidore not only compiles *florilegia* of earlier authorities but also becomes an authority who will be quoted throughout the Middle Ages. Both in the content and the method of his work, he illustrates the intellectual filtering common to many medieval authors. Authoritative explanations of the world around one are to be found in revered books. These books are timeless, never out of date; if the reality one sees around oneself does not seem to correspond to the models described on parchment, it is the evidence of the senses that must be questioned, not the authorities. Yet the authoritative books must be reread, reworked, reinterpreted in order to make sense of the reader's ever-changing world.

Isidore's numerous works include chronicles, biblical commentaries, theological tracts, and the *Etymologies,* which were perhaps *the* best-seller of the Middle Ages, surviving in close to one thousand medieval manuscripts.[1] They comprise a vast encyclopedic text into which Isidore poured knowledge gleaned from the Bible, Latin poets and geographers, and church fathers. Isidore's ambitious intellectual program represents an attempt to grasp the rational order of God's creation: to order human knowledge. The universe, for medieval Christians, was a rational creature. Created by God in six days, its structure was a reflection of divine wisdom. To study the universe was to study God's reason. History, too, had a rational, divinely ordained structure. Isidore, one of the great systematizers among medieval chroniclers, was conscious of living on the cusp of a new era. He witnessed the definitive break of his native Spain from its Roman past and celebrated the legitimacy of its Visigothic kings, newly converted from Arian heresy to Catholic orthodoxy. Modern scholars know Isidore as an encyclopedist, a compiler of the wisdom of the ancients into digests that will be used by countless medieval readers. His works show little originality in their content; this was an age when originality and innovation were to be shunned, not sought out. Yet what impresses, throughout Isidore's huge corpus of works (especially in his magnum opus, the *Etymologies,* or *Origins*), is a will to order the universe, to offer an organized, coherent summary of human knowledge.[2] While Isidore was compiling and constructing the sophisticated filtering system that generations of Christians would use to help perceive and understand the world around them, at the other end of the once-Roman world, Muhammad and the first generation of Muslims were creating a new religious community that would in time dominate most of that world. In order to understand how medieval Christian writers perceived Muslims, the Christian views of history and religious deviancy epitomized in the works of Isidore must first be understood.

Apocalypse Later: Isidore's Vision of Christian History

History, to the Christian writer (as to the Jew and the Muslim) is the working out of God's plan for humanity. For the three religions, the world has a beginning in time, the moment of God's creation. The subsequent history of humanity is a drama of the tumultuous relations between God and his people, with key human actors for God (prophets, saints, mahdî) and against him (false prophets, heretics, Antichrist). History has not only a beginning but an end: the final cataclysm of destruction and redemption. While in other religions God is timeless and man's history essentially cyclical, for the three Abrahamic monotheistic faiths, history is linear and the study of history is a window on the divine plan for humankind.[3]

Ever since the fourth century, when Eusebius, bishop of Caesarea and adviser to Constantine, penned his *Ecclesiastical History* and his *Chronicle,* two historical traditions were inextricably linked: biblical history and Roman imperial history.[4] During the age of Roman persecution of Christians, Christian writers had vilified Rome as the whore of Babylon, reincarnation of the despised enemy of the Old Testament, the Babylonians who in their arrogance constructed the tower of Babel and later destroyed the Temple of Jerusalem and led the Jews into captivity. Eusebius, writing to glorify Constantine and his Christian Roman empire, overhauled Christian historiography. He provided an unbroken narration of human history from Abraham to his own day, calculating the periods between key biblical events. In the fifth century, Augustine of Hippo divided world history into six ages, following a Jewish tradition that, just as the world was created in six days, it would last six long "days" and be destroyed on the seventh, but Augustine refrained from calculating the lengths of these ages.[5]

True to his passion for ordering knowledge, Isidore, in his *Chronica maiora* (composed in 615 and reworked in 624), became the first Christian chronicler to calculate the lengths of each of the six ages, fusing sacred and profane historiography to produce the first Christian universal chronicle.[6] The first of the six ages had stretched from the creation of Adam to Noah (a period of 2,242 years, according to Isidore's calculations); the second, from Noah to Abraham (942 years); the third, from Abraham to David (940 years); the fourth, from David to the Babylonian captivity (555 years); and the fifth, from the Babylonian captivity to the birth of Christ (549 years).[7] Isidore (like his predecessors) placed himself in the sixth age, which was meant to stretch from the birth of Christ to his second coming: "it is 5813 years from the beginning of the world to the present era, which is the fifth year of the Emperor Heraclius [610–41] and the fourth of the most religious prince Sisebut [612–21]."[8] Since he placed the beginning of the sixth age in the year 5228 after the Creation, this means that 586 years of the sixth age had gone by (he seems to be counting from the death, rather than

the birth, of Jesus). As for what is to follow, Isidore simply says, "the remainder of time cannot be known to human investigation"; citing Acts he
says, "it is not for you to know the times or the seasons, which the Father
has put in his own power."[9]

While the six-age structure gives prominence to biblical history (key
biblical people or events mark the beginning and end of each age), much
of what Isidore places into the chapters of his *Chronica majora* reflects an
imperial Roman conception of history. His narration of the first three ages
is brief and largely based on the Bible, whereas his entries for the fourth
age are largely a succession of kings of Israel: political and dynastic history
take the upper hand. This tendency is accentuated in his description of the
fifth age, where the organizing principle is the succession of Persian, Mace-
donian, and Roman rulers. While the birth of Christ is supposedly the
great event separating the fifth age from the sixth, Isidore in fact makes the
break between Julius Caesar and Augustus, even though Augustus's reign
begins before the birth of Christ. With the sixth age, Isidore rests firmly in
the tradition of Roman imperial history: each emperor has a brief paragraph dedicated to his reign, while various other events and people (church
councils, holy bishops, Germanic invaders, heresiarchs) are relegated to the
end of each paragraph. Toward the end of the chronicle, as he approaches
his own age, events in Spain become increasingly prominent, taking up
more space in each successive chapter: one of the key events of the reign
of the emperor Mauricius, for Isidore, is the teaching and preaching of
Isidore's brother Leander.[10] Yet the imperial structure remains until the last
chronological chapter (§120), dedicated to the reign of Heraclius.[11]

If the world chronicle forces Isidore to adopt a Roman-centered chronology, his other major historical work, *On the Origins of the Goths*, focuses
on rehabilitating the Visigoths. It was the Visigoths who had sacked Rome
in 410; historians since Augustine had cast them in the role of divine
scourge, a role well known to all steeped in the reading of the Old Testament: the Visigoths were to the Romans as the Assyrians and Babylonians
had been to the Jews of old; this role seemed to fit them all the more since
they were Arian heretics. But in 589, at the Third Council of Toledo, Reccared, king of the Visigoths, announced his conversion to Catholicism and
the end of the (heretical) Spanish Arian church. Now that the Visigoth Reccared was both master of Spain and Catholic, the history of his Visigothic
ancestors needed a face-lift. Two Spanish bishops set out to rewrite the history of the Visigoths: John of Biclaro and Isidore of Seville. For John, Rec-

cared is a new Constantine; like the first Christian emperor, he presides over church councils and vanquishes enemies with the help of God.[12] Isidore attempts a legitimation on a much grander scale: his *On the Origins of the Goths* traces the glorious history of the Goths from the time of Noah to their current "marriage" with Spain.[13]

This optimistic view of the present colors Isidore's view of the future: there is no sense, in any of his historical works, of the imminence of the world's end, of the coming of Antichrist. Pope Gregory the Great, at the height of the Lombard invasions of Italy (c. 590), had proclaimed "in this country where we live the world no longer announces its end but demonstrates it."[14] Other Latin writers of the fifth and sixth centuries had seen either the crumbling of Roman hegemony or the spread of heresy (or both) as the work of Antichrist, sure signs that the end was near.[15] For Isidore, on the contrary, a new age of Christian peace is dawning, a hoped-for end to war and heresy.

Yet history (for Isidore and for all Christians) was a one-way voyage with predestined terminus: one day, the world would end; Antichrist would come; Christ would judge mankind. In the *Etymologies,* Isidore explains that the Antichrist is he who will come "against Christ."

> He will impersonate Christ when he comes and will contend against him. And he will oppose the Sacraments of Christ so that the gospel of his truth may be weakened. And he will repair the temple at Jerusalem and will attempt to restore all the ceremonies of the Old Law. But the Antichrist is also he who denies that Christ is God. He is therefore the contrary of Christ. Therefore all who depart from the church and who cut themselves off from the unity of the faith are Antichrists.[16]

The term "Antichrist" could have two meanings for Christians. First, it referred to *the* Antichrist, he who was coming at the end of time to lead the faithful astray and who often (as here) has both heretical and Jewish tendencies: heretical in that he claims to be Christ and leads Christians astray, Jewish in that he denies that Christ is God and attempts to rebuild the temple and reinstate Jewish practices (prophecies to be remembered by Christians who watch circumcised Muslims who denied Jesus' divinity building mosques on Jerusalem's temple mount). Second, the word "Antichrist" (or at times, "precursor of Antichrist") could be applied to various enemies of the church—particularly heretics: had not John said, after all,

"Such is the Antichrist: the person who denies the Father and the Son"?[17] To later Christians, Muslims, who reject the Trinity and deny that Jesus was God, seem to fit this definition perfectly.

One of the key biblical passages for understanding Antichrist is the so-called Little Apocalypse of the Synoptic Gospels:

> Take heed that no one leads you astray. Many will come in my name saying "I am the Christ" and they will lead many astray. And when you hear of wars and rumors of wars, do not be alarmed; this must take place [Dan.2:28–29], but the end is not yet. For nation will rise against nation [2 Chron. 15:6] and kingdom against kingdom [Isa. 19:2]. . . . When you see the Abomination of Desolation spoken of by the prophet Daniel [Dan. 2:28–29] set up where it ought not to be [Dan. 11:31], standing in the holy place [Dan. 9:27]—let the reader understand. . . . For in those days there will be such tribulation as has not been from the beginning [Dan. 12:1] of the creation which God created until now, and never will be. . . . And then if anyone says to you, "Look, here is the Christ!" or "Look, there he is!" do not believe it. For false Christs and false prophets will arise [Deut. 13:2], and show great signs and wonders, to lead astray if possible the elect.[18]

The text could be cited further, and other important biblical texts could be used (the Prophets, the Apocalypse), but the essential scenario for the last days is clear: false Christs and false prophets will come, performing miracles and leading good Christians astray, performing acts of blasphemy, setting up the "abomination of desolation" in "the holy place." These events will fulfill the prophecies of the Old Testament, reechoed verbatim (as so often) in the Gospels. Ardent Christians (such as Gregory the Great) from the first century to the twentieth have seen their own tribulations and sufferings as signs that the end is near; each century has also known writers (such as Isidore) with cooler heads or more optimistic temperaments who saw the end as comfortably far in the future. In the first centuries of the Christian era, the Antichrist was associated with that "whore of Babylon," the Roman Empire—and particularly with the more vicious persecutors of Christians, such as Nero.[19] After the conversion of Constantine, Christian historians gave Rome a positive role in the divine plan; now the enemy was heresy. Many now associated the "false Christs" and "false prophets" of the Bible with heresiarchs: Hilary, bishop of Poitiers (d. 367) brands Arius as an

Antichrist.[20] Just so, many writers of the Middle Ages will see Muhammad as a "false prophet" and "false Christ," feeling sure that the Muslim invasions are the catastrophes predicted by the Bible.[21]

Saracens and Arabs in Isidorian Ethnology

Understanding the medieval Christian conception of history is crucial to understanding how Christians subsequently perceive Islam. It is equally important to understand how Christian writers such as Isidore envisaged the geography and ethnography of the world around them, in particular how they described the Arabs, Ishmaelites, or Saracens.

For Isidore, human geography is a consequence of human history: the confusion of peoples, languages, and customs in the world is the direct consequence of the Fall, the flood, and the confusion of the languages at Babel. We all descend from Adam, and indeed from Noah; our ancestors all spoke the same language, Hebrew, until God destroyed the tower of Babel and created the confusion of languages. For Isidore, again, the confusing diversity of humanity was rationally explicable and could (at least in theory), be traced to a unified origin, to a human ancestor, Noah. While he incorporated many details from classical Roman ethnographic tradition, he hung them on a biblical framework, imposing order on chaos.[22]

Isidore showed this same vision of historical ethnography in book 9 of the *Etymologies*.[23] He says that the world contains seventy-two or seventy-three peoples, each with its own language, each traced back to one of Noah's three sons, Ham, Japeth, or Shem. This schema allowed Isidore (and his readers) to identify and classify people in an apparently rational and comprehensible framework. He writes in the *Chronica*, "in the second year after the flood, when Shem was one hundred years old, he begat Arphaxad, from whom the Chaldean people (*gens*) has sprung."[24] Isidore uses the genealogies of Genesis 10–11; in *Etymologies*, he mentions only the names of those men who were founders of peoples: Heber, of the Hebrews, or "Ishmael, son of Abraham, from whom come the Ishmaelites, whose name now has been corrupted into Saracens (*Saraceni*), as if from Sarah, and Agarenes (*Agareni*) from Hagar."[25]

Ishmael, according to Genesis, was Abraham's first-born son, born of Hagar, Sarah's handmaid. The angel of the Lord who announced to Hagar the birth of her child tells her "he will be a wild man; his hand will be against every man, and every man's hand against him; and he shall dwell in the presence of all his brethren" (Gen. 16:12). Abraham's wife, Sarah, later bears a child, Isaac; when Isaac is weaned, his parents have a feast, and Sarah sees Ishmael mocking his younger brother (Gen. 21:9). Sarah tells Abraham, "Cast out this bondwoman and her son: for the son of this bondwoman shall not be heir with my son" (Gen. 21:10). God tells Abraham to heed Sarah, consoling him by announcing that "of the son of the bondwoman will I make a nation." This is the same message God sends to Hagar in despair in the desert (Gen. 21:13, 18). Indeed, Ishmael lived to father twelve sons, "twelve princes according to their nations" who "dwelt from Havilah unto Shur, that is before Egypt, as thou goest toward Assyria" (Gen. 25:16–18). Already in the first century C.E. Jewish and Christian writers identify the twelve sons of Ishmael with the twelve tribes of the Arabs; Eusebius makes the same identification.[26] If Agarenes, Saracens, and Ishmaelites are three synonyms denoting the same people (descendants of Shem via Ishmael), they are distinct, for Isidore, from the Arabs, descendants of Ham (according to the *Etymologies*). This perhaps reflects Isidore's lack of information; earlier authors used the four terms interchangeably.[27] The Arabs were, of course, of little direct concern to Isidore, writing in Spain at the turn of the seventh century: the only other information about them that a diligent reader could glean from the *Etymologies* is that they pierce their ears and that among their numbers are heretics who believe in reincarnation.[28] Other writers were aware that some Arabs practiced the Jewish customs of circumcision and abstention from pork and that they worshiped a large stone[29]; some said that they were idolaters who practiced human sacrifice.[30] An anonymous pilgrim from Piacenza who visited the holy land c. 560–570, claims to have witnessed the Saracens worshiping an idol made of white marble and to have seen it turn black at the rising of the moon.[31] Isidore says nothing about the Arabs' ferocity in battle, unlike Eusebius and other Eastern writers who describe them as blood-thirsty cannibals, "robbers of Arabia," or "wolves of Arabia."[32] For Rufinus of Aquilea, author of the *Ecclesiastical history* (fourth century), Saracens were dangerous, barbarous marauders; yet one of their queens, Mauvia, converted to Christianity, showing that there was hope for them.[33] But if Arabs and Saracens, for Isidore, are obscure and distant peoples of merely academic interest, within a century they will be the new masters of Spain, and European Christians will scour the Bible, the church fathers, and Isidore's *Chronica* and *Etymologies* for information about them. Isidore uses his reading of the Bible and of Jerome to try to impose order not only on the chronology of history but also on ethnology: history is the key to understanding the *origins* (and hence, to a large degree, the *natures*) of the world's peoples (*gentes*).

Isidore's Typology of Religious Error:
Pagans, Heretics, Antichrist, and Jews

If Isidore seems unable to escape the Roman, imperial structuring of history, he nevertheless shows a Catholic churchman's preoccupation with religious error: paganism and especially heresy. He places the creation of pagan idolatry near the beginning of the second age: "in these times the first temples were built, and certain princes among the nations began to be adored as gods."[34] He later (§45–53) discusses Prometheus, Atlas, Mercury, Jove, and other humans who were worshiped as gods. Isidore develops this idea in more detail in *Etymologies* 8[35]; after the death of such men, he explains, their followers crafted images (*simulacra*) of them, "so that they could have some solace in the contemplation of images, but their descendants, persuaded by demons, gradually slipped into this error [idolatry]."[36] Who was the human inventor of such idolatry? Isidore has two nominees: "The Jews say that it was Ishmael who first made an idol (*simulacrum*) of clay. The Gentiles however say that Prometheus first presented an idol he had made out of clay and that with him was born the art making idols and statues."[37] Here, too, Isidore is combining the classical scholarship of Lactantius with the biblical exegesis of Jerome.[38] Jerome, in turn, probably relied on Jewish exegetes for some of whom Ishmael made the first idols and for this was expelled from the house of his father Abraham.[39] Paganism, for Isidore, is idolatry, the worship of images; these images are inhabited by demons, and the devil himself encourages this pagan worship so as to turn men away from the worship of the divine name. (*Etymologies* 8.11.14). Isidore goes on to catalog the names of dozens of pagan gods, names he has gleaned from his reading of classical literature and the Bible: a few Near Eastern and Egyptian gods scattered in among dozens of Greek and Roman divinities.

In the *Chronica* paganism is replaced, in the sixth age, with a far more pernicious enemy: heresy.[40] The first heretic was Simon Magus, whose story falls in the midst of the description of Nero's rule and horrific persecution of Christians: "In these times Simon Magus proposed a contest with the apostles Peter and Paul, saying that he had some great power from God. He proposed to fly to the Father and indeed flew in the air for half a day, held up in the air by demons. Finally, with Peter cursing them in God's name and Paul praying, Simon lost control and fell. When he died, Nero had Peter crucified and Paul killed by the sword" (§247). The story of Simon Magus and his confrontation with the apostle Peter is attested in many medieval sources.[41] All the apocryphal accounts agree that Simon produced miracles that led the faithful astray and impressed Nero: he could change sex and age, turn into a dragon, make statues move and talk. Yet these are illegitimate miracles performed through the aid of demons; Simon's goals are self-glorification and sexual depravity. When put to the test, Peter and Paul are able to defeat Simon by praying and making him fall down in midflight. Simon is the first heresiarch and becomes a model that other heresiarchs are perceived to follow: a false message, demonically inspired miracles, sexual debauchery with his followers, and ultimately, death and defeat dealt by God through the agency of his saints. Isidore emphasizes this in his list of heresies in the *Etymologies:* the first Christian heretics in his list are "the Simoniacs, so called from Simon, expert in the art of magic, whom Peter cursed in the Acts of the Apostles, because he wanted to buy the grace of the Holy Spirit from the Apostles with money" (8.5.2). Isidore is well aware of the variety of Christian heresy; indeed, he lists dozens of heresies and heresiarchs in *Etymologies* 8. Yet Simon, for Isidore as for many medieval writers, is the father of heresy: a model whose errors later heresiarchs will typologically reenact, just as saints typologically reenact the deeds of Christ and the apostles.[42] By this "careful arrangement of [heretics'] ideas as the antithesis of Christianity," as Brian Stock suggests, Christian authors "attempt to fit a new, troubling experience . . . into an acceptably conventional framework."[43] In other words, they tried to make sense of the doctrines or practices that they rejected by connecting them to earlier, discredited errors; Christian authors have the same reflex when confronted with Islam.

Heresy holds a prominent place in the rest of Isidore's *Chronica.* He discusses the origins of Arianism, Donatism, and many other heresies: virtually every chapter now contains references to some heretical group. The East is the hotbed of heresy: Syria, Egypt, Constantinople. Moreover, among those he accuses of heresy are several of Constantinople's most illustrious emperors: Constantine, accused of a deathbed conversion to Arianism[44]; Constans, an Arian who persecutes Catholics[45]; and Justinian, condemned as a Monophysite.[46] This preoccupation with heresy reflects the concerns of Isidore the bishop, who fought both Monophysitism and Arianism in Spain, but it also reflects the point of view of a royal propagandist for the Visigothic monarchy: if the Visigothic kings of old could be censored for their Arianism (and Isidore does not hesitate to do so[47]) so could the Roman emperors of Constantinople. Moreover, Reccared's dramatic conversion marks an end to the Visigoth's heresy; no such event cleanses Byzantium's reputation. Religious legitimacy and political legitimacy go hand in hand, and Visigothic Toledo, for Isidore, lays equal or better claim to them than does Constantinople. Visigothic kings Leovigild and Reccared built Byzantine-style churches and aped Byzantine court ritual; Isidore is giving their successors a theoretical legitimacy meant to rival that of Byzantium.[48] Eusebius had heralded Constantine's reign as the beginning of an age of Christian peace; yet for Isidore this end of the period of persecution marks the beginning of the age of heresies.[49] Reccared would succeed in inaugurating an era of Christian peace where Constantine had failed. In his *Etymologies,* he copies an optimistic note from his brother Leander: the universal Catholic church "is not like the coteries of heretics isolated in a few scattered regions; it is spread out across the whole earth."[50] Heresy is still the enemy, but one whose days are numbered: it is now a minor, local problem, one that upright Catholic bishops should be able to solve.

Isidore and the Jews

Yet Reccared's conversion did not completely eliminate religious divisions in Spain: there is still Judaism. Isidore's *Against the Jews,* addressed to his sister Florence, is less a polemical attack on Judaism than an attempt to explain Christian doctrine using only the Old Testament.[51] In the first of the tract's two books, Isidore devotes a chapter each to fifty-one key Christian doctrines, designed roughly to fit the chronology of Christ's life; the point is to show that Christ's birth, mission, death, and resurrection, in all their important details, were predicted by the Hebrew prophets. In book 2 he traces the history of the church, explaining that Christians no longer follow the ritual practices imposed by the Old Testament because the old law of Moses has been replaced by the new law of Christ. The old, "carnal" sacraments (circumcision, animal sacrifice) have been replaced by their new, better, spiritual equivalents (baptism, the Eucharist).[52] The Jews blindly refused to recognize Christ; they killed him and were punished by the destruction of Jerusalem and dispersion; they continue blindly to continue in the old law, but "at the end of the world the Jews will believe in Christ."[53] As with much of his geographical lore, his ideas on Judaism are bookish, based on his reading of Jerome rather than on any contact with real Jews[54]; he is unaware, for example, that Jews have not practiced animal sacrifice since the destruction of the temple in 70 C.E.[55] He has no knowledge of the Talmud.[56] He seems to be attacking the Judaism of the Old Testament, rather than that of seventh-century Spain.

If Isidore's "proofs" of Christian doctrine strike the modern reader as singularly unconvincing, such belief in the logical necessity of Christian doctrine is part of his fight for Catholic unity against doubt and division. The unconverted Jews represented doubt incarnate; their very existence threatened Isidore's triumphant vision of Catholic history. Thus Isidore had to present the Jews' refusal to accept a Christian reading of the Old Testament as illogical, "hard of heart."[57] Isidore draws this contrast between Christian reason and unthinking Jewish habit when (in the *Etymologies*) he defines the difference between church and synagogue:

Indeed our Apostles never said "synagogue" (*synagoga*) but always "church" (*ecclesia*), either in order to distinguish between the two or because there is a difference between a congregation (where the word synagogue comes from) and a convocation (whence the word church). For as sheep tend to congregate (*congregari*), whence we speak of flocks (*greges*), to be convoked is more fitting for those who use reason, as do men.

(*Etymologies* 8.1.8)

Christians are rational, as befits men; Jews congregate like irrational sheep. Despite his dependence on Jerome, Isidore is much more virulently anti-Jewish than the earlier church fathers: he may well have played a key role in the formation of Visigothic anti-Jewish policy. Reccared himself had passed a law forbidding Jews to have Christian slaves or to have sexual intercourse with Christian women; the children of any such unions were to be baptized. No Jew was to be in a position of authority over Christians.[58] In these measures, Reccared is echoing earlier Visigothic legislation,[59] and the concern is not to convert Jews or inhibit the practice of their religion: it is rather to keep the boundaries firm between Christianity and Judaism. The same concerns underlie laws attempting to prevent "judaizing": King Chindasuinth (642–53) dictates the death penalty for Christians who practice circumcision or other Jewish rites.[60] In 612, King Sisebut, noting that Reccared's laws prohibiting Jews from owning Christian slaves were not being enforced, reiterated them and imposed harsher penalties.[61] In the fourth year of his reign (615–16), it seems, he ordered the Jews of his kingdom to convert to Christianity. Spanish bishops had very mixed feelings about this: the Fourth Council of Toledo, under Isidore's leadership, criticized Sisebut for his policy yet reaffirmed that those who had been forcibly baptized were now Christians and had to remain so. Isidore criticized Sisebut's policy in his *On the Origins of the Goths*.[62]

Isidore was "obsessed with Judaism."[63] Why? We have seen that paganism and heresy, for Isidore, had been dealt their death blows. The end of Arianism produced the unity of Spain, the marriage of the Goths and Hispania. The only stain on this unity was the continued persistence of one group of infidels: while numerically Jews could surely not be a threat to the Visigothic kingdom, psychologically they may have been. The much-hailed conversion of Reccared had not succeeded in bringing hoped-for unity and peace to Spain. In the search for scapegoats, eyes turned to the one continued group of voluntary outsiders, the Jews; it was certainly much more comfortable for King Sisebut to blame the Jews for his (and his predecessors') failures to unite Spain in peace than to find fault with himself or his nobles.[64]

Subversive Christology:
Jewish Responses to Christian Disdain in the Early Middle Ages

In subsequent centuries, such Christian attitudes toward Jews were at times reflected in Christian attitudes toward Islam. Perhaps a closer parallel can be drawn between *Jewish* attitudes toward Christianity and Christian attitudes toward Islam. Jews in Christian Europe, like Christians (and Jews) under Muslim rule, were minorities struggling to preserve their traditions and communities amid disdain, ridicule, and pressures to convert. Some Jews forged an aggressive theological defense against Christianity, just as many Christians forged one against Islam. As early as the second century, Jews introduced liturgical condemnations of *minim* (heretics) in an effort to keep Christians out of Jewish services.[65]

Jewish polemics against Jesus prefigure Christian (and Jewish) polemics against Muhammad. Scattered references in the Talmud refer to Jesus: "Jesus the Nazarene practiced magic and led Israel astray."[66] Elsewhere the Talmud gives its readers the spectacle of Jesus tormented in hell, condemned to wallow for eternity in a boiling pile of dung for having mocked the words of the Sages and Prophets.[67] Another passage in the Talmud affirms that Jesus, as a sorcerer and as a seducer of Israel, was justly condemned and executed; after all, did not the Torah enjoin us to kill whomever should bid us to worship other gods, even if that person was a brother, daughter, son, wife, or friend?[68] Several Jewish texts throughout the Middle Ages echo this judgment.[69] The various hostile Talmudic traditions are elaborated upon in the early Middle Ages and by the ninth century are found together in a Hebrew text, the *Toledoth Yeshu* (Generations of Jesus).[70] Jesus, this text tells us, is the illegitimate child of Mary and Joseph. He sneaks into the temple at Jerusalem to learn the name of God. The knowledge of this name gives him the power to perform miracles: to cure the sick, revive the dead, walk on water, fly through the air. Judas Iscariot then learns the divine name and enters into combat with Jesus; the two fly through the air fighting equally until Judas manages to soil Jesus; this makes him fall down and forget the divine name. Eventually, Jesus is brought to trial and condemned to death. After Jesus' execution and burial, a gardener steals his body and reburies it in his garden. Jesus' followers, finding the tomb empty, proclaim his resurrection. Subsequently, the gardener produces Jesus' corpse and "all Israel . . . bound cords to the feet of [Jesus], and dragged him round the streets of Jerusalem."[71] It is hard to find a more potent symbol for the utter demise of one's enemy than to have his corpse defiled by filth, dragged through the streets, or boiled in dung.[72] The *Toledoth* makes no attempt to deny Christian claims that Jesus performed miracles; rather, it illegitimizes them by branding them as sorcery, black magic. As Mary Douglas has noted, many societies draw the distinction between beneficial magic, performed by and for the authorities of the "in" group, and harmful, black magic, performed by outsiders in an attempt to disrupt order and authority.[73] In this the *Toledoth Yeshu* bears striking parallels to the Christian legends of Simon Magus—and to twelfth-century Christian portrayals of Muhammad (see chapter 6).

This view of Jesus is more apologetical (i.e., defensive) than polemical (offensive): clearly, it would be dangerous to communicate this view of Jesus to Christians. Indeed, these legends about Jesus outraged Christians who found out about it and led to the condemnation and burning of the Talmud and other postbiblical Jewish texts several times in the Middle Ages: these texts were specifically prohibited twice in seventh-century Spain.[74] Anti-Jewish polemicists from the ninth century to the twentieth have dredged up these texts and exploited them in order to flame Christian hostility toward Jews.

Christians claim that Jesus brought a message that both continues and supersedes that of Moses; Muslims claim that Muhammad brought a message that both continues and supersedes that of Jesus. Just as some Chris-

tians vilified Muhammad, some Jews attacked Jesus, branding him as a sorcerer, imposter, and heretic. For the reader of the twenty-first century,
prone to ecumenism and tolerance, these legends can be a source of em-
barrassment to the heirs of the communities that produced them and offensive to those whose sacred traditions are vilified. Yet these legends bear
examination, because they show how an embattled, despised religious minority created walls and boundaries between itself and the dominant
(Christian or Muslim) majority. Because he had a detailed and disparaging
biography of the founder of the majority religion, with derogatory explanations for its principle rites and holidays, the Jew (or Christian) could
protect himself from doubt, could construct a wall of contempt between
himself and Christianity (or Islam). To the haughty disdain of the majority
he would respond with an equal and opposing scorn.[75]

While some of these hostile Jewish descriptions of Christianity can be
(and have been) explained as reactions to Christians' anti-Judaism, this
begs the question: what explains the virulent hostility to Judaism of so
many Christians over the centuries? Why are Christians much more hostile
toward Jews, with whom they have much in common, than with (say) Buddhists or animists, with whom they have much less in common? It is precisely because Christians and Jews are fighting for rightful ownership of a
common spiritual heritage that their disputes can be so bitter. Each claims
to be sole legitimate heir to Moses and Abraham; each claims exclusive
rights to the correct interpretation of the Torah: those who are "too close
for comfort" provoke "uncharacteristic and bitter fury."[76] When Islam steps
forward as a third claimant to that heritage, the attacks from Jews and
Christians will be harsh.

ISIDORE CONSTRUCTED an ordered vision of human history and human
knowledge. It was a vision, he hoped, that offered at least a dull reflection
of the perfect order of the divine mind. In his great project, the *Etymologies,* he distilled and drew together human knowledge in an encyclopedia of unprecedented scope, using language as the bridge for the unity
of knowledge. In his *Chronica,* Isidore drew together biblical and classical
history into a single framework of the six ages of the world. This unity of
human cultures is even more clearly symbolized in the genealogical ethnography that pervades both the *Chronica* and the *Etymologies.* Yet within
this unity lie a plethora of distinctions, so many pieces in a divine jig-
saw puzzle. And beyond geography and ethnography, the fundamental
division between a unified Christianity and a disunified cacophony of pagans, heretics, and Jews.

I explore in this chapter the paradox of Isidore's method. He seems slavishly traditional, in that his pen writes little that he has not found in the works of earlier authorities. Yet he uses the words of Augustine and Orosius to create a vision of history significantly different from theirs. He weaves together Genesis, Jerome, and classical scholarship to create a new Christian ethnography. Isidore is an active, selective reader, bowing to the accepted authorities while he appropriates them to forge a new vision of the world.

Nothing in Isidore's *Eytmologies* or his historical works could, of course, predict or account for the meteoric rise of Islam and its rapid conquest of an empire stretching from the Indus to the Atlantic. From the perspective of the twentieth-first-century historian, the rise of Islam and the Muslim conquests comprise one of history's great watersheds. Medieval Christian writers could not acknowledge this, because it would have cost them too much to abandon their Christian view of history and geography. Just as Columbus insisted that he had sailed to Asia and found the garden of Eden rather than abandon his notions of geography, so medieval writers would stretch their old language to accommodate Islam, to squeeze it into pre-existing categories rather than rethinking those categories.[77] When looking at Muhammad and his Muslim followers, they would try to figure out where they fit in the well-established religious spectrum: obviously not Catholic Christians and apparently not Jews, were they the followers of Antichrist? Were they heretics? Were they pagans? Why had God permitted their tremendous conquests? What role had he chosen for them in Christian history? Truth, they thought, was to be found in the books of respected Christian authorities. This is why I focus this first chapter on Isidore: first, because later Christians will have the same reflex: to understand the world around them by delving into the works of respected *auctores:* a word that (tellingly) means both "authors" and "authorities." Moreover, Isidore himself quickly accedes to the rank of *auctor:* from the Carolingian authors of the ninth century to Parisian authors of the twelfth and thirteenth centuries, Isidore's works (especially the *Etymologies*) are cited as proof texts.[78] Never mind that all these books were composed before the rise of Islam and that none of them could therefore reflect the slightest knowledge about it. Truth was eternal, and the structure of God's plan was rational and constant; the revered writings of old remained their surest guide. Error, apparently multifarious, nevertheless reflected the constant opposition between God and Satan. These are the principles behind all the willful misunderstandings and distortions of Islam examined in the chapters that follow.

These beleaguered Christians took what little they knew of these new invaders and tried to make sense of them by poring over the ethnographic, historical, and religious categories of the Bible and of Isidore, Augustine, and others. They would find a series of images of Saracens, or Arabs, who are descendants of a common ancestor, Ishmael. Ishmael is variously portrayed in these sources as bastard son of Abraham, the first idolater, a magician, and especially "a wild man" whose "hand will be against every man, and every man's hand against him."[79]

Few and far between were the authors who attempted to understand Islam on its own terms, based on its own sacred texts. To do so would be to fall into the devil's trap, to take the first step toward being seduced by their error.

Chapter 2

༺྾ঞ

ISLAMIC DOMINION AND THE RELIGIOUS OTHER

Recite in the name of your Lord who created, created man from clots of blood!
Recite! Your Lord is the Most Bountiful One, who by the pen taught man
what he did not know.

Koran, Sûra 96

THUS, ACCORDING to Muslim tradition, began the divine mission of
Muhammad, Messenger of God. "Recite!" (*Iqrâ'*): an order given by
God to his prophet, an order to communicate his word to the Arab people
and to the world.[1] Within a century from this revelation, Islam became the
dominant religious and political force in much of the former Roman and
Persian empires. In chapters 3 and 4, I show how Christians of the eastern
and western parts of the former Roman empire explained and understood
this monumental change. But first, in this chapter, I explore what it looked
like to the first generations of Muslims.

In the first chapter I examine seventh-century Christian conceptions of
divine history and religious other; in this, we will examine the development of Muslim doctrines concerning theodicy and the religious other in
the Koran, the Hadîth, and other key early Muslim texts. We will see how,
for many early Muslims, the rise of Islam and its tremendous successes
against Christians were proof of God's favor: God allowed a small and pure
band of his devotees to subdue two large and powerful but decadent empires. Judaism and Christianity were corrupt, superseded versions of the
true religion, Islam; their adherents were to be tolerated, but were not to be
considered equal to Muslims.

What follows will not be new to scholars of Islam. My purpose here
is twofold: first, to show how Muslim notions of divine history and the

religious other develop within the early Muslim community; second, to present the Koranic and traditional accounts of events in Muslim history— particularly concerning the prophet Muhammad—that are subsequently reused, twisted, and attacked by many Christian writers.

Muhammad and the Early Muslim Community, According to the Koran and Tradition

Our starting point for understanding Muslim sacred history and Muslim portrayals of the religious other is the Koran. The revelation of this "recitation" (Qur'ân, anglicized as Koran), according to Koranic scholars, took place as a series of revelations (Sûras) over twenty years, from about 610 until shortly before Muhammad's death in 632. The 114 Sûras reflect the changing circumstances and needs of the Muslim community over the period, as they went from a handful of persecuted monotheists in Mecca to a unified community in Medina to the dominant force in the Arab peninsula.

Yet the central message of the Koran is unchanging: God asks mankind for *Islam*: submission to his will. To one who has submitted (*muslim*), God promises eternal paradise. To him who turns away from God, the flames of hell await. The mandates of Islam, unlike those of medieval Christianity, are not sacramental: there are (at least in theory) to be no ordained priests, no sacraments, no holy intercessors (alive or dead) between God and the individual. The fundamental duties of every Muslim are the same, the most important of which are the so-called five Pillars of the Faith: first, the adherence to and the recitation of the *shahâda*: "There is no God but God, and Muhammad is his Messenger!"; second, the performance of the *salât*, a series of five prayers, at set hours each day, preceded by ritual ablutions; third, the offering of alms to the poor; fourth, fasting from dawn to dusk during the entire month of Ramadan; fifth, making the pilgrimage to the Ka'ba at Mecca.

The austere and simple message of the Koran is supplemented by the Hadîth (tradition), in the form of sayings attributed to Muhammad compiled primarily in the ninth century C.E. To these, over the centuries, were added ever more numerous and elaborate stories of Muhammad's life and miracles. These stories (similar to the miracles attributed to the Virgin Mary in the Christian tradition), often frowned on by theologians, were (and are) widely read and loved. Particularly popular was the story of Muhammad's celestial voyage (*Mi'râj*), vaguely alluded to in the Koran (17:1), a tour of heaven and hell described in increasingly baroque detail throughout the Middle Ages and beyond.[2] The *Sîra* (biography) of Muhammad compiled by Ibn Ishâq (c. 704–c. 767) and reworked by Ibn Hishâm (d. 828 or 833) became the fundamental source of information about his life.[3]

WHEN MUHAMMAD received the order to recite, his first revelation, around 610, he was about forty years old. He was born in Mecca, a town on the caravan routes of central Arabia centered around the Ka'ba, a temple devoted to the supreme God (Allah) and his three daughters, goddesses whose statues adorned the sanctuary. Little of Muhammad's previous life indicated his future spiritual role: born into the prestigious and powerful Quraysh tribe of Mecca, orphaned at the age of six, brought up by an uncle, he eventually became a successful merchant, accompanying caravans to Roman Syria, marrying a widow, Khadîja. Later legends will embellish this sober description of his youth: his father emanates a celestial light at the hour of his conception; the young Muhammad miraculously saves his people from a terrible drought; two angels cut him open, take out his heart, cleanse it with snow and replace it.[4] Legend also tells of how, when the young Muhammad accompanied a caravan, a pious Christian monk named Bahira recognized in him his future glory as a prophet.[5] The Koran contains none of this; it makes only vague reference to the spiritual turmoil that preceded Muhammad's call.[6] On the contrary, the Koran emphasizes the simplicity and humanity of Muhammad; that is what makes the message all the more miraculous. The Hadîth dramatize this by having Muhammad fall on the ground and contort as he receives revelations via Gabriel, overpowered by the awesome presence of the Divine Word.[7]

Ibn Hishâm's edition of Ibn Ishâq's *Life of Muhammad* incorporates information from a variety of traditional, oral sources.[8] It describes the night of Muhammad's first revelation, during the month of Ramadan when he was forty years old. The archangel Gabriel came to him and ordered him "Recite!" When Muhammad asked him, "What shall I recite?" Gabriel squeezed Muhammad so tightly that he thought he would die. Finally Gabriel recited the first revelation (Sûra 96, quoted at the beginning of this chapter). When Gabriel departed and Muhammad awoke from his vision as if from a dream, "it was as though these words were written on my

[Muhammad's] heart." He was so confused and troubled by the revelation that he decided to commit suicide by throwing himself off a mountain, but when he went out to do so, he heard a voice from heaven proclaiming "O Muhammad! Thou art the apostle of God and I am Gabriel." He looked up and saw the angel, "in the form of a man with feet astride the horizon."[9] He went home, still uncertain of his mission, and told his wife Khadîja what had happened. She told him to rejoice and be of good heart and went to her cousin Waraqa, a learned Christian who, upon hearing the details of Muhammad's vision, proclaimed that he was indeed "the prophet of this people."[10]

At first Muhammad only shared his revelations with his wife Khadîja and a few close associates. Then, probably in 612, he began to proclaim his revelations publicly to his fellow Meccans. He told them of the power and glory of God, and of the beauty of his creation. God created the earth and heavens; God created man; and God created the Koran. In return, man owes him gratitude and submission:

> It is the Merciful who taught the Koran.
> He created man and taught him articulate speech. The sun and the moon
>   pursue their ordered course. The plants and the trees bow down in ado-
>   ration. . . .
> He laid the earth for His creatures, with all the fruits and blossom-bearing
>   palm, chaff-covered grain and scented herbs. Which of your Lord's
>   blessings would you deny? . . .
> Pearls and corals come from [the oceans]. Which of your Lord's blessings
>   would you deny?
> His are the ships that sail like mountains upon the ocean. Which of your
>   Lord's blessings would you deny?

> (Koran 55:1–25)

God's earth is beautiful, bountiful, good. God created it for his creatures for their benefit and enjoyment. We are far, here, from the asceticism of an Augustine. The senses are not the snares of temptation; they are the means of our participation in God's glorious creation. The City of Man and the City of God are one, if only we will bow down (as do our fellow creatures, the sun, moon, plants, and trees) and submit to the will of God. Submit before it is too late, for the end of time, the final judgment, may come sooner than we think:

When the sky is rent asunder; when the stars scatter and the oceans roll
together; when the graves are hurled about; each soul shall know what
it has done and what it has failed to do.

(Koran 82)

Submission to God's will, *Islam,* involves humility and gratitude before
God, acknowledgment that these gifts come from him. It also involves solidarity with one's fellow man. God is generous, merciful, compassionate:
these adjectives are used to invoke him hundreds of times in the Koran.
Man must strive to be likewise: he must share his wealth with the poor, for-
give those who have wronged him, refrain from fighting with his fellow
creatures. The early Sûras of the Koran lash out at the false piety of the
rich:

Have you thought of him that denies the Last Judgment? It is he who
turns away the orphan and who does not urge others to feed the poor.
Woe to those who pray but are heedless in their prayer; who make a show
of piety and give no alms to the destitute.

(Koran 107)

To those who give to the poor and submit humbly to God's will, however, God's gifts are theirs to enjoy, in proper gratitude and moderation:
owning without avarice, dining without gluttony, making love without debauchery. Though Sufis later practiced the same sorts of ascetic feats of
prowess as Christian hermits and monks, asceticism never was to have the
dominance in Islam that it did in Christianity.

This difference is manifest in the Christian and Muslim conceptions of
heaven. Both Christianity and Islam assert that we are to resurrect with our
bodies at the end of time, and for both, the punishments of the damned in
hell are quite physical: "Flames of fire shall be lashed at you, and molten
brass. There shall be none to help you" (Koran 55). Yet the Koran, unlike
most Christian texts, lavishes more description on the joys of heaven than
on the torments of hell, and they are joys that ascetically minded Christians would dare not hope for in the Hereafter:

But for those that fear the majesty of their Lord there are two gardens
(Which of your Lord's blessings would you deny?) planted with shady
trees. Which of your Lord's blessings would you deny?

Each is watered by a flowing spring. Which of your Lord's blessings would
   you deny?
Each bears every kind of fruit in pairs. Which of your Lord's blessings
   would you deny?
They shall recline on couches lined with thick brocade, and within their
   reach will hang the fruits of both gardens. Which of your Lord's bless-
   ings would you deny?
They shall dwell with bashful virgins whom neither man nor jinnee will
   have touched before. Which of your Lord's blessings would you deny?
Virgins as fair as corals and rubies. Which of your Lord's blessings would
   you deny?
Shall the reward of goodness be anything but good? Which of your Lord's
   blessings would you deny?

(Koran 55)

When Muhammad first made his mission public, he met with ridicule. The Meccans mocked his revelations, saying that he invented them. Some said a mortal teacher taught him: "We know they say 'a mortal taught him.' But the man to whom they allude speaks a foreign tongue, while this is eloquent Arab speech."[11] The doubters asked for proof, for miracles:

> They say: "We will not believe in you until you make a spring gush from the earth before our very eyes, or cause rivers to flow in a grove of palms and vines; until you cause the sky to fall upon us in pieces, as you have threatened to do, or bring down God and the angels in our midst; until you build a house of gold, or ascend to heaven: nor will we believe in your ascension until you have sent down for us a book which we can read."
>
>   Say [God instructs Muhammad]: "Glory to my Lord! Surely I am no more than a human apostle."
>
> (Koran 17:90–94)

While later pious legends ascribe all sorts of miracles to Muhammad (splitting the moon in two, making water gush forth in the desert, etc.),[12] the Koran emphatically stresses that God had ordained that he would produce only one miracle through Muhammad: the Koran itself, composed by no human hand but by God himself, whose clarity, beauty, and profundity are inimitable.[13] Further proof of its miraculous status is that Muhammad was *ummi* when he revealed it, a word interpreted by most Muslim commentators (from the third Muslim century onward) as "illiterate."[14] The Koran challenges the pagans and their idols to create a single verse that will match its own divine beauty; they are sure to fail (Koran 2:21).

Meccan resistance to Muhammad's message hardened as the Koran attacked the cult of idols venerated at the Ka'ba. For a fleeting moment, according to Ibn Hishâm, Muhammad proffered reconciliation with the idolaters, devotees of the three Meccan goddesses: "Have you thought on Allât and al-'Uzzâ, and, thirdly, on Manât? They are exalted birds and their intercession is desired indeed."[15] In Muhammad's desire to reconcile Islam with his compatriots, he had compromised its monotheism. Muslim tradition tells us that the angel Gabriel came to him and told him that it was Satan who placed those words into his mouth, that these satanic verses must be removed, and the following condemnation of the three goddesses must be put in their place: "They are but names which you and your fathers have invented: God has vested no authority in them. The unbelievers follow vain conjectures and the whims of their own souls."[16] The story of the "Satanic verses," from later Muslim tradition, shows Muhammad's desire to accommodate, to save even those who will not receive his message. While the message of the Koran is harsh, the messenger sometimes tries to soften is harshness, and is reprimanded: "Are you [Muhammad], then, going to melt away your soul in sorrow for them that they do not believe in this Teaching?" (Koran 18:6). The Koran rebukes the Prophet for his soft-heartedness and his impatience; other prophets, it tells him, accepted God's will with patience and equanimity.[17]

As the Meccans' resistance to Islam hardened, so did their persecution of the Muslims. A band of Muslims took refuge in the Christian kingdom of Ethiopia in 615, but Muhammad remained in Mecca. The revelations from this period remind the Muslims that Muhammad is not the first prophet to be spurned by his people; indeed, every prophet faced the same ridicule and rejection. The Koran tells the stories of earlier prophets such as Noah, Abraham, Joseph, Jonah, Moses, David, John the Baptist, Jesus, and others. Each of them came to his own people with the same message from God, asking for *islam*, submission: cease from worshiping idols; desist from pride and evil; bow down to the one true God, giving him thanks and praise. Each of these prophets gained a small band of devoted followers, who were persecuted by the idolaters.

This concept of "prophet" (*rasûl*) is different from that of Judaism or Christianity, encompassing a variety of Old and New Testament persons that Jews and Christians would not call "prophets." Some of the details of their lives differ in the Koran from those given in the earlier scriptures; this, of course, will become a subject of contention for Jewish and Christian polemicists. The Koran imposes unity on sacred history: if God is One and unchanging, so is the essential message of his prophets—and so is the eternal resistance of the damned. Even when confronted by the clear evidence of miracles performed by Moses, Jesus, and other prophets, they refused to believe the message. For this reason, Muhammad performed no miracles other than producing the Koran: "We refrain from sending Signs [miracles] because the men of former generations treated them as false" (Koran 17:61).

As the resistance of the Meccans became more intense, the people of Medina (or Yathrib) sent an embassy to Muhammad, offering to make him their leader. Muhammad accepted and left with his followers on the emigration, or *hijra*, in 622 ; this crucial event marks the beginning of the Muslim calendar. The Medinese pagans converted to Islam; Muhammad guaranteed religious freedom to Medina's Jews. Muhammad was now a political leader as well as a religious leader; he was confronted with the difficulties of incorporating the Meccan emigrants into the community of Medina, with difficult relations with Medina's Jewish tribes, and with hostility from both local Bedouins and the Meccans. The Sûras from this period reflect the change in circumstances: they are longer, less prone to poetic description of hellfire and the orchards of delight, full of specific legal injunctions on everything from alms tax (*zakât*) to marriage and divorce.

The Koran, like the Torah, is among other things a code of conduct, of laws; in neither is there a distinction between "religious" and "secular" law. The Koran, it seems, confirmed and modified much of existing practice, rather than creating a new code of law. The changes or reforms tend to be in the direction of logic, morality, and piety, and at times involve codification of what had previously been voluntary Muslim practice: the moral injunction to give alms becomes an annual "alms tax" (*zakât*). The Koran also shows traces of slow, progressive installing of reform; an example concerns the consumption of alcohol: first it is drunkenness during prayer that is prohibited, then alcohol in general is discouraged, finally it is condemned outright as evil.[18]

The Koranic legislation about marriage, divorce, and inheritance is similar: an attempt to reform and redirect existing Arab practice, rather than starting from a tabula rasa. Throughout, the emphasis is on protection of the weak against the depredations of the powerful; the latter are reminded that hellfire awaits the evildoer. Orphans are to be protected: their property is to be given to them when they become adults; their wards are to provide for them. Slave girls must not be forced into prostitution. Laws of inheritance are meant to ensure the rights of all parties. Married women are to maintain their own personal property, and the dowry that their husbands give them is to be considered the wives' property; in case of divorce, the husband must restore his wife's property. In order to convict a woman of a charge of fornication, four witnesses are needed. Divorce must be followed by a waiting period of at least three months (until the end of her pregnancy, if she is pregnant) before expelling the divorced wife from one's home; a man must provide for his former wife, particularly if she is nursing his child. Because of this concern for the material well-being of all parties (and in particular, of the women and children), polygamy is discouraged: "if you fear you cannot maintain equality among [multiple wives], marry one only." (Koran 4:3), later adding: "Try as you may, you cannot treat all your wives impartially" (4:128). Monogamy is apparently the ideal. Traditional Arab polygamy, however, is not abolished, but merely restricted to a maximum of four wives.[19]

This is a maximum by which Muhammad himself did not abide; the Koran (33:49) gives the Prophet special exemption from the restrictions on marriage; he had as many as nine wives at one time. This, to ascetically minded Christian authors, will be scandalous; they will use it to portray the Prophet as driven by lust. Yet Muhammad did not marry until the age of twenty-five and then remained monogamous for another twenty-four years, until Khadîja's death in 619. Perhaps more significant is that his polygamy begins in Medina, where he has become an important political and military leader: like many an Arab potentate before him, Muhammad used marriage to forge important political alliances and to reflect his political and economic prestige. It is in this context that the Koran orders the Muslims to obey their Prophet as political leader and judge. At this point, too, the Koran verifies his right to more than four wives and specifies in particular his right to marry Zaynab, divorced wife of his disciple and adopted son Zayd (33:37–38). This story, too, will be twisted by the hostile pens of Christian polemicists, will be used to supplement their image of Muhammad as lustful; the prophet's polygamy corresponded to their preconceived image of Antichrist. Whereas Saint Paul discouraged marriage, conceding only that is better to marry than to burn in hell (1 Cor. 7:8), the Koran encouraged single Muslims to marry (24:32); there was nothing wrong with marriage and sex, as long as it stayed within the bounds of propriety and mutual respect.

The Medina period was also marked with the continued—and indeed increased—hostility of the Meccans. War broke out between Mecca (led by the Quraysh) and Medina, piecemeal at first: Meccans attacked and persecuted Muslims, and the Muslims retaliated by attacking Meccan caravans. In 624 Muslims defeated the Meccans in a full-fledged battle at Badr. The following year, the Meccans defeated the Muslims in battle of Uhud; the Prophet himself was wounded and the situation looked bleak for the Muslims. In the wake of Uhud, the carefully constructed alliance in Medina began to crumble at the edges: in particular, some of the surrounding Bedouins, as well as the Jewish tribes of Medina, went over to the Meccan side; against them, Muhammad staged a series of punitive expeditions.

In the midst of this struggle, Sûra 2 of the Koran orders the Muslims to change the *qibla,* the direction of prayer, from Jerusalem to the Ka'ba in Mecca. Some scholars have suggested that this represents a break with Judaism following the collapse of the Muslim-Jewish alliance in Medina. The Koran explains that the Ka'ba was built by Abraham and his son Ishmael.[20] Abraham had been a monotheist (*hanîf*), and Islam was a continuation of his religion, *hanîfiyya.*[21] Ishmael, far from being the rejected illegitimate son portrayed in Genesis, is, for the Koran, the first and favored son of Abraham, and the Ka'ba is the oldest and most holy shrine to the One God, predating Solomon's temple at Jerusalem. This highlights the urgency of victory over the Meccans; the Ka'ba must be cleansed of idolatrous filth, returned to the pristine cult of the God of Abraham. The *Hâjj,* the ritual pilgrimage to the Ka'ba, was also instituted by Abraham and should be practiced by the faithful in its original form, cleansed of paganism.

Despite the defeat at Uhud, the Medinese were able to impose a blockade preventing Meccan caravans from trading to the north. The Quraysh, hoping to deliver a deathblow to Islam, enlisted the aid of many Bedouins and organized a major offensive against Medina in 627. The outnumbered Muslims responded by constructing a large defensive ditch around Medina that prevented the Meccan horse and cavalry from approaching the city walls. A combination of defensive fighting, occasional sorties, and negotiation with groups of Bedouins weakened the Meccan alliance, which gradually disbanded; the Meccans were unable to break the Medinese blockade. The following year, Muhammad and his Muslims marched toward Mecca with the intention of making the *Hâjj.* They were met outside the city by a group of Quraysh who negotiated to let them make the pilgrimage the following year, in exchange for a ten-year truce. Islam's star was rising, and many of the Meccans' allies went over to the Muslims. In 630, allies of the

Quraysh attacked some Muslims; this became the pretext for Muhammad to lead an army of ten thousand into Mecca, which surrendered without bloodshed. The Muslims marched into the Ka'ba and destroyed the idols and statues of the polytheists: Abraham's shrine was purified. The remaining pagan Bedouin tribes soon became Muslim; the entire Arab peninsula was unified through Islam, under the political and military leadership of Muhammad. "When God's help and victory come, and you see men embrace His faith in multitudes, give glory to your Lord and seek His pardon. He is ever disposed to mercy" (Koran 110).

This is all a very different story, of course, from the early struggles of Christianity: Jesus put to death by Rome as a criminal; his followers, a Christian minority in a pagan empire, persecuted for centuries. No wonder early Christians looked upon political and military power as evil, Rome as a reincarnation of the whore of Babylon. Later Christian authors write Rome into the divine plan (and subsequently, in the case of Isidore, write it out and replace it with the Goths), but there is really no positive image of political power in the New Testament. Medieval Christian kings will look back to the Old Testament for role models: the ancient Jewish kings, especially David. The Torah offers a mitigated view of earthly power: it glories in the victories that God gives his kings, yet describes the shame and humiliation of Israel's defeat at the hands of Babylon.

Things look different from the perspective of early Islam. God crowned Muslims with success from the beginning, it seemed: there was no need to vilify earthly power or to explain away political and miliary success. Christian writers from the seventh century to the twentieth reproach the Prophet for his political and military success, arguing that prophets do not spread the Word through the sword.[22] While Muslim texts portray Muhammad as passive in his role of messenger, humbly transmitting the word of God, he is aggressive in pursuing the interests of Islam, in forging the Muslim state. There is no contradiction here: one must humbly submit to God's will but firmly and unhesitatingly serve his law.

Muslims were encouraged to use political and military means for the expansion of Islam: outside the *dâr al-Islam* was the *dâr al-Harb,* the theater of war, open for the expansion of Islam. Muslim tradition affirms that Muhammad sent letters to the king of Ethiopia, the Roman governor or Egypt, and the Roman and Persian emperors, inviting them to convert to Islam.[23] Muhammad himself had organized expeditions into Syria in 626 and 629. Muhammad would not live to see the conquest of Syria. In 632 he made the pilgrimage to Mecca and returned to Medina, where he became ill. He died later the same year, his head in the lap of his beloved wife 'Â'isha.[24]

The Koran says nothing about the political order that was meant to follow the prophet's death. Many of the Bedouins decided that their treaties had been made with Muhammad personally and that they no longer owed either allegiance or the zakât to anyone. Muhammad's associates, however, declared that Abû Bakr was to be Muhammad's khalîfa (caliph), or successor. Meccans and Medinese rallied around him and fought to resubmit the Bedouins to the Islamic state.[25] When Abû Bakr died in 634, he was succeeded by 'Umar (634–44), who led the reunited Muslims north into Roman territory.

The Muslim invasions were not an irruption of a new and foreign people into the fertile crescent. Arabs had long been confederate members of the Roman (or Byzantine) military forces; they had founded and settled many of the cities of Syria: Petra, Hims, Harrân, Edessa.[26] Trade between Roman Syria and the Bedouins of the Arabian peninsula had been constant, punctuated by sporadic military clashes. What was unprecedented in 634 was that the tribes of the peninsula were no longer feuding rivals but united allies.

Moreover, Byzantine Syria and Persia, the two great rival empires, were both weakened by their recent war. The emperor Heraclius had scored a Pyrrhic victory for Constantinople, a victory of little comfort to the inhabitants of Byzantine Syria. Heraclius was hoping to regain control over his eastern provinces and to reassert (by compromise or by force) Constantinople's control over Christians it considered heretical, who had succeeded in establishing ecclesiastical independence: Armenian and Egyptian Monophysites and Syrian Jacobites. (Monophysites affirmed that Christ had only one nature, rejecting the "orthodox" Duophysite doctrine of distinct divine and human natures in Christ). The emperor also had plans to punish Jews for their alleged role in helping the Persian invaders in the recent war. The various inhabitants of the region felt battered by war and fearful of the reestablishment of Constantinople's power.

Thus the Muslims' strength and unity coincided with Byzantine weakness, and in the years between 634 and 638 the Muslims captured all of Byzantine Syria.[27] The Muslims won two key pitched battles that marked definitive defeat for the Byzantine forces in Syria: at Ajnâdayn (634) and Yarmûk (636). Other than those two battles, the Muslims encountered only weak and sporadic resistance. Most of the cities of the region surrendered after mere token resistance that allowed them to negotiate advantageous terms of capitulation. By the death of 'Umar in 644, the Muslims controlled all the fertile crescent and Egypt and much of Iran; they were poised to push their conquests further over the coming decades: west across the Maghreb and (in 711) into Visigothic Spain. At the same time Muslim troops pushed east through Iran and across the Oxus and Indus. Umayyad Caliph Walîd I (705–15) ruled an empire that stretched from what is now Pakistan and Afghanistan to Morocco and Portugal.

All this confirmed the Muslims' belief that God was on their side; as a seventh-century patriarch of Jerusalem complained, they boast that they are subduing the whole world.[28] This self-assured sense of divine mission certainly was a key factor in the success and rapidity of the conquests. At least as important was the freedom of religion guaranteed to most of its non-Muslim subjects.

Islam and Other Faiths

This freedom of religion was not granted toward pagan idolaters. Apart from the brief episode of the satanic verses, Muslim doctrine on idolatry is clear: it is evil. Idols must be eliminated, and Muslim troops often destroyed them and their temples. Arab tribes who converted to Islam were asked to destroy their own idols as proof of their clear break with the past.[29]

Muslim attitudes toward Judaism and Christianity have always been ambivalent. The Koran affirmed that the Torah and Gospels were divinely inspired scriptures that had been revealed by God through his prophets. While pagans were to be forced to convert, Jews and Christians, as People of the Book (*ahl al-kitâb*), were assured the right to worship.[30] The Koran expresses reverence for the main figures of the Jewish and Christian traditions: Moses, David, the Virgin Mary, Jesus, and others. It enjoins respect for some of the main elements in Old Testament law: to refrain from pork, practice circumcision, and so on. Many passages in the Koran emphasize the common heritage of these three faiths, all related to that of the original *hanîf*, Abraham. The Koran lambasts Christians and Jews who claim that only members of their sect will be admitted to heaven. The Koran makes no such exclusivist claims for Muslims: good Christians and Jews will have their place in heaven as well.[31] "Be courteous when you argue with the People of the Book, except with those among them who do evil. Say: 'We believe in that which is revealed to us and which was revealed to you. Our God and your God is one. To Him we surrender ourselves' " (Koran 29:46).

Yet there were conflicts with Jews in Medina, and it is in this context that the Medinese Sûras assert that Islam is the true uncorrupted form of the religion of Abraham, that Judaism has been sullied by the worship of the golden calf in Sinai, by failure to abide by God's law, and by willfully "altering words from their proper meanings."[32] The Koran echoes the Christian polemical attack on "blindness" of the Jews: "Those to whom the burden of the Torah was entrusted and yet refused to bear it are like a donkey laden with books. Wretched is the example of those who deny God's revelation."[33] Jews (and Christians), it seems, misinterpret their scripture so as to deny the antiquity of Islam and the prophethood of Muhammad. Later Muslim authors will accuse Jews (and Christians) of falsification of scripture (*tahrîf*): deliberately expunging prophecies relating to Muhammad from the Torah and Gospel.[34] Judaism in its present form is a corrupted, imperfect version of the true religion revealed to Abraham and Moses. It is to be tolerated but never to be granted equal footing with Islam.

The same can be said for the Koran's view of Christianity.[35] The Christian doctrines of the Trinity and incarnation are rejected.

> People of the Book, do not transgress the bounds of your religion. Speak nothing but the truth about God. The Messiah, Jesus the son of Mary, was no more than God's apostle and His Word which He conveyed to Mary: a spirit from Him. So believe in God and His apostles and do not say: "Three." Forbear, and it shall be better for you. God is but one God. God forbid that He should have a son! His is all that the heavens and the earth contain. God is the all-sufficient Protector. The Messiah does not disdain to be a servant of God, nor do the angels who are nearest to him.
>
> (Koran 4:169–71)[36]

Jesus was a prophet, a pure and holy man born miraculously from a virgin; but he was merely a man, not a god. The Crucifixion is rejected as well.

> And for their [the Jews'] saying, "We killed the Messiah, Jesus the son of Mary, the messenger of God," though they did not kill him and did not crucify him, but he was counterfeited for them; verily those who have

gone different ways in regard to him are in doubt about him; they have no knowledge of him and only follow opinion; and certainly they did not kill him, but God raised him to Himself.[37]

Christians, like Jews, have strayed from the pristine purity of their faith, have corrupted the teachings of the Gospel. For Ibn Ishâq, Muhammad was the Paraclete promised by John (15:26); the Christians stubbornly refuse to acknowledge him.[38] Followers of both religions are to be left free either to stay in their religious traditions or to embrace Islam; there shall be no compulsion for them.

If the errors of Christians and Jews do not justify forcible conversion, they do justify wars of conquest:

> Fight against those who do not . . . practice the religion of truth, those who have been given the Book, until they pay the tribute (*jizya*) off-hand, being subdued. The Jews say that 'Uzayr (Ezra) is the son of God,[39] and the Christians say that the Messiah is the son of God; that is what they say with their mouths, conforming to what was formerly said by those who disbelieved; God fight them! How they are involved in lies! They take their scholars and their monks as Lords apart from God, as well as the Messiah, son of Mary, though they were only commanded to serve one God, besides Whom there is no god, glory be to Him above whatever these associate with Him! They would extinguish the light of God with their mouths, but God refuses to do otherwise than perfect His light, though the unbelievers are averse.
>
> (Koran 9:29–35)

This Sûra is from the Medinese period, when Muslims were fighting to dominate Christian tribes in the northern Arabian peninsula.[40] It is be used to justify war against Christian states (in particular the Byzantine empire). Muslims came to see the world as divided in two: the *dâr al-Islam,* the world of Islam, and *dar al-harb,* the domain of war. It is a licit—indeed holy—part of the Muslim's spiritual struggle (jihad) to expand the domain of Islam by war. The Christian and Jew may be forced to submit to the paying of a poll tax (*jizya*) from which Muslims are exempt: thus they acceded to the status of *dhimmi,* protected minorities This would help encourage Muslim rulers to be tolerant, for it was more lucrative for them to have *dhimmi* subjects than Muslim ones. Yet the *dhimmi* was a second-class subject, meant to "pay tribute" and be "utterly subdued."[41]

In the wake of the Muslim conquests, little changed for the average Christian or Jewish resident of ex-Byzantine Syria. In Damascus, for example, the same family that had administered the city under Constantinople now did so for their new Muslim masters. Bureaucratic apparatuses were left in tact, and the language of administration continued to be Greek (or Persian in the former Persian empire). In the two centuries that followed, the Near East, from Egypt to Iran, became the theater of a tremendous though gradual cultural transformation: out of Greek, Persian, Arabic, Syriac, and Indian elements, a new Islamic civilization was forged.

Early Christian writers had constructed vast theological edifices in part from the need to justify their new faith in the face of Judaism, classical paganism, and Neoplatonic philosophy. Similarly, Muslim theology developed, over the course of the first centuries of Islam, in close contact and rivalry with Christian theology and Greek philosophy. It is no surprise that much theology in this period (both Christian and Muslim) bears the marks of this contention. Muslims wrote works of polemics and apologetics against Christianity that served the same purpose as Christian anti-Jewish texts: to immunize the faithful against the theological errors of the other and to convince new converts to reject the vestiges of their old religion.[42] Even when not directly addressing the rival religion, the theologian often betrayed a defensive attitude, as if he were already imagining the counterarguments of his rival. When Jâhiz, writing in the eighth century, set out to prove that Muhammad was indeed a prophet, he had potential Christian and Jewish criticisms in mind.[43]

Yet Muslim authors did not limit themselves to apologetics; they also actively attacked what they considered the grossest errors of Christian theology. The Christian doctrines of the Trinity and Incarnation offended Muslims (and Jews); it was blasphemous to worship Jesus, a human being created by God, as if he were God. It was scandalous to introduce Trinitarian divisions into God's indivisible unity. These two central doctrines are attacked in the Koran, and Muslim polemicists vigorously refuted them, paying less attention to more minor doctrinal differences with Christianity.[44] The Christians were "associators": instead of worshiping the One True God, they gave him a bevy of associates as minor deities: Jesus, the saints, the monks and priests.[45]

When Muslim intellectuals grappled with Christian and philosophical objections to Muslim doctrine, on the whole the mood was triumphalist: after all, had not God shown his preferences by granting Islam such stunning successes? As a seventh-century Muslim reportedly told a Christian monk, "It is a sign of God's love for us and pleasure with our faith that he has given us dominion over all regions and all peoples."[46] Muslim tradition held that Muhammad had sent a letter to Heraclius inviting him to convert to Islam. Caliph 'Umar II (717–20) is said to have sent such a letter to Byzantine Emperor Leo III.[47]

The letter attributed to 'Umar (in the version that has come down to us) seems in fact to have been written by a Muslim writer of the ninth century.[48] It provides a good example of Muslim polemical views of Christianity as they had by then developed. The author argues that the Christians have falsified their scriptures; that Jesus had never claimed to be God, but rather a messenger sent by God who had foretold the coming of Muhammad; that Jesus taught monotheism and not Trinitarianism. For all these arguments, he cites biblical proof texts (with varying levels of accuracy). He attacks the cult of relics and the cult of the cross and images. He gives a brief defense of Muslim doctrine against Christian arguments and then concludes by invoking the miraculous spread of Islam:

> In this way, with him in whom we trust, and in whom we believe, we went off, barefoot, naked, without equipment, strength, weapons or provisions, to fight against the largest empires, the most evidently powerful nations whose rule over other peoples was the most ruthless, that is to say: Persia and Byzantium.
>
> We marched against them with our small number, and our weak resources. And God enabled us to triumph over them and to take possession of their territories. He allowed us to settle down in their lands and houses, gave us their riches, when we had no other might or power than the Religion of Truth, thanks to God's power, mercy and help. From then on, He never ceased to grant us His favors, overwhelming us night and day again and again until we reached our present state which we receive from His generosity, His overflowing grace and His power. . . .
>
> As for us, we find in God's Revelation to our Prophet that He Himself said: "He it is who has sent His messenger with Guidance and the Religion of Truth to make it prevail over all religion."
>
> (Koran 9:33)[49]

Islam's meteoric rise indeed seemed miraculous: a handful of warriors from the desert subduing the richest and most populous parts of the world's most powerful empires. Surely God favored Islam and wished new subjects to convert. Most of them will (gradually, over several generations) conclude that this is so; most will convert to Islam. Those who refuse to convert, who choose to remain Christian, must answer the formidable question: Why has God permitted the stunning successes of Islam?

Perhaps the most dramatic and powerful refutation of Christian doctrine and affirmation of Muslim Christology was not to be a dialogue in a caliphal court or a theological tract relegated to an obscure library: it was carved into the Dome of the Rock mosque, in the holy city of Jerusalem.[50] An inscription says the Umayyad Caliph 'Abd al-Malik built it in 692, although it is unclear whether this refers to the beginning or the completion of its construction.[51] It is the first monument of Muslim architecture, built on the site of the second Jerusalem temple, which had been destroyed by Roman armies in 70 C.E. In rebuilding on the site of the temple associated with the ancient kings Solomon and David, the Umayyad caliphs laid claim to their heritage, source of legitimacy in the eyes of their subjects—Jewish, Christian, and Muslim. The choice of site made a powerful statement: Islam is here to stay; it continues and supersedes its predecessors, Judaism and Christianity. The inscriptions running along the exterior proclaim, in Koranic verses, the unity of God and the mission of his prophet Muhammad; the inscription on the interior, in contrast, contains all the Christological verses of the Koran, emphasizing Jesus' role as a human prophet, asserting that God cannot have a son. On the temple mount of Jerusalem, a short walk from the Church of the Holy Sepulcher, the inscriptions on the Dome of the Rock clearly proclaim that Muslims are the true heirs to Jesus, not the Christians who have set him up as a God alongside the one true God. The mosque was "meant as a message of power to Christians, whose defeated rulers had their crowns hanging in the sanctuary."[52] A message perhaps all the more urgent in light of recent Muslim military defeats against Byzantium. Christians (whether or not they could read the inscription) understood the message (see chapter 3).

The same triumphal message was painted on the walls of the eighth-century Qusayr 'Amra palace. There, in a mix of Byzantine and Persian traditions, are depicted the crowned kings of the world (Byzantium, Persia, Abyssinia, Visigothic Spain, etc.), identified in Arabic and Greek, making fealty to the Umayyad Caliph Walîd I. The message here is more overtly political: the Umayyad caliphate is now heir to the imperial and cultural traditions of Rome and Persia; like the earlier empires, it claims universal sovereignty.[53]

If a resident of, say, Damascus in the 630s could think he was merely exchanging a Byzantine overlord for an Arab one, a century later it was clear that more fundamental changes were afoot: Damascus was the capital of an emerging Islamic civilization. More and more Christians were converting to Islam; Arabic was being increasingly used. No hard demographic evidence exists to tell us when Muslims passed from being a minority to a majority, but educated guesses are around 825 for Iran, 900 for Egypt, Syria, and Iraq.[54] While we have stories of prominent individuals who actively sought out conversion to Islam, in many cases the "conversion" was probably passive: by not seeking the liminal Christian sacraments of baptism and the Eucharist, many ceased to be Christian without choosing to "convert" to Islam.[55] The number of *dhimmi* gradually, steadily diminished, and the number of Muslims grew in proportion.

For the Muslim, this was the rational, normal order of things. God had rewarded his faithful with dominion over the richest lands of the earth. He had shown Islam's superiority to Christianity (and Judaism) twice: first through the Koran, then by making Jews and Christians submit, as *dhimmi,* to the Muslim yoke. Their weakness and submission were appropriate to their inferior, secondary status in the eyes of God. More and more of them, moreover, were seeing the light and converting to Islam. There was still, of course, the weakened but still important Christian power of *Rûm* (Rome), with its capital, Constantinople, that resisted repeated Muslim attacks. Muslims prayed to have it delivered to Islam, and some day it would be. It was easy for a Muslim of the first Islamic centuries to reconcile himself with God's plan.

It was not so easy for a Christian. A triumphalist vision of history was excluded: the careful constructions of Isidore (and of other Christian thinkers like him) seemed to crumble into dust. What did it feel like to be one of the *dhimmi?* To be tolerated and disdained, viewed as a relic of a bygone era? How could a Christian of Syria construct a vision of theology and of history that would comfort him in his decision to refuse to join the tide of converts? What about the Christian in Constantinople? How did he feel about this new Islamic empire setting itself up on the ruins of his empire? To these questions I turn in chapter 3.

Chapter 3

❧✿❧

EARLY EASTERN CHRISTIAN REACTIONS TO ISLAM

God, who exacts his due and who determines sovereignty among people on the earth, will give power to whom He chooses. He may appoint even the dregs of mankind to be their rulers. When He saw that the measure of the Romans' sins was overflowing and that they were committing every sort of crime against our people and our churches, bringing our [Jacobite] Confession to the verge of extinction, He stirred up the Sons of Ishmael and enticed them hither from their southern land. This had been the most despised and disregarded of the peoples of the earth, if indeed they were known at all. Yet is was by bargaining with them that we secured our deliverance. This was no small gain, to be rescued from Roman imperial oppression.

Ninth-century Syrian chronicler Dionysus of Tel-Mahrē, as preserved in a
chronicle of the thirteenth century

DIONYSUS OF TEL-MAHRĒ expresses the ambivalence felt by many Syrian Christians as the Muslim armies conquered the Middle East.[1] Most Christian writers sought to explain the invasions with the traditional tools of Judeo-Christian historiography: the invaders were scourges sent by God to punish bad Christians for their sins. For Dionysus, a Syrian Monophysite, the scourge is sent against the Byzantine church as punishment for its Duophysite heresy and for its persecution of good (Monophysite) Christians. For Byzantine writers, on the contrary, the punishment falls on the Monophysites for *their* heresy. Some writers, by contrast, will attribute the invasions to more venal (often sexual) sins. All hoped that proper repentance would turn away the Saracen scourge, and few bothered to inquire into the religious beliefs of the invaders.

Over time, however, it became clear that the new Muslim rulers were here to stay. Muslims affirmed their power, proselytized among Christians and Jews, and dotted the landscape with new mosques; only then did Christians begin to take Islam seriously as a religious rival and to attempt to define it in Christian terms. Some authors ascribed an apocalyptic role to Islam; its rise and its winning of new Christian converts were proof that it was the religion of Antichrist and that the last days were at hand. Some authors branded Islam as heresy, falsely derived from Christian doctrine. In an attempt to stem the tide of conversions to Islam, they denigrated it using the familiar traditions of antiheretical polemics. A few Christians attacked Islam and its prophet in public, deliberately provoking the Muslim authorities into inflicting the death penalty; thus they became new martyrs whose hagiographers attempted to boost the flagging Christian morale.

All these authors struggled with the same troubling questions: why should God allow the Muslims to conquer (and maintain) huge territories and to reduce their Christian inhabitants to the status of *dhimmi?* Was it because God preferred Islam? Indeed, that was the point of view of Muslims and of the increasing numbers of Christian converts who swelled the ranks of Islam. That could not, of course, be the response of the authors who chose to remain Christian; they needed other explanations. In other words, they had to adapt the concepts of Christian theology and Christian historiography to explain Islam to their Christian readers. In so doing, they had to convince their readers of the superiority of Christianity, of the need to remain steadfast in the ancestral faith.

The Scourge of God:
The Arab Conquests as (Temporary) Punishment for Christian Sins

Historians now recognize the Muslim conquests of the Sassanian Persian empire and of large swathes of the Roman (or Byzantine) empire as a fundamental watershed of world history. This was not clear to those who lived through the conquests, the largely Christian inhabitants of the Middle East. They had seen their share, after all, of conquerors, most recently in the back-and-forth struggles between Persian and Roman empires that had so weakened both. From Constantinople, the invasions must have seemed the latest of a series that had lasted several centuries: Rome had lost its western provinces to Germanic barbarians and had weathered the coordinated assault of the Avars and the Sassanian Persians. The Arab invasions, like the previous incursions, were seen as God's punishment of his people for their sins. Yet the imperial army and the Virgin Mary had always protected Constantinople.[2] God was merciful; would he not allow a properly chastened Christian empire to regain its dominions?

Hence it should not be surprising that the earliest Christian commentators on the Muslim conquests have little to say about Islam or its prophet. One searches in vain in these texts for the words "Muslim" or "Islam," or indeed for any indication that the invaders have religious motives. The earliest Syriac texts, for example, speak of "kings" rather than caliphs, "Arabs" (*Tayy*) rather than Muslims.[3] Muhammad is mentioned rarely, and primarily as a military and political—rather than a spiritual—leader. Several chroniclers supposed that the new Arab invaders must have been idolaters like the Arab tribesmen of an earlier era.[4]

At the very height of the invasions, on Christmas day, 634, the Christians of Jerusalem, unable to go to recently conquered Bethlehem for the customary Christmas Mass, stayed in Jerusalem and heard a sermon by their patriarch, Sophronios. He spoke of the invasions and of the fear that they struck into the hearts of Jerusalem's Christians: this was punishment for "countless sins and very serious faults."[5] Just as Adam and Eve were banished from the earthly paradise by the angel's flaming sword (Gen. 4.24), Sophronios says, so are Christians prevented by the sword of the Saracens from approaching Bethlehem on Christmas. Just as the pagan gentile "slime" had once prevented King David from reaching Bethlehem so the "godless Saracens" now keep the Christians away.[6]

The invaders, for Sophronios, present a formidable military threat but a negligible spiritual menace: he does not bother to find out what their religious beliefs and practices are. Rather, the invaders represent the scourge of God so familiar to readers of the Old Testament: God, angry with his people, punishes them by sending godless barbarians to conquer them. The path to victory, as always, is repentance:

> Therefore I call on and I command and I beg you for the love of Christ the Lord, in so far as it is in our power, let us correct ourselves, let us shine forth with repentance, let us be purified by conversion and let us curb our performance of acts which are hateful to God. If we constrain ourselves, as friendly and beloved of God, we should laugh at the fall of our Saracen adversaries and we would view their not distant death, and we would see their final destruction.[7]

Sophronios looks forward to the imminent destruction of the Saracens, whose role in the divine scheme of history he limits to a brief cameo appearance as divine chastisement, an unpleasant but necessary interlude in the reign of the Christian Roman empire.[8] Over the next several years, the Muslim invaders showed no signs of going away. Sophronios himself had to surrender Jerusalem to the caliph 'Umar; in the last of his sermons to come down to us, he bewails the desolation wreaked by the Saracens and predicted by the prophets; the Saracens, he complains, boast that they are subduing the whole world.[9]

Other church leaders took a similarly dim view of their new overlords. Maximus the Confessor, in a letter written from Alexandria between 634 and 640, bemoaned the losses inflicted by the barbarian invaders: "What could be more dire than the present evils now encompassing the civilized world? To see a barbarous nation of the desert overrunning another land as if it were their own, to see our civilization laid waste by wild and untamed beasts who have merely the shape of a human form."[10] These "beasts," for Maximus, are Jews and followers of Antichrist; this is all he says about their religious orientation. Repentance by Christians is what is needed to repulse the invaders.

The late seventh-century writings of Anastasius, a monk of Saint Catherine's monastery on Mount Sinai, present a similar view.[11] Anastasius devoted much of his work to fighting his spiritual enemies. These adversaries are not Muslims but rather Monophysite heretics; it is their error that he attacks in his polemical work the *Hodegos*. He does, in his prolific writings, at times allude to the tribulations brought about by the Arab invasions and even describes (accurately) the arguments that some of these "Arabs" level against Christianity. Yet not once does he refer by name to Islam, Muslims, Muhammad, or the Koran. Monophysitism is a much larger preoccupation for Anastasius; this heresy, indeed, seems to be the root of the errors of the Arabs, and the Arab invasions themselves are punishments for the Monophysitism of Heraclius.[12]

While the Saracens are beneath serious theological refutation for Anastasius, he does not hesitate to put them in the devil's camp. Anastasius's *Dièghèmata Stèriktiká* is a collection of pious stories, many of them involving Eucharistic miracles; others, the snares of devils and witches.[13] The Saracens figure prominently as the demons' chief allies. A group of Saracens attacks an icon, which bleeds; the attackers all die.[14] Demons accompany Saracens on their raids, but the Saracens are worse, for at least the demons are awed by the power of the Eucharist.[15] But what of the Saracen cult? Anastasius reports that two Christian sailors ventured to Mecca where the Saracens "have their stone and their cult." The Saracens sacrificed goats and camels; that night, the sailors saw a horrible woman rise out of the earth and eat the heads and feet of the animals. The sailors proclaimed: "Look at their sacrifice! It did not go up, towards God, but down. And that woman is their erroneous faith!"[16] In this curious story, Anastasius imputes an unwitting cult of demons on the Saracens; only in the dark of night, when all the Saracens are gone, is the true object of their veneration revealed. Lest there should be any doubt about the demons' alliance with the Saracens, Anastasius tells of a certain John of Bostra who interrogated demonically possessed girls in Antioch. The demons told him (through the mouths of the girls) that the three things they feared most were the cross, baptismal water, and the Eucharist; that, they continued, is why they preferred the religion of their "companions," the Saracens, who rejected all three.

Anastasius attempts to erect a wall of difference between Islam and Christianity. He is not ignorant of the similarities between the two faiths; he is painfully aware of them. This is why he stresses the differences, the quasi-magical powers of the sacraments, as the most effective way to repel the demonic forces. Anastasius tells that "thirty years ago" he had been in Jerusalem and had seen the Egyptians clearing away rubble from the Temple Esplanade; at night, he claims, he saw demons helping them. He felt it necessary to write this down, he says, because some people say that what is being built there now (i.e., the Dome of the Rock mosque) is the Temple of God.[17] In Jerusalem, as at Mecca, only the nighttime appearance of demons alerts the cautious Christian that the Saracens are really (if perhaps unwittingly) in alliance with the devil, not God.

Two eighth-century Byzantine writers followed Anastasius's lead in presenting Muhammad's monotheism as a veneer covering his true idolatry. For Nicetas of Byzantium, Muhammad was in fact a devotee of the goddess Khabar: it is her idol the Muslims actually worship in Mecca.[18] Georges the Monk gives a fraudulent translation of the Arabic *Allahu akbar!* (God is great!) that *dhimmi* would constantly hear intoned from minarets. He transcribes it as *Allah wa Koubar,* and he says that it means "God and Koubar"; the latter, he explains, is the Saracens's name for the moon and Aphrodite.[19] The hostile Christian can twist even a simple affirmation of God's greatness into a call for Saracen idolatry.

Precursors of Antichrist

For some Christian authors, the Arab invaders were something more than a mere divine chastisement: they were actors in the divine drama of the last days. In other words, the invasions represented the beginning of the end of time, as predicted by the Hebrew prophets, the Gospels, and the Book of Revelation. The author of an anonymous anti-Jewish text, the *Doctrine of Jacob Recently Baptized* (634), sees the Arab conquests as anything but temporary. He interprets the four beasts described by the prophet Daniel, in the quite standard way, as four successive world empires, the last of which is Rome. Yet for him, the current invasions mark the end: "If the fourth beast, that is, the Roman Empire, is reduced, torn asunder and shattered, as Daniel said, verily there will be no other, except the ten claws and the ten horns of the fourth beast, and afterwards a little horn, completely different, which has knowledge of God. Immediately there will take place the end of the universe and the resurrection of the dead."[20] The ten claws and ten horns are traditionally seen as a series of persecutors of God's people; the *Doctrine* here identified the Arabs as the eleventh, little horn. To receive such an important role in the drama of the final days, the new invaders must have some *religious* significance. Justus, one of the interlocutors in this fictive dialogue, tells of a letter he received from his brother, Abraham of Caesarea, about "a deceiving prophet [who] appeared amidst the Saracens." Abraham heard from an old scribe that this prophet "is deceiving. For do prophets come with swords and chariot? Verily, the events of today are works of confusion."[21]

Yet to other Christians the situation did not look so bleak. If the Melkite church (i.e., the Duophysite "orthodox" church now under Muslim dominion) saw its power and prestige diminished by the Arab conquests, adherents of rival churches on the other hand seemed to breathe a collective sigh of relief. No longer subjected to pressure (and intermittent persecution) from Constantinople, they were granted broader religious freedoms by their new Muslim rulers. Sebeos, an Armenian Monophysite, wrote in 661 that Muhammad was learned in the law of Moses, taught the knowledge of God of Abraham to Arabs, who "abandoning the reverence of vain things, . . . turned toward the living God, who had appeared to their father Abraham."[22] God granted to Arabs the lands he had promised to Abraham, and gave them victory over the impious Byzantines. Other seventh-century chroniclers also painted Islam in positive terms. One, having described how Abraham constructed a shrine to God in the desert, asserts: "the Arabs do nothing new when they adore God in this place, but continue the ancient usage, as is proper for people who honor the ancestor of their race."[23]

Sebeos, like the anonymous author of the *Doctrine of Jacob Recently Baptized,* created a niche in history for the Muslim conquerors by using Daniel's four-empire scheme; contemporary Jewish authors did the same.[24] But for Sebeos the "Ishmaelites" represented not one of the horns of the beast, but the fourth beast itself, in other words, the last great world empire, an honor generally reserved for Rome.

The invasions could look quite different depending on one's perspective: an orthodox Christian safe in Constantinople bewailing the loss of territory, a Melkite thrust into the role of *dhimmi* by the new masters, or a Monophysite happy to be liberated from Byzantine oppression. Yet members of all the Christian communities eventually had to face an unpleasant fact: Islam was here to stay. God's scourge showed no signs of wishing to go away or to convert to Christianity. On the contrary, society was becoming slowly Arabized, in language and in social customs, and more and more Christians were converting to Islam. Greek- and Syriac-speaking Christians had begun to feel like foreigners in their own lands. Gradually, Islam came to be seen as a *religious,* and not merely *military,* threat. Christian writers needed to come to terms with it and offer arguments to refute it, not in order to convert Muslims to Christianity but to slow down the tide of conversions from Christianity to Islam.

THE CRISIS in Christian minds would have been accentuated by the construction of the Dome of the Rock mosque, a refutation of the Christian vision of history anchored firmly in the bedrock of Jerusalem, spiritual center of the Christian world. Surely the chroniclers who had portrayed the Muslim invaders as an ephemeral divine chastisement were wrong. Confronted by this symbol of Muslim political and spiritual might, in the midst of the rising tide of conversion and Arabization, a new, darker vision of God's plan was forged: the anonymous Syriac author of the *Apocalypse of Pseudo-Methodius* (c. 692) presented the Muslim domination as part of the drama of the last days.[25]

The work bears the title *Apocalypse of Pseudo-Methodius* because it purports to be the work of Methodius, bishop of Olympas (d. c. 311). The preface explains that this "apocalypse" or "revelation" was granted to Methodius by the Lord, who "sent to him one of his powers, to the mountain of Šingar, and He showed him all the generations and the kingdoms one by one."[26] In other words, God revealed the course of military and political history to Methodius, from Adam to the world's end. In this vision, the Muslim invasions become both the punishment God metes out to sinful Christians and the "testing furnace" meant to try the true Christians before the ultimate Christian victory. By attributing the *Apocalypse* to the respected church father Methodius and by placing it in the fourth century, the anonymous author passes off his *descriptions* of the Muslim invasions as authoritative, divinely inspired *predictions* of the invasions and hopes in turn to lend credibility to his predictions of imminent Christian victory over the "pagan" Ishmaelites.

While the *Apocalypse of Pseudo-Methodius* presents the sweep of world history using the same notion of six millennia employed by Isidore,[27] its major preoccupation is to explain Muslim hegemony and the conversion of Christians to Islam in Christian terms. Just as God gave the Holy Land to the Jews to punish the sins of its previous inhabitants, "So too with the sons of Ishmael, it is not because God loves them that He allows them to enter into the kingdom of the Christians, the like of which has never been done in any of the former generations."[28] What are the unprecedented sins being punished? For this author, they are not Christological but sexual, described in lurid detail: men dress in drag as harlots in the market place and fornicate with each other; men take their sons and brothers to whorehouses to share the same prostitutes; men fornicate with men and women with women, and so on. The punishment is described in detail as well: Methodius "predicts" the scope and magnitude of the conquests of the Ishmaelites, couching them in terms of apocalyptic destruction: rape and pillage, fire and tempered steel, and—worst of all—tribute and taxes.

Yet, far from being a sign that God has abandoned Christians or that he prefers the Ishmaelites, the invasions are a just, even mild, punishment for the sexual sins of Christians. The only other mention of such sexual deviance in the *Apocalypse of Pseudo-Methodius* is during the second millennium, when "the women were openly running after the men and, like mares in a wild herd, the women, and the men too, had gone mad in an excess of fornication."[29] The punishment then was the flood; in comparison, seventh-century Christians suffering under the yoke of the Ishmaelites could feel that they were getting off with a light sentence.

The Muslim invasions are not the first time the Ishmaelites have sown havoc: in the fifth millennium they overran the promised land "like locusts; they used to walk naked; they ate flesh from the vessels of flesh and drank the blood of animals."[30] In order to make the Ishmaelites (and conversion to Islam) abhorrent to its readers, the *Apocalypse of Pseudo-Methodius* dehumanizes them; this becomes even clearer in the descriptions of the more recent Ishmaelite invasions:

> These barbarian rulers are not men, but sons of destruction, and they set their faces toward destruction. They are spoilers, and they are sent for desolation. They are ruination, and they come forth for the ruin of everything, being abominable people who love abomination. At the time of their coming forth from the desert, they will tear open pregnant women; and they will take babies by force from their mothers' arms and dash them against the rocks like unclean animals. They will sacrifice the ministers within the temple, and they will sleep with their wives and with the captive women inside the temple. They will make the sacred garments into clothing for themselves and their sons. They will tether their cattle in the shrines of the martyrs and in the burial places of the saints. They are insolent and murderous, shedders of blood and spoilers; they are a furnace of trial for all Christians.[31]

Even the mass conversions of Christians to Islam is "predicted" by Methodius, as part of this "furnace of trial."[32] Paul himself had predicted "that in the latter times some shall depart from the faith, giving heed to seducing spirits, and doctrines of devils."[33] These "latter times," the world's final days, have come; the mass, voluntary apostasy of Christians is proof of it. During this period, the *Apocalypse* makes clear, the good Christian who perseveres will suffer more persecution than the bad Christian who apostatizes. Why?

> It is so that they might be tested, and the faithful might be separated from the unfaithful, and the tares and those who are rejected from the choice wheat, because that time will be a furnace of trial. And God will be patient while His worshipers are persecuted, so that by means of the chastisement the sons might be made known, as the Apostle proclaimed beforehand, "if we are without chastisement, whereof all are partakers, then ye are bastards, and not sons."[34]

This period of punishment and trial, a rod that a loving father uses to discipline his wayward children, was almost over: God had declared that the Ishmaelites' dominion would last "ten weeks of years"—in other words, seventy years.[35] It is unclear what the author considered the beginning of the seventy-year dominion: perhaps the invasions of Syria in 634–36. The message to Christians of 692 (the probable date of composition[36]) is clear: hang on for a few more years, patiently enduring the "furnace of trial," and you will see vindication and revenge.

The *Apocalypse* describes with relish the imminent demise of the Ishmaelites. The "King of the Greeks" (i.e., the Byzantine emperor), will arise "as a man who shakes away his wine,"[37] and will rout the Ishmaelites in battle and submit them to servitude, destroying Arabia and Egypt. "And all the fierce anger of the king of the Greeks will run a full course with those who had denied Christ."[38] This is a clear warning to those who might be considering apostasy and a promise of sweet revenge for those Christians who remain true to their faith. For the Christian faithful, the Greek Christian victory will usher in "the final peace of the end of the world: there will be joy on the whole earth; men will dwell in great peace; the churches will be renewed; the cities will be rebuilt, and the priests will be set free from tax."[39]

Yet the victory over the Ishmaelites and the subsequent peace are merely the prelude to harsher invasions: the barbarians of the North, Gog and Magog—wild men who eat scorpions, kittens, miscarried fetuses, and human flesh—will pour out of the mountains and wreak havoc for "a week of calamity" until God sends one of his angels to destroy them, and the king of the Greeks will rule in Jerusalem for ten and a half years.[40] Yet even this is but a prologue to the real drama of the end: it is at this time that the Antichrist is born. I will not here expound in detail his description of the birth, career, and ultimate defeat of Antichrist and of the final coming of Christ: suffice it to say that the earlier invaders (Ishmaelites, Gog, Magog, and the rest) have all been swept from the stage and none is mentioned.

What are we to make, then, of the role of the Ishmaelites in this Christian vision of history, a vision crafted, perhaps, in response to the Dome of the Rock? Clearly (although the *Apocalypse* does not actually use the term), the Ishmaelites are prominent among the various precursors of Antichrist. The persecution they inflict on Christians is both punishment for Christian fornication and a "furnace of trial" for the selection of worthy, steadfast Christians. The good Christian can look forward to the imminent end of this persecution, but the subsequent peace will be brief and will be followed by harsher persecution.

The anonymous Syriac author hoped against all reason for a sudden miraculous military recovery of the Byzantine empire; yet the "ten weeks of days" passed, and the Muslim empire endured. Various later Christian apocalyptic writers (some of them directly inspired by *Apocalypse of Pseudo-Methodius;* others, not) would recalculate the allotted time, usually putting the end of Muslim rule in the near future. The difference between Sophronios's view of the Arab invaders as a divine chastisement and the *Apocalypse of Pseudo-Methodius's* portrayal of them as forerunners of the Antichrist is one of degree, not nature; they are given a more prominent role in God's plan to correspond with their enormous political, military, and spiritual successes. Yet the *Apocalypse* (like Sophronios) shows little interest in or knowledge of Islam: if this is a response to the Dome of the Rock, it is to the symbolic enemy presence in the holy city. No attempt is made to refute the Islamic Christology inscribed in the stones of the new building; the Ishmaelite is described repeatedly as "pagan," with no effort to understand his religion. He is irretrievably other, barbaric—what he believes cannot be of interest to the steadfast Christian.

Muslims Branded as Heretics by Christian Apologists and Polemicists

As a strategy for stemming the tide of apostasy, the crude caricatures of the *Pseudo-Methodius* were singularly ineffective: the tide of conversion to Islam continued to rise. Clearly a closer look at the spiritual adversary was needed. While writers of apocalypses continued to fan the flames of hope down the centuries, other writers confronted Islamic doctrine directly and attempted to refute it. Their texts in theory fall into the categories of apologetics (defenses of Christianity) and polemics (attacks on Islam), though in practice the two broadly overlap. There are a handful of Christian anti-Muslim writers during the first Muslim century: of these the best known (and most influential over the subsequent centuries) was John of Damascus (d.749).

Yuhannâ b. Mansûr b. Sarjûn, better known as John of Damascus, bridged two worlds.[41] Melkite presbyter and monk, John wrote extensively in Greek on a variety of theological issues. Yet he was also one of the chief financial administrators of the Umayyad caliphs 'Abd al-Malik (685–705) and Walîd I (705–15). John's family had long been prominent in Damascus; indeed, it was probably his grandfather, Mansûr b. Sarjûn, who surrendered the city to Khâlid b. al-Walîd in 635. John's father, apparently, was an Arabic Christian who spoke no Greek; one Greek writer praises John for having learned Greek so fast.[42] John himself wrote in Greek; many of his works were subsequently translated into Arabic and seem to have been read and used by Muslim writers.[43] He was anathematized by Byzantine bishops, who appreciated neither his opposition to iconoclasm nor, perhaps, his role in the administration of Byzantium's chief political and military adversary. He left Damascus around 725 to become a monk in the Palestinian monastery of Mar Sabbas; there he wrote many of his works. His departure from the Umayyad court has been the subject of much legend and speculation.[44] It may be that he felt unwanted or at best redundant in a court increasingly Muslim, where Arab had recently replaced Greek as the language of administration. The pressures to convert—political, economic, and social—were stronger than ever, and the tide of conversions to Islam was continuing to rise.[45]

John occupied a key—and at times awkward—position at the intersection of the Christian and Muslim worlds. Yet in his works, which run to more than fifteen hundred pages in the modern edition, barely a dozen pages deal directly with Islam: a short chapter of his *Fount of Knowledge* and the brief *Disputation Between a Saracen and a Christian*. If page count is a reliable gauge, iconoclasm is a much larger preoccupation for John than is Islam.[46] Yet his dozen pages on Islam provide a key glimpse at the formation of an apologetic Christian response to Islam, and they were to be read and reread by scores of later Christian writers as they attempted to come to terms with Islam.

Near the end of his life, in 743, as a monk of Mar Sabbas, John completed his *Fount of Knowledge,* a vast theological compendium consisting of three parts: the first on philosophical ideas, the second on heresies, and the third on the orthodox faith.[47] Part 2, *On the heresies,* in some manuscripts is an independent text: it describes one hundred heresies in as many chapters. Of these, the first ninety-seven are largely derivative, copied with little change from earlier compendia; only the last three chapters, on iconoclasm, the Aposchites, and Islam, seem to be the original work of John of Damascus.[48] The place of his description of Islam should be kept in mind: Islam is the last of one hundred heresies that have plagued the church. John will deploy against Islam the Trinitarian arguments habitually leveled against Jacobites and Nestorians, arguments for free will deployed against the Manicheans, and arguments in defense of crucifixes and icons from the iconoclastic dispute.[49] From John's perspective, Islam is not a new religion but the last in a long line of deviant Christianities.

John devotes the last of his hundred chapters, much longer than the others,[50] to "the religion of the Ishmaelites, which still dominates today, leading the people astray, precursor (πρόδρομος) of the Antichrist."[51] He places the Ishmaelites in the context of biblical genealogy: they are the descendants of Hagar (hence called Hagarenes) and of Ishmael (hence Ishmaelites). They are also called the Saracens, he says, because Sarah sent Hagar away empty (this etymology is based on an untranslatable Greek pun).[52] These people, he says, were idolaters who "venerated the morning star and Aphrodite, whom notably they called *Khabar* (Χαβάρ) in their own language, which means 'great' [*akbar*, in Arabic]; therefore until the times of Heraclius they were, undoubtedly, idolaters." During the reign of Heraclius, he continues, "a false prophet appeared among them, surnamed Mamed (Μάμεδ), who, having casually been exposed to the Old and the New Testament and supposedly encountered an Arian monk, formed a heresy of his own."[53] This "Arian monk" is no doubt meant to be Bahira, who, rather than merely recognizing the prophet's divine mission, seems to play a role in the formation of the prophet's "heresy." John makes him an Arian heretic in order the better to discredit Islam by associating it with familiar errors already attacked in previous chapters of *Against the Heresies.*[54]

John goes on to say that "Mamed" pretended that God had revealed scriptures to him, pronouncements "worthy only of laughter."[55] He summarizes, accurately and briefly, Muslim doctrines regarding the unity of God, Creation, and the role of Jesus as human prophet (but not God). Rather than attempting to refute these doctrines, John calls into question the legitimacy of the revelation. "Although he includes in this writing [the Koran] many more absurdities worthy of laughter, he insists that this was brought down to him from God."[56] What is absurd and risible in Islam, for John, is its rejection of the divinity of Christ, of the Crucifixion, and of other fundamental Christian doctrines. Here John turns and interrogates a hypothetical Muslim adversary, asking him to produce witnesses to prove the legitimacy of the prophet's revelation. He contrasts Muhammad to Moses, who received the law on Mount Sinai in full view of the people. The Ishmaelites' law requires witnesses for weddings, land sales, and other transactions; why do they not ask for witnesses to prove that the Koran is truly revealed by God?

Such arguments are unlikely to convince a real Muslim, who could retort that Christians accept the Gospels and the books of the Hebrew prophets without any witnesses. The very lack of theological sophistication in this argument shows that this is not so much polemical (i.e., an offensive attack on Islam) as apologetical (a defensive strategy designed to slow down the defection of Christians to the Muslim camp). He seems to be furnishing arguments that could be deployed by Christians wishing to defend their faith to Muslim interlocutors and is certainly not offering an attack Muslim thinkers could take seriously. He needs to convince his reader of the efficacity and irrefutability of his arguments, in response to which, he asserts, his Muslim opponents were "surprised and at a loss"; "they remain silent because of shame."[57]

The practical, defensive nature of his apologetics becomes even clearer in the two sections that follow, offering aggressive counterarguments against two common Muslim objections to Christianity. "They call us *associators,* because, they say, we introduce beside God an associate to Him by saying that Christ is the Son of God and God."[58] John responds with two arguments, defensive and offensive. First, the defensive argument: the prophets announced Christ's coming and the Gospels confirmed it; if we are wrong, they are wrong. Second, the offensive argument:

> Again we respond to them: "Since you say the Christ is Word and Spirit of God, how do you scold us as *associators?* For the Word and the Spirit are inseparable each from the one in whom this has the origin; if, therefore, the Word is in God it is obvious that he is God as well. If, on the other hand, this is outside of God, then God, according to you, is without word and without spirit. Thus, trying to avoid making associates to God you have mutilated Him. . . . Therefore, by accusing us falsely, you call us *associators;* we, however, call you *mutilators* (κόπτας) of God."[59]

In other words, by depriving the divinity of the Word and the Spirit, Muslim "mutilators" deprive God of his key attributes. Such Trinitarian arguments, based on triads of divine attributes, are to become standard fare in Christian polemics against Islam. Here John gives a simplified version of such an argument, primarily, it seems, to provide the Christian with a handy insult word to bandy back against any Muslim who accuses him of being an associator. He makes no attempt (as some later polemicists will) to prove the truth of the Trinity; he indeed asserts elsewhere that it is an incomprehensible and inexplicable mystery.[60]

He next says that Muslims "defame us as being idolaters because we venerate the cross, which they despise."[61] Here again, he offers both an offensive argument and a defensive one. How is it, he asks his imaginary Muslim opponent, that you rub yourself up against a stone and kiss it? The adoration of the Ka'ba, he suggests, smacks of idolatry: "This, then, which they call 'stone' is the head of Aphrodite, whom they used to venerate and whom they call *Khabar* (Χαβάρ), on which those who can understand it exactly can see, even until now, traces of an engraving."[62] How can the Muslim compare this to veneration of "the cross of Christ, through which the power of the demons and the deceit of the devil have been destroyed"?[63] John redeploys the traditional image of pagan litholatry ascribed to pre-Islamic Saracens by Jerome, Isidore, and other writers; the suggestion is that if one scratches the monotheism of the Muslim, one finds a pagan stone-worshiper. The accusation is meant to be deployed defensively, to ward off the charge that Christian veneration of Crucifixes was idolatry.

Having provided these key defensive arguments to parry the most common Muslim thrusts against Christianity, he goes on to try to discredit the Koran in the eyes of his Christian readers. He dwells on the Koranic laws involving polygamy and divorce and on the marriage between Muhammad and Zaynab. After a brief description of Muslim laws on circumcision and the prohibition on drinking, the *De haeresibus* ends abruptly; if John ever wrote a conclusion to the text, it has not survived. He makes no effort to synthesize at the end of his description of one hundred heresies.

John's brief *Disputation between a Saracen and a Christian* shows the same practical concern for providing the beleaguered Christian with practical, defensive arguments to be deployed against Muslim proselytizers. A Saracen and Christian debate over issues of free will, Creation, Christology, and baptism. The Saracen tries to trick the Christian into making untenable statements; at each instance the Christian recognizes the trap being laid for him and cleverly avoids it: he maintains, for example, that God Himself gives man his free will but that man and the devil (and not God) are the authors of evil. John presents common Muslim arguments against key points in Christian theology and provides simple, ready-made refutations of those arguments. As always in such fictive dialogues, the protagonist easily has the upper hand: the facility with which he refutes the Saracen and the latter's unbound admiration for his arguments take us into a fantasy world. In response to one of the Christian's arguments, "the Saracen, having understood and being impressed, said: 'That is the way it is, indeed.'"[64] And at the end of the *Disputation*, "the Saracen was very much amazed and surprised, and, having nothing to reply to the Christian, departed without challenging him any more."[65] This happy ending is revealing: the goal is not to convert the Saracen but to silence him, to be left alone, in peace, to practice one's ancestral faith. John's dozen pages on Islam represent not polemics as much as apologetics: the defense of a beleaguered Christian community struggling for survival at the center of an expanding, confident Muslim empire. He casts Islam in the familiar role of Christological heresy, and thus devotes much of his attention to attacking Muslim Christology.[66] He calls Islam a "forerunner to Antichrist"; yet he paints no apocalyptic scenarios: indeed, he used the same term to refer to the heresiarch Nestorius.[67] Though in another work John prays for an end to the Ishmaelites' rule and a return of Byzantine power,[68] unlike the author of the *Apocalypse of Pseudo-Methodius* he seems to have little real hope that it will come to pass; while the pseudo-Methodius dehumanized the "Ishmaelites," John plays an important role in their government; while the pseudo-Methodius was stubbornly ignorant of Muslim doctrine, John studies it and explains it to his reader—in order to refute it.

Martyrs

The indigenous Christian populations of the Near East reacted to Muslim dominion in several ways. The majority of them converted to Islam gradually over the first three Islamic centuries.[69] Those who remained Christians explained Islam as a temporary divine chastisement, as a part of the cataclysm of the last days, or as a worldly, heretical deviation from the Christian truth. The authors whose works I have examined wrote for Christian audiences in order to urge them to remain true to Christianity. While theological debate was possible with Muslims, most Christians in such cases stuck to apologetics and avoided making polemical attacks against Muhammad and the Koran. For to do the latter would have been dangerously overstepping the limits of Muslim tolerance.

Some Christians deliberately overstepped those boundaries and were put to death for doing so. A handful of Christians became martyrs either for attacking Muhammad and the Koran or for converting from Islam to Christianity (which, as apostasy, was a crime punishable by death). Revered as saints by their Christian communities, their lives (and especially deaths) were recorded by hagiographers who recounted miracles performed by the martyrs in order to prove their sanctity. It is often impossible to separate truth from hagiographical legend: some of the martyrdoms certainly occurred; others are mere pious fictions. Yet even the latter provide a key glimpse into the vision of Islam crafted by the hagiographers.

A number of these hagiographical texts tell of prominent Muslims who converted to Christianity and then were put to death by the Muslim authorities: such is the case of the *Passion of Anthony Ruwah*.[70] Anthony was a

Muslim official in the court of 'Abbāsid Emir Hârûn al-Rashîd; his main pastime, if we are to believe his *Passion,* was harassing the Christian monks of the Damascene monastery of Saint Theodore. One day Anthony shot an arrow at the icon of the saint; Theodore repelled the arrow, which wounded Anthony in the hand. After a series of visions confirmed the miracle, a chastened Anthony journeyed to the Jordan River to be baptized. Upon his return to Damascus, his family denounced him as an apostate. Finally, he was brought before the caliph, who offered him wealth and honor if he would reconvert to Islam. Anthony refused and was beheaded on Christmas day, 799. Miraculous signs appeared in the sky that night to confirm his status as martyr for the true faith.

It is hard to know what truth, if any, lies behind this story. But it is easy to see how this text could be heartening to discouraged Christians living as *dhimmi* under Muslim rule. God has not forsaken them: he continues to produce saints and miracles. He continues to defend them by turning their persecutors into allies. The choice given to Anthony by the caliph—wealth and worldly honor on the one hand, martyrdom on the other—carries a polemical message: Islam is the religion of this world; Christianity, the religion of the next. The Christian reader is reassured that he is right after all and his encouraged to endure the rather minor "martyrdom" of life as one of the *dhimmi* in return for the celestial rewards Christ is saving for him. This message was a popular one; Theodore Abû Qurrah mentions Anthony as a well-known saint, and his cult was venerated across sectarian lines by Christians not only in Syria but also as far away as Georgia and Ethiopia.[71]

Hagiographers also wrote of Christians who had converted to Islam, repented, returned to Christianity, and were subsequently martyred.[72] Other martyrs were Christians who (deliberately or not) incurred the death sentence for attacking Islam. Bishop Peter of Capitolias was martyred for vilifying Muhammad as a "false prophet and Antichrist," proclaiming, "Anathema on Mouamed and his fables and on everyone who believes in them!"[73] Similar stories were told about Romanos the Neomartyr and Michael the Sabaïte.[74] There were other stories of prominent Arabs who apostatized, were martyred, and developed flourishing cults: Abo of Tbilisi (d. 786), Pachomios (d. c. 800), and 'Abd al-Masîh (d. c. 860).[75]

Gregory of Decapolis (early ninth century) relates secondhand a story he heard from a general named Nicholas about the conversion and martyrdom of a Saracen named Ampelon nephew of the "Caliph of Syria."[76] Ampelon, like Anthony Ruwah, benefited from a miracle as a result of his blasphemous aggression. He ordered his servants to lead twelve camels into the church of Saint George, so he could have the pleasure of watching them trample the altar. A priest pleaded with him to desist, but in vain; Ampelon insisted. His servants reluctantly carried out their orders, and the camels dropped dead as soon as they entered the church. Ampelon, stunned, ordered his servants to remove the dead camels and went away. Later that day he returned (camel-less) to the church as priests were consecrating the Eucharist; they bade him enter and witness the "wondrous miracle." But Ampelon recoiled in horror, for what he saw in their hands was not bread but a bloody child, which they were ripping apart and placing into a chalice before sharing it with the assembled faithful. Furious, Ampelon went to the bishop after the mass and asked him what he had been doing; performing the holy sacrifice with bread, the bishop answered. Ampelon accused him of homicide, telling him what he had seen. The bishop, awed, told the Saracen that he had benefited from a vision; he then explained the mystery of the Eucharist to him. Ampelon asked to be baptized, but the bishop, afraid of the repercussions, told him to go to the Sinai and be baptized there. Ampelon departed for the Sinai the same night, was baptized, and became a monk. Three years later, having decided that he "wishes to see Christ," he deliberately set out in search of martyrdom. He returned to the caliph, told him of his conversion, and bade him to convert as well. The caliph first ridiculed him, then tried to give him gifts and fine clothes to persuade him to desist. Ampelon replied:

> Sell the clothes which you have prepared and give [the money] to the poor. And you, give up the worldly scepter of your kingdom, so that you may achieve eternal life. Do not place your faith in present things, but hope for the future. Do not believe in the pseudo-prophet Moameth, that filthy, abominable son of perdition; believe rather in Jesus Christ of Nazareth crucified. Believe in the consubstantial trinity, one divinity, Father, Son, and Holy Spirit, consubstantial and inseparable Trinity.
>
> (PG 100:1209)

The consequence of this, of course, was that Ampelon got his wish to see Christ: he was taken outside the city and beheaded. The story of Ampelon serves the same purpose as that of Anthony Ruwah: to reassure its reader that the success of Islam is due to its worldliness. The Christian, for whom this world is only a trial, an exile, should patiently accept his subordinate social status, remain steadfast in his ancestral faith, and await his celestial reward.

Christianity Defended in the Language of Muslim Theology

While John of Damascus portrayed Muslim doctrine from a Greek Christian perspective as a Christological heresy, his pupil Theodore Abû Qurrah (d. c. 820) attempted to justify Christianity in the terms of Muslim theology.[77] Abû Qurrah played a role in the intellectual fervor of early 'Abbasid Baghdad: he was one of the *mutakallimûn* (theologians) who pondered and debated the relations between revealed truth and reason; he was a Christian *mutakallim* who, in the free-wheeling intellectual atmosphere of the day, could argue philosophy and theology with Muslims in the caliph's court. Nestorian Katholikos Timothy I argued theology with Muslims in Baghdad and even, in 781, with the caliph al-Mahdî himself.[78] Some of Abû Qurrah's works show a practical, apologetic aim: he denies that Islam had supplanted or abrogated Christianity in God's favor just as Christianity had supplanted Judaism;[79] he defends Christian veneration of images against the charge of idolatry.[80] He wrote his *Refutation of Outsiders,* he says, because when he came out of the Church of the Holy Sepulcher in Jerusalem with some friends, a group of Muslims accosted them and began questioning them about their faith.[81] Theodore's *On True Religion* is much more ambitious: it purports to prove the superiority of Christianity over other religions through rational, objective criteria.[82] It was well enough known to be the object of a rebuttal by the Muslim *mutakallim* al-Murdâr.[83]

Abû Qurrah starts with a philosophical proof of the creation of the universe and of the existence of a creator, God. His point of departure is a Neoplatonic view of the universe: the effects of God as creator are evident in the order and harmony among the elements of the universe. He concludes that God as cause must be greater than his effects: he must be eternal, unchanging, good, wise, and so on.: here he provides a long list of the divine attributes commonly accorded to God by Muslim thinkers.

Having established certain truths about God from a rational, nonsectarian perspective, he then asks which religion is true: he briefly describes each of nine prominent religions. Only one of these religions can be true, he says, but how are we to tell which one? He imagines a man from a remote mountainous region coming down into a city, seeing that people have different religions, and trying to determine which one he should choose. He proposes to compare the scriptural tenets of each of these religions with the philosophical truths about God enumerated in the beginning of his treatise. Unsurprisingly, he will conclude that only Christianity is consistent with what an objective, philosophically minded person can ascertain about God. His arguments are both apologetical (in defense of the Trinity, for example[84]) and polemical (he criticizes Islam for condoning violence and for promising sensual rewards in this life and the next). Islam, like most other religions, spread with the military and political power of its adherents; base, worldly reasons (political ambition, greed, etc.) play a prominent role in encouraging conversions to Islam. Not so for Christianity, says Abû Qurrah: it spread far and wide despite the best efforts of the Romans to extinguish it; this shows that its adherents are inspired only by a desire for God and for the rewards of the world to come, not by earthly ambitions.[85]

Abû Qurrah's *On True Religion* rejects Islam's spiritual claims directly and unequivocally. Yet it does so in a very different way from the other texts I have examined. Abû Qurrah places himself in a (fictional) nonsectarian viewpoint and attempts to prove the superiority of Christianity in rational, objective terms. While his teacher John of Damascus portrayed Islam in Melkite terms as a Christological heresy, Abû Qurrah attempts to justify Christianity through the vocabulary and ideas of the *mutakallimûn* of 'Abbasid Baghdad. He calmly accepts the existence of Islam on the political and social level: we are all seekers of truth, he seems to be saying to Muslims; you just happen to be wrong. Abû Qurrah, like the anonymous Christian who wrote the first Arab apology for Christianity a few years earlier, was an Arab who thought and wrote using the vocabulary of the Koran and the intellectual categories of his Muslim contemporaries.[86] The Muslim intellectuals of Baghdad are not the horrible barbarians of Sophronios or pseudo-Methodius; they are his companions. Yet they are companions who have erroneously picked the wrong religion for understandable but insufficient reasons. Islam is the religion of enjoyment of this world; Christianity is the religion of the next. In this way, it seems, Abû Qurrah hopes to persuade his Christian readers to remain faithful to Christianity while at the same time explaining to them the success of Islam.

Over the following centuries, many Arab writers, Muslim and Christian, would continue to write apologetics and polemics in which scriptural citation and philosophical notions were mustered to attack (or defend) key elements of Christian and Muslim theology. The defense of the Trinity remained a cornerstone of Christian apologetics: God is one and at the same time three. Some authors would (as John of Damascus and Abû Qurrah had done) assert the impossibility to comprehend this mystery: it is like trying to shoot arrows at the stars.[87] Other apologists would cite the Bible to show it, create analogies to elucidate it, or even attempt to prove it (or at least explain it) through triads of essential divine attributes borrowed from the vocabulary of Greek philosophy.[88] The latter strategy involves defining three essential characteristics of divinity and associating them with the three persons of the Trinity. God is eternal, rational, and living (for example); or he is good, wise, and powerful.[89] This strategy, a staple of Christian-Muslim apologetics, would be enthusiastically adopted by Spanish Christian writers in Arabic and (in the twelfth and thirteenth centuries) in Latin and Catalan.[90]

In addition to disputations with real adversaries (or, preferably, with more docile, fictive ones), polemical or apologetical letter exchanges between Muslims and Christians became common. Muhammad, according to Muslim tradition, sent letters to various rulers, expounding Islam and inviting them to convert. Similar letters were attributed to several early caliphs. According to the Byzantine chronicler Theophanes, caliph 'Umar II (717–20) "sent a doctrinal letter to the Emperor Leo [III (717–41)], thinking to persuade him to apostatize."[91] Ghevond, an Armenian chronicler writing, it seems, in the tenth century, gives what he claims is the text of 'Umar's letter, although it is in fact "a clumsy attempt by an Armenian historian to reconstruct the Muslim text from a number of responses to it made by Leo in the course of his answer."[92] The Muslim's letter survives in an independent Arabic tradition, however; there seems to have been a real correspondence between a Muslim and a Christian, even if (as seems probable) it took place in the ninth century and was later attributed to Leo and 'Umar.[93] Even if there is some historical basis for this correspondence (and that is far from certain), Ghevond (or his source) has clearly padded Leo's letter to make it into a thoroughgoing refutation of Islam.[94] It may well be that a ninth- or tenth-century Christian polemicist composed both letters and attached to them two illustrious names: what could be more satisfying to a Christian reader than to see how a famous Byzantine emperor had refuted Islam and bested an early caliph?

Similar questions of authenticity surround the much more widely read *Risâlat al-Kindî*, supposedly an exchange of letters, in Arabic, between two prominent members of the 'Abbasid court. A Muslim (unnamed in the text, but whom a later tradition identified as Allah al-Hâshimî), presents Islam to a Nestorian Christian friend (traditionally referred to as 'Abd al-Masih al-Kindî[95]) and invites him to convert; in reply, al-Kindî presents a long, detailed refutation of Islam and defense of Christianity and invites al-Hâshimî to convert. In fact, both letters were probably written by one

Christian author. The letter ascribed to al-Hâshimî presents Islamic doctrine in an unconvincing way and makes only feeble attacks on Christianity; like the Muslim disputants in John of Damascus's *Disputation,* al-Hâshimî is there to lend an air of authenticity to the refutation, a fictitious witness to a Christian theological triumph.[96] The "Muslim" devotes more space to the praise of Christian monks than to the defense of Islam.

The *Risâlat al-Kindî* is both polemical and apologetical: it attacks Muslim doctrine and provides a defense of key Christian doctrines that would be distasteful to Muslims. The author shows a good knowledge of Islam and of the Koran: the Muslim's letter presents Abraham as the first Muslim; the Christian retorts by saying that Muhammad himself said that *he* was the first Muslim and provides a citation from the Koran to prove it.[97] He defends the Trinity while affirming God's unity; far be it from a true Christian to say that "God is the third of three."[98] Does not God, in the Bible, refer to himself in the plural?[99] God has many attributes, he asserts, two of which are eternal: life and knowledge. Life corresponds to Christ ($\lambda \acute{o} \gamma o s$, *kalima*), knowledge to the Holy Spirit ($\pi \nu \epsilon \hat{\upsilon} \mu \alpha$, *rûh*); thus the Trinity can be proven from a reflection on God's nature.[100]

The Christian next launches a concerted attack against Muhammad, in order to prove that he was no prophet. He recounts Muhammad's biography in as acerbic and derogatory a fashion as possible, showing all the while a good knowledge of the Koran and early Muslim historiography. He notes that Muhammad had first been an idolater and had enriched himself through trade and through his marriage with Khadîja. Wishing to rule over his tribe, he decided to pretend to be a prophet; his companions, gullible nomads who knew nothing of the signs of prophecy, believed him. He and his followers enriched themselves through war and pillaging. These acts, for the Christian writer, are enough to prove that Muhammad was not a prophet; the failures of some of the expeditions (especially the battle of Uhud) even more so: a true prophet would have foreseen (and avoided) defeat.[101]

This Christian monk is particularly shocked by Muhammad's sexual life, which he attacks with gusto. Muhammad himself, he says, claimed to have the sexual powers of forty men. He presents a catalog of Muhammad's fifteen wives, dwelling on the scandals surrounding Zaynab and 'Â'isha.[102] Did not the apostle Paul proclaim that "he that is unmarried careth for the things that belong to the Lord, how he may please the Lord: But he that is married careth for the things that are of the world, how he may please his

wife" [1 Cor. 7:32–33]? Is this not even more true of a man with fifteen
wives, a man, moreover, constantly involved in planning war? "How could
he, with this continual and permanent preoccupation, find the time to fast,
pray, worship God, meditate and contemplate eternal things and those
things appropriate to prophets? I am certain that no prophet was as attached to the pleasures of this world as was your master."[103]

The Christian monk then explains "the signs of prophecy which oblige
one to recognize the title of prophet and of apostle to him who shows
them."[104] The Muslim notion of *rasûl* differs from Christian and Jewish notions of "prophet." The Christian author does not acknowledge this, again
suggesting that his real audience is fellow Christians and not his fictitious
Muslim correspondent. The two signs of prophecy are revelation of things
unknown (past and future) and performance of miracles. Muhammad foretold nothing, whereas the Hebrew prophets, Christ, and the apostles did.
Muhammad produced no miracles, as the Koran expressly states; the miracles attributed to him are false.[105]

In much of this, the Christian author compares (explicitly or implicitly)
Muhammad with Jesus: Christ shunning sex and worldly power, Muhammad eagerly pursuing both; Christ prophesying true things, Muhammad
failing to foresee his defeats in battle; Christ producing miracles, Muhammad none. He carries this contrast into his description of Muhammad's
death. Muhammad, he says, ordered that his companions not bury him after his death, for angels would come within three days to carry his body up
to heaven. At his death, his disciples did as he had ordered: "after they had
waited for three days, his odor changed and their hopes of his being taken
up to heaven disappeared. Disappointed by his illusory promises and realizing that he had lied, they buried him."[106]

Having slandered the messenger, the Christian author of the *Risâlat al-
Kindî* next attacks the message: the Koran. What kind of law is it, he asks,
that your master brought you? It is not divine law: that was brought by
Christ; it is not natural law: that God revealed to Moses. It must then, he
suggests, be satanic law. He tries to prove this through comparisons between the Koran on the one hand and the Old and New Testaments on the
other. The arbitrary and unconvincing nature of this argument again suggests that the text is meant for sympathetic Christian readers. The author
argues that, far from being revealed by God, the Koran was composed by
Muhammad with help from a heretical Christian monk named Sergius
(also called Nastûr or Nestorius) and from two Jews, 'Abd Allah b. Sallâm
and Ka'b al-Ahbar. Moreover, he says, varying versions of the Koran existed

until the time of the caliph 'Uthman, who ordered a definitive recension. All this, he says, proves that the Koran is not divinely revealed scripture.[107]

He next attacks Muslim ritual. Why ritually wash before prayer, he asks: "you wash your bodies, but your hearts are impure and stained with sin, just like those of the hypocrites Christ denounced in the Gospel of Matthew." He attacks, for similar reasons, the Ramadan fast, male and female circumcision, Muslim laws regarding marriage and divorce, the prohibition of eating pork. He next gives a long diatribe against the pilgrimage rites at Mecca, comparing them to idolatrous rites of India. He provides a detailed tirade against jihad, or holy war, saying that it contradicts Koranic injunctions against using force in matters of religion. Those who die in war will not go to heaven as martyrs; the only true martyrs are those who peacefully and willingly gave up their lives for God.[108]

The final part of the *Risâlat al-Kindî* is an apologetical presentation of key Christian doctrines. Al-Kindî defends the Trinity and Christian veneration of the cross. He presents a brief and standard catalog of the Old Testament passages said to predict Christ's coming. He defends Christians against the common Muslim charge of falsification of the scriptures *(tahrîf)* by citing passages from the Koran that praise the Torah and Gospels. Besides, he notes, how would it be possible for so many Jews and Christians, spread over the earth and speaking many different languages, to modify the text of holy writ?[109] He then gives a sort of Christian catechism, narrating the life of Christ according to the Gospels (citing the Koran when it agrees with the Gospel account) and presenting key Christian doctrines. He compares the mission of the Apostles—preaching and miracle-working—with the holy war of the Muslims. He closes his letter by inviting his Muslim friend to convert to Christianity.[110]

The *Risâlat al-Kindî* reflects the same irenic, friendly atmosphere of free exchange between court intellectuals enjoyed by Theodore Abû Qurrah; the two letters purport to be between friends who have talked many times about spiritual and philosophical topics. Both texts accept that Islam is here to stay; neither descries any apocalyptic saviors on his temporal horizon. Yet the anonymous Christian monk who forged the *Risâlat al-Kindî* is much less interested in philosophical argumentation than is Abû Qurrah and more interested in vilifying Muhammad and the Koran. Both authors, like the anonymous hagiographers of the martyrs, portray Islam as a religion of this world, whose devotees are enthralled to power, wealth, and sex. Christianity is the spiritual religion which, in place of such base rewards, offers eternal life. These authors, despite their pretensions of converting thoughtful Muslims, are writing for Christian readers, hoping to instill in them a sense of religious superiority that will help them cling to their Christianity even while accepting their subordinate role in Muslim society.

Toward an Uneasy Status Quo: Religion and Identity in the Eastern Mediterranean

A socially subordinate role for Christianity could be shown to make sense: by tapping into ascetic traditions, these authors could portray Christianity as the otherworldly religion, its adherents, unconcerned with the city of man, neither rich nor powerful. It is unsurprising that Eastern Christian authors from this period wrote few chronicles of world history: having rejected pseudo-Methodius's apocalyptic vision of history, what vision could they now comfortably adopt?

From Byzantium things looked slightly different: there Theophanes penned his *Chronicle* in about 815. In the tradition of Eusebius, he narrates the history of the world from the Creation to his own day. By 815 it is clear that the Middle East's new Muslim rulers are here to stay; their successes must be explained in the context of Christian history.

For Theophanes, Muhammad, "the leader and false prophet of the Saracens," is important enough to merit a brief biographical sketch.[111] Like Isidore, Theophanes sees biblical genealogy as a key to understanding the Arabs' (or anyone else's) place in the divine plan: he says that they are the descendants of Ishmael through Nizaros. Theophanes claims that the Jews had first flocked to Muhammad, thinking he was their long-awaited Messiah; when they saw him eating camel (a forbidden food), they realized their error, yet some of them stayed with him out of fear "and taught him illicit things directed against us, Christians."[112] Theophanes describes Muhammad's marriage to Khadîja and his travels in Palestine where he sought out the writings of Jews and Christians. Muhammad had an epileptic seizure, and at this Khadîja became distressed; he soothed her by telling her: "I keep seeing a vision of a certain angel called Gabriel, and being unable to bear his sight, I faint and fall down."[113] Khadîja sought the advice of "a certain monk living there, a friend of hers (who had been exiled for his depraved doctrine)"; this heretical monk seems to be based on the Muslim legends of Waraqa and Bahira. The monk told Khadîja that Muhammad was indeed a prophet to whom the angel Gabriel came in visions. With such beginnings, his "heresy" soon was spread by force. Theophanes recounts that Muhammad promised to all who fell fighting the enemy a paradise full of sensual delights: eating, drinking, and sex. He said "many other things full of profligacy and stupidity."[114]

Theophanes, fully aware of the religious motivations behind the Muslim conquests, characterizes Islam as a heresy composed of a mixture of Jewish and Christian elements; he later refers to Mecca as "the place of their blasphemy."[115] He is less clear about why God allowed these Muslim heretics to conquer vast territories. At times he blames the corruption and ineptitude of Byzantine officials, such as the eunuch who refuses to pay Arab mercenaries who had been defending Roman Syria from the Muslims; the mercenaries quickly switch sides and act as scouts for the invading Muslims.[116] Yet he also describes divine portents of the impending disasters: an earthquake in Palestine, a sword-shaped sign hanging in the southern sky.[117] When the caliph 'Umar enters Jerusalem as a conqueror, clad in a dirty camel-hair garment, according to Theophanes, the patriarch Sophronios proclaims: "Verily, this is the abomination of desolation standing in a holy place, as has been spoken through the prophet Daniel."[118]

For Theophanes, the primary dramatic cause of the spectacular losses of Roman territory to the Arabs is Heraclius's embracing of the Monothelite heresy (according to this doctrine, Christ had a single, unified will, rather than separate divine and human wills).[119] This fall from grace is all the more dramatic as Heraclius had (for Theophanes) been the champion of orthodoxy, thanks to whom Constantinople had crushed its Avar and Persian enemies and recovered the true cross from the Persians. God and the Virgin had watched over Heraclius and guaranteed his success until the emperor inexplicably turned heretic, at which point they abandoned him to the Arab invaders. Moreover, it is the fault of wicked Monophysite Syrians that Heraclius was dragged into the nets of heresy:[120] how could the ravaging of Syria by Arab armies be anything but God's just and terrible punishment? The Monothelite heresy rent the church in two, pitting the heretical forces of Heraclius and the Constantinopolitan patriarch Sergius against the orthodox, led by Sophronios and the Roman popes.

> And while the Church at that time was being troubled thus by emperors and impious priests, Amalek rose up in the desert, smiting us, the people of Christ, and there occurred the first terrible downfall of the Roman army, I mean the bloodshed at [Ajnâdayn (634) and Yarmûk (636)]. After this came the fall of Palestine, Caesarea and Jerusalem, then the Egyptian disaster, followed by the capture of the islands be-

tween the continents and of all the Roman territory, by the complete loss of the Roman army and navy at Phoinix, and the devastation of all Christian peoples and lands, which did not cease until the persecutor of the Church [Sergius?] had been miserably slain in Sicily.[121]

For Theophanes, the Islamic conquests are clearly part of God's plan: they are foretold by prophets and by natural disasters, and Muhammad's life corresponds to that of previous heresiarchs. Just as God had in previous times sent Amalek from the desert to smite Israel when it went astray, so he did again in the reign of Heraclius.[122] Yet Theophanes seems at a loss to draw any broader or clearer conclusions. He suggests no role for Islam in the apocalyptic drama of the last days, nor does he make any reassuring predictions of its imminent demise. Apparently baffled by Islam's continuing success, Theophanes does not pretend to know what God has in mind. This may come, in part, from the chronicle genre, in which the author often limits himself to narrating events year by year, rather than trying to explain the underlying causes of history. Yet the very fact that Theophanes and other writers of the period retreated into the safe conventions of the chronicle genre perhaps shows their inability to explain these events as part of a Christian divine plan.[123]

Islam provided a series of troubling, but not unique, intellectual problems for Theophanes, as well as for the other writers whose work is discussed in this chapter. If God's faithful suffered new setbacks at the hands of Muslims, it had suffered them before, at the hands of Amalek and Babylon, Roman persecutors, barbarian invaders, and wily heresiarchs. If Islam challenged accepted Christian orthodoxies by presenting a new blend of Christian and non-Christian beliefs and practices, it merely showed itself to be heresy, along the lines of the innumerable heretical groups that had preceded it. While Islam's success in conquering and converting most of Christendom challenged the assumptions of a triumphalist tradition of Christian historiography, darker traditions of Antichrist and Apocalypse could explain these troubling events. One could trace the history of these Eastern Christian reactions further, looking at texts from the rest of the Middle Ages and beyond. I have not done so in part because it has already been done.[124] But the principal reason is that I am most interested in tracing the history of Latin European responses to Islam: it is these early Eastern Christian texts about Islam, in particular Theophanes, pseudo-Methodius, and especially the *Risâlat al-Kindî*, that are translated into Latin and read and used by scores of European writers.

Terence Hawkes has said that "a colonist acts essentially as a dramatist. He imposes the 'shape' of his own culture, *embodied in his speech,* on the new world and makes that world recognizable, habitable, 'natural,' able to speak his language."[125] The same could be said for the *colonized,* in this case for Eastern Christians during the first two Muslim centuries. Refusing to acknowledge the fundamental and irreversible nature of the advent of Islam, they imposed the familiar forms of the old Christian Roman commonwealth on the new world of Islam, casting their adversaries (especially Muhammad) in familiar and despised roles, roles that allowed the Christian writer to hope for a happy ending. The negative "orientalist" portrayals of Islam that Edward Said denounces in his *Orientalism* as the ideological underpinnings of French and British colonialism in fact have their origins in the defensive reactions of Christian "orientals," unwitting subjects of the new Muslim empire.

The same range of reactions to Islam's successes will be replayed—with about a century's lapse—in the western Mediterranean, particularly in Spain, which fell to Muslim invaders in 711.

Part Two

FORGING POLEMICAL IMAGES
(EIGHTH–TWELFTH CENTURIES)

A S THE MUSLIM conquests swept across North Africa and, in 711, into Spain, European Christians sought, like their Eastern brethren, to explain the role of these events in the scheme of Christian history. In the centuries that followed those conquests (see chapter 4), Christian *dhimmis* in Spain created a polemical image of Islam much like that forged by the Christians of the Near East and for much the same reasons: to discourage apostasy, to defend their status as protected minorities, or to deny the legitimacy of their Muslim rulers. Many of the Arab texts written by Eastern Christians, in particular the *Risâlat al-Kindî*, found receptive readers among Iberian Christians.

Europe North of the Pyrenees showed little interest in Islam before the first Crusade of 1095–99. Chapter 5 examines how chroniclers of the first crusade portrayed Saracens as idolaters who had polluted the holy city of Jerusalem with their profane rites, in particular through the adoration of a silver idol of Muhammad in the Temple of Solomon, an idol the crusaders supposedly demolished. This image, albeit wildly inaccurate, helps justify and glorify, for these authors, the violence of the Crusade. Other authors throughout the Middle Ages, particularly the poets of *Chansons de Geste*, offer a similar image of Saracen idolatry, often with similar motives.

The twelfth century also saw another image of Islam emerge in Latin Europe: Islam as a heretical variation of Christianity (see chapter 6). Various twelfth-century authors presented Muhammad as a heresiarch in the tradition of Arius and others. While some authors did this through the compilation of colorful, scandalous, largely imaginative biographies of Muhammad, writers in Spain continued to develop the traditions of Arab Christian apologetics, giving them a sharper, more polemical edge, encouraged by the Christian conquest of much of Muslim Spain. This Spanish tradition, imported north by writers such as Petrus Alfonsi and Peter of Cluny, informed the more learned responses to Islam in the following centuries.

From the eighth century to the twelfth, Eastern Christian polemical views of Islam were imported to Spain, where they were reworked and brought to northern Europe. At the same time, the contrasting image of Islam as pagan idolatry was created by European chroniclers and poets. By the end of the twelfth century, European writers had created the essential portrayals of Islam that would be elaborated upon, reworked, and deployed for different purposes for centuries to come.

Chapter 4

WESTERN CHRISTIAN RESPONSES TO ISLAM (EIGHTH–NINTH CENTURIES)

WHILE THE FIRST generations of eastern *dhimmis* came to terms with their new lot, the Muslim empire continued to expand: eastward to the Indus and westward across northern Africa. In 701 the conversion of masses of Berbers to Islam brought most of northwestern Africa under Muslim dominion. In 711, in the midst of a Visigothic dynastic crisis, the Berber general Târiq ibn Ziyâd crossed the straits of Gibraltar to Spain and routed a Visigothic army, killing Rodrigo, last king of the Visigoths. By 720 Muslims had subjected most of the Iberian peninsula to their rule. In the 720s and 730s Arab and Berber forces fought and raided north of the Pyrenees, well into what is now France. Over the course of the next several centuries, Arab navies based in Spain and North Africa conquered most of the major islands of the Western Mediterranean (Sicily, Sardinia, Corsica, the Balearics) as well as a large portion of Puglia on the Italian mainland; a band of Arab corsairs established a small foothold in Provence (at Fraxinetum); others raided and plundered cities and monasteries along the Mediterranean coasts of Europe, making occasional ventures inland, sacking Saint Peter's in Rome in 846 and the monastery of Monte Cassino in 881. These incursions were not a unified effort to conquer Europe. The Muslim world was increasingly fragmented, both politically and religiously, and these raids by pirates and fortune-seekers were the fruits of individual ambition and greed, not of a coordinated Muslim expansion.

European Christians reacted to these events in a variety of ways, as did their Eastern brethren. It is one thing to describe the conquests of a rival power from the safety of seventh-century Constantinople or of an eighth-century Northumbrian Monastery, and quite another to be thrust unwillingly into the role of *dhimmi* in an increasingly Muslim and Arab Damascus or Córdoba. We find the same developments among Spanish *dhimmi* as among Eastern ones: they initially portray Muslims primarily as military

71

enemies, divine chastisement for Christian sins. Only as more and more Christians convert do Christian authors attack Islam as a religious adversary.[1]

Islam as Seen from Northumbria

For Bede (c. 673–735), monk at the Northumbrian monastery of Jarrow from his childhood, the Saracens were a distant and obscure threat. The conversion of the Berbers took place when he was almost thirty. Before then, the Saracen invasions had primarily been at the expense of the Persian empire and its eastern neighbors (about whom a Northumbrian monk could scarcely be expected to have much knowledge or interest) and against the Byzantine empire, which Bede disliked for the same reasons Isidore had: he opposed its universalist political pretensions and saw it as prone to all sorts of heresy.[2] Only in later years, as Saracens conquered Spain and raided Italy and Gaul, did Bede see them as dangerous.

Constantinople's enemies shed few tears over the Muslim conquest of two-thirds of the Byzantine empire (see chapter 3); they tended to portray its new Arab overlords in sympathetic terms. The same holds true for Bede, as can be seen in his *De locis sanctis* (On the holy sites). Bede meant this seventh- (or eighth-) century Baedecker to describe the sites of the Holy Land to the potential (or armchair) pilgrim. He draws his descriptions from venerated authorities such as Orosius and Isidore (as well as, of course, the Bible), but also relies on Arculf, a Frankish bishop who made the pilgrimage between 679 and 682, and whose experiences were recorded just a few years later by Adamnan of Iona.[3] Bede weaves together two kinds of sources; respected, established authorities and recent (by seventh-century standards) reports of one who had been in the Holy Land.[4] In reading this work, one has little sense of turmoil in this newly conquered, changing society, nor would one sense that the Arabs are the military enemies of Byzantium. His description of Arabia, land of odoriferous myrrh, is taken largely from Isidore; there is no sense that these Arabs are more important players on the world scene than they had been a century before.[5] Yet Bede is aware of Saracen dominion over much of the near East, aware that *Mavias rex Sarracenorum* (the Umayyad caliph Mu'âwiya) rules from Damascus, where Christians continue to frequent the Church of Saint John the Baptist and "the king of the Saracens" builds and consecrates "another one for his own people," a new Saracen "basilica."[6] Whereas Bede's source,

Adamnan, specified that this was a "church for infidels" (*ecclesia incredulo-rum*) Bede does not; his reader would presumably conclude that this good Saracen king was a Christian.[7] His name, "Mavias," is curiously close to that of the fourth-century Christian queen of the Saracens.[8]

Indeed, in another passage of *De locis sanctis* King Mavias invokes Christ as "savior of the World." When he describes Jerusalem, Bede says that the Saracens constructed a "house" for their prayers; since Arculf made his pilgrimage before the construction of the Dome of the Rock, this probably refers to an earlier structure.[9] Bede tells of a miracle that Arculf recounted involving a group of Jews and a group of Christians who supposedly fought over the ownership of the shroud that had covered Jesus' head at his burial. The "Saracen king Mavias" intervened by casting the cloth into a fire and proclaiming "now let Christ the Savior of the world, who suffered for the human race, who had this shroud (which I now hold in my arms) placed on his Head in the sepulcher, judge by the flame of the fire between you who contend for this cloth."[10] The cloth rose unharmed from the fire and floated to the Christian group. Not only does God intervene to produce a miracle to defend the Christian community against the claims of the Jews, the good Saracen king calls up the miracle and professes his belief in Christ's roles as savior and miracle worker. In Muslim Jerusalem, under the shadow of the new mosque, it is the Jews who are perceived as the threatening enemy, and the Saracen king as ally.[11]

Yet Bede does not always portray Saracens as quasi-Christians. He gives a different view in his commentary to Acts 7:43, where God upbraids the Israelites for lapsing into idolatry. Among other foreign gods, they worship "the star of Remphan." This star, Bede explains, is "Lucifer, into whose cult the race of the Saracens is enslaved in honor of Venus."[12] In the eighth century "Lucifer" refers to the morning star (i.e., the planet Venus) rather than to the devil; yet this association with the devil will suggest itself to Bede's later medieval readers. The way to understand the Saracens is to comb the Bible for references to them. Having done so, Bede can assign to them an appropriate niche in Christian history. Here Bede seems not to suspect that the religion of Saracens may have changed and the cult of Remphan fallen into disrepute; the Bible, after all, was his surest guide to truth in the world around him. In true Isidoran style, he etymologically explained the derivation of *Agareni* from the Hebrew *ger* (enemy); who could thus be surprised at the Agarenes' hostility toward Christendom?[13] Over the next several centuries, the authors north of the Pyrenees who have anything to say about Islam will (with a few exceptions) describe the Saracen invaders in the same way: a violent scourge of God, vaguely associated with idolatrous cults. The origins and details of these idolatrous cults are obscure and provoke little interest. It was enough to know that they were idolatrous *perfidi* (infidels) who someday would allow the true faith to be preached, as did pagan king Ethelbert of Kent; they might convert, perhaps even destroying their own idols in a dramatic show of piety, as did the high priests of the Northumbrians and East Saxons in Bede's *Ecclesiastical History of the English People.*[14]

The *Ecclesiastical History* was Bede's magnum opus. While Isidore had celebrated the rise of Catholic Visigothic Spain, Bede chronicled the triumphant story of the fluorescence of British Christianity and celebrated the lives of the Roman and Irish monks, bishops, and missionaries who made it possible. In this drama of the English church, the distant incursions of non-Christian warriors onto Christian soil receive only brief mention, as so many small dark clouds on the horizon. Bede does however note:

> In the year of our Lord 729, two comets appeared around the sun, striking terror into all who saw them. One comet rose early and preceded the sun, while the other followed the setting sun at evening, seeming to portend awful calamity to east and west alike. Or else, since one comet was the precursor of day and the other of night, they indicated that mankind was menaced by evils at both times. They appeared in the month of January, and remained visible for about a fortnight, pointing their fiery torches northward as though to set the heavens aflame. At this time, a swarm of Saracens ravaged Gaul with horrible slaughter; but after a brief interval in that country they paid the penalty of their wickedness [*perfidia*]. During this year the man of God Egbert departed to our Lord on Easter Day as I have mentioned, and immediately after Easter, on the ninth of May, King Osric of Northumbria departed this life after a reign of eleven years.[15]

The twin comets are divine signals of coming catastrophe, east and west: in the west, the deaths of Kings Egbert of Kent and Osric of Northumbria; in the east, the Saracen invasions of Gaul. Yet these Saracens subsequently received due punishment in Gaul itself; some historians have suggested that Bede is referring to the defeat of 'Abd al-Rahmân by the forces of Charles Martel at Poitiers, though it may well refer instead to the Battle of Toulouse (721), in which Eudes, duke of Aquitaine, routed Emir al-Samh.[16] Here was a "dreadful plague" (*grauissma lues*), reminiscent of the trials and punishments faced by the Hebrews in the Old Testament, followed by a satisfying vindication of Christian superiority. Moreover, Bede specifies that the Saracens are punished for their *perfidia,* a term he and other contemporary writers usually use to denote religious error: pagan, Jewish, or heretical (though it can on occasion mean "treachery" in a nonreligious sense).[17] Their punishment seems to be more for their religious error than for their devastating raids on Christian Gaul; indeed, for Bede, the brutality of the Saracens is probably the direct consequence of their *perfidia.* After all, his *Ecclesiastical History* tells of other groups of *perfidi* who wage violent war until they are converted: the Kentish before the arrival of Augustine of Canterbury, the Angles, Picts, and others.

In a Europe continually ravaged by war and invasions, the Saracens were one among a number of non-Christian interlopers. Christian European writers showed little curiosity about the religion of these invaders, be they Saracens, Vikings, or Magyars. They all seemed to be part of the terrible tribulations through which God was putting his people; none provoked (it seems) the slightest suggestion that its religious beliefs and practices could be worth investigating—much less imbued with the slightest legitimacy.

The advantage that the Saracens held over other distant invaders (say, the Magyars), from the point of view of a monk and scholar like Bede, was that one could find out about them by looking in the Bible. After all, the Bible, says Bede, is superior to all other writings in antiquity, utility, and authority.[18] It is in his biblical commentaries that Bede shows that he indeed is aware of the breadth and importance of the Saracen invasions. Genesis 16:12 described Ishmael as "a wild man" whose "hand will be against every man." Like many of his contemporary Eastern brethren, Bede saw this as a clear reference to the Saracen conquests: "Now how great is his hand against all and all hands against him; as they impose his authority upon the whole length of Africa and hold both the greater part of Asia and some of Europe, hating and opposing all."[19] Bede's view of the Saracens changed over time. In his early years he could portray Mu'âwiya as a distant and sympathetic king who protected his Christian subjects and built churches for his people. As the Saracen invasions moved ever further west—and then north into Europe—Bede portrayed them as no better than the other "pagan" persecutors that plundered Europe: rod of divine chastisement that would in the end either be crushed or converted.

Bede's growing awareness of the Saracens as they push west is apparent in the *Chronica maiora* that he included in his *De temporum ratione.* Following in Isidore's footsteps, he divides world history into six ages, organizing the sixth under the reigns of successive Roman (and Byzantine) emperors. As did Isidore, Bede appends several chapters on the Antichrist and the last judgment, which are meant to dissuade apocalyptic speculation on the part of his readers; nowhere in the events he describes does Bede see the signs of the end. Bede narrates the occasional military and political event succinctly, saving most of his efforts for the recounting of the doings of saints, popes, bishops, missionaries, heresiarchs, and church councils.

Bede's account of the reign of Heraclius provides some telling examples of his method and interests. He devotes twenty-three lines (in the Patrologia Latina edition) to the martyrdom of the monk Anastasius, decapitated by the Persian emperor Chosroes, then fourteen lines to the mission of Paulinus of York to King Edwin of Northumbria, then seven to a controversy between the Pope and the Scots about the dating of Easter. Here are the three subjects that Bede finds worthy of commemoration during the reign of Heraclius. In the context of Anastasius's martyrdom, he does indeed mention in passing that Heraclius defeated the Persians but makes not the slightest allusion to his defeats against the Arabs at Ajnâdayn (634) or Yarmûk (636). Bede only notices the Muslim conquests as they reach the Western Mediterranean. He notes in his chapter on the reign of Constantine IV (668–85) that "Saracens invaded Sicily and returned to Alexandria with great booty."[20] Emperor Justinian II (685–95) "made peace with the Saracens, by sea and by land, for ten years. But the Saracens took the province of Africa from the Roman Empire . . . and captured and destroyed Carthage."[21]

The final chapter in his history of the sixth age is dedicated to the reign of Leo III (717–41) and is largely devoted to the Saracens: their failed assault on Constantinople and their raids on Sardinia, which had depopulated the island. The Lombard king Liudprand found there the bones of Saint Augustine, which had been brought to Sardinia from North Africa to save them from destruction by "barbarians"; *which* barbarians (Vandals? Saracens?) he does not say. Liudprand took the saint's bones back to his capital, Pavia, where he had them reburied with great honor.[22] This final episode of Bede's universal history is painted in chiaroscuro: in the face of barbarian onslaughts, the capital of the empire is in danger, and the bones of the great church father have had to retreat from his native Africa to Sardinia and finally to northern Italy; a dark scenario indeed. Yet confronting this disorder are the newly catholic Germanic kings of Europe: men like Liudprand who maintain the political order and show proper deference to the church and its saints. The transference of Augustine's bones is both an admission of defeat (Christendom has lost North Africa) and an assertion of a new Christian order, in which Germanic kings (and not the emperors of Constantinople) are the new protagonists.

Other Latin writers portray the Saracen invaders in similar terms. The *Chronicle of Fredegar* (c. 658), earliest Latin chronicle to mention the Arab victory over Heraclius, describes the invasions in semiapocalyptic terms: Heraclius is warned by astrologers of his impending defeat at the hands of a circumcised race; he opens the mythical gates of the north (built by Alexander the Great), unleashing a hoard of northern barbarians on the Saracens, but to no avail.[23] In the early eighth century, the *Apocalypse of Pseudo-Methodius* was translated into Latin, offering hopes of an imminent, dramatic end to the Saracen invasions.[24] Yet in their descriptions of the fresh waves of Muslim raids into Europe during the ninth century, Christian chroniclers continue to portray Muslims as scourges of God for their sins, as formidable military opponents, but *not* as religious adversaries. For Carolingian chroniclers, the Goths lost Spain on account of their own sins, and hegemony over former Gothic territory (Septimania, Catalonia) has naturally passed to the Franks: the *Chronologia regum Gothorum* asserts the end of Gothic rule and the ascendancy of Charlemagne, while the *Chronicon moissiacense* portrays the Arab conquest of Spain as punishment for the sins of Visigothic king Witiza.[25] Yet, whether chronicling the sack of Benevento or Charles Martel's victory at Poitiers, they have nothing to say about the religious beliefs and practices of these "Saracens."[26] The same is true of Liudprand of Cremona's tenth-century descriptions of the depredations wrought by the Saracens of Fraxinetum.[27] Even pilgrims to the Holy Land say little about the religion of the Saracens: eighth-century pilgrim Willibaldus prayed alongside Muslims in the church at Nazareth that had been divided (following a common Muslim practice) between Christians and Muslims. Yet he refers to them as "pagans" and grumbles that they really want to destroy the church.[28]

The historian of the twenty-first century is aware of the vast cultural and religious differences between Arab Muslims and Picts or Vikings; he is aware that Islam would survive and flourish, while the invaders from northern and eastern Europe would become Christians and integrate into the societies they had previously attacked. The Northumbrian or Frank of the eighth century could not know this: he saw God's scourge falling on him from all sides and sought an explanation in the sins of Christians; he was not interested in studying the different beliefs of these "pagan" invaders. Boniface, in a letter to King Ethelbald of Murcia, portrayed the

Saracen invasions as punishments against the Christians of Spain and Provence for the sin of fornication.[29] Yet the Saracens were not the only such scourge: Zacharias wrote to Boniface of the "tribulation" wrought by "Saracens, Saxons, and Frisians."[30]

Eighth-Century Spanish Chroniclers on Islam

One would expect a very different view of Islam in the writings of Spaniards thrust into the role of *dhimmi*. Indeed, ninth-century writer Paul Alvarus, who wrote in Muslim Córdoba in the 850s, was much better informed about Islam than Bede and far more hostile. Muhammad, for Alvarus, was an Antichrist, and in his readings of the Prophets and of Revelation, Alvarus saw the clear predictions of Islam and the Muslim conquests. Alvarus wrote in defense of the Córdoba martyrs, Christians (mostly monks) who publicly insulted Islam and its prophet in a deliberate attempt to provoke the Muslim authorities into executing them for blasphemy—or, in the eyes of Alvarus, martyring them. Alvarus forged an aggressively anti-Muslim theology of history, with which he tried (unsuccessfully) to convince his fellow Christians to support and revere the martyrs.

Yet Alvarus and his fellow apologists (Eulogius, Speraindeo) were the first Spanish Christians, it seems, to attack Islam theologically and to give it a clear (and negative) place in the divine plan. Earlier Spanish Christian writers described the Muslim conquest of Spain without coming to terms with it: they had even less to say than Bede about why God would permit the stunning Saracen military successes. Spanish chroniclers of the eighth century simply described the conquest without explanation, as if unable to comprehend why God should will it to happen.

Two Latin chronicles survive from eighth-century Spain, both anonymous and untitled; scholars know them by their dates of composition: the *Chronicle of 741* and the *Chronicle of 754*.[31] Both are in fact continuations of universal chronicles: just as John of Biclaro wrote a continuation of the Eusebius/Jerome chronicle to bring it up to date, the *Chronicle of 741* picked up where John left off, whereas the *Chronicle of 754* brought Isidore's *Chronica majora* up to date. Here, a priori, should be good examples of how eighth-century authors managed to fit the rise of Islam into Isidore's (and John of Biclaro's) Christian view of history. These chroniclers, like Isidore (as Kenneth Wolf notes) "were faced with the task of explaining how it was that a long-standing peninsular power should have yielded to foreign domination. Yet unlike Isidore they did not enjoy the luxury of identifying with the victors."[32]

The chroniclers' view of history can be seen in their presentation of two key events: the Muslim conquest of Syria and the conquest of Spain. The *Chronicle of 741* describes the reign of Heraclius in detail: his rebellion against Phocas, his setbacks and ultimate victory against the Persians, and the invasions of the Saracens. Heraclius warns his brother Theodore not to fight against them, for being expert in astrology he could foretell disaster. Theodore does not listen and is routed. Subsequently, the Saracens "firmly took hold of the provinces that they had invaded and founded a kingdom at Damascus, the splendid Syrian city."[33] There is no attempt to paint these events in dark colors. Saracen rule in Syria, it seems, is no less (or more) legitimate than had been that of Heraclius before. As for the leader of these Saracens, he is identified as "Mahmet by name, born of the most noble tribe of that people, a very prudent man who could foresee future events."[34] The chronicler also explains that the Saracens "revere *[colunt]* him with such honor and reverence that they affirm in all their sacraments and all their writings that he is God's apostle and prophet." The verb *colere* could be misleading (it can be translated as *revere* but more frequently means *worship*); otherwise this passage offers a succinct and accurate account of Muhammad's place in Islam, with no suggestion of contestation or disapproval. In short, the reader is not asked to be shocked or saddened by the Saracen conquest of Syria. The chronicler presents a confrontation between Heraclius and Muhammad in which neither is demonized, and one is left with no sense of why God would favor one rather than the other.

The *Chronicle of 754* offers a more detailed, dramatic, and moralized version of the same events. Heraclius's defeat seems to be divine punishment not (this time) for heresy or sexual debauchery but for hubris. "Seduced," after his victory over the Persians, "by the praise of his people who heaped the honor of victory not on God but on Heraclius himself he feared that rebuke which was being gravely presaged in his recurring visions."[35] For the emperor had recurring dreams of an invasion of rats from the desert and foresaw impending disaster in the course of the stars. The Saracens again become the divine scourge punishing the emperor and his people, who do not give due credit to God.

The Saracen invaders are portrayed in a far more negative light than in the *Chronicle of 741*. The *Chronicle of 754* says that they succeeded "more through trickery than through the power of their leader Muhammad, and devastated the neighboring provinces, proceeding not so much by means of open attacks as by secret incursions. Thus by means of cunning and fraud rather than power, they incited all of the frontier cities of the empire and finally rebelled openly."[36] The *Chronicle of 754,* unlike the *Chronicle of 741,* makes sense of the conquest of Syria by portraying it as the scourge of an unholy band of invaders for the hubris of the emperor Heraclius.

Turning to the Muslim conquest of Spain, however, neither of the two chronicles makes the slightest attempt to explain its place in the march of Christian history. Both chroniclers narrate the events following the Muslim conquest of Syria matter-of-factly, alternating paragraphs devoted to the reigns of Muslim caliphs, Byzantine emperors, and Visigothic kings. The reader of the *Chronicle of 741* would have no reason to think that the Muslim conquest of Spain was of special importance. In a section devoted to the reign of the caliph Walîd I (705–15), the chronicler recounts the Muslim conquests in Asia Minor (Romania), India, and the Mediterranean islands. The conquest of Spain receives one sentence: "In the western regions the Kingdom of the Goths, for so long and so solidly established in Spain, was invaded by a general named Mûsâ, with his army, was conquered and made to pay tribute."[37]

The *Chronicle of 754,* again, is much less laconic about the matter. It had, in the tradition of Isidore and John of Biclaro, celebrated Gothic rule in Spain, eulogizing its bishops (including Isidore, who bests a heretical Syrian bishop in a debate) and praising its kings for having the good sense to follow the advice of their bishops. An exception is King Egica (687–702) who "oppressed the Goths with cruel death. Moreover, bubonic plague spread mercilessly at this time."[38] Yet Egica's son and successor, Witiza, is "most clement"; he reinstates those whom his father had oppressed.[39]

The *Chronicle of 754* recounts the conquests of the caliph Walîd (including that of Spain) in virtually the same words as the *Chronicle of 741.*[40] But the chronicler follows that passage with a description of how, in 711, Rodrigo "rebelliously seized the kingdom at the instigation of the senate." He pulled together an army to fight Mûsâ and Târiq, "who had long been raiding the province consigned to them and simultaneously devastating many cities." Rodrigo met them in a pitched battle and "the entire army of the Goths, which had come with him fraudulently and in rivalry out of ambition for the kingship, fled and he was killed. Thus Rodrigo wretchedly lost not only his rule but his homeland."[41] The evils that befell Spain seem to be due to the political treachery of Rodrigo.

The disastrous consequences are described in lurid detail: slaughter, pillage, devastation:

> Who can relate such perils? Who can enumerate such grievous disasters? Even if every limb were transformed into a tongue, it would be beyond human nature to express the ruin of Spain and its many and great evils. But let me summarize everything for the reader on one brief page. Leaving aside all of the innumerable disasters from the time of Adam up to the present, which this cruel, unclean world has brought to countless regions and cities—that which, historically, the city of Troy sustained when it fell; that which Jerusalem suffered, as foretold by the eloquence of the prophets; that which Babylon bore, according to the eloquence of the scriptures; that which finally Rome went through, martyrially graced with the nobility of the apostles—all this and more Spain, once so delightful and now rendered so miserable, endured as much to its honor as to its disgrace.[42]

In a rapture of melodrama, the author puts the Goth's fall to the Arabs on a par with history's great disasters. Yet even if the sack of Saragossa is ordained by the "judgment of God" (*iudicio Dei*), the causes for the catastrophe seem not to be divine disfavor but rather the evil machinations of the Arab invaders and of a few bad apples among the Goths: not only Rodrigo but also Oppa, son of the evil king Egica. "After forcing his way to Toledo, the royal city, [Mûsâ] imposed on the adjacent regions an evil and fraudulent peace. He decapitated on a scaffold those noble lords who had remained, arresting them in their flight from Toledo with the help of Oppa, King Egica's son. With Oppa's support, he killed them all with the sword."[43] The intrigues of men like Oppa, along with the cowardice of others (such as Sindered, bishop of Toledo, who fled to Rome[44]), allow the Saracens to establish their "savage reign" (*regnum efferum*).

What can follow such a somber scene? The chronicler next recounts, with some satisfaction, Mûsâ's fall from grace and his humiliation by the caliph Walîd. Yet in the chapters that follow, the chronicle does not demonize the Arab rulers of Spain. On the contrary, it recounts their intrigues and military ventures much in the same way it had that of the Visigothic kings, censuring some rulers as greedy or inept while praising others for their justice and valor. The chronicle's center of gravity has shifted: events are now dated by the regnal years of the Muslim caliph, the Spanish emir, and the Byzantine emperor, yet the chronicler has less and less to say about events in Constantinople and almost nothing to say about other parts of the world. Damascus and Córdoba are now the centers of the chronicler's world. He indeed mentions the Franks, but only as adversaries of Spanish Muslim armies.

Only in the description of these confrontations between Spanish Muslims and Frankish Christians is there a sense that the author's allegiances do not lie with his Muslim overlords. Both the *Chronicle of 741* and the *Chronicle of 754* describe briefly and impartially the 721 Battle of Toulouse, in which Eudes, Duke of Aquitaine, routed Emir al-Samh.[45] But when the *Chronicle of 754* describes Charles Martel's victory over 'Abd al-Rahmân at Poitiers, which is traditionally dated to 732 but may in fact have been fought in October 734[46] (and which the *Chronicle of 741* does not relate), the author seems to be rooting for the Franks. "The northern peoples remained immobile like a wall, holding together like a glacier in the cold regions, and in the blink of an eye annihilated the Arabs with the sword." Originally identifying them as simply the "people of Austrasia," the chronicler then twice refers to these "northern people" as "the Europeans" (*Europenses*), inflating the battle's significance: this, it seems, is a confrontation between Europe and the Arabs. This may explain why the author expresses unaccustomed anger at the Franks for sheathing their swords and stopping the battle at nightfall, thus permitting the "Ishmaelites" to escape back to Spain.[47] The next emir, 'Abd al-Malik, made an expedition to the Pyrenees to subdue rebellious Christians but met with no success: "After launching further attacks here and there in those remote places with his strong army and losing many of his soldiers, he was convinced of the power of God, from whom the small band of Christians holding the pinnacles was awaiting mercy."[48] These are tempting tidbits for the historian in search of the ideological roots of the *reconquista*: the author describes in purple prose the horrors of the Arab conquest of Spain, cheers on Charles Martel at Poitiers, and alludes to small bands of Christians clinging to rocky outposts in the Pyrenees, waiting for God's help against the Saracens. Yet these isolated passages are outweighed by the straightforward narratives of the battles and political intrigues of Arab rulers. Furthermore, the author does not once express any animosity toward the *religion* of these Arabs: indeed, he says nothing at all about it.[49]

The reader of either of these eighth-century chronicles is given little reason to hope for an imminent end to Saracen rule in Spain; indeed, both authors steer clear of any apocalyptic speculation. The final chapters of a universal chronicle (as in those of Isidore and Bede) are the appropriate place for speculating on the course of history and the coming end of the world. Isidore and Bede used these chapters (as is traditional) to caution their readers against apocalyptic fervor; occasional chroniclers used them, on the contrary, to argue for the imminence of the end. Both eighth-century chronicles avoid the issue altogether. The *Chronicle of 741* ends abruptly with the accession of the caliph Hisham (724–43); it is as if the author, unable to draw any conclusions from his narrative or to see any wider logic in God's plan for history, simply left the task of completion for a successor.

The *Chronicle of 754* does indeed conclude with a chapter on the calculation of chronology. But rather than speculating on the number of years remaining in the sixth age until the time of Antichrist, he works out exactly how many years elapsed between the Creation and the birth of Christ (5,196 or 5,200); he offers the pros and cons for each figure, invoking the authority of Eusebius, Isidore, and Julian of Toledo. He calculates that 5,950 (or 5,954) years have elapsed between the Creation and the composition of his chronicle. This would mean (though he does not say it) that only 50 (or 46) years remain before annus mundi 6000, a year of apocalyptic significance according to many Christian authors. Yet this author steers clear of any evocation of the implications of this, retreating into an excursus on the annus mundi date of Christ's birth, as if preferring the safe, academic tallying of past history to the contemplation of the uncertain future.

These two eighth-century chroniclers recorded the events of their time without explaining how they fit into God's scheme of history. Their old Visigothic world had crumbled around them, and their new Berber and Arab overlords were locked in constant internecine struggles: a major revolt of Spanish and African Berbers in 740, and recurring uprisings in various Spanish cities; rebellion and civil war seemed to flare up at every turn, with ever-shifting alliances between groups of Berbers, native Christians, and *muwalladun* (recent native converts to Islam).[50] Can these writers be blamed for failing to see order in the chaos around them? The two chroniclers, writing in Latin for a Christian audience, limit themselves to narrating the more prominent of these intrigues. Drawing perhaps from their own experiences, but also from earlier Arabic chronicles, these two authors are already bilingual, bicultural—at least partially Arabized. Indeed the two chronicles show the process of cultural and linguistic Arabization that many Iberian Christians were probably undergoing; for this reason historians refer to the Christian communities of Muslim Spain as "Mozarab" (from the Arab *musta'rib*, "Arabized").[51] Both chroniclers were probably churchmen; both begrudgingly accepted their new status as *dhimmi* without showing the slightest interest in the religion of their new Arab overlords. Like their counterparts in seventh-century Syria, they viewed their new masters as political and military rivals, not as religious ones. Indeed, for both groups of Christians, small heretical sects seemed to pose a greater spiritual menace than Islam: the iconoclasts for John of Damascus, Monophysites for Anastasius of Sinai, Migetius for several eighth-century churchmen in Spain.[52] The increasing conversions of Syrian Christians to Islam in the eighth century prodded Christian churchmen to take notice of Islam and attempt to combat it theologically; the same scenario will be replayed in ninth-century Spain.

Churchmen like these chroniclers, in Spain as elsewhere in the Muslim world, became pivotal players in the political and cultural exchange between Muslim ruling elite and Christian majority. In the wake of the conquests, Muslim rulers left *dhimmi* communities largely intact, free to organize not only their cult but also justice and finances, including collection of the *jizya* (poll tax). The leaders of these communities (usually bishops, for Christians) would mediate between their Christian flock and their Muslim overlords. Close cooperation was essential to all concerned: the Christians preserved their rights and freedoms; the Muslim rulers received the poll tax and maintained their rule peacefully; and the bishops saw their importance and authority confirmed from both below and above.

The Umayyad emirs and caliphs of Córdoba, like other Muslim rulers, understood the political importance of *dhimmi* leaders: after all, the majority of their subjects were Christians until well into the ninth century, if not later.[53] So the emirs and caliphs brought the most important bishops into their court, seating them prominently among the courtiers during embassies with foreign dignitaries and during other state occasions.[54] What better way to affirm their legitimacy in the eyes of their Christian subjects than to turn their bishops into so many bright planets revolving around the sun of emiral power? Moreover, this was in the best tradition of Damascus and Baghdad, those distant caliphal courts whose grandeur the Cordovan rulers tried so hard to imitate. Perhaps this, too, helps explain the lack of polemical texts written against Islam in the first century of Muslim rule in Spain: those Christians who knew Arabic and who must have known something about Islam were in no position to attack the religion of their benefactors. A tactful refusal to broach doctrinal issues was in the best interests of all concerned.[55] To do so would be to risk undermining their own precarious status as privileged intermediaries between Muslim rulers and Christian masses. The only Christian Spaniard who is said to have written a (now lost) polemic against Islam is Felix, bishop of the Pyrenean diocese of Urgel, outside of Córdoba's political and military grasp.[56]

Crisis of Ninth-Century Mozarabs: The Córdoba Martyrs

While eighth-century Spain was marked by war, chaos, and uncertainty, the ninth century (despite scattered rebellions) saw the clear and steady ascendancy of the Umayyad emirate of Córdoba. 'Abd al-Rahmân I, refugee from the *fitna* that overthrew the Umayyad caliphate of Damascus and replaced it with the 'Abbasid caliphate of Baghdad, declared himself emir of al-Andalus in 756. By the reign of his great-grandson, 'Abd al-Rahmân II (822–52), the Umayyad hold on Spain was firm. 'Abd al-Rahmân II set out to make his provincial capital, Córdoba, into a new Damascus or Baghdad: he built up his palace complex, minted coins, imitated the style and ceremony of the 'Abbasid court, imported luxury items, and patronized scholars, poets, and musicians from the East. He brought from Baghdad the poet and singer Ziryab, who became so popular and so widely imitated as a fashion plate, that one historian has compared the impact of his arrival to that of the Beatles in the United States.[57]

Suddenly, Spanish Christians were confronted with the large-scale importation of high Islamic culture. The situation is very different from Syria, where Arabs had participated in Greco-Semitic culture long before Muhammad, and where Islamic court culture gradually evolved out of a mix of Syriac, Greek, Arab, and Persian elements. This culture had been, on the whole, absent in Spain during the first century of Muslim rule: Spanish Christians considered their new masters to be formidable militarily and politically but not culturally or religiously. Indeed, it was Muslim muftîs such as Yahyâ b. Yahyâ who (in the first half of the ninth century) warned Muslims not to celebrate Christian holidays such as Christmas.[58] Suddenly Christian Spaniards were confronted with massive onslaught of imported culture; suddenly their Arab Muslim overlords had culture, literature, music: and it all risked making the tired Latin culture of the Christians look pale by comparison.

Latin writers of the period watched these developments with alarm. Eulogius remarks:

Córdoba, however, once called Patricia, now called the Royal City, because of his ['Abd al-Rahmân's] residence, has been exalted by him
above all, elevated with honors, expanded in glory, piled full of riches,
and with great energy filled with an abundance of all the delights of the
world, more than one can believe or express. So much so that in every
worldly pomp he exceeds, surpasses, and excels the preceding kings of
his race. And meanwhile the church of the orthodox groans beneath his
most grievous yoke and is beaten to destruction.[59]

For the first time in Spain, the Muslims were gaining the upper hand culturally and intellectually, not only militarily: it was a cultural dominance
they would maintain until well into the thirteenth century. Paul Alvarus
complained that Christian youths no longer studied the Latin writings of
Bible and church fathers; instead:

> The Christians love to read the poems and romances of the Arabs; they
> study the Arab theologians and philosophers, not to refute them but to
> form a correct and elegant Arabic. Where is the layman who now reads
> the Latin commentaries on the Holy Scriptures, or who studies the
> Gospels, prophets or Apostles? Alas! all talented young Christians read
> and study with enthusiasm the Arab books; they gather immense li-
> braries at great expense; they despise the Christian literature as unwor-
> thy of attention. They have forgotten their language. For every one who
> can write a letter in Latin to a friend, there are a thousand who can ex-
> press themselves in Arabic with elegance, and write better poems in this
> language than the Arabs themselves.[60]

The chroniclers of 741 and 754 read Arabic chronicles: their great-
grandchildren were composing Arabic poems in Abd al-Rahmân's Córdoba. This acculturation bode ill for the Latin church, according to the
worried ruminations of Eulogius and Alvarus. While the bishops were being drawn into the politics and culture of the court, the monasteries remained steadfast bastions of Latinity and of resistance to acculturation.
Speraindeo (hope in God), Eulogius's and Alvarus's teacher and abbot of the
Cordovan basilica of Saint Zoilus, wrote a polemical disputation against Islam in the 820s or 830s, in which he reviled the Muslim idea of heaven as a
brothel (lupanar); he also composed passiones of two Christians who had
been put to death by Muslim authorities in the 820s, whom he considered

martyrs.⁶¹ These men, like the Syrians of John of Damascus's day, were seeing the world around them change, becoming foreigners in their native
land, no longer speaking the same language as their children. This "colonization" is more sudden in Spain than it had been in the Near East; the "anticolonial" reaction against it, on the part of Eulogius and others, will be all
the more violent. And the Andalusian bishops will be caught in the middle.

This tension exploded in the 850s, producing the Cordovan martyrs
movement.⁶² The spark that ignited this powder keg was a casual discussion between Muslims and a Christian priest by the name of Perfectus. One
day in 850, according to Eulogius's *Memoriale sanctorum*, some Muslims
asked Perfectus what he thought of Jesus and Muhammad; he responded
that Christ was divine but that he did not dare say what the Christians
thought of Muhammad, lest he anger his interlocutors. They told him to
go ahead and speak without fear. He explained (in Arabic) that for him
Muhammad was one of the false prophets announced in the Gospel: "For
there shall arrive false Christs, and false prophets, and shall show great
signs and wonders; insomuch that, if it were possible, they shall deceive the
very elect" (Matt. 24:24). Matthew was specifically predicting the career of
Muhammad, affirmed Perfectus, who described the Muslim prophet in the
following terms: "seduced by demonic illusions, devoted to sacrilegious
sorcery, he corrupted with his deadly poison the hearts of many idiots and
condemned them to eternal perdition. Lacking any spiritual wisdom, he
made them subjects of Prince Satan, with whom he will suffer the most
abominable punishments in hell. And to you, his disciples, he showed the
path that leads to the inextinguishable flames where you will burn with
him."⁶³ Perfectus went on to condemn the lasciviousness of Muhammad
and of his law. The Muslims were outraged, but they let him go his way.
Several days later, he was brought before the *qâdî* (judge) and questioned;
he spent the next several months in prison. On April 18, 850, the *qâdî* summoned him again, asking him to retract his blasphemies and to convert to
Islam. Perfectus reiterated his insults against the prophet and was sentenced to death. This, at least, is Eulogius's version of the story.⁶⁴ His
Memoriale sanctorum is an apologetical hagiography of the martyrs: he certainly embellishes Perfectus's speech and blackens his antagonists. Yet some
aspects of it seem quite realistic: the Muslims show, rather than hostility
toward Christianity, curiosity (perhaps mixed with mild disdain). They are
shocked by Perfectus's hostility. Christian belief held an honored if subservient place in Muslim theology, just as the Christian bishop held an

honored but subservient place in the emir's court. There is however no room in Christian theology for lesser revelations; all prophets outside of Christianity are false prophets, devotees of Satan who must be fought. This is confirmed, for Perfectus, by Muhammad's endorsement of polygamy and promise of beautiful houris in paradise; what could contrast more dramatically with the celibacy of the Christian monk or bishop?

Perfectus was not the first Christian to be executed for blasphemy; there were isolated similar cases in Syria and Iraq, as well as two earlier cases in Spain in the 820s. Perfectus's case could well have remained another isolated martyrdom, but it did not. The following year saw fifteen executions: ten of monks from nearby monasteries.[65] Most of these monks deliberately sought out martyrdom, going to the qâdî and insulting Islam and Muhammad (whom they referred to, according to Eulogius, as a precursor of Antichrist, *praeuium Antichristi*).[66] This spontaneous martyr movement was unprecedented anywhere in the Muslim world. Other martyrs were offspring of mixed marriages (usually Muslim father and Christian mother) who were legally considered Muslim; if they practiced Christianity, they were apostates and subject to the death penalty according to Muslim law. Such illegal practices had been tolerated, it seems, previously; but now these children of mixed marriages, caught in the middle, were forced to choose which side they were on.

Caught in the middle, too, was the rest of the Christian community, especially its bishops. The martyr movement rocked Córdoba, and the fragile alliance between Muslim rulers and Christian subjects threatened to come tumbling down. This indeed, was one of the objectives of the martyrs (or at least, of their apologists): to break the links between the Christians and the "Chaldeans," to erect an impenetrable wall of violence and hatred between Muslim ruler and Christian subject. This corresponds to the logic of what Edward Said describes as the anticolonial "resistance culture": to demonize the "occupying" power and discredit those who collaborate with it, using violence to dramatize the opposition between the "us" and the "them."[67]

In November 851 the bishops tried to regain control of the situation. Reccafred, metropolitan of Seville, wanted to put a stop to the martyrdoms and restore the fragile alliance between the emir and his Christian subjects. According to Alvarus, "Bishop Reccafred pounced on the Churches and the clerics like a violent tornado and locked up as many priests as he could in prison."[68] Reccafred and the other churchmen who refused to defend the martyrs, Alvarus continues, are cowards who grovel before the emir; they fear for their bodily safety but not for the salvation of their souls.[69] They are not men (*homines*); they are midgets (*homunculi*).[70]

Among the prisoners are Saul, the bishop of Córdoba, and Eulogius, who begins his *Memoriale sanctorum* in prison. The priests are freed on November 29. It is at this time, according to Alvarus, that Eulogius refuses to celebrate mass, "in order to avoid getting mixed up in Reccafred's errors."[71] By this symbolic act, Eulogius breaks with the ecclesiastical hierarchy because it has chosen the side of the oppressors, not that of the martyrs. The crisis has split the Christian community; it seems there are now *two* churches: one obedient to the archbishop, which confirms the condemnation of the martyrs during a council in 852,[72] and a separate, "donatist" clergy that defends the martyrs and refuses to recognize episcopal authority.[73] In 852 the new Umayyad emir Muhammad I (852–86) banishes Christians from his court, provoking fresh resentment against the martyrs.[74]

The martyrs were clearly unpopular with Córdoba's Christians: indeed much of Eulogius's and Alvarus's energy is directed at convincing their fellow Christians of the sanctity of the martyrs and the evilness of the Muslim authorities. It was, as Kenneth Wolf notes, "clear to everyone, even Eulogius, that the martyrs of Córdoba were not martyrs of the ancient Roman cast":[75] they deliberately sought out death; they had been free to practice Christianity; they produced no miracles, as even their devotees admitted. The apologists were fighting an uphill battle, as most Cordovan Christians resented the trouble wrought by the martyrs, whom they deemed fanatics; were they not "killed by men who venerated both God and a law"?[76] This, for Eulogius and Alvarus, is fuzzy theological thinking; there can be no truth (or half-truth) outside of Christianity. If Christian Cordovans entertain such dangerous errors, the fault lies with the bishops who fail to guide their flock. The privileged role accorded to the bishops in the emirate is, for the two apologists, scandalous. Alvarus opens his *Indiculus luminosus* by praying that God help him play the role of "dog who barks for You against the rabid wolf."[77] Alvarus is on God's side, whereas those who preach peace with the oppressors shirk their duty; they are "dumb dogs; they cannot bark."[78]

These churchmen can't "bark," according to Alvarus, because their worldly interests are closely tied to those of their Muslim rulers. Indeed, the prominent role played by leading churchmen in the Umayyad administration may explain the lack of polemics against Islam. (John of Damascus wrote his apologetical works only after quitting the government of Umayyad Damascus and retiring to the monastery of Mar Sabbas.) Alvarus and Eulogius are the first Latin writers to give Islam a place in God's plan: for Alvarus, in particular, the martyrdom of Cordovan Christians are "the persecutions of Antichrist." "Whoever denies that there is persecution to-day in these lands is either asleep, dazed by the yoke of slavery, or else, swelling with pride like the pagans, he crushes with his insolent foot Christ's humble catechumens."[79] In other words, the Christian had to pick sides: either Christ or the Antichrist. In Alvarus's spiritual universe, there is no room for compromise: for mixed marriages, bishops in the emir's court, obedient and subservient *dhimmi.*

For Eulogius, Muhammad is a *praecursor Antichristi* because he rejects Christ's divinity.[80] According to Eulogius, Perfectus, the first of the Cordovan martyrs, identified Muhammad with the false prophet announced by Matthew (24:24). In his *Liber apologeticus martyrum,* Eulogius repeats the same charge, citing other New Testament passages to prove his case.[81]

But it is Alvarus who weaves an elaborate exegetical argument to identify Muhammad as the Antichrist, or rather as a *praecursor Antichristi,* since he affirms (in the conservative tradition of Augustine) that there are many Antichrists. Since many accept that Domitian, Nero, and Antiochus are *praecursores Antichristi,* he asks, how can they not see that Muhammad is one too? I will not venture too far down the twisted lanes of Alvarus's exegesis of Daniel, Job, or Revelation, in which he tries at the same time to prove that Muhammad is an Antichrist and to slavishly follow the traditional interpretations of church fathers such as Gregory the Great.[82] I consider only one example, his exegesis of Daniel 7:23–27.[83] In this passage, the prophet has a dream in which he sees (among other things) four beasts. The description of the fourth beast is what interests Alvarus:

> The fourth beast shall be the fourth kingdom upon earth, which shall be diverse from all kingdoms, and shall devour the whole earth, and shall tread it down, and break it in pieces. And the ten horns out of this kingdom are ten kings that shall arise: and another shall rise after them; and he shall be diverse from the first, and he shall subdue three kings. And he shall speak great words against the most High, and shall wear out the saints of the most High, and think to change times and laws: and they shall be given into his hand until a time and times and the dividing of time. But the judgment shall sit, and they shall take away his dominion, to consume and to destroy it unto the end. And the kingdom and dominion, and the greatness of the kingdom under the whole heaven, shall be given to the people of the saints of the most High, whose

kingdom is an everlasting kingdom, and all dominions shall serve and obey him.

(Dan. 7:23—27)

In Daniel's description of this beast, Alvarus sees the career of the Antichrist Muhammad and his disciples. This eleventh king who arises after the others, "diverse from the first," who subdues three kings, is it not Muhammad, who vanquished the Greeks, the Romans, and the Goths? "And he shall speak great words against the most High": did he not deny the divinity of Christ, thus, according to Saint John, showing himself to be an Antichrist?[84] He "shall wear out the saints of the most High": is this not a prediction of the persecutions inflicted by the Muslims, in particular of the martyrdoms of Córdoba? He will "think to change times and laws": did he not introduce the Muslim calendar and the Koran? "And they shall be given into his hand until a time and times and the dividing of time" (*tempus et tempora et dimidium temporis*); this predicts the present period of persecution under the Muslim yoke and happily affirms that it will last only a limited period of time. I will spare the reader Alvarus's labyrinthine calculations of this period; suffice it to say that he concludes that Muslim rule is destined to last 245 years and that only 16 remain.[85] Like the pseudo-Methodius, Alvarus paints the present in apocalyptic colors while holding out the hope of the imminent end of the persecutions. It is logical that the persecutions of the enemy are hardening, but the good Christian who perseveres will live to see a better day. Unlike pseudo-Methodius, however, Alvarus does not foresee the end of time, only the end of Muslim rule. Edward Said has shown how resistance cultures reshape history, creating a historiography of resistance to oppose the triumphalist historiography of the dominant regime. In the same way, pseudo-Methodius, Alvarus, and Eulogius oppose the Muslim triumphalist view of history with an apocalyptic vision promising Christian vengeance.

In order to prove that Muhammad is indeed Antichrist, one has to know something of his biography. Alvarus and Eulogius are of course not about to ask the Muslims themselves; who would trust a life of Antichrist written by his acolytes? On the contrary, Eulogius discourages dialogue with Muslims; one must learn about the false prophet from trustworthy Christians: which is to say, for Eulogius, from Christians untainted by contact with Muslims.[86] In 850 Eulogius travels to Pamplona; he brings relics of the third-century martyr Acisclus for Pamplona's bishop.[87] In the nearby monastery of Leyre, he discovers a brief biography of Muhammad in a

Latin manuscript. He copies it and includes it in his *Liber apologeticus martyrum*.[88] This short text shows some knowledge of Islam: it describes Muhammad's marriage with Khadîja, the role of Gabriel in the revelation of the Qur'an, the titles of various Qur'anic Sûras, and Muhammad's marriage to Zaynab. All these events, however, are presented in the worst possible light, twisted almost beyond recognition by the hostile pen of the author. Muhammad's death is described in a manner that has nothing to do with Muslim tradition, but comes straight out of Christian traditions about Antichrist:

> Sensing his imminent destruction and knowing that he would in no way be resurrected on his own merit, he predicted that he would be revived on the third day by the angel Gabriel, who was in the habit of appearing to him in the guise of a vulture, as Muhammad himself said. When he gave up his soul to hell, they ordered his body to be guarded with an arduous vigil, anxious about the miracle which he had promised them. When on the third day they saw he was rotting, and determined that he would not by any means be rising, they said the angels did not come because they were frightened by their presence. Having found sound advice—or so they thought— they left his body unguarded, and immediately instead of angels, dogs followed his stench and devoured his flank. Learning of the deed, they surrendered the rest of his body to the soil. And in vindication of this injury, they ordered dogs to be slaughtered every year so that they, who on his behalf deserve a worthy martyrdom here, might share in his merit there. It was appropriate that a prophet of this kind fill the stomach of dogs, a prophet who committed not only his own soul, but those of many, to hell.[89]

A rotting corpse, which is subsequently desecrated by beasts: a vicious and emphatic image. If one imagines Muhammad as Antichrist one imagines that he occupies the same role in Islam that Christ occupies in Christianity. It seemed self-evident to many of these Christian polemicists that Muhammad had claimed to be the Messiah and that he had claimed he would resurrect. A rotting or desecrated corpse was presented as evidence that he was *not* on God's side.[90] This line of reasoning is shared by the Cordovan authorities who let the cadavers of executed Christians rot to prove they were not saints.[91] It does not matter, for Eulogius, that no Muslim believes that Muhammad is the Messiah, or that he never predicted that he would resurrect: this image of Muhammad the Antichrist gives the Christian reader a simple and comprehensible explanation of the role of Islam in the divine scheme; it helps him live with Islam and inoculates him against doubt and the desire to convert. Muhammad's fate evokes that of the biblical queen Jezebel, adept of Baal and enemy of God, whose "whoredoms" and "witchcraft" finally receive proper punishment when she is pushed from a window and her cadaver is trampled by horses and eaten by dogs.[92]

Eulogius deforms Muhammad's biography to fit the standard biographies of Antichrist. He is certainly not ignorant of what Muslims say about their prophet; he simply chooses to present the elements of Muhammad's life that fit the image of Antichrist. One of the favorite topics of Christian polemicists is sex: Muhammad's wives, Muslim polygamy, and the celestial houris promised to the faithful. All this is foreign to the ideal of Christian celibacy and to Christian ideas of heaven, but it fits well with the doctrines traditionally attributed to Antichrist. Eulogius has more trouble explaining the Koran's affirmation of the virginity of Jesus' mother. Here, again, his solution is a gross deformation: "I will not repeat the sacrilege which that impure dog [Muhammad] dared proffer about the Blessed Virgin, Queen of the World, holy mother of our venerable Lord and Savior. He claimed . . . that in the next world he would deflower her."[93] This outrageous claim, it seems, is Eulogius's invention; I know of no other Christian polemicist who makes this accusation against Muhammad. Eulogius fabricates lies designed to shock his Christian reader. This way, even those elements of Islam that resemble Christianity (such as reverence of Jesus and his virgin mother) are deformed and blackened, so as to prevent the Christian from admiring anything about the Muslim other.

The goal is to inspire hatred for the "oppressors," and (as wartime propagandists have long known) there is little better way to do so than to accuse the enemy of murder and rape. If most Cordovans seem ready to tolerate Islam with a sort of ecumenical open-mindedness, Eulogius sets out to show that the Muslim is not a friend but a potential rapist of Christ's virgins. He not only imagines that Muhammad wants to deflower the Virgin Mary but also supposes that the Cordovan authorities want to force Christian virgins Flora and Maria to become prostitutes. In his *Documentum martyriale* he writes to these two prisoners to encourage them to endure their tribulations with patience. Forget, he tells Flora, the love of your father and of your people, because God, the king, desires you. He tells the two virgins not to worry if their lustful oppressors touch them with their filthy hands and force them to commit impure acts; they will not be defiled, because they will commit the acts against their will.[94] This is a rape of virgins consecrated to God, a rape that, it seems, exists only in Eulogius's fevered imagination, but that underlines, for him, the brutality and lust of the Muslim, qualities that make him irrevocably other.[95]

Time and again, Eulogius and Alvarus insist on two key faults of the Muslim other: their lust and violence. One of the chief objectives of these apologists is to show that the Muslim authorities (and not the martyrs) were responsible for the executions. Eulogius seeks to prove that the Muslims are violent by nature. In the biography of Muhammad that he inserts in his *Liber apologeticus,* Eulogius emphasizes the cruelty of the pseudo-prophet and of the Arabs in general: "He ordered his believers to take up arms on his behalf, and, as if with a new zeal of faith, he ordered them to cut down their adversaries with the sword."[96] For Eulogius, the "Chaldeans" perpetuate the violence of their founder; the martyrs of Córdoba are simply their most recent victims.

To better inscribe these events in the annals of sacred history, Eulogius evokes the tribulations of Israel under the yoke of slavery, as well as the martyrdoms of the primitive church. In the trials of Israel described in Lamentations, Eulogius sees the reflection of his own age: "Our inheritance is turned to strangers, our houses to aliens. . . . Servants have ruled over us: there is none that doth deliver us out of their hand."[97] In order to prove, in his *Liber apologeticus martyrum,* that Christians are indeed undergoing persecution, he describes the destruction of Cordovan churches and violent attacks on priests[98] To accentuate the difference between the Christian us and the Muslim other, he deploys (as does Alvarus) animal metaphors: Saracens are savages, beasts, not men like us.[99]

For Eulogius, the good Christian does not seek out a modus vivendi with the Saracen; nor should he condemn the martyrs or discourage those seeking martyrdom. On the contrary, he should openly preach the gospel and accept death if it comes. Eulogius eventually becomes a martyr himself: along with Leocritia, an apostate Muslim who had taken refuge with him, he is executed on March 11, 859. Eulogius chose the path of martyrdom, and Alvarus contented himself with the role of Eulogius's hagiographer. Córdoba becomes peaceful, the modus vivendi between Christians and Muslims is gingerly reestablished; the more extreme Christians emigrate to the Christian kingdoms of the North; and the remaining Christians try to forget about the martyrs.[100] A Galician boy named Pelagius is martyred in 925, supposedly for refusing the sexual advances of the caliph 'Abd al-Rahmân III;[101] an apostate woman and a French priest are martyred in 931;[102] but there is evidence of only a single native Cordovan Christian actively seeking out martyrdom after 859.[103]

One of the principal tasks of the polemicist or war propagandist is to convince the people of the alterity of the enemy. Should we consider this voluntary martyrdom as the last desperate act of a few Christians who saw their culture, language, and religion dissolving into the mass of Muslim culture, as a last-ditch effort to affirm and resuscitate Christian Latin culture? If indeed this was their goal, they failed miserably: the strife caused by the martyrs probably encouraged Christians to convert to Islam, rather than discouraging them. The fifty-odd dead, mostly monks and priests, represented that many fewer priests and bishops for al-Andalus, where they were already in short supply. Eulogius himself, according to Alvarus, had been named bishop of Toledo in 851; he chose martyrdom over episcopal duty.[104] Indeed, the martyrs were motivated more by a yearning for personal salvation than by a desire to help the Christian church as a whole.[105]

The apologists for the martyrs direct their fiercest anger and apoplexy not at the Muslims but at Christians who consort with Muslims, in particular for churchmen who follow the orders of the emir.[106] The bishops were indeed caught in the middle, none more so than Bishop Saul of Córdoba. Saul was imprisoned with Eulogius and other clerics in 851 and fled the city in 853, to return sometime before 858.[107] Alvarus lashes out at Saul accusing him of not fully supporting the martyrs. By choosing neither one side nor the other, Saul earned the contempt and mistrust of both. Alvarus rejects the very role of bishop in the emirate: he compares the fees that Saul paid to the palace officials to obtain the office of bishop to the thirty solidi that Judas was paid; paying the church's money to the infidel in this way, he affirms, is simony.[108] Saul's superior, Reccafred, metropolitan of Seville, placed himself more firmly in the camp of the emir, and drew even sharper criticism from the martyrs' apologists.

The Cordovan martyr movement was not the origin of these tensions between purity and segregation on the one hand and toleration and acculturation on the other. Indeed these tensions exist wherever Islam and Christianity (and, for that matter, Judaism) coexist. The martyrs merely provided a particularly dramatic and violent response to these tensions, and in so doing made cooperation nearly impossible (for a time) between Muslim authorities and Christian churchmen.

The problems of Christian courtiers' accommodation or hostility toward Islam continue after the martyrdoms. A good example is Samson, abbot of Pinna Mellaria (Peñamelaria), a Cordovan monastery that had illegally recovered relics of the martyrs. Samson was summoned to the emir's court in 863, in order to translate from Arabic into Latin a letter to the Frankish king Charles the Bald. Yet he soon fell into disfavor: Samson's enemies charged that he passed military secrets to the Franks; a Christian punished for insulting Muhammad claimed that Samson urged him to do so. Christian clerics close to the court subsequently accused him of heresy. Having decided that it was better to change one's location than one's mind, he fled to the monastery of Martos and wrote his *Apologeticus,* a long defense against the charges of heresy.[109]

In his *Apologeticus,* Samson pours his bile out on Christian courtiers who milk their flocks to buy gifts for the emir and his family, who participate in drunken orgies in court.[110] The aged Avernus went so far as to have himself circumcised, surrendering his old, tough foreskin to the surgeon's knife.[111] This is accommodation gone too far: for Samson it is a prelude to apostasy; for Alvarus it was the mark of the Antichrist.[112] Other court Christians went so far as to denounce churches whose altars illegally housed relics of the recent martyrs.[113] Samson reserves much of his bile for his accuser, Malagan bishop Ostegesis, whom he nicknames *Hostis Ihesu* (enemy of Jesus). Ostegesis, he says, extorts as much money as possible out of his flock so that he can live a life of drinking and debauchery in the caliph's court. He ruthlessly draws up censuses of Christians in order to provide the emir with accurate tax rolls. He deals with recalcitrant taxpayers by flogging them, naked, through the streets.[114]

One cannot accept at face value this angry and venomous portrait of prominent Cordovan Christians in the years following the martyr crisis. Yet they again point out the difficulties faced by Christians in the emiral court. Christians were losing their distinctive Latin culture: none of the prominent court Christians, it seems, was capable of translating a letter to the Frankish king into Latin; an abbot from a nearby monastery had to be summoned. Christian authors of the following centuries translate Orosius and Isidore into Arabic for Christian readers who presumably cannot read Latin.[115] Ostegesis did indeed write his accusations against Samson in Latin, but he apparently had a hard time of it, and Samson took pleasure in mocking him for his poor Latin.[116] Loss of Latin, cultivation of Arabic letters, eager participation in court culture, circumcision: all this amounted, for writers like Samson, Alvarus, and Eulogius, to a prelude to apostasy.

Bishop Ostegesis epitomized this treachery, for Samson. We do not have Ostegesis's response to these accusations, but we can imagine what it might be. In acting against the cult of the new martyrs, he was striking a blow against the fanatical, donatist factions among Christian Cordovans, not simply showing his loyalty to the emir. In taking census of Christians in his diocese, Ostegesis undoubtedly had his own financial interests (as well as those of the emir) in mind. Yet this may also be his way of affirming the existence and importance of the Christian community of Malaga: yes, these Christians exist; they are still important; here they are. He is trying to prevent, perhaps, a sort of "conversion by slippage": many nominal Christians were happy (for tax purposes and in order to be better assimilated into Islamic society) not to be recognized as Christians. Rather than making the difficult decision of choosing to reaffirm their Christianity or to actively embrace Islam, they preferred to benefit from their ambiguous status. Ostegensis forced them to recognize their Christian identity, and they did not appreciate it.[117] This "conversion by slippage" is the fate of most Andalusian Christians in the next century or so. If lukewarm Christians of 850 don't mind hiding their Christian identity, their children and grandchildren are less and less likely to define themselves as Christian and to seek out the necessary initiatory sacraments from the diminishing supply of priests and bishops.[118]

Alvarus fulminated against Christian youths who preferred Arabic poetry to Latin letters; his own son, it seems, composed Arabic poems. Hafs ibn Albar, according to one of his Muslim contemporaries, was the most intelligent and most Arabized of the Andalusian Christians. Hafs translated the Psalms from Latin into Arabic verse. He also composed the *Book of Fifty-Seven Questions,* an Arabic apology of Christianity that (although it is now lost) seems to have been much less virulent than his father's.[119] Rather than vilifying Islam, as his father had, he crafted apologetical works that aimed to defend and justify Christianity in the eyes of both Christians and Muslims.[120] Mozarab Christians had found the spirit of polite apologetical dialogue familiar to oriental Christians. The father's diatribes were soon forgotten: Alvarus's *Indiculus luminosus* and *Life of Eulogius* each survive in one tenth-century manuscript; of Eulogius's none remain.[121]

In al-Andalus, tact and diplomacy reign. In 969 John of Gorze, monk and emissary of emperor Otto I, came to Córdoba hoping to win a martyr's crown. He brought letters in which Otto attacked Islam. The Cordovan Christians managed to cool John's suicidal ardor and convince him not to deliver his incendiary letters.[122] In the following centuries, Mozarab Christians sought to defend their place in the *dâr al-Islâm* rather than questioning or attacking it. Martyrdom, it seems, had lost its charm.

The *Crónicas Asturianas*:
A Reborn Gothic Kingdom Destined to Expel the Chaldeans?

While the generations of Cordovan Christians that followed the martyrs learned to live peaceably with their Muslim cohorts, other Christians emigrated, some of them going to the fledgling northwestern kingdom of Asturias. Mozarabs—and particularly Mozarab churchmen—provided a key link between Muslim south and Christian north. When Alfonso III needed to negotiate a peace treaty with Muhammad I in September 883, he sent Dulcidius, a Mozarab priest from Toledo. Dulcidius did not return empty-handed; he arrived in Oviedo in January 884, bringing with him the bodies of Eulogius and Leocritia, as well as manuscripts containing (among other texts) the complete works of Eulogius.[123] Dulcidius and other Mozarab churchmen played a key role in forging a new royal ideology for the Asturian kings, anointed successors to the Goths of old, destined to drive the Saracen invader from Spain. This ideology is expressed in three chronicles produced between 883 and 890: *The Prophetic Chronicle, The Chronicle of Albelda,* and *The Chronicle of Alfonso III.*[124]

The Prophetic Chronicle was written in April 883, nine months before the arrival of Eulogius's relics. It predicted the imminent demise of Arab hegemony in Spain and proclaimed that the Asturian King Alfonso III (866–910) "will soon reign in all Spain"[125] This chronicle, preserved in slightly varying forms in several codices, is a hodgepodge of prophecy, narrative history, and regnal lists of Spanish Muslim rulers. It also contains a genealogy of Muhammad, as well as the same brief life of Muhammad that Eulogius had inserted in his *Memoriale sanctorum.* Yet the ideological purpose of this eclectic composition is clear: the author seeks to prove that Muslim rule in Spain will soon come to an end and that the Goths will reign again in the person of Alfonso III.

The Prophetic Chronicle opens with a prophecy based very loosely on Ezekiel 38–39. Ezekiel had predicted battles between Gog and Israel; the anonymous chronicler associates Gog with the Goths (as Isidore and others had done before him) and changes "Israel" into "Ishmael." He goes on to explain that these prophecies have been partially fulfilled: God sent the Ishmaelites into Spain "on account of the sins of the Gothic people" but allotted the Ishmaelites only 170 years of rule over the Goths.[126] Here again is the Old Testament scenario of God turning away from his chosen people mired in sin. He later says that God punished them for not showing proper penance for their sins and for not following the teachings of the church councils, expelling them from the promised land.[127] He carefully calculates the reigns of the Muslim rulers in Spain from the invasions of Târiq and Mûsâ to the Emir Muhammad I (852–86). The chronicler, writing in April 883, predicts that 884 will be the year in which Alfonso delivers Spain from the "pagan" invaders.[128]

This chronicle clearly shows the exportation to the Asturian north of the strident attitude of the supporters of the martyr movement. Alvarus had predicted the imminent demise of Muslim rule in Spain; now a Mozarabic chronicler in Oviedo hooks his apocalyptic hopes onto the military prowess of an Asturian king. This prophecy also has parallels with Eastern texts like the pseudo-Methodius: Muslim conquerors have been sent by God as punishment for the sins of Christians but will eventually be overthrown by a heavenly ordained Christian king. Yet the *Prophetic Chronicle,* unlike pseudo-Methodius, does not predict the end of time, contenting itself (as had Alvarus) with the end of Muslim rule in Spain. While the vision is similar to Alvarus's, the methods are much cruder: Alvarus erected intricate exegeses of various prophetic texts, working closely with the previous interpretations by Gregory the Great and others. *The Prophetic Chronicle* proffers clumsy prophecies based on deliberate misreadings of Ezekiel.

Dulcidius and Sebastian, bishop of Orense, collaborated (at the king's bidding) to create, in the late 880s, a more nuanced and more frankly royal version of this historical vision in the *Chronicle of Alfonso III.*[129] Their chronicle purports to be a continuation of Isidore's *Origins of the Goths,* and as such its ideological purport is clear: Spain's marriage with the Goths was not over, it was merely undergoing a temporary separation. The Asturian monarchy would restore Gothic hegemony. The Muslim conquest was the punishment against the moral depravity of a few Gothic kings, notably Witiza, who had practiced polygamy and forced priests to marry.[130] The pivotal player in this succession between Goths and Asturians is a certain Pelayo (Pelagius), former sword bearer of Kings Witiza and Rodrigo.[131] Pelayo, fleeing the tyranny of the "Chaldeans" who forced Spaniards to pay tribute to the "King of Babylon," took refuge in a Cantabrian cave that housed a shrine to the Virgin.

This mountain shrine becomes the stage for the dramatic confrontation between the virtuous Pelayo and his Muslim adversaries: a "pagan multitude" of 187,000 comes to dislodge Pelayo and a small band of companions. The Muslim army is accompanied by the epitome of cowardice and complicity, the wimpish Oppa, son of King Egica according to the *Chroni-*

cle of 754; here he is a Mozarabic bishop. Oppa tries to convince Pelayo to surrender, telling him how futile it is to resist to such an enormous army. Pelayo haughtily rejects Oppa's plea, saying "Christ is our hope that through this little mountain, which you see, the well-being of Spain and the army of the Gothic people will be restored."[132] In the ensuing battle, the Virgin hurls back the stones catapulted at her sanctuary, and the handful of Christian soldiers rout the "Chaldean" multitudes.

This battle (subsequently known as Covadonga), whether or not it ever took place, would become the cornerstone of the ideology of *reconquista:* Pelayo provided a genealogical link (real or fictitious) with the Gothic past and the clear sense of a mission to reinstate Gothic hegemony over the entire Iberian peninsula. Knowledge of the religion of the Muslim other was available and at times was used (the *Prophetic Chronicle* incorporates the *Life of Muhammad* from Eulogius's *Liber apologeticus martyrum*) but was not essential. The Mozarab chroniclers who helped forge this prophetic vision certainly knew of the martyr movement in Córdoba, yet they say nothing about it: the protagonists in this new drama are the Asturian kings, and the martyrs are of no apparent use to Asturian royal ideology. Potentially, Oviedo's ideologues could have made good use of the martyrs (and of the writings of their apologists) to paint the Cordovan emirs as persecutors of Christians. Surprisingly, neither they nor later Spanish chroniclers exploited the martyrdoms in this way: they are scarcely if ever mentioned by later Iberian authors. What these chroniclers *did* inherit and adapt from Eulogius and Alvarus was the ability to see their own struggles through the magnifying lens of the Old Testament prophets. The Muslims were the Chaldeans, who ruled from Babylon, and whose oppressive reign was ordained by God to punish the sins of the chosen people.[133] Yet God had not completely abandoned his people, and a renewed Christian monarchy would restore its hegemony over the promised land.

Three Cordovan Martyrs in Paris

Oviedo was not the only ninth-century Christian capital to revere the martyrs of Córdoba: the monastery of Saint Germain des Prés, dear to Frankish king Charles the Bald, had relics of three martyrs brought back from Córdoba.[134] True, the monks of Saint Germain, Usuard and Odilard, had originally wanted the relics of Saint Vincent; to this end they set off for Valencia in 857, despite (or perhaps because of) the frequent Viking incursions against Paris and the surrounding area. The two monks narrated their travels to another monk, Aimoin, who recorded their adventures in writing. As Aimoin tells the story, Usuard and Odilard, unable to find the relics they wanted in Valencia but having been told of the Cordovan martyrs, set off for Córdoba in search of fresh relics. There they met Eulogius (Aimoin praises his *Memoriale sanctorum*), negotiated with Bishop Saul and others, and managed to obtain the decapitated body of Aurelius, the head of his wife, Nathalie (also known as Sabigotho), and the body (complete with head) of George, along with a letter from Bishop Saul to King Charles certifying the authenticity of the relics. For the occasion, Eulogius composed a text narrating the passion of the three saints; here again, texts accompany relics. With this haul they made their way back to Paris, or rather, to the nearby villa of Esmans, where the monks of Saint Germain were taking refuge from the Vikings. These martyrs duly perform miracles, Aimoin tells us, along the route—not in Spain, but from Béziers to Esmans. King Charles was delighted to receive the martyrs.

Several things are striking about Aimoin's description. First is the equivalence between the new Cordovan martyrs and the martyrs executed by Rome: while the monks set out in search relics of Saint Vincent of Saragossa (d. 304), the newer martyrs will do just fine as a substitute. This they prove themselves by obligingly performing miracles. Furthermore, Aimoin has nothing to say about Islam or about the particular crimes for which the martyrs were killed. This is all the more striking in that Usuard and Odilard went to Córdoba, met Eulogius, Saul, and others, and even read the *Memoriale sanctorum*. Yet on the few occasions Aimoin refers to Muslims it is as "Saracens," "pagans," or "ministers of the devil": vituperative terms, indeed, but ones that draw no distinction between Roman pagans of old and Cordovan Muslims of his own day. Whatever the two may have learned about Islam on their trip to Córdoba he does not deem worth reporting.

The martyrs performed miracles in their new home. This is standard in such translation narratives: the miracles confirm the bona fide sanctity of the relics and verify that the saints are happy in their new home. Yet it is ironic that these saints, who produced no miracles in Spain (as even Eulogius begrudgingly admits),[135] would do so in Gaul. The martyrs were unpopular and controversial in Córdoba, widely despised as troublemakers—so much so that even their advocates could not pretend they produced miracles. They became less controversial with each step of the monks' journey from Córdoba to Paris. By the time they reached Saint Germain they were bona fide miracle workers like any other self-respecting martyrs. The three martyrs were revered in their new Parisian home, but revering the martyrs did not necessitate any knowledge of Islam. On the contrary, the less one knew of the peculiar conditions of the Córdoba martyrdoms, it seems, the more apt one was to revere the new saints and trust in their miraculous powers. For Aimoin, the three martyrs were victims of "pagan persecution," just like the Parisians who weathered the repeated attacks of pagan Vikings. At roughly the same time as he wrote his account of the translation of the three martyrs, Aimoin also wrote a collection of miracles of his monastery's patron saint, Germain, who performed miracles to protect his monks and to kill the pagan Vikings who defiled his church. Clearly the monks of Saint Germain were looking for powerful protectors against "pagan" enemies and were uninterested in learning about the differing natures of their "pagan" errors. When Usuard compiled his *Martyrology,* whose hundreds of manuscripts were to spread all over Europe, he made note of the three martyrs whose bodies he had brought back; he also mentioned twenty-seven other Cordovan martyrs, including Eulogius.[136] But nothing in his brief mention of these martyrs told the reader that their deaths were any different or any more recent than that of the hundreds who died at the hands of the Romans, whose feast days (i.e., calendar dates of martyrdom, without mention of years) Usuard dutifully records.[137]

It is of course possible that these monks communicated what they had learned of Islam to others; they may have spoken with Paschasius Radbertus, who in his exegesis of Matthew, asserts that the Saracens "were wickedly seduced by some pseudo-apostles, disciples of Nicholas so to speak, and composed for themselves a law from the Old as well as the New Testament, and so perverted everything under the cult of one God, unwilling to agree with us or the Jews in any respect" He adds that "many think" that they are followers of the Antichrist, which makes the military success of Islam explicable for a Christian exegete: they are clearly predicted in the Apocalypse of Saint John.[138]

The three martyrs housed in Saint Germain would continue to be revered there until the eighteenth century; thanks to the influence of Usuard's *Martyrology,* the names of the Cordovan martyrs would be remembered on their feast days in monasteries throughout Europe, by monks who would not have the slightest reason to suspect that they had not been put to death by the imperial agents of Decius or Diocletian rather than 'Abd al-Rahmân or Muhammad I. In Spain, by contrast, their cult would remain unpopular; other than the mention made of several feast days in the tenth-century *Calendar of Córdoba,* their names rarely appear in the martyrologies of Spanish monasteries. There is little evidence of a cult of their relics surviving later than the ninth century either in Córdoba or in Oviedo.

SPANISH CHRISTIANS confronted by the rise of Islam reacted in various ways, much along the lines of their Eastern brethren a century earlier. Churchmen begrudgingly accepted their role as *dhimmi* and chronicled the military and political destinies of their new overlords without commenting on their religious beliefs. Theologically, these writers could explain Islam's military successes only as punishment for the sins of heretical or morally depraved rulers (Heraclius, Witiza, Rodrigo); they had plenty of models in the Bible and in earlier Christian historiography to guide them. Yet their new role of protected, second-class minority was unprecedented: nothing in the writings of earlier Christians described anything remotely like it. If Islam tolerated Judaism and Christianity as expressions of valid (though superseded) revelation (as Christians in theory tolerated Judaism), there was no place in the Christian scheme of history for a later legitimate revelation. Christians had no solid theological grounds for showing the same tolerance toward their Muslim overlords that they received from them. As a result, these Arabized churchmen, some of whom held important positions in the Umayyad administration, preferred to keep an awkward silence about the religion of their new overlords and benefactors.

For Alvarus, these assimilated churchmen were errant sheepdogs who refused to bark against the ravenous wolves, the Chaldean followers of Antichrist. In defending the actions of the Cordovan martyrs, Eulogius and Alvarus branded Muhammad as a heresiarch and false prophet, Islam as a heretical deviation of Christianity. Passive acceptance of *dhimmi* status was anathema; those Christians who participated in the life of the Chaldean court were consorts of the devil. In response, Alvarus, glossing the prophet Daniel, offered the vague hope of the imminent end to Muslim rule in Spain.

While this strident anti-Muslim ideology seemed necessary to defend the actions of the martyrs, northern Christians by and large ignored Islam rather than anathematizing it. Even the royal Asturian chronicles, written by Mozarab Christians who revered the martyrs and brought Eulogius's relics and writings from Córdoba to Oviedo, show scant interest in the refutation or vilification of Islam. They justified their conquests against the Umayyads as a reestablishment of Gothic hegemony, not as a holy war against Chaldean heretics. When Aimoin and Usuard brought the relics of Cordovan martyrs to Paris, they did their best to minimize the religious differences between the Muslim victimizers of the new martyrs and the pagan executors of the martyrs of old. At Saint Germain in the ninth century, as in Jarrow in the eighth, the Saracens were among the more distant of the many groups of barbarians whose armies menace Christendom, whose religious beliefs inspire little curiosity.

Supposing that an assiduous reader in northern Europe in the year 1000 wished to know something about the religious beliefs of the Saracens, what could he find? If he had access to one of the three manuscripts of Eulogius's passion of George, Nathalie, and Aurelius, he would learn that the Saracens followed the teachings of a pseudoprophet who had himself been instructed by demons.[139] He would have no access to manuscripts of other works by ninth-century Spanish writers on Islam. In Paschasius Radbertus's exegesis of Matthew, he could read that the Saracens had been seduced by false prophets into following Antichrist. He would be unable to read the works of the Eastern writers whose works are discussed in chapter 3, with the exception of the pseudo-Methodius (translated into Latin in the eighth century by a Frankish monk named Peter[140]) and of Theophanes's *Chronographica,* which Anastasius the Librarian translated into Latin in the 870s.[141]

Benjamin Kedar has traced the textual history of some of these early Latin texts about Islam, along with that of other numerous brief mentions of the beliefs and customs of the Saracens; "it is evident," Kedar says, "that a considerable amount of information about the Saracens did reach Catholic Europe between the mid-seventh and early eleventh century."[142] Yet this information, if perhaps "considerable" in aggregate, was quite thinly spread. Moreover, there was no way for the reader to distinguish between accurate and inaccurate information.

Over and against these meager references in a handful of manuscripts in a few libraries scattered across Europe, the reader in the year 1000 would have a wealth of information readily available in the many manuscripts of the Bible, Jerome, Isidore, and Bede; there, of course, he would learn that the Saracens were pagan idolaters and stone-worshipers. It should thus come as no surprise that when (in the eleventh and twelfth centuries), Latin authors began to take an interest in the religion of the Saracens, they described it (in increasingly lurid detail) in the familiar and despised guise of pagan idolatry.

Chapter 5

৵৵

Saracens as Pagans

They run to an idol of Apollo in a crypt,
They rail at it, they abuse it in vile fashion:
"Oh, evil god, why do you cover us with such shame?
Why have you allowed this king of ours to be brought to ruin?
You pay poor wages to anyone who serves you well!"
Then they tear away the idol's scepter and its crown.
They tie it by the hands to a column,
They topple it to the ground at their feet,
They beat it and smash it to pieces with big sticks.
They snatch Tervagant's carbuncle,
Throw the Mahumet into a ditch,
And pigs and dogs bite and trample it.

Chanson de Roland

This is the religion of the Saracens, as it is portrayed in many European texts of the Middle Ages. In the *Chanson de Roland,* the Saracens destroy their own idols when they prove themselves powerless against the army of God.[1] These idols of gold, inlaid with precious stones, to whom the Saragossans had offered the symbols of power (scepter and crown), provide a vivid and concrete (though completely imaginary) focus for the military activities of the valiant Christian knight. The crusader, in Spain or Syria, can strike stoutly and with a clear conscience, for the Saracens' idolatry is proof plenty that "Pagans are wrong and Christians are right" (l. 1015).

Scores of medieval texts, in Latin, French, and other languages, paint Saracen religion in the familiar hues of classical Roman idolatry: their

Saracens prostrate themselves and sacrifice to idols inhabited by demons. Medieval sculptures and paintings also portray Saracen idolatry in nearly identical visual terms as classical Roman idolatry: often the acolyte's dark skin and turban are the only characteristics that allow the viewer to distinguish him as a Saracen.[2] Earlier Latin texts described Saracen religion in terms of pre-Islamic Arab litholatrous paganism. Eastern Christian authors who knew more about Islam attacked the cult of the Ka'ba for its supposed continuation of pre-Islamic pagan rites in honor of Venus. Yet none of these earlier authors imagined Saracen religion in such vivid terms. It is only in the twelfth century that various European authors provide the Saracens with a panoply of idols, in stone and precious metals, inhabited by demons who endow them with magical powers. This is not mere "literary convention," as Norman Daniel claims.[3] This portrayal of Saracen idolatry grows out of a propagandistic effort to justify and glorify the actions of the first and second Crusades. Yet the earliest vivid description of Saracen idolatry predates the first Crusade by a century; it comes from the pen of a nun writing about a Cordovan martyr.

Saracens in Pagan Garb: Hrotsvitha of Gandersheim and the *Passio Thiemonis*

The Cordovan martyrs' persecutors were stripped of their Islamic garb by the martyrs' Frankish hagiographers. Hrotsvitha, nun at the abbey of Gandersheim at the turn of the millennium, will go a step further and clothe them in the familiar attire of classical Roman idolaters. In a long poem glorifying the martyr Pelagius, Hrotsvitha does acknowledge that the Saracens allowed Christians to practice their ancestral religion, yet asserts that they inflicted the death penalty on anyone who blasphemed the gods they made of gold.[4] The good Christians who longed to gain the martyrs' palm would insult the marble idols before which the Saracen prince prostrated himself and burned Sabaean frankincense (which Hrotsvitha associates with Arabs thanks to her reading of Isidore).[5] The Saracen king Abderahemen ('Abd al-Rahmân III, 912–61), "stained with bodily lust" (*luxu carnis maculatus;* l. 74), attempts to seduce Pelagius, a Christian boy. Pelagius rejects the king's advances, proclaiming:

> *It is not proper for a man purified through baptism in Christ*
> *To bow down his unsullied neck to a barbarous love,*

Nor for a Christian anointed with holy oil
To be captured by the kiss of the Demon's filthy associate.
Therefore embrace licitly the stupid men
Insane and rich, who frolic with you on the lawn;
Let the slaves which are your idols be your friends.[6]

The king then warns Pelagius that he is blaspheming against "our idols," and that the punishment for such blasphemy is death by decapitation. Urging the boy to be respectful and cooperative, he bends down again to kiss his neck. Pelagius hits him in the face; blood stains the king's beard. Furious, the king has his men hurl the boy over the city wall to the banks of the river below; miraculously, the boy falls gently and is unharmed. The king's men then find that they are unable to harm the boy's body with their weapons. Finally, Christ allows his head to be cut off, so that the angels may bring the new martyr to heaven. These miracles are the standard fare of the *passiones,* as is the final miracle that follows the boy's death: the king orders that the boy's body be burned, but Pelagius's severed head announces that God will not allow the flames to hurt it.

For Hrotsvitha, 'Abd al-Rahmân's homosexual desire is directly inspired by the demons whose idols he worships: his subsequent urge to destroy the beautiful young boy he cannot possess shows him as a quintessential despot. Hrotsvitha affirms that the military success of this Saracen king implies no merit of his own; it is a divine punishment decreed by the "secret Judge." Over and against this demonically inspired despot whose "barbaric rite" consists of idolatry, homosexuality, and the destruction of his enemies, is the righteous boy Pelagius, soldier (*miles*) of the celestial king. It is common in the martyrologies to portray martyrs as soldiers (*milites*) or gladiators (*athleti*) of Christ, fighting against the demonical forces of paganism. Yet Hrotsvitha goes a step further when she evokes armed struggle to resist the evil forces of paganism. The valiant people of Galicia spurn the pagan law: they are Christ's devotees and "rebels against the idols." It is this resistance—both political and religious—that inspires a demonic fury in the king and has him set out, "sword aflame," to subdue the rebellious province.[7]

This is a potent ideological cocktail. The Saracen pagan king, inspired by the demons whose idols he worships, lusts after pure Christian boys and decapitates them when they do not surrender their bodies to him. In fury, he directs his flaming sword against those Christian provinces such as Galicia whose people rebel against the cult of the idols. The interior Christian

minority and the exterior Christian enemy are both threatened by this diabolical power. Hrotsvitha makes no call to war, does not urge Christian
knights to aid their oppressed Spanish brethren. But it is easy to see how
this view of the pagan other could (and would) subsequently be used to
justify war against Saracen "pagans"—and against Wendish or Lithuanian
pagans closer to Gandersheim.[8] Many earlier authors assumed that the
Saracens or Arabs continued to observe the same cults as had their pagan
ancestors. Yet Hrotsvitha is the first Latin author to describe this paganism
in lurid detail and to use it to justify resistance against Saracen rule. This
strategy will become common two centuries later, as the writers on the first
Crusade glorify and justify the killing of Saracens by Christian knights.[9]

The *Chronicles of the Archbishops of Salzburg* includes the story of Archbishop Thiemo, who died in the Crusade of 1101.[10] Thiemo, we are told,
along with Duke Welf of Bavaria, led a group of Bavarians and Swabians
toward Jerusalem, which was already under the rule of crusader Godfrey.
As they approached the holy city, these crusaders were surrounded and defeated "by an innumerable multitude of gentiles *[ethnici]*." These pagans
were led by three brothers from Corosan "who in their ferocity were more
tyrannical and in their cult more pagan than Decius"—a Roman emperor
best known for his brutal persecutions of Christians. The "pagans" were
angered by the recent victory of the crusaders and eager to wreak vengeance on Christian pilgrims.[11] They led Thiemo and other pilgrims away
into slavery. One day their king discovered that Thiemo had been trained
as a goldsmith, so he asked him to repair a golden idol. Thiemo asked for a
hammer and approached the idol. He addressed the demon inhabiting the
idol, ordering it in the name of God to leave the statue.[12] When the demon
uttered blasphemies, Thiemo smashed the idol with his hammer. This led
to his martyrdom: he was thrown into prison, brought out the next day,
put on an ass, whipped, and brought to an arena before the throngs; there
the king accused him of sacrilege. Thiemo responded that the idols were
not gods but demons, and preached that the king should desist from the
worship of Saturn, Jove, and the obscene Priapus. The king responded by
ordering that all Thiemo's fingers be cut off, as well of those of his followers, and that their limbs then be lopped off. As the king drank the martyrs'
blood, Thiemo commended his soul unto God, and the crowd saw a choir
of angels descend to take up the souls of the martyrs. Nearby, we are told,
was an idol named Machmit, whom the pagans were wont to consult as an
oracle. A demon began to speak through Machmit, saying that this had
been a great victory for the Christians, "whose glory grows against us

daily."[13] He warned the pagans not to attempt to stop the Christians from burying their saint. Thiemo was buried in a church and miracles ensued: he healed the blind, deaf, lepers, and possessed, both among Christians and among pagans. Woe to those who attempt to violate his sanctuary; they face immediate death. For this reason, we are told, the pagans held Saint Thiemo in respect and did not pester any of his pilgrims.

The story of Thiemo presents a vivid portrait of the enemy that the crusaders went off to fight, as they imagined him; or at least as their chroniclers imagined them. The picture is shocking both for its hostility and for its wild inaccuracy, its Technicolor horror: a king who worships golden idols, seeks out Christian pilgrims, and delights in ripping off their limbs and drinking their blood. This portrait (like Hrotsvitha's portrait of 'Abd al-Rahmân) is pieced together with images from the stories of the early martyrs of the church, stories very familiar to clerical authors through the daily monastic reading of the martyrologies.[14] Not that all readers of this story believed it. Otto of Friesing came across the story and retells it in his *Chronicle of Two Cities*, but immediately rejects it as impossible: the Saracens would not have asked Thiemo to worship idols since "the Saracens universally are worshipers of one God. . . . They are cut off from salvation by one thing alone, that they deny that Jesus Christ . . . is God and the Son of God, and hold in reverence and worship as a great prophet of the Supreme God, Mahomet, a deceiver."[15]

The Pagan Adversaries in the Chronicles of the First Crusade

While few of the Latin chroniclers of the first Crusade imagine their Saracen enemies in quite as vivid and hostile terms, they do not present them in ways that contradict this image. The epic descriptions of battles against the Saracens demanded a vivid and colorful enemy, one against whom war was just and victory was glorious. Almost all these chroniclers describe them as pagans, and most of them present the crusaders' victory as part of the age-old struggle with paganism, as part of the culminating events that would result in the eradication of paganism and—for some—the second coming of Christ. Their idols are at times called Jupiter, Apollo, or Mahomet; chroniclers of the first Crusade occasionally refer to their adversaries as *Mahummicolae*: "Muhammad-worshippers."[16] Fighting against pagans, crusaders could claim to be wreaking vengeance for the pagans' Crucifixion of Christ and their usurpation of his city; when they fell in battle, they could claim the mantle of martyrdom. The fight against paganism had a long history, one in which Christianity was sure to emerge victorious.

Many scholars have described how the first Crusade represented a radical new form of piety, a strange mixture of pilgrimage and military ardor: humbly submitting to God's will while aggressively attacking one's enemy.[17] The paradoxical nature of the Crusade is epitomized in the image of the barefoot knights in procession around the walls of Jerusalem, days before they capture it. In the words of crusader and chronicler Raymond d'Aguilers, "it was ordered that . . . the priests prepare themselves for the procession, with crosses and relics of the saints and that the knights and all strong men follow them with trumpets and banners and barefoot, and that the armed men should march barefoot."[18] If this strange hybrid, this armed pilgrimage, needed justification in the eyes of Christians back home in Europe, its success was a resounding vindication: clearly the Christian knights had been right to cry out "Deus lo volt!"; clearly it was God's will that the crusaders take Jerusalem back from the "pagans." Yet the novelty of the endeavor, and its success, forced Christian writers to contemplate how the Crusade fit into the divine plan.

A number of participants wrote firsthand accounts of the Crusade; these were soon read and reworked by monastic writers in Europe.[19] The anonymous *Gesta Francorum* consistently refers to the crusaders' foes as "pagans" and twice has its leaders swear oaths by their God "Machomet."[20] Yet, other than this, it has little to say about who these pagans are, what their religious rituals are, or why the Christians are justified in taking land from them. Other Christian writers felt a need to explain the Crusades, to place them in Christian history and eschatology as a key part of the long, hard fight against paganism: a fight, however, that the Bible promises will, in the end, result in Christian victory.

Only one of the chroniclers of the first Crusade, Guibert of Nogent, acknowledged that the Saracens were monotheists and Muhammad their prophet not their God (I examine Guibert's portrayal of Muhammad in chapter 6). For the rest, it is pagan idolaters that the crusaders went off to fight, in order to take Jerusalem back from them and to wreak vengeance on them for the Crucifixion—as well as for their subsequent blasphemies against Christ. Time and again, the chroniclers of the first Crusade cite the eradication of paganism as one of the key motives behind the Crusade. Raymond d'Aguilers, for example, says that by God's mercy his army "stood forth over all paganism."[21] Raoul de Caen, in the preface to his *Gesta Tancredi* (which narrates the exploits of Tancred de Hauteville), says that his subject is "that pilgrimage, that glorious struggle, which added to its in-heritance our holy Mother Jerusalem, which extinguished idolatry and re-stored the faith."[22]

To understand how the image of Islam as paganism helps justify the Crusade, I examine in detail one account written by a participant in the first Crusade, Petrus Tudebodus. Tudebodus asserts (as do most of the chroni-clers) that the pilgrims' amazing victory against enormous odds was the work of God, not man; that Christ awarded the fidelity and valor of his army by granting it victory over innumerable pagans. This victory over pa-ganism is part of the divine plan and a signal that the end of time is near. Tudebodus frequently compares the army of God with the apostles, implic-itly and explicitly: both spread the Christian faith, fought paganism, and received the palm of martyrdom. To a modern reader these appear drasti-cally different: preaching the Gospel and passively accepting execution on the one hand, waging war on the other. Tudebodus will try to present these as essentially similar acts: the crusaders are the new apostles and martyrs, ushering in a new age for Christ and his church.

This purpose is clear from the first sentences of Tudebodus's *History:*

> In the year of our lord [1095],[23] when that end grew near which the Lord each day shows to his faithful, and which He particularly shows in the Gospel, saying "If any man will come after me, let him deny himself, and take up his cross, and follow me" [Matt. 16:24] there was a great commotion in all the regions of Gaul. If anyone wished zealously and with pure heart and mind to follow God and to faithfully bear the cross after him, he should not hesitate to quickly set out on the way to the Holy Sepulcher [*via Sancti Sepulchri*].[24]

Tudebodus here puts the Crusade in an eschatological context. The end, he says, was drawing near (though he is careful to avoid saying exactly *how* near): he connects that end with the injunction to take up one's cross and follow Christ. God's command, which before could be understood only in its spiritual sense (Eulogius cited it to justify the Cordovan Christians who sought out martyrdom[25]) was now literally being fulfilled before Tudebo-dus's eyes, as crusaders sewed on the cloth crosses that symbolized their pilgrimage vow and followed Christ by setting off for his city.[26]

Throughout his *History,* Tudebodus in this way describes the crusaders in language taken straight from the Gospels, implicitly likening them to the apostles and martyrs. He has Pope Urban II, at the council of Clermont, say that "anyone who wishes to save his soul should not hesitate humbly to set off on the way of the Lord and the Holy Sepulcher."[27] He puts in Urban's mouth words of scripture, urging his listeners to follow the injunctions that Christ gave to his disciples:

> Brothers, it is proper that you suffer many things in Christ's name, that is to say misery, persecution, poverty, illnesses, nudity, hunger, thirst and other things of this kind, as He himself said to his apostles: "It is proper that you suffer many things in my name. And do not be ashamed to speak before men; I myself will give you a mouth and eloquence and a great reward will follow you."[28]

Won over by Urban's eloquence, Tudebodus asserts, these new apostles flocked to Constantinople from all over Europe.

Those who die are described as martyrs, and here again descriptions of their martyrdom—like that of Thiemo's—are often modeled on those of the apostles and early martyrs of the ancient church, who refused to offer sacrifice to Roman idols and were subsequently put to death.[29] At Nicaea, Tudebodus recounts, a bishop preaches to a band of crusaders besieged by Turks, using Jesus' injunction to the apostles: "Be everywhere strong in the faith of Christ, and fear not those who persecute you. As the Lord said: 'Fear not those who kill the body; indeed they cannot kill the soul.'"[30] This "persecution" lasts eight days, after which the Turks take the castle. We are told, in language redolent of the martyrologies: "Those who refused to renounce God were given the capital sentence, . . . these first happily accepted martyrdom for Christ's name."[31] Throughout the remainder of his narrative, Tudebodus emphasizes that the Christian dead are martyrs.[32]

If the crusaders are the new apostles, the Saracens play the role of the pagan Roman persecutors: their paganism and barbarism are a necessary foil to the steadfast devotion of the crusaders/apostles. They are "our enemy and God's, . . . saying diabolical sounds in I know not what language."[33] The geographical and ethnic distinctions between these enemies are vague; at one point Tudebodus describes a castle "full of innumerable pagans: Turks, Saracens, Arabs, Publicans, and other pagans."[34] Many of the place-names are familiar from the Bible: Tudebodus and other chroniclers associate the pagans with the places where Antichrist is born and raised, Babylon and Corosan.[35]

Nothing illustrates Tudebodus's attitudes better than the scenes that come from his imagination, those he could not have seen. In the midst of a battle outside Antioch, for example, when the momentum turns in favor of the crusaders, Tudebodus tells us: "The women of the city came to the windows of the wall; the Christian women, seeing the miserable fate of the Turks, secretly clapped their hands, as was their custom."[36] They clapped their hands because they were on the Christians' side; they did so "secretly" so that their glee would not be noticed by the Turks inside the city or out. If this "secret clapping" could not be seen by the Turks, it presumably could not be seen by Tudebodus below, in the heat of battle. The scene is imagined by Tudebodus and is meant to dramatize the solidarity (real or imagined) between the Christians inside and their self-appointed liberators outside.

In many of Tudebodus's fictive scenes, we see most clearly how he conceives of his pagan enemies: how they worship, how they see the Christian crusaders, how they see (or fail to see) their place in God's plan. Other chroniclers also indulge in such imaginary dialogues in the enemy camp; indeed, some of these passages are almost identical to those in Tudebodus. Unrestrained by facts, these authors paint a vivid image of their adversaries. Tudebodus, in particular, uses these scenes to show the continuity of pagan resistance to Christianity—and in particular to the crusader/ apostles; yet he has the pagans acknowledge that their days are numbered, that their defeat at the hands of God and his warriors is inevitable.

Tudebodus, like the anonymous hagiographer of Thiemo, portrays the deaths of crusaders in terms taken from hagiography. This is easiest to do, of course, for the deaths he did not witness: he can imagine them as they *should* have happened. Rainaldus Porchetus, a crusader taken captive by the Turks of Antioch, Tudebodus says, is taken to the top of the walls and told to urge the crusaders to pay a large ransom for his return. Instead Rainaldus exhorts the crusaders to persist, telling them to value his own life as nothing and that the city's defenders will be unable to hold out much longer. This advice earns him the praise of his comrades and death at the hands of his captors. After Rainaldus's admonition to the crusaders from atop the walls of Antioch, the "Amiralius" of the city bids him: "Renounce your god whom you worship and in whom you believe, and believe in Malphumet and our other gods. If you do this, we will give you anything you ask: gold and silver, horses and mules, and many other trappings which you might desire. And we shall give you wives and land, and much honor."[37] This of course is the standard choice given to potential martyrs (as seen in the *passions* discussed in chapter 3): power, wealth, and sex on one hand, the crown of martyrdom on the other. Rainaldus of course makes the right choice, responding only by praying fervently to God. The angry Turkish admiral has his head cut off, and angels take the martyr's soul up to heaven. Still furious, the admiral has all the pilgrims (i.e., crusader captives) in the city rounded up, stripped naked, and burned in a mass martyrdom. The Crusade, for Tudebodus, makes historical, theological, and moral sense as part of a continuing struggle against paganism; the response of the good Christian—in the eleventh or twelfth century as in the third or fourth—is to resist the temptations of this world and steadfastly to face martyrdom.

Martyrs, of course, are saints who produce miracles. While the *Passion of Thiemo* described standard miracles of cures and protection, Tudebodus's martial martyrs produce a military miracle. After the Christians capture Antioch, they find themselves besieged in the city by a Muslim relief army led by Kurbuqa, the Atabeg of Mosul (whom Tudebodus calls Curbaan).[38] One night during the siege, Tudebodus tells us, a priest named Stephen has a dream in which Christ comes to him, complains of the sins of the crusaders (who, in particular, are sleeping with pagan women), and urges penance on them. In return, Christ promises, he will send to the aid of the crusaders "blessed George, and Theodore, and Demetrius, and all the pilgrims who have been killed in this voyage to Jerusalem."[39] Sure enough, when the battle ensued, "innumerable armies came out of the mountains, on white horses, with white insignia *[vexilla]*. Seeing this army, [the crusaders] did not know who they were, until they recognized that this was the aid from Christ, as He ordered them according to the priest Stephen. Their leaders were saint George, and blessed Demetrius, and blessed Theodore."[40] The martyrs get to have their cake and eat it too: through death at the hands of pagans, they earn the palm of martyrdom; through a military miracle, they come back to rout the pagan host. And what more appropriate general for this celestial army than the knightly Saint George, who himself, as Tudebodus reminds us elsewhere, also "in the name of Christ accepted martyrdom from perfidious pagans."[41] While intervention by celestial armies is a common topos in both Muslim and Christian accounts of the Crusades, only Tudebodus uses it to prove the sanctity of the new martyrs.[42]

The most vivid depictions of the foe come from the scenes imagined inside the enemy camp. Just before this battle, Tudebodus describes a military council in Curbaan's camp. Curbaan proclaims that the Christian soldiers plan to expel the pagans from Asia minor and Syria, beyond Corosan and the (fictive) Amazon river.[43] He dictates a letter, describing his plight, to "the Caliph our bishop, our king and sultan and most strong soldier" in Corosan, swearing "by Machomet and by the names of all the gods" that he will defeat the Christians and conquer all the lands from Antioch to Puglia.[44]

At this point Tudebodus indulges in high melodrama. He has Curbaan's mother arrive in tears, begging him, "in the names of the gods," not to fight with the Franks.[45] When Curbaan replies that his army is bigger and stronger than that of the Christians, his mother retorts that their God fights for them; as proof she cites King David (i.e., the Psalms): "disperse the nations that do not invoke Your name."[46] She goes on to explain:

> These Christians are called the sons of Christ, and by the mouths of prophets are called "children of promise" [Gal. 4:28] and by the apostles "heirs of Christ" [Rom. 8,17]; they are those to whom Christ already granted his promised inheritance, saying: "From where the sun rises to the west will be your borders; no one will dare to stand against you."[47]

If Curbaan obstinately insists on fighting God's army, he will lose, she says in tears, and will die within a year. Here we have a pagan woman citing scripture to try to dissuade her son from fighting against God's army, a prominent pagan testifying to the superior power of Christ over her gods. When Curbaan is still not convinced, she brings in arguments from pagan wisdom:

> Dearest son, over a hundred years ago it was discovered in our pages, and in all books of the pagans, that the Christian nation would be over us and would everywhere defeat us, and reign over pagans, and our nation would everywhere be subject to them; but I did not know if it is to be now or rather in the future. And I, sorrowing, did not desist from following you to Aleppo, that beautiful city, where, pointing and acutely investigating, I looked at the stars in the sky, and sagaciously deliberating and with sedulous mind observing the planets, and the twelve signs of the zodiac, and innumerable lots, in all these things I saw that the Christian nation would be victorious everywhere.[48]

Curbaan, incredulous, says he thought Bohemund and Tancred were the crusaders' gods, and that they each consume two thousand cows and four thousand pigs for lunch. His mother responds that they are mere mortals but that the God who protects them is the invincible creator of heaven and earth, whose will no one may oppose. But Curbaan will not be daunted, and his mother leaves in grief.[49]

This melodramatic scene has been largely overlooked by historians: it is, after all, useless in attempting to reconstruct the events of the Crusade. It is crucial, however, for seeing how Tudebodus makes sense of the Crusade: unobstructed by mere facts, he can fabricate the enemy he desires. The passage brings together several key elements in his justification of the Crusade. One is the apocalyptic element: the time has come for Christians to take back the Holy Land and defeat pagans everywhere. This is evident not only through careful exegesis of the prophets, but even through the pagan arts of astrology and necromancy. In addition, Curbaan's mother emphasizes God's protective relationship with his army. She describes the crusaders in biblical language, as both the new apostles coming into Christ's inheritance and as the army of Israel, whose enemies the Lord disperses.

A key scene in all the chronicles of the first Crusade, of course, is the siege of Jerusalem itself, in which several chroniclers describe a confrontation between Christ and Muhammad. When the Christians laid siege to Jerusalem, they made a penitential pilgrimage around the city, armed and barefoot. According to Tudebodus, when the Muslims of Jerusalem saw the procession, they brought onto the city wall an idol on a lance (or perhaps some sort of stick—*asta* is the Latin word), covered with a cloth.[50] How the Christians knew this was "Machomet" is not explained. The crucifix, confronted with the idol of Machomet, began to bleed miraculously. Here the idol Machomet combats Christ on the crucifix, and the crucifix is destined to win. The Amiravissus (apparently the pagan ruler of Jerusalem) subsequently laments the imminent fall of his city and twice invokes Machomet and the other gods.[51]

Tudebodus's descriptions of Saracen paganism form a key element in his justification of the Crusade. Christianity has from the beginning been locked in a struggle with paganism: now the time has come—predicted both in scripture and in the stars—when Christ will vanquish the idols once and for all, and his people will come into his inheritance. The army of God is painted in the colors of the Bible, described both as the righteous army of Israel and as the new apostolate.[52] The confrontation between God's army and the pagan army, like that between the crucifix and the idol of Machomet, can have only one outcome: victory for the Christians. Themes essential to Christian history—pilgrimage, martyrdom, and the fight against idolatry—combine to form a powerful justification of the Crusade.

Raymond d'Aguilers (like Tudebodus) underscores the enemy's testimony to the superiority of Christianity. Raymond describes a series of truces and alliances with Muslim leaders as if this implied that the rulers recognized the superiority of Christianity. Thus when legates come from the king of Babylon (the Fatimid caliph of Egypt), "seeing the marvels that God worked for his followers, they glorified Jesus, son of the Virgin Mary, who treads potent tyrants underfoot for His poor followers."[53] Similarly, the king of Caesaria, as he provides a market for the crusaders, acknowledges "I see that God has chosen this people."[54]

Almost all the chronicles place great importance on the crusaders' barefoot procession around Jerusalem days before they capture it. Tudebodus has a crucifix bleed when confronted with an idol of Machomet. Here is how Raymond D'Aguilers describes the Saracens' reaction to it: "The Saracens and Turks went around inside the city, ridiculing us in many ways, putting many crucifixes on yokes *[patibulis]* on top of the walls, inflicting upon them lashes and insults."[55] The pagans, according to Raymond, are reenacting the Passion, retorturing Christ. Here is a striking parallel to the accusations made against Jews in the later Middle Ages: that they torture and mutilate crucifixes, icons, the Eucharist, or even Christian children; the Jews are accused of ritually reenacting the Passion. Those stories, like this one, will be used to sanction acts of horrible violence: many a pogrom, from the thirteenth century to the twentieth, will be justified by such trumped-up accusations.[56] For Raymond, this torturing of crucifixes, it seems, provides a justification for the terrible vengeance the crusaders are about to wreak on the defilers. When he describes the massacre of Jerusalem's inhabitants after its capture, it is as a glorious, if perhaps overzealous, revenge:

> We came to the temple of Solomon [i.e., the Dome of the Rock], where they [the Saracens] used to sing their rites and festivals. But what happened there? If we speak the truth, we will be beyond belief. Suffice it to say that in the temple and porch of Solomon one rode in blood up to one's knees, and up to the horses' reins. This was truly a judgment [of God], that that place should receive their blood, since it endured for such a long time their blasphemies against God. . . . I say that this day saw the weakening of all paganism, the confirmation of Christianity, and the renovation of our faith.[57]

For Raymond d'Aguiliers, the Crusade—in all its bloodiness—is justifiable first and foremost as *vengeance*. The pagans, who crucified Christ, who continue to crucify him in effigy, and whose rites pollute the sacred places of Jerusalem, deserve to have the wrath of God fall on them in the form of the crusaders' sword. For Raymond as for Tudebodus, the Saracens' supposed paganism is a key element in vindicating the Crusade.

I focus on Tudebodus and Raymond d'Aguilers because theirs are the two chronicles of the first Crusade (along with the *Chanson d'Antioche*, which I discuss below) in which Saracen paganism is such a central element of defense. If less central in the other chronicles, it is nonetheless omnipresent (except in the chronicle of Guibert de Nogent).

Even Anna Comnena, the Byzantine princess whose *Alexiad* chronicles the reign of her father, the emperor Alexius Comnenus, purveys the same image of Saracens as idolaters. For Anna, the barbarians of Egypt and Libya "worship Mahumet with mystic rites" while the "Ishmaelites" worship Chobar, Astarte, and Ashtaoth.[58] Anna, who is able to describe in detail the theological errors of Bogomils and other Christian heretics, and whose work bristles with citations of Homer and Thucydides, is completely in the dark about the religious beliefs and practices of the Turks. Even Byzantine writers (such as Georges the Monk and Nicetas of Byzantium) who knew more about Islam than Anna presented Muhammad's monotheism as a veneer covering his true idolatry.[59]

Many of the Latin chronicles, like that of Tudebodus, contain imagined scenes of the enemy in colloquy. One fictive scene common to several of these chroniclers is a poetic lament put in the mouth of the Amiravissus, supposedly the pagan ruler of Jerusalem, when he sees that his city is about to fall to the crusaders. Robert the Monk, for example, has the Amiravissus (whom he names Clement) lament:

> We used to vanquish, and now we are vanquished; we used to be happy of heart, and now we are afflicted with sadness. Who can hold back the tears from his eyes and hold back the sobs breaking out of his heart? How long I have taken great pains to bring together this army; I have spent much time in vain. At great cost I brought together the most powerful soldiers in all the Orient, and led them to this battle; and now I have brought them and their price to the end. . . . O Mathome, Mathome, who worshiped you with greater magnificence, in shrines of gold and silver, with beautifully decorated idols of you, and ceremonies and solemnities and every sacred rite? But here is how the Christians often insult us, because the power of the crucifix is greater than yours: for it is powerful on heaven and earth. Now it appears that those who

confide in it are victorious, while those who venerate you are vanquished. But it is not the fault of our lack of care, for your tomb is more adorned than his with gold, gems, and precious things.[60]

One can see why this would make satisfying reading for the Christians back in Europe. The fictive lament not only inserts melodrama and pathos into the narrative but also drives home the superiority of Christianity to paganism: the pagans are doomed to defeat against God, no matter how many armies they assemble or how much gold and precious stones they lavish on their false gods. Here the center of Saracen worship is the tomb of Mathome, rather than an idol, but the message is the same: the false god is confronted by the crucifix, and the crucifix wins. Once more, a powerful pagan is brought low as he acknowledges the awesome power of God.

Another equally fictitious but equally important event in several chronicles of the first Crusade is the discovery of an idol of Mahomet in the temple of the Lord, or temple of Solomon (where Raymond d'Aguilers gruesomely described knights riding in blood up to their knees). Raoul de Caen wrote his *Gesta Tancredi*, in mixed prose and verse, sometime between Tancred's death in 1112 and Raoul's before 1131. Raoul glorifies (and exaggerates) Tancred's military achievements during and after the first Crusade.[61] He describes Tancred encountering a huge silver idol of "Mahummet" in the temple, piously destroying it, and confiscating the silver:

> *On a high throne sat a cast idol*
> *of heavy silver, . . .*
> *Tancred saw this and said: "For shame!*
> *"What does this mean? What is this sublime image?*
> *"What does this effigy mean, these gems, this gold?*
> *"What does this royal purple mean?" Now Mahummet*
> *Was crowned in gems and dressed in royal purple, and he glowed with gold.*
> *"Perhaps this is an idol of Mars or Apollo:*
> *"Is it Christ? These are not the insignia of Christ,*
> *"Not the cross, not the crown of thorns, not the nails, not the water from*
> * his side.*
> *"Therefore this is not Christ: rather it is ancient Antichrist,*
> *"Mahummet the depraved, Mahummet the pernicious.*
> *"O if this companion is here now, he will be here in the future!*
> *"Now I will crush both Antichrists with my foot!*

"For shame! The companion of the Abyss holds sway in the Arc of God."

. . . .

"It will tumble down quickly, without doubt it will yet tumble!"

. . . .

Immediately it was ordered, you will see it already done,
Each soldier gladly fulfilling the order
It was broken, dragged down, smashed, cut down.
The material was precious but vile the form
Thus destroyed, the vile was made precious.[62]

The temple of Solomon has become the center of the cult of the pagan idol of Mahummet; for Raymond d'Aguilers, the "blasphemies" that the Saracens performed in the temple (the Dome of the Rock) called down the righteous vengeance of God in the form of a bloody massacre. But Raymond did not say what these "blasphemies" were; Raoul provides a vivid image of them: a silver idol of the pagan god Mahummet. Tancred, first thinking the statue might be one of Mars or Apollo, finally realizes that it is Mahummet, whom he also calls Antichrist. The destruction of this profane image, intruder in the temple of the Lord, provides a dramatic, vindictive climax to the first Crusade. Other chroniclers recount more or less the same story; for Fulcher of Chartres this idolatrous worship of Mahomet had polluted the temple.[63] Robert the Monk more graphically accuses the Saracens of having defiled the altars and baptismal fonts by smearing them with blood from circumcisions.[64] This notion of "pollution" of the holy places of Jerusalem is a justification and a rallying cry: when Edessa falls to Zanqî, Bernard of Clairvaux and other preachers decry the pollution of the Holy Land by "heathen filth" *[spurcitia paganorum]* and call for purification through Christian swords.[65]

From Chronicle to Epic? The *Chansons de Croisade*

If Islam is seen in the familiar and despised guise of ancient paganism, then the struggles of Christians against it will be seen as part of the continuing struggle against the pagan persecutions of Roman days. With the notion of opposing paganism, naturally came the ideal of martyrdom: the chroniclers compared the struggle with the "pagan" Saracen to the struggle against the ancient pagans of Rome. The patent falseness of these stories is obvious to anyone with a rudimentary knowledge of Islam. It was anything but obvious, however, to those who read these stories: to them (as, perhaps, to many of the crusaders themselves) the stories rang true. They helped them make sense of the struggles they faced, the risks the ran, the death they or their comrades faced. They helped glorify the enterprise of the Crusade and put it solidly in the context of Christian history, of the divine plan.

The goal of the chronicler/polemicist, in other words, was to show that the Crusade was not new, that it had been predicted by earlier Christians, and that it would play an important role in the apocalyptic scenario of the last days: this mission is dramatically embodied in the *Chanson d'Antioche,* an epic describing the first Crusade through the conquest of Antioch.[66] The anonymous author of the *Chanson* makes the Crusade central to Christian eschatology by having Christ himself predict it. The narrative opens with the Crucifixion: Christ, speaking to the good thief crucified at his side, predicts the eventual arrival of the crusaders: A "new people," he foretells, the Franks, will avenge the Crucifixion, liberate the Holy Land, and eliminate paganism.

> *Friends, said Our Lord, know*
> *That from across the sea a new people will come*
> *They will exact vengeance for the death of their Father*
> *No pagans shall remain from here to the East*
> *The Franks will liberate all the earth*
> *And for those who were taken and killed in this manner*
> *Material weapons will secure our salvation.*[67]

Here again, the paganism of the Saracens is a key element in the theological justification of the Crusade: the pagans killed Jesus, and the crusaders will wreak vengeance on the pagans for the murder of their "father." The Jews were frequently blamed for the Crucifixion, and it is during the first Crusade that the call for revenge will lead crusaders to massacre Jews in Europe.[68] But the pagan Romans were blamed for the Crucifixion as well, and the crusaders will wreak vengeance against them: the Saracens must be pagans in order to be appropriate objects of vengeance. The crusaders' historical model was the capture of Jerusalem by the Roman emperor Titus, in revenge (as was commonly believed in the Middle Ages) for the killing of Jesus; in the same way the architect of the contemporary Romanesque church of Moissac celebrated the Crusade by modeling the porch on Titus's first-century triumphal arch.[69]

Unsurprisingly, the *Chanson* gives us a vivid picture of Saracen idolatry, along with a glowing account of the idols' destruction, heralding the imminent demise of paganism. As in other texts concerning the conversion of idolaters, the ultimate and most satisfying testimony to the impotence of the idols is their repudiation and destruction by their own devotees (or, in the story of Thiemo, the recognition of Christian superiority by the idol Machmit itself).

The center of the pagan cult, for the *Chanson d'Antioche*, is Mahomes, an idol held in midair by magnets.[70] A defeated Saracen general, Sansadoines, strikes the idol, knocking it down and breaking it after it has shown itself powerless to secure victory for its devotees. Here again, the pagan enemy himself realizes the powerlessness of his idols and destroys them with his own hand. Sansadoines then predicts to the Saracens that they will be defeated by the Christians who will "break the walls and palisades of Mieque [Mecca], will take Mahomet down from the pedestal where he is placed, [and will take] the two candelabra that sit there."[71] At the end of the poem the crusader Godfrey of Bouillon vows to take "Mahomet of Mieque" in virtually the same words.[72] The conquest of Mieque, the Saracens' cultic center, will mark the ultimate defeat of paganism.

The *Chanson d'Antioche* describes, in vivid detail, an embassy to Mieque, which is ruled over by three brothers:[73] hymns are sung to the golden idol Mahomes as the "Apostle Califes of Bauda" (presumably Baghdad) presides over a grand "parlement." The Saracens, through enchantment, have caused a demon, Sathanas, to inhabit the idol of Mahomes, which now speaks to them. "Christians who believe in God," says Sathanas/Mahomes, "this lost people, have no rights on earth, they have taken it in great error. Let God keep heaven; the earth is in my fiefdom *[baillie]*."[74] The Califes de Bauda then announces a "rich pardon that Mahons will give us," a sort of inversion of the indulgences that Urban II granted the crusaders. The caliph says that Mahons will allow every man who fights the Christians to have twenty or thirty wives, or as many as he wishes. Those who die in battle will take to the gates of heaven two bezants in one hand and a rock in the other; with the bezants they can buy their way into heaven, or if that fails, with the rock they can force their way in.[75] Again an inversion or parody, this time of the hope of martyrdom proffered to the Christian crusader. The pagan enemy, it seems, is a deformed mirror image of the righteous crusader, devoted to the devil rather than God, granted indulgences by the caliph of Baghdad/Mecca rather than the Pope, hoping to buy or fight his way into heaven.

As with Tudebodus and the *Passion of Thiemo,* the pagan adversaries are themselves made to acknowledge—both before and after the conflict—the inevitability of their defeat at the hands of the Christians. Sansadoines predicts that the Christians will take Mecca. Later in the poem, his fears are confirmed by a dream, which he narrates to Corbaran (Kurbuqa, the Curbaan of Tudebodus): he stands before Antioch and sees "out of Antioch issued a leopard and a boar, a snake, bear, and dragon, to devour our people."[76] Solimans, one of Corbaran's men, responds that Mahons is very powerful and would never let this happen to his people. As in Tudebodus, Corbaran is warned but heeds not the warnings. Soon after Sansidoines leaves, Corbaran's mother arrives and (as in Tudebodus) warns him to desist: his defeat is predicted by the stars.[77]

Corbaran himself, as he sees his defeat, calls one last time on Mahomet, this time to curse and threaten him:

> "Oh, Lord Mahmet! How I used to love you
> And to serve and honor you with all my might!
> If ever I may return one day to my country
> I will burn you and reduce you to dust
> Or I will have you trampled by horses."[78]

Once again, Christian victory over paganism culminates in the pagan leader's rejection and destruction (even if, as here, only threatened) of his idols. In the *Conquête de Jérusalem,* the caliph himself decapitates the idol Mahon.[79]

Armed with self-righteousness, the Christian soldier could strike with a clear conscience, knowing that he was fighting for Christ against paganism. Convinced that he was fighting for the restoration of the lands and rights of the ultimate feudal Lord, he could cry out with King David (as with crusader chroniclers Baldric of Dole and Guibert of Nogent): "O God, the heathens are come into thy inheritance!"[80]

The Persistence of the Image of Saracen Paganism

As the victorious crusaders settled down to rule in the Levant and made alliances with local Muslim rulers, they came to recognize that Muslims were monotheists, not pagan idolaters. The chronicles written about the later Crusades only occasionally contain images of Saracen idolatry or polytheism.[81] Yet the image of the pagan persecutors of virtuous Christians lives on in many texts; an anonymous thirteenth-century Franciscan chronicle, for example, describes how Baybars, the "Sultan of Babylon," captured two Franciscan friars and invited them to "worship Muhammad according to the rite of the Saracens"; when they refused, he martyred them.[82]

While the imagined idolatry of the Saracens is particularly vivid in these chronicles of the first Crusade, it was also present even among Byzantine writers. In the ninth century, a time of Byzantine military recovery in Asia Minor, the church created a ritual formula of abjuration, which converts from Islam to Christianity had to proclaim publicly before being baptized. This formula contained a twenty-two-point condemnation of supposed Islamic doctrines; the strangest of these is the following:

> And before all, I [the convert] anathematize the God of Muhammad about whom [Muhammad] says "He is God alone, God made of solid, hammer-beaten metal; He begets and is not begotten, nor is there like unto him any one."[83]

This is, curiously enough, based on a translation of Koran 112; an accurate translation except for one key word, samad, which means "solid"or "eternal" in the Koran but here is rendered "of solid, hammer-beaten metal" (ὁλόσφυρος).[84] Emperor Manuel I Comnenus (1143–80), fully aware of how ridiculous it is to accuse Muslims of worshiping a ὁλόσφυρος God, ordered the clause struck from the formula of abjuration. From Manuel's standpoint, it seems, Muslim converts should be asked only to renounce the errors of Muhammad, not the true, eternal God, who was after all the same as the Christian God. Manuel succeeded in having the formula altered, but only in the face of strong resistance by conservative church members offended at the suggestion that the Muslim god was the same as their own. These Byzantine church leaders need to affirm the religious alterity of Islam in order to keep the boundaries clear between religious truth and error: better to associate Islam with pagan idolatry than to suggest that it venerates the eternal God. Other Byzantine writers follow suit: John Vekkos (late thirteenth century) accuses Muhammad's followers of reveling in orgiastic rites in the Christian holy places they now occupy.[85] Fourteenth-century writers Philotheos and Cantacuzenos claim that the Turks have revived the polytheistic idolatry of the ancient Greeks.[86] It is not always clear how seriously such charges were meant; fifteenth-century writer Doukas equates the altars of Latin priests with the pagan altars of

ancient polytheism: surely this is more polemical exaggeration than anything else.[87] Other Byzantine writers referred to their Turkish enemies as
"Persians," "Medes," "Huns," "Chaldeans," or more generally as "barbarians"
—not as much to suggest religious deviance as to inspire Greek chauvinism
against the barbaric Orient by evoking the enemies of another age.[88]

Back in Europe, the image of the Saracen as idolater lives on, particularly in the *Chansons de Geste,* the French epic poems glorifying the exploits of Charlemagne and his knights. The *Chanson de Roland* portrays
the Arabs or Saracens as pagans who worship a triad of idols: Mahumet,
Apollin, and Tervagant.[89] The Saracen knights invoke the aid of these idols,
whose images adorn the banners they carry into battle. Their idols, of
course, prove to be powerless to stop the Christian's victory: despite the
death of the hero Roland, Charlemagne, with the help of the angel Gabriel,
routs the combined forces of all paganism. When Roland cuts off the right
hand of the Saracen king Marsile in battle, the king flees home to Saragossa
and his people vent their anger against their idols: they hurl Mahumet
from the parapets into a ditch where it is sullied by dogs and pigs (in the
passage quoted at the beginning of this chapter). When the Christian warriors takes Saragossa, they smash with hammers the idols they find in the
"sinagoges" and *"mahumeries"* (ll. 3661–65).

The ideology of the *Chanson de Roland* is the same as that of the crusading chronicles with which it is roughly contemporary. Yet the poet has
freer rein to portray the valorous exploits of the Christian army and their
indomitable two-hundred-year-old king Charlemagne, with his flowing
white *"barbe fleurie."* The enemy is portrayed in equal and contrasting
color: the *Amireil* of Babylon, older than Virgil or Homer (ll. 2614–16),
leads an army recruited from the entire non-Christian world, from pagan
eastern Europe to Persia to Africa, under the banner of their triad of pagan
gods.[90] His recruits include monstrous semihumans: the Micenes have
large heads and spines on their back; the soldiers from Occian have skin as
hard as steel armor; those from Malprose are giants (ll. 3214–64). The individual soldiers have names that express their evilness and deformity or that
associate them with biblical enemies of God.[91] They include such colorful
figures as "Siglorel, the sorcerer who was once in Hell: Jupiter led him there
by sorcery" (ll. 1390–92), the kind of enemy whose slaughter calls for no
justification. The same is true for Chernuble de Munigre, who comes from
a land inhabited by demons, where the sun never shines and rain never
falls (ll. 979–83). When Archbishop Turpin sees Abisme, "black as pitch,"
approach carrying a banner with a dragon on it, he proclaims: "This Sara-

cen seems quite heretical to me; it would be much better if I were to kill him." (ll. 1484–85). And who would not feel righteous pleasure when Roland kills Valdebrun, who had once taken Jerusalem through treachery, sacked Solomon's temple, and murdered the patriarch at the baptismal fonts (ll. 1566–68)?

The goal of the poet here is the same as that of the filmmaker portraying quintessential bad guys: to allow the reader (or viewer) to enjoy the violence, to revel in the blood and killing, without remorse. Only by dehumanizing the adversary, making him sufficiently "other," is this possible. Yet he cannot be made too other, for it is not valorous to slaughter mere beasts. Hence the paradoxical, mixed nature of the Saracen host in *Roland*: alongside the monstrous creatures are virtuous knights who seem to be mirror images of their Christian adversaries, for whom the poet can proclaim (of Baligant): "God! What a knight, if only he were Christian!" (l. 3164). It is the religion of the Saracens that makes them irretrievably other, even if Baligant seems a mirror image of the valiant Charlemagne.

This ideology of the other, reproduced in scores of later epics, in French and subsequently in other languages, present essentially the same image of Saracen paganism. Since the pioneering work of Paul Bancourt in 1982, a tremendous amount of work has been done on the image of the Saracen in these *Chansons de gestes*.[92] Some modern scholars (notably Norman Daniel) have dismissed this portrayal of Saracen idolatry as mere literary convention: no one believed this of the Muslims; they were only creating a caricatural "bad guy" as a foil for the epics' forthright Christian knights.[93] While Daniel is certainly right to point out the element of playful exaggeration in some of these texts, he is wrong in asserting that the writers and readers of these epics knew better. Some writers, indeed, did know better; many, however, did not. Many writers, in Latin as well as the vernacular, in chronicles, legal treatises, plays, and other texts, continued to portray Saracens as pagan devotees of Apollo, Jupiter, Mahomet, and other "demons."

"Saracen" as a Synonym for "Pagan"

A measure of how complete the assimilation of the image of Saracen as pagan became is that even the pagans of antiquity were referred to as "Saracens" who worship Mahomet. Many medieval authors refer to pagan idols by the name of Muhammad, in various corrupted forms (Mahomet, Mahon, Mahoum, Mawmet). In the *Chansons de Geste*, he is invoked as a god or described as an idol hundreds of times.[94] Yet this is not merely a convention of the French epic poets; many other authors refer to Muhammad in the same terms. To give just a few of the many possible examples: the thirteenth-century Hereford map refers to the golden calf worshiped by the Israelites during the exodus as a "Mahom."[95] Even the *Decreta* of the Council of Vienne (1311) refer to the Saracens worshiping Muhammad.[96] In English plays of the fourteenth century, one finds Alexander the Great, Julius Caesar, and Pontius Pilate all swearing by or worshiping "Mahound"; "Mahon" is a pagan idol in many middle English lives of saints.[97] Jean Mandeville describes a Roman idol of Jupiter as a *"maumette."*[98] The twelfth-century *Roman d'Alexandre* tells of Alexander the Great entering a *"mahomerie"* full of idols; his enemy, the amiral de Babilone, adores the god Mahon.[99] Ranulph Higden knew that Muhammad was a man, not an idol, and that he indeed had forbidden the cult of idols; his English translator Trevisa (d. 1402) renders this as "he forbeed þe paynims mametrie."[100]

So much is the Saracen associated with the pagan for medieval writers, that the very word "Saracen" (in its Latin and Romance vernacular cognates) or *"Moro"* (the Castilian Spanish equivalent) are used to mean "pagan"—even when referring to pagans of antiquity. Thus the twelfth-century epic *Floovant* refers to the Frankish king Clovis as a "Saracen" before his conversion to Christianity.[101] Another *Chanson de Geste, Gormont et Isembart* describes Danish marauders as "Sarrazins" devoted to the god Apollin; their leader, Gormont, "li Arabis" is called both "Antecrist" and "Satenas."[102] Fourteenth-century writers refer to the pagan Lithuanians as "Saracens."[103] Even learned legal scholars of the thirteenth century refer to Saracens as pagans; for the decretalist Azo, Saracens "worship and adore innumerable gods, goddesses, and demons."[104] "Saracen" and "pagan" are such intertwined terms that when Peter Abelard (in the twelfth century) composes his *Dialogue of a Philosopher with a Jew and a Christian,* he portrays the "pagan" philosopher as a sort of cross between an ancient Roman and a contemporary Muslim, as one who is circumcised yet cites Ovid.[105]

Some authors struggled to explain the origins of the term "Saracen." The thirteenth-century *Estoire du Saint Graal,* in recounting the wanderings of Joseph of Arimathea with the Holy Grail, tells how he and his family

came to a city named Sarras, between Babylon and Salamandre. It is from this city the Saracens first came; and they are called "Saracen" after this city of Sarras. And do not believe those who say that they are named after Sarah, the wife of Abraham, because this is an invention and does not seem reasonable. It is not unknown that Sarah was a Jewess and her son, Isaac, was a Jew and all his descendants were Jews. Since for the smaller part one takes the whole, and since the Jews descend from Sarah it does not seem right that the Saracens took their name from her, but rather that they took their name from that city named Sarras, since it was the first city where this people learned what they should worship and where they invented and founded the sect that the Saracens subsequently maintained until the arrival of Mahomet, who was sent to save them, although he damned himself before and them after through his gluttony. Before his sect was established in Sarras, the people did not know what to worship. Thus they worshiped whatever they fancied, and what they worshiped one day they did not worship the next. But then they began to worship the sun and the moon and the other planets. [106]

The anonymous author describes pagan idolaters of the first century C.E. as "Saracens" but distinguishes their (pre-Islamic) paganism from the law that Muhammad later established. Rejecting the familiar etymology of Saracen from Sarah, he invents a city, Sarras, to provide an alternative explanation. Later in the romance, Joseph converts the Saracen king, in part through a dramatic confrontation with the demon inhabiting an idol of Mars: through the power of the cross, Joseph makes the demon destroy the Saracen idols.

The point of all this is that for many western Europeans throughout the Middle Ages, Saracens were pagans, and pagans were Saracens: the two words become interchangeable. When, in the early fifteenth century, Firmin le Ver composes his Latin-French dictionary, he defines "Saracenus" as "paganus," noting that it derives "from Sarah, as in born from Sarah" (*a Sara dicitur, quasi ex Sara genitus*); for paganus he gives the French equivalents "sarrasin, paiens, mescreans."[107] The examples could be multiplied almost indefinitely; they have already been well cataloged in the works of Paul Bancourt, Michael Paull, and others. The image is so common that writers on Islam who know better—from the twelfth century on—go to great pains to explain that the Saracens *are not* pagans.[108]

For the polemicist-chroniclers of the first Crusade, this portrayal placed the Crusade firmly in an old and familiar place in Christian history, as part of the age-old struggle against pagan demon worship. While it would be impossible to make sweeping generalizations about what purpose (if any) this image served in each of the later medieval texts just mentioned, for the most part they accepted the version of history proffered by the crusader chroniclers: the struggle against the Saracen-pagans of the Middle Ages was a continuation of the struggle against the Saracen-pagans of Christ's day. The idolatrous other is an essential foil for Christian virtue. If the image of idolatry comes in part from the reading of the ancients, perhaps it also stems from a projection of *Christian* practice onto the imagined enemy. After all, images and relics played an important role in medieval Christianity; Saints were often invoked to succor their devotees and to smite the enemy. When the saints failed to do so, their relics were often punished, "humiliated"; it was perhaps natural for Christians to assume that the Saracens practiced similar rites.

The Saracen idols play a key role in many of the liturgical dramas of the thirteenth and fourteenth centuries. In Jean Bodel's *Jeu de Saint Nicolas*, first performed in December 1200, the main protagonists are less the nameless humans (Christian and Saracen) than the icon of Saint Nicolas who is opposed by the "mahommet" (i.e., idol) of Tervagan.[109] In a blending of the exotic and the ridiculous, the (nameless) king of the Saracens leads an army recruited from mythic lands such as Orkenie, "from beyond Grey Wallengue, where dogs crap gold" (ll. 362–63), or Oliferne, a burning land replete with precious gems (ll. 368–72), or "beyond the Dry Tree," where people use millstones as coins (ll. 373–76). The king is particularly devoted to his idol of Tervagan, which he covers with gold (l. 136). The king asks Tervagan to show him who will win the upcoming battle with the Christians: "If I must win, laugh; if I must lose, cry" (ll. 181– 82); enigmatic, the demon-inhabited idol cries and laughs simultaneously, signifying that the Saracen king will win the battle but lose his Saracen faith. Here we leave the world of epic (where the Christian army invariably wins) and enter that of hagiography;[110] in the wake of the loss of Jerusalem and the failed third Crusade, perhaps conversion miracles seem more plausible than crusader victories. The Saracen military victory is complete, the only Christian survivor being an (again, nameless) "Preudome" captured while praying to his icon of Saint Nicolas, which the Saracens mistake for a "mahommet." Yet Nicolas produces a miracle for the king: he appears in a dream to three robbers who have stolen the king's treasure and frightens them into bringing it back. The king acknowledges the power of the saint and converts, along with all his men. He orders his seneschal to expel the idol of Tervagan from the "sinagoge"; before destroying the idol, the seneschal addresses these words to it, reminding his audience of the idol's prophecy at the beginning of the play:

> *Tervagan, you will in time see the fulfillment of your prophecy*
> *When you laughed and cried*
> *In your pain.*
> *What lies you tell me!*
> *Down with you! You have no right to be up there!*
> *We do not care a whit for you! (ll. 1522–27)*

As the idol comes crashing down on the stage, the audience's devotion to Saint Nicolas is vindicated; he proves himself more powerful than the "mahommets" of the Saracens.

In the English mystery plays, Saracen idolatry plays the same role as foil to Christian piety. In the York cycle of mystery plays, the pharaoh is a devotee of Mahownde pitted against Moses, follower of the true God.[111] This opposition typologically prefigures the whole spiritual conflict that these plays seek to dramatize: a continual struggle between the followers of Christ and the satanically inspired devotees of Mahownde. In the Chester cycle, a pagan named Balaam predicts that the incarnation of Christ will lead to the destruction of the "mawmets"; the pagan king Balak responds "Mahound giue the mischance!"[112] In a parallel prophecy, angels announce that when the infant Christ flees into Egypt, the "mahumetis" will fall.[113] Herod subsequently introduces himself as "prince of Purgatorre . . . and cheff capten of hell . . . Reysemelyng the fauer of thatt most myght Mahownd; From Jubytor be desent and cosyn to the grett God."[114] Herod and the other villains of the drama claim an eclectic (and often deliberately comic) allegiance to Saracen idols, classical Roman deities, and the forces of hell. The devils worship Mahound, as do the Jews (especially the Pharisees); it is the scheming of Jewish devotees of Mahound that leads to Christ's Crucifixion.[115] In the Townley mystery cycle, Pontius Pilate is a Jewish devotee of Mahowne who calls on "Sir Lucifer" and hails his soldiers as descendants of Cain.[116] The soldiers who torture Christ mock him in the name of Mahowne and ridicule his pretensions to be savior of mankind; the soldiers express doubts about Christian doctrine that the audience is not allowed. The sharp dichotomy between the forces of good and evil served its didactic and doctrinal purpose: doubt about Christian doctrine could only come from demonic inspiration. Those who rejected Christianity—Jews, Saracens, and pagans—are united in their diabolic hostility toward Christ and his followers. By making the outsider object of scorn, the need for Christian unity is stressed.

The same image of Saracen paganism is found in late medieval saints' lives written in Middle English.[117] In the *Life of Saint Katherine,* for example, the emperor Maxentius invites the saint to forsake Jesus Christ and worship "our" gods "Mahon and Teruagant."[118] The emperor is described thus:

> *Sarrazin he was ful strong,*
> *Wiþ cristendom he seyd nay,*
> *For alle þat leued on Jhesu Crist*
> *He stroyd hem boþe ni3t & day.*[119]

Yet in Saint Katherine, the "Saracen" Maxentius has found his match: her faith withstands his pleading, promises, and torture; she dies a martyr. The death of Christians at the hand of their Saracen enemies is as much a victory as the exploits of Charlemagne in the *Chanson de Roland.*

The *Life of Saint Katherine* has brought us full circle, back to martyrology, where the chapter began with a look at Hrotsvitha's "Pelagius." Yet the similarities between the two texts should not blind us to an essential difference that shows how deeply the topos of Saracen paganism anchored itself in the European worldview in the three centuries between the two texts. Hrotsvitha dressed Pelagius's persecutor, ʿAbd al-Rahmân, in the familiar and despised garb of a classical pagan idolater. The author of the *Life of Saint Katherine* does precisely the opposite: he paints the classical Roman emperor Maxentius as a familiar literary personage, the evil Saracen king who worships idols of Mahound and Tervagant and who persecutes Christians.

The persistence of this image—across a wide variety of texts in numerous European languages—has surprised many modern critics and historians; it is all the more astonishing in that it persists in the face of more reliable information about Islam. A reader of William of Tyre's *Historia rerum in partibus transmarinis gestarum,* for example, would learn that the Saracens revered Muhammad as a prophet and rejected worship of idols. Yet an illuminator of one of the manuscripts of a French translation of William's text tells a different story. He portrays a group of Saracens worshiping a naked, shield-bearing idol in the temple of Jerusalem (see illustration).

Illumination from a thirteenth-century manuscript of William of Tyre's *Histoire d'Outremer*, showing (bottom right) Saracens worshiping a naked idol. (Baltimore, Walters Art Gallery manuscript 10137.f.1r. Reproduced with the permission of Walters Art Gallery.)

Which version of Saracen religion is the reader to believe: the monotheism described in the text or the idolatry vividly depicted in the miniature?[120]

This sort of confrontation of images of Saracen religion becomes more
common as more information about Islam and its prophet reaches Europe.
Some authors will even try to accommodate both versions: William of
Malmesbury, writing in about 1125, knows that the Saracens are monotheists yet still believes they erected a statue of Muhammad in the temple
of Jerusalem.[121] Even King Alfonso VI of León and Castille describes the
mosque of Toledo as the "habitation of demons" (though not, indeed, of
idols).[122] The twelfth-century *Pseudo-Turpin Chronicle,* a medieval "best-
seller,"[123] has one Saracen explain that Mahoumet is their messenger sent by
God but another invokes him as "my God." The same chronicle tells us that
Mauhoumet made an idol of himself in Spain, used his necromancy to fill
it with demons, and set it up to protect the Saracens from Christian attack.[124] Hence the reader might believe that Mauhoumet is at the same time
a man whom the Saracens accept as their prophet and an idol that this false
prophet made of himself.

The idols of Mahomet live on into the twentieth century in the festivals
of small towns in Spain, many of which involve annual ritual reenactments
of the reconquest of the town from the Muslims. In a number of these
fiestas of "Moors and Christians," a squadron of local inhabitants dressed
up as *Moros* take over a mock citadel and set up a "Mahoma"—a dressed-
up effigy meant to represent Muhammad—on the walls. In the mock siege
that follows, the Christian troops take over the citadel and destroy the Mahoma. In some of the fiestas, the Mahoma, filled with fireworks, explodes
in a spectacular (and somewhat dangerous) pyrotechnic finale. In the second half of the twentieth century, many of the towns, in a post-Vatican-II
spirit of ecumenism, banished Mahoma from these festivities as an embarrassing travesty of Islam.[125] Yet eight centuries after the *Chanson de Roland*
describes the Saracens of Saragossa toppling the idol Mahomet into a ditch,
eight centuries after Raoul de Caen imagines Tancred destroying a gilded
idol of Muhammad in the temple of Solomon, Valencian villagers reenact
this imaginary idol-destruction as a central part of their dramatization of
the *reconquista.*

While the image of the pagan Saracen lives on in the *Chansons de geste,*
liturgical drama, and saints lives until the fifteenth or sixteenth centuries
(and in village fiestas until the twentieth), assuring the Christian readers of

the truth of their own religion, it dies quickly among those who have closer contact with Islam. Among the chronicles of the Crusades, only those dealing with the first Crusade portray Saracens as idolaters. Spanish Christians from the eighth century on had known enough of Islam not to present it as idolatry; other Western writers, using knowledge of Islam gleaned from Spanish and Eastern sources, will increasingly portray it as a variant, heretical version of Christianity. These Latin authors, like their earlier Eastern and Spanish counterparts, will make sense of Islam by painting its prophet in the familiar hues of a diabolically inspired heresiarch.

Chapter 6

ᥴᕉᖆᕲᖆ

Muhammad, Heresiarch (Twelfth Century)

*According to popular opinion, there was a man, whose name, if I have it right,
was Mathomus, who led them [the Orientals] away from belief in the Son and
the Holy Spirit. He taught them to acknowledge only the person of the Father as
the single, creating God, and he said that Jesus was entirely human. To sum up
his teachings, having decreed circumcision, he gave them free rein for every kind
of shameful behavior. I don't think this profane man lived a very long time ago,
since I find that none of the church doctors has written against his licentiousness.
Since I learned nothing about his behavior and life from writings, no one should
be surprised if I am willing to tell what I have heard in public by some skillful
speakers. To discuss whether these things are true or false is useless, since we are
considering only the nature of this new teacher, whose reputation for great crimes
continues to spread. One may safely speak ill of a man whose malignity transcends and surpasses whatever evil can be said about him.*

Guibert de Nogent, *Dei gesta per Francos*, 1109

*I wonder why, when you abandoned your paternal faith, you chose the faith of
the Christians rather than that of the Saracens, since you have always been
brought up with them and have conversed with them, . . . you have read their
books, you understand their language.*

—Petrus Alfonsi, *Dialogi contra Iudaeos*, 1110

I N 1109 Guibert de Nogent, at the opening of his chronicle of the *Deeds
of God through the Franks* (Dei gesta per Francos), contrasts the valor
and religious zeal of the Franks with the moral turpitude of the Orient,

nest of heresies from the time of Arius onward. This contrast justifies and glorifies the Frankish exploits in the Holy Land. Guibert is aware that Muslims "contrary to what some say, do not believe that he [Muhammad] is their god, but a just man and their patron, through whom divine laws were transmitted."[1] Guibert looked for a theological refutation of Muhammad's doctrine among the writings of the church fathers; he found none, which led him to believe that Muhammad (or Mathomus, as he calls him) lived after the fathers wrote. Guibert would prefer to speak of Mathomus from the security of patristic authority; but, *faute de mieux,* must merely recount what the common people say about him. He gives a brief biography of Mathomus, hostile and mocking, similar to those of Theophanes (see chapter 3) and to the ninth-century *Historia de Mahometh pseudopropheta* (see chapter 4). Guibert's Mathomus is a colorful scoundrel whose acolytes provide a satisfying enemy for the Frankish knights. Guibert is one of several early twelfth-century Latin authors to portray Muhammad in this way.

Guibert in 1109 noted the lack of reliable information and sound theological refutation of Islam; the following year, Petrus Alfonsi purported to provide exactly that: based on his knowledge of Arabic and his familiarity with Arabic Christian polemics against Islam (in particular the *Risâlat al-Kindî*), he inserted a brief refutation of Islam into his *Dialogues against the Jews* (Dialogi contra Iudaeos). His polemic soon became one of the most widely read Latin theological texts on Islam. One of its readers was Peter the Venerable, abbot of Cluny, who in 1142–43 traveled to Spain, where he commissioned a Latin translation of the Koran; he subsequently wrote two treatises of learned polemics against Islam, in which he branded Muhammad as a heresiarch.

While the Saracen idolater flourished in the manuscripts and in the imaginations of twelfth-century Europe (in Crusade chronicles, *Chansons de Geste,* and many other texts), the various texts I examine in this chapter present another image that developed at the same time: the Saracen as heretic, blind follower of the arch-heresiarch Muhammad. It is tempting to brand the Saracen idolater as the imagined enemy of the knightly layman while seeing the heresiarch Muhammad as the fruit of the theological hostility of the clerical class. The paganism of the song of Roland would be the "popular" image of Islam, whereas the heresy of Muhammad would be the "learned" image, even (for Norman Daniel) the "official" point of view of the church. Yet the situation is far from being so simple. Latin chroniclers of the Crusade, nothing if not "clerical" in outlook, ascribed pagan idolatry to the Saracen enemies of the crusaders. And "popular opinion" (*plebeia opinio*) to which Guibert of Nogent refers paints Muhammad as a heresiarch. When one examines the texts closely, the distinction between "learned" and "popular" blurs.

As Christians began to learn about Islam and to take it seriously as a spiritual threat, they tried to come to grips with it in Christian theological terms. They studied it in order to place it in their preestablished taxonomy of error, the better to refute it. For the great majority of these authors, from John of Damascus in the eighth century to Paul Alvarus in the ninth, Islam was a heresy. It thus should not come as a surprise that when twelfth-century Latin authors tried to come to terms with Islam, they also classified it as heresy and tried to refute it using the well-worn tools of antiheretical argument. Twelfth-century polemicists such as Petrus Alfonsi or Peter of Cluny placed themselves in a long tradition of polemics against the Saracen "heresy," a tradition well established in Eastern Christendom and in al-Andalus. These polemics wear the "learned" tag without much problem.

Yet other texts began to circulate in Latin in the twelfth century that cannot easily be classified as either "learned" or "popular," either "clerical" or "lay." This is particularly true of four polemical lives of Muhammad in which the prophet of Islam is painted not only as a heresiarch but also as a trickster and magician: Embrico of Mainz's *Vita Mahumeti*, Gautier de Compiègne's *De otia Machometi*, Adelphus's *Vita Machometi*, and the brief biography that Guibert of Nogent inserts into his *Gesta*. In these four texts, a real (if limited) "learned" knowledge of Islam and of Muhammad's life is inextricably mixed with imaginary "popular" images of the trickster of folklore. This newfound fascination with a largely imaginary trickster Muhammad reflects not only a growing concern with Islam but also growing uncertainties as to how to distinguish "real" reform from heresy in the turbulent spiritual atmosphere of the twelfth century.[2]

Plebeia Opinio: The Use and Abuse of Vicious Legend

These four hostile biographies of Muhammad are similar enough to warrant discussing together. None of them seems to be the source or archetype for the other three. They indeed base their image of Muhammad on earlier Eastern and Latin texts that portrayed him as a pseudoprophet and heresiarch. Yet they go much further than the earlier texts, making him into a colorful scoundrel who dupes the credulous Saracens through magic and fake miracles. These texts are written by clerical authors who claim to be working from oral sources and who consciously distance themselves from the "popular" material they deploy so well. One of these writers, named Adelphus, distances himself from his text by attributing it to the untrustworthy Greeks, with their fabulous imaginations; he opens his *Vita Machometi* with the following disclaimer:

> The Greeks are the inventors or writers of almost all the arts. Their wit—ancient and modern—fills many Latin books. There is no story so fabulous that it does not contain some pure truth to be found hiding inside it, if it is sought out eagerly using that light which Latin vigilance can strike from the Greeks' flint. Among these sayings of the Greeks are those which they relate about the Saracens. These I have collected as so many encyclopedic curiosities and have disposed them in proper style in the present work.
>
> I frequently heard the Saracens invoke that horrendous monster Machomet by the sound of their voice, so that they can worship him in their bacchanalia, calling on him and worshiping him as a god. Astounded, I came back from Jerusalem to Antioch, where I found a certain little Greek man (*Greculus*) who knew both Latin and the Saracen language. From him I carefully sought to learn what I should believe about the birth of this monster.[3]

Adelphus, it seems, went to Jerusalem either with the first Crusade or sometime shortly thereafter, returning via Antioch. It is the contact with Islam that piques his curiosity. More precisely, it seems to be the call of the muezzin, the voice invoking Muhammad and "adoring him as a god," that makes him seek to learn more about Islam. His "Greculus" teaches him to call Muslims "Agareni" rather than "Saraceni" (since they descend from Hagar rather than Sarah) and tells him of the life and deeds of Machomet. Adelphus seems anything but confident in the truth of what he narrates; he prefers to attribute the scurrilous tale to his Greculus. He reiterates this at the close of the *Vita:* "Enough has been said about Machomet, the Nestorius of the Agarenes, based on what the Greek told me. If anyone says these things are false, he shouldn't blame me, but attribute it either to his own ignorance or to the inventiveness of the Greeks."[4]

Gautier de Compiègne has another way to distance himself from his narration: he tells us that a Saracen convert to Christianity narrated the life of Muhammad to a canon in the Cathedral of Sens. This canon then related the tale to Warnerius, Gautier's abbot, and now Gautier undertakes to write it down. Gautier thus asserts at the same time a knowledgeable source (the converted Saracen) and a long enough line of transmission to avoid personal blame for inaccuracies in his text. Guibert makes no claim to veracity, contenting himself with repeating what the common people (*vulgus*) say about Muhammad; yet, he says (as if in defense), "One may safely speak ill of a man whose malignity transcends and surpasses whatever evil can be said about him."[5] Three of the four authors thus show that they are diffusing popular, vulgar legend: they distance themselves from their material, while at the same time they exploit its potential to defame the Saracen enemy.

Like earlier hostile biographies of Muhammad (John of Damascus, the *Risâlat al-Kindî.,* Theophanes, or the *Historia de Mahometh pseudopropheta*) the four twelfth-century texts are based on deliberate distortions of Muslim traditions. Here, however, the Muslim tradition is more distant and the distortion more marked; these are texts meant to denigrate Islam to readers that were unlikely ever to meet a Muslim, not to *dhimmis* who had daily contact with Muslims. The authors are thus freer both to make Muhammad conform to the typological image of a heresiarch and to paint him in vivid colors as a scoundrel.

Bahira, the Christian monk who (according to the Hadîth) recognized in the young Muhammad the future prophet, was made by hostile Eastern Christians into an Arian or Nestorian heretic who schooled Muhammad in doctrinal perversion (see chapter 3). He plays a prominent role in the four twelfth-century biographies. For Gautier this nameless saint (*sanctus*) is a positive character, forced into helping Muhammad in order to avoid the persecution of Christians and destruction of Solomon's temple. For the other three authors, however, this hermit is the real scoundrel and mastermind of the Saracen heresy: Adelphus calls him Nestorius, equating him with the heresiarch of the same name.[6] Guibert does not name him, but compares him with Arius;[7] Embrico simply calls him Magus. This false, heretical hermit seeks to become *pontifex* of Jerusalem (for Embrico) or patriarch of Alexandria (for Gautier); spurned because of his heretical views, he goes off into the desert and plots revenge. At this point the hermit meets Muhammad and recognizes him as future spiritual and political leader of his people. This is based on the traditions of Bahira's meeting with Muhammad, here presented in as hostile a manner as possible. For Guibert, the "ancient Enemy," the devil himself, comes along and tells the hermit to look for the young "Mathomus" and to ally himself with him. Muhammad is of ignoble birth: Adelphus makes him a swineherd.

Muhammad's marriage with Khadīja (though she remains unnamed) is maligned in all four of the texts as mismatched in age and social rank. For Guibert, the hermit arranges the marriage; Adelphus has Machomet marry the Queen of Babylon. Both Gautier and Embrico emphasize that Muhammad married his former employer's wife. Gautier has Muhammad trick her into the marriage by proffering bogus dire predictions in order to dissuade her from marrying a young noble; Muhammad talks her into marrying him by speaking like a "a second Cicero" (l. 170); the marriage gives rise to lewd jokes: "She who used to be on top is now lying underneath" (l. 246). Embrico goes further and has the Magus and Mammutius (as he calls Muhammad), through magic, kill Mammutius's former master before arranging the marriage with his widow.[8] Three of the four texts make Muhammad an epileptic, following the lead of Theophanes, who claimed that Muhammad invented his visions of Gabriel to explain his epileptic fits.[9] Gautier, Guibert, and Embrico all tell a similar story, having the hermit reassure the doubtful wife that Muhammad's visions are indeed genuine.

In order to win converts to his cause, a heresiarch needs to perform miracles. Here the four texts depart completely from (deformed) Muslim tradition to portray Muhammad as a trickster and magician who dupes his followers by performing false miracles. According to Gautier, Machomis hides milk and honey in hollows that he has cleverly carved at the top of a mountain. He then tells his people:

> *Let us go up the mountain which you see here, he said*
> *Perhaps a heavenly voice will ring out*
> *For thus did Moses once receive on the mountain*
> *The tables of the Law from God.*

(Gautier, ll. 765–68)

They climb to the top of the mountain, where Machomis prays:

> *If it pleases you then to soften the rigor of the Law*
> *As Gabriel taught me you would do*
> *Deign to give the world an unaccustomed sign*

(ll. 807–9).

He then "discovers" the milk and honey, which all accept as a true sign of divine favor. (Adelphus has him perform a similar bogus miracle with water.) Machomis quickly gives an exegesis of the miracle:

> *The honey means that bitterness will recede from the law*
> *The milk, that God will nourish us as his children*

(ll. 827–28)

In other words, the bitterness of Christian law will be replaced by the sweetness of a new law. Emboldened by this miracle, Machomis again prays to God:

> *We pray that, just as high on a mountain*
> *Christ gave laws to his disciples*
> *And as Moses received the Law on a mountain,*
> *written by the finger of God,*
> *Just so may God deign to certify in writing*
> *The law by which he wishes humanity to live.*

(ll. 831–36)

Here Machomis compares himself to Moses, sets himself up as a new (but, of course, false) divinely ordained lawgiver for his people; Adelphus has Nestorius invoke Moses in the same way.[10] This sets the stage for another bogus miracle. Machomis, according to Guibert, had raised a bull, training him to come and kneel before him when he heard his master's voice. He then wrote a book of laws and tied it to the bull's horns and hid the bull in a cave on top of the mountain. On hearing Machomis's voice raised in prayer, the bull comes and kneels before him: the people, astonished at this further sign of God's favor, take the book from its horns and accept it as their new, divinely authored law. Gautier and Adelphus recount the same sham miracle in similar terms.[11]

These authors do not deny that Muhammad produced miracles: indeed the miracles they have him perform are more numerous and various than those attributed to him by the Hadîth (the Koran attributes none to him). Yet they are all produced by trickery and magic: Muhammad (or his ally the hermit) is supposed to be expert in the black arts of magic. For Adelphus,

> *This swineherd was a supreme magician, student of diabolical doctrine, of the evil art, a very learned man in necromancy, from whom "no herb nor root lurking in dark places escaped."*[12]

This serves to explain how such a vile heresiarch could develop such a huge following. Muhammad in these texts is similar to the Jesus of the *Toledoth Yeshu:* duping the people through false miracles, he leads them from the true faith to a new and depraved cult.[13]

> *He performed so many wonders [mirabilis] among his people, that they liked to invoke him as a god. That is how good his magic [mathesis] was.*
>
> (Adelphus, ll. 303–4)

For Embrico, the magician (and real villain) is Mammutius's mentor and ally, whom he calls simply Magus (the magician):

> *He sought the praises of men by means of magic fraud,*
> *So that through his zeal he might corrupt the Church.*
>
> (ll. 87–88)

In either case, the "magic fraud" of Islam's founder serves to explain to the reader both the diabolical nature of Islam and its tremendous success in winning converts. The reader is placed in an omniscient position: he can see that the miracles are false but can understand how they seduce the multitude of gullible Saracens.

A scoundrel and heresiarch deserves an ignominious death. Three of the four texts have Muhammad attacked and devoured by pigs: for Embrico, God strikes him dead first; for Adelphus, they attack him when he is out hunting; for Guibert:

> Since he often fell into a sudden epileptic fit, it happened once, while he was walking alone, that he suddenly fell into a fit; while he was writhing in this agony, he was devoured by pigs, so that nothing could be found but his heels. While the true Stoics, that is, the worshipers of Christ,

killed Epicurus, lo, the greatest lawgiver tried to revive the pig, but the pig itself lay exposed to be eaten by pigs, so that the master of filth appropriately died a filthy death. He left his heels fittingly, since he had wretchedly fixed the traces of false belief and the foulness in deceived souls.[14]

Mathomus's heels, for Guibert, become the supreme relics of Islam; attacking false relics (in general, closer to home) was one of Guibert's favorite pastimes. For Adelphus, only the arm is left after the pigs have had their fill. The story is supposed to explain why Saracens do not eat pork.[15]

Guibert asserts that the Saracens worship the relics of their prophet; Embrico and Gautier describe this worship in vivid terms:

> *And his people, believing that his spirit to the stars*
> *had passed, dared not submit his body to the earth.*
> *They established therefore an ark of admirable workmanship:*
> *In this they placed him as best they could.*
> *For, as is told, [the ark] seems to hang*
> *With Machomus' members lying inside*
> *So that without any support it hangs in the air,*
> *And without any chains holding it from above.*
> *And if you ask them by what artifice it does not fall,*
> *They erroneously repute it to Machomus' powers.*
> *But in fact it is covered in iron,*
> *Placed in the center of a square building*
> *Made out of magnetic rock, on all four sides*
> *The measurements are the same inside and out.*
> *By nature it attracts the iron to itself equally*
> *So that it is unable to fall in any direction.*
>
> Gautier, ll. 1059–74

Through a final posthumous phony miracle, Muhammad dupes the naive Saracens into revering him. Embrico tells the story in similar terms. Gautier places the tomb in *Mecha*, an appropriate name since Muhammad was an adulterer (*mechus*); others, Gautier tells us, place his tomb in Babel, also appropriate since Muhammad's effrontery matched that of the builders of the tower of Babel (Gautier, ll. 1077–86). This imagined cultic center of the Saracen world, the floating tomb of Muhammad at Babel/Mecca, is a sort of mirror image of the crusaders' Jerusalem, an anti-Jerusalem: just as Christian pilgrims journey to Christ's tomb in Jerusalem, Saracen pilgrims flock to the floating tomb of their false prophet and god. It is also meant to explain the power and attraction of Islam to the numerous Saracens.[16]

THE PARALLELS between these four accounts should not obscure the differences between them. Guibert and Adelphus are concerned with the Crusades; both wrote brief prose biographies of Muhammad in order to show the true nature of the Christian knights' enemies in the Holy Land. Embrico and Gautier wrote much longer lives in verse. Each recounts the above events in a slightly different order. Yet the similarities remain striking, not only in the details of the story they tell (epilepsy, false miracles, etc.) but also in their broader concerns. None of the four authors uses the term Antichrist to describe Muhammad, and not one of them has him claim to be messiah or predict he will resurrect. All portray him as a heresiarch and false preacher, showing how much all four are preoccupied with the issues of reform and heresy closer to home. Twelfth-century Europe was crawling with preachers who claimed to be inspired by God and exhorted their listeners to return to an earlier, purer faith. Some of these preachers were hailed as reformers by Popes and bishops; others were condemned as heretics. How was one to tell the difference? Hagiographers and heresiologists tried to grapple with this question. All four authors insist on the spiritual heritage of Muhammad: while he himself claims affinity to Moses and Christ, the authors assert his affinity with the great heresiarchs of old, in particular Arius and Nestorius.

Most of the chroniclers of the first Crusade used the image of Saracen idolatry as a key element to justify and glorify the actions of the crusaders (see chapter 5). Adelphus and especially Guibert use the image of Oriental heresy as a more sophisticated strategy for the same ends. Guibert places his brief life of Muhammad near the beginning of his *Dei gesta per Francos,* as a part of a brief narration of the history of Jerusalem and of oriental Christendom from the time of Constantine to the moment the crusaders set out for Jerusalem. After the glorious foundation of the basilica of Jerusalem by Helen, mother of Constantine, the East slides slowly but surely into heretical error:

> The faith of Easterners, which has never been stable, but has always been variable and unsteady, searching for novelty, always exceeding the bounds of true belief, finally deserted the authority of the early fathers.

Apparently, these men, because of the purity of the air and sky in which they are born, as a result of which their bodies are lighter and their intellect consequently more agile, customarily abuse the brilliance of their intelligence with many useless commentaries. Refusing to submit to the authority of their elders or peers, "they searched out evil, and searching they succumbed" [Ps. 63:7]. Out of this came heresies and ominous kinds of different plagues. Such a baneful and inextricable labyrinth of these illnesses existed that the most desolate land anywhere could not offer worse vipers and nettles.[17]

Orientals are clever, flighty intellectuals whose brilliant circumlocutions carry them off into heresy, contrasted implicitly to the stodgy, earthbound, authority-respecting Latins. Is it any wonder, Guibert continues, that virtually all the heresiarchs were Orientals, from Mani and Arius forward? These Orientals continue to defend their errors through reasoning (*ratiocinatio*): the use of leavened bread in the Eucharist, the lack of proper deference to the Pope, clerical marriage, and Trinitarian errors regarding the procession of the Holy Spirit.[18] It is because of these errors, Guibert affirms, that God allowed the Eastern empire to fall to the Arab invaders. It is at this point that Guibert narrates Muhammad's biography, placing him in a dual role: both as divine scourge sent to punish the heretical Eastern Christians, and the latest and worst of a long line of oriental heresiarchs. Heresy is a noxious Eastern import. The ideological point is clear: the conquests of God's army, of valorous and pure Christians from the West, are justified and necessary: both against the Saracen followers of Muhammad and against the weak and perfidious Greeks. Like some of the nineteenth-century orientalists denounced by Edward Said, Guibert uses the image of the flighty and sensual Oriental to affirm the right—indeed the duty—of the vigorous stolid European to appropriate his lands and to rule over him.

Adelphus's narration is remarkably similar to Guibert's. Where Guibert describes the decline of Eastern Christendom from the time of Helen's Jerusalem, for Adelphus, it seems, the decline started when Saint Peter left Antioch for Rome: it is then that the "enemy of the human species" began spreading the poison of heresy, "one root with innumerable branches" (Adelphus, ll. 34–51). Among those many branches, Adelphus continues, mixing his metaphors, a fox broke into the vineyard of Christ, a wolf appeared to ravish God's flock: Nestorius, whom Adelphus makes into Machomet's mentor. For Adelphus, as for Guibert, Muhammad's error is one particularly violent strain of that omnipresent oriental plague, heresy.

Guibert, like Isidore and Bede, uses the Greeks' heresy to denigrate them and deny them political legitimacy. A fortiori, Muslim rule is even more illegitimate: Guibert tries to make this clear by emphasizing Muhammad's similarity to Arius. The law of Muhammad, he stresses, is "neither the antiquity of Moses nor the more recent Catholic teachings."[19] Instead, it is a law based on lust, which authorizes, he says, libidinous sexual relations not only with numerous wives and consorts but also with beasts. For Gautier, too, Machomis's goal is to "soften the rigor of the law," in particular to permit lechery. In the same vein, Embrico has his Magus enjoin Mammutius:

> *The Gospels must be changed; their law is difficult,*
> *It deems us void of sense and foolish*
> *Since it prohibits us from adultery and wantonness*
> *And it destroys marriage between blood relatives*
> *It forbids or enjoins many things through its inept rules*
> *Which you will condemn when you give more appropriate ones.*
> *For adultery and making love you will establish by law;*
> *Let food abound and let love be set free!*
> *But you should close your decree with this ending:*
> *That whatever was prohibited should now be permitted.*

(ll. 711–20)

Muslim law is a travesty of Christian law, a negation of it, an anti-Christianity: "Let everything be now permitted that was before prohibited." The reasons for the instigation of this new law are the Magus's diabolical anti-Christianity and Mammutius's desire for power and sex. Accusations of sexual debauchery were often made against heresiarchs; Jerome makes such charges against Simon Magus, Nicolas of Antioch, and Priscillian. Le Mans chroniclers charged that Henry of Lausanne seduced boys and women, performing obscene acts that are described in detail.[20] Whatever information might have reached these authors about Muslim polygamy or about the promised sexual delights of the next world could only confirm these prejudices, as so much proof that the Saracens heresy is like that of other past and current heresies.

Guibert makes clear that Saracens consider Muhammad to be their wholly human prophet, not a god. The other three authors try to accommodate the popular belief that Muslims worshiped Muhammad as their God. Adelphus concludes his biography by proclaiming, "This is Machomet, who is honored as a teacher [doctor] by the Hagarenes, is called king and prophet and is worshiped as a god" (Adelphus, ll. 318–19). Gautier says that because of Muhammad's military success, the Saracens thought he must be God; Embrico asserts that Libyans worship Muhammad in his floating coffin.[21] Thus the images of Saracen idolatry examined in chapter 5 could be accommodated with a cursory knowledge of Muhammad's life. In this way, William of Malmesbury, writing in about 1125, can assert the Saracens are monotheists yet still maintain that they had erected a statue of Muhammad in the temple of Jerusalem.[22]

These twelfth-century authors, like their predecessors, do not see Islam as an independent phenomenon, a distinct religion. Rather, they see the law of the Saracens as part of a panoply of diabolically inspired error that threatens the souls of Christians and the hierarchy of the church. Faced with this perceived threat (from Saracens, Waldensians, Cathars, Jews, or others), many twelfth-century authors responded with hateful slander, not refuting their adversaries but vilifying them, denigrating them so that their readers could not take them seriously. There were other twelfth-century Christians, however, who attempted a more serious rebuttal of Islamic doctrine.

Mozarabic Christian Polemics Against Islam: Eleventh to Twelfth Centuries

As Europe north of the Pyrenees confronted new heresies and sent waves of crusaders to face the Saracen infidels, Spain too faced military and religious turmoil. Wars of conquest, often motivated (or at least justified) by ideologies of crusade and jihad, pitted the Christian rulers of the north against the new Almoravid Muslim dynasty. These conflicts provoked emigration and conversion of large numbers of religious minorities: many Muslims moved south, many Christians and Jews went north into the expanding Christian kingdoms. Large religious minorities remained in the urban areas: Muslims and Jews in the newly conquered Christian towns, Christians and Jews in the Almoravid empire. Some converted to the majority religion, responding to a mix of social and economic pressure and spiritual turmoil; others clung to the faiths they had been born into.

This atmosphere produced a number of polemical and apologetical works between Judaism, Christianity, and Islam. At least five Christian writers wrote polemics against Islam in twelfth-century Spain: four of these authors are (or are said to be) converts to Christianity, two from Judaism and two from Islam. All of them show knowledge of Islam, of the Koran, and the Hadîth; all of them know (and continue) the traditions of Eastern Christian anti-Islamic polemics embodied in the *Risâlat al-Kindî* (a text with which many in Spain were familiar).[23] Moreover, all five of them, it seems, were written in Christian territories recently wrested from Muslims —at least three of them in Toledo, which had been conquered by Alfonso VI in 1085.

These texts, which attest to the frequency of interfaith disputation and polemic in Spain in the eleventh and twelfth centuries, survive for the most part in fragmentary form. Three of them survive only as fragments cited by Muslim authors. The Cordoban Muslim al-Khazrajî was prisoner in Toledo from 1145 to 1147. There, "one of the Goths," a Christian priest, wrote to him, sending him a brief polemical tract against Islam; al-Khazrajî responded with his own refutation.[24] In the early thirteenth century, a writer known simply as "the Cordoban Imâm" (*al-Imâm al-Qurtubî*) refuted two other Toledan works of Christian apologetics: one, *Tathlîth al-wahdânîyah*, written by a convert from Islam to Christianity, the other the *Mashaf al 'âlam*, probably written by a Mozarabic priest named Augustine.[25] A fourth text, the *Liber denudationis*, written in Arabic in the twelfth century, survives only in a sloppy and much abridged Latin translation in one sixteenth-century manuscript.[26] The fifth text is the brief anti-Islamic chapter that Petrus Alfonsi inserts into his *Dialogues against the Jews* (1110) and that is based almost entirely on the *Risâlat al-Kindî*. I do not attempt to give a thorough analysis of these texts here; that has been done elsewhere.[27]

These five texts illustrate that Spain (and in particular Toledo) had become a center of polemical exchange between Christians, Muslims, and Jews. The role of converts in these disputes is central. The anonymous author of the *Liber denudationis* claims to be a convert from Islam: he describes his former religion as "blindness and stupidity," out of which God led him.[28] Petrus Alfonsi similarly describes his former religion (Judaism) as a "tunic of iniquity" that he shed when he was baptized in 1106 under the protection of his godfather Alfonso I of Aragon in the cathedral of Huesca—a building that had itself undergone a conversion, as it had been a mosque only ten years earlier.

The Christian authors of these polemical exchanges paint Islam as a heretical deviation from Christianity, attacking Muhammad as a false prophet who feigned a spiritual mission to satisfy his lust and ambition. They attack the Koran as contradictory and illogical. They ridicule Muslim polygamy and the promise of sexual pleasure in heaven. They defend the Bible against the charge of falsification and craft quasi-rational "proofs" of the Trinity. In all of this, these Mozarab authors are continuing the apologetical and polemical traditions they found in earlier Eastern texts such as the *Risâlat al-Kindî*. Yet at the same time they develop these arguments in new ways, showing a familiarity with contemporary Arabic science and with Latin theologians such as Hugh of Saint Victor and Abelard.[29] These authors define and explain Islam to Christendom; their strategies would subsequently be adapted by their readers, Latin polemicists against Islam in the twelfth and thirteenth centuries.

Muhammad is the chief scoundrel for these Christian writers. Petrus Alfonsi's anti-Islamic polemic is part of the *Dialogues against the Jews,* a fictive discussion between the author's new Christian persona (Petrus) and his former, Jewish one (Moses). Just as the *Risâlat al-Kindî* has the (fictitious) Muslim correspondent, al-Hâshimî expound Islamic doctrine in order for the Christian to refute it, Alfonsi's Moses presents a summary of Muslim belief and asks Petrus why he didn't choose to convert to Islam. The centerpiece of Petrus's response is an acerbic and derogatory biography of Muhammad, who "through heated fraud feigned to be a prophet," proffering "an inane doctrine."[30] Closely following the *Risâlat al-Kindî*, Petrus recounts that Muhammad had first been an idolater and had enriched himself through trade and through his marriage with Khadîja. Wishing to rule over his tribe, he decided to pretend to be a prophet; he and his followers enriched themselves through war and pillage. Muhammad's loss and injury at the battle of Uhud show that he was not a true prophet, for otherwise he would have foreseen and avoided them. The three signs of prophecy, Petrus says, are "probity of lifestyle, performance of miracles, absolute truth in everything he says."[31] Muhammad, for Petrus, fails on all three accounts.

> Purity of lifestyle was for Mahomet violence, for by force he ordered that it be preached that he was prophet of God. He joyed in theft and rapacity. He burnt so with the fire of lust that he did not blush to pretend that the Lord ordered him to soil another's marriage bed through adultery, as we read about Zaynab, daughter of Ias, wife of Zayd: "God," he said, "orders you, Zayd, to divorce your wife." Once [Zayd] divorced her [Mahomet] copulated with her continually.[32]

Where the *Risâlat al-Kindî* had merely reproduced the Koranic passage referring to the Zaynab affair without comment,[33] Alfonsi wishes to drive his lesson home: Muhammad is not only violent and lustful (and hence he lacks the signs of prophecy) but also does not stoop to falsifying bogus revelations in order to satisfy his basest desires. The *Liber denudationis* recounts the story in greater detail; the main point, for the anonymous author, is to undermine the validity of the Koran: how could one pretend that God is the author of such debased and self-serving revelations?[34]

Alfonsi, following the *Risâlat al-Kindî,* uses the legend of Muhammad's failed resurrection to help explain the successes of Islam:

> After Muhammad's death, everyone wished to abandon his Law. He himself had said that on the third day his body would be borne up to heaven. When they realized that this was a lie and saw his corpse rotting, he was buried and the greater part [of his followers] abandoned [Islam]. 'Alî, the son of Abû Tâlib, one of Muhammad's ten associates, took over the kingdom at Muhammad's death. He coolly predicted and hotly admonished the people to believe, and said that they had not properly understood Muhammad's words. "Muhammad," he said, "did not say that he would be resurrected before his burial or while men watched. He said rather, that after the burial of his body the angels would, with no one knowing, bear him up to heaven. Therefore, when they did not immediately bury him, he began to decompose, so that they might bury him immediately." By means of this argument ['Alî] kept the people for a while in their original error.[35]

Here Muhammad functions as Antichrist (although Alfonsi does not use the term), promising (but failing) to rise from the dead on the third day: his rotting corpse is presented as evidence of his error. Yet 'Alî's clever lie keeps the people in error; hence Alfonsi is able both to denigrate Muhammad and explain the success of Islam.

Both Alfonsi and the *Liber denudationis* portray Islamic ritual and belief as a confused hodgepodge of heretical Christianity, heretical Judaism, and idolatrous survivals. Both stress the role of Muhammad's heretical teachers. For the *Liber denudationis,* they are the monk "Boheira" (i.e., Bahira), the Jew 'Abd Allâh ibn Salâm, and the Persian Salmân al-Fârisî; for Alfonsi, Muhammad was educated by a Jacobite heretic named Sergius (who, he says, had been condemned by a council of Antioch) and by two Jewish heretics, Abdias (perhaps 'Abd Allâh b. Salâm) and Ka'b al-Ahbâr.[36] For this reason, both authors suggest, Muslim doctrine contains a mixture of truth and error, its ritual a blend of Jewish practice and paganism.

As an example of the latter, both authors portray the pilgrimage rites at Mecca as vestiges of paganism. For the *Liber denudationis,* the practice of kissing the black stone of the Ka'ba is nothing more or less than idolatry.[37] Alfonsi rejects as groundless the Muslim tradition that the Ka'ba was constructed by Abraham and Ishmael. Instead, he gives his own peculiar version of its history:

> The two sons of Lot, Amon and Moab, honored this house, and the two idols were brought there by them, one made of white stone, the other of black stone. The name of the one, that was of black stone, was Merculicius, the name of the other was Chamos. The one which was of black stone was erected in honor of Saturn, the white one in honor of Mars. Twice in the year their devotees came up to these idols to pray to them, to Mars when the sun was in the first degree of Aries (because Aries is the honor of Mars). When Mars leaves Aries, as was the custom, they threw stones. [They came] to Saturn when the sun entered the first degree of Libra, because Libra is the honor of Saturn. They burned incense, naked and with heads tonsured; this is still celebrated in India today, as I said. Indeed the Arabs adored idols with Amon and Moab. Then Muhammad, coming after a long time, was not able to remove the original custom, but by a change in the custom he permitted them to make the circuit of the house covered with seamless garments. But lest he seem to enjoin sacrificing to idols, he constructed a likeness of Saturn in the corner of the house. And so that his face might not appear, he placed it so that the back side was facing out. The other idol, that of Mars, because it was sculpted in the round, he put underground and placed a stone on top of it. He ordered the men who convened there for prayer to kiss these stones and, bent over and with heads tonsured, to throw stones backwards between their legs. In bowing down they bare their rears, which is a sign of the original law.[38]

Alfonsi stops short of calling Muslims pagans, but he implies that their monotheism is sullied by the vestiges of these pagan rites. He associates real elements of the Muslim Mecca cult (lapidation, wearing of seamless garments, the Ka'ba itself) with Talmudic descriptions of the pagan cults of Merqulis (at whose idols devotees threw stones) and Baal-Peor (to whom one bared oneself and defecated); these are linked through the story of Lot's sons, Amon and Moab, in a twist that seems to be Alfonsi's own innovation.

Both the *Liber denudationis* and Petrus Alfonsi assert that the Koran is not the fruit of a true revelation, since it was composed by Muhammad's followers after his death. Furthermore, they affirm that it cannot be divinely inspired since it contains many logical contradictions and many injunctions that are clearly immoral; the Hadîth, too, show the same faults. Both polemical texts, like the *Risâlat al-Kindî* before them, stress that according to the Koran, Muhammad produced no miracles. These texts dismiss and ridicule various of the miracles attributed to Muhammad by popular Muslim tradition.[39] How can Muslims claim that Muhammad split the moon, asks the author of the *Liber denudationis,* when the moon, being ethereal, can neither fall nor be split? Furthermore, since the moon controls the tides, the disastrous consequences of its fall would have been noted worldwide; such was not the case.[40]

But it is Muslim sexual mores, once again, that become the favorite target for the polemicists' ridicule. Both authors dwell on Muhammad's marriage with Zaynab, and the Koranic revelation said to have validated it; for both, this is proof that the Koran, far from being divinely inspired, is manipulated by Muhammad to serve his own base desires. The *Liber denudationis* dwells on the supposedly sordid details of Muhammad's other marriages.[41] The *Liber denudationis* (like the *Risâlat al-Kindî* and *al-Qûtî*) attacks Muslim divorce law, which allows a man to remarry the wife he has divorced only after she has had sexual intercourse with another man.[42] And all these texts ridicule the Muslim idea of heaven, dwelling on the sexual delights that Muhammad promised there. The *Liber denudationis* even goes so far as to claim that Muslims believe that in the next life each Muslim in paradise will be awarded for his virtue by an elongation of his penis: it will be so long, in fact, that he will need seventy Christians and seventy Jews to carry it before him![43]

These arguments are unlikely to carry weight with Muslims; they are meant rather to inspire in their Christian reader disgust and ridicule for Islam. Muhammad is a heretic and a heresiarch for these authors, as he was for Guibert de Nogent, Gautier de Compiègne, Embrico of Mainz, and Adelphus. Yet the Mozarabic authors base their caricature on knowledge of Islam and write for Christians who are in daily contact with Muslims. They cannot content themselves with fabricating wildly inaccurate tales of the trickster and magician who dupes the Saracens through false miracles. They need to provide their readers with an image of Islam that seems realistic at the same time that it is repellent.

These authors also need to provide their Christian readers with defensive arguments to parry the polemics of Muslims. They need, in particular, to be able to defend the Bible, the incarnation, and the Trinity. The *Liber denudationis* refutes the charge of *tahrîf* (falsification of the scriptures) by relying on arguments found in oriental Christian apologetics such as the *Risâlat al-Kindî:* it cites passages from the Koran that praise the Torah and Gospels. It also argues that it would be impossible for so many Jews and Christians, spread over the earth and speaking many different languages, to modify the text of the holy writ.[44]

To defend the incarnation to Muslims is a more difficult task. All five of the Mozarabic texts argue for the possibility or plausibility of the incarnation based on analogies to events attested in the Koran (and hence accepted by Muslims). The Koran acknowledges that God spoke directly to Moses through the intermediary of the burning bush.[45] Both the *Tathlîth al-wahdânîyah* and the priest Augustine's *Mashaf al-'âlam* argue that God is present, incarnated, in Jesus in the same way that he was present in the burning bush.[46]

The Trinity is the most common object of scorn among Muslim critics of Christianity. Early Eastern Christian apologists defended the Trinity, and at times claimed to be able to prove it, by identifying it with an essential triad of divine attributes (see chapter 3). Both the *Tathlîth al-wahdânîyah* and Petrus Alfonsi use such arguments to "prove" the Trinity. In the sixth of Alfonsi's *Dialogi,* Moses asks Petrus who the three persons of the Trinity are. Petrus responds that they are substance, wisdom, and will (*substantia, sapientia,* and *voluntas*). Having claimed to prove the existence of God the creator through the evidence of his creation, Petrus goes on to prove the existence of the Trinity:

> Since indeed it is proven that substance truly exists and that it is the creator of all things, the beginning of all beginnings, and the maker of all things made, it is necessary that it have wisdom and will, namely that it know what it wishes to do before it does it, and that it also will to it do, because, before the work comes forth in appearance, it is first formed in the imagining soul, and this imagination is wisdom. And since it thus knew, either it did it or it did not do it. It did not do it if it did not will it. If indeed it did it, then it willed it. And this is the will. Thus the creator of the world could not create anything, before there existed in Him both knowing and willing.[47]

Moses responds "that is true." Petrus concludes from this "Thus God is substance, wisdom, and will."[48] Moses asks if wisdom and will are insepara-ble from and coeternal with God; Petrus responds yes, since to imagine God without either wisdom or will would be to ascribe accident to him.

Moreover, God could not have created either wisdom or will, since he needs both wisdom and will in order to create. Petrus equates substance with the Father, wisdom with the Son, and will with the Holy Spirit; the rationalistic explanation of the Creation, for Alfonsi, requires the existence of the Trinity. *Tathlîth al-wahdânîyah* gives essentially the same argument, though its triad differs slightly: it is power, knowledge, and will.[49] Both authors are working within a well-established tradition of Arab Christian apologetics; both emphasize supposedly rational and scientific proofs. Reason (*ratio*) can disprove Judaism and Islam and prove the essence of Christian truth.

Of these five texts, four, written in Arabic, continue the traditional apologetical strategies of *dhimmi* Christians, strategies examined in chapters 3 and 4. Yet there seems to be a resurgence in these texts, which now have a sharper, polemical edge, sparked perhaps by the Christian conquest of Toledo and the Almoravid response. A free, aggressive tone is possible in Christian Toledo—without the disastrous personal consequences that it would have entailed in Umayyad Córdoba. Moreover, it is these texts, and texts like them (in particular the *Risâlat al-Kindî*) that Latin Christians will consult when they wish to learn about (and refute) Islam.

The most widely read and influential of these texts was the anti-Islamic chapter of Petrus Alfonsi's *Dialogues against the Jews*. Alfonsi composed them in 1110 and subsequently immigrated to England and then to France; from there, his *Dialogues* circulated among monastic readers interested in Old Testament exegesis, Judaism, and Islam. Sixty-three extant manuscripts of the *Dialogues* (along with another sixteen manuscripts containing adaptations of the text) testify to its popularity. Vincent de Beauvais included an abbreviated version of the text in his *Speculum historiale* (c. 1250), which survives in more than two hundred medieval manuscripts. Several scribes recopied only the anti-Islamic chapter, and the Dominican Humbert of Romans, in his *Tract on the Preaching of the Crusade,* recommends it alongside the Latin translation of the Koran as essential reading for understanding the religion of the adversary. Dozens of medieval writers on Islam based their descriptions of Muhammad's life, of Muslim law, and of the pilgrimage rites at Mecca on Alfonsi's *Dialogues*.[50] The popularity of Alfonsi's work contributed to the increasing tendency to link anti-Jewish and anti-Muslim polemics: whereas earlier anti-Jewish polemicists had contented themselves largely with arguing for Christian interpretations of the Torah and the Prophets, Alfonsi focused on the Talmud and the Koran as two illegitimate pseudorevelations that formed the bases for two erroneous religions. Both Talmud and Koran, for Alfonsi, could be attacked through scriptural and rational-scientific argumentation, and key elements of Christian doctrine (the Creation and the Trinity) could be proven. The Muslim or Jew, since he is rational, could be brought to the Christian truth, as Moses is in Alfonsi's *Dialogues.* This linkage of anti-Jewish and anti-Muslim argumentation and this insistence on the irrationality of both rival faiths represents a crucial turning point in the portrayal of both Islam and Judaism in medieval Europe.

Peter of Cluny Attacks Saracen Heresy

One of Petrus Alfonsi's readers was Peter the Venerable, abbot of Cluny, who used Alfonsi's tract in the anti-Muslim and anti-Jewish polemical tracts he composed in the 1140s and 1150s.[51] A comparison of the two authors' approaches shows the cultural gulf that separates them, one an Andalusian with a philosophical education and the other a Burgundian monk steeped in the reading of the Bible and the church fathers. Alfonsi, true to the traditions of Christian Arab apologetics, presents Christianity as the foremost among the three monotheistic faiths. He uses his philosophical and scientific knowledge to attack the writings of rival faiths and to attempt to prove the doctrines of his own. Here he is one not only with the spirit of interreligious apologetics in the Arab world (in Spain and elsewhere) but also with the spirit of the twelfth-century renaissance in Latin Europe, where theologians increasingly apply logic and science in order to explain or prove Christian doctrine. Peter of Cluny, on the contrary, models his approach to Islam on that of the church fathers to the multiple heresies of antiquity; he wants to provide a definitive refutation of Saracen "heresy" worthy of being placed alongside the antiheretical treatises of Augustine or Jerome. For this he uses the *Risâlat al-Kindî* and Alfonsi's *Dialogues,* but his approach is quite different from either of theirs.[52]

In 1142–43 Peter traveled to Spain and assembled a team of translators. He had Robert Ketton produce a full, Latin version of the Koran, which was subsequently given extensive marginal annotations; it is the first translation of the Koran into Latin, indeed probably the first complete translation into any language.[53] Other translators produced Latin versions of other Muslim texts and of the *Risâlat al-Kindî.* Using this collection of texts (often referred to as the *Collectio toletana*), Peter himself composed two anti-Islamic tracts: the first, his *Summa totius haeresis Saracenorum,* describes and vilifies Islam to a Christian readership; the second, the *Contra sectam siue haeresim Saracenorum,* attempts to refute Islam on its own terms and enjoins its Muslim readers to convert to Christianity.

Peter of Cluny offers a rare opportunity of seeing a medieval mind at work—rare because we know what he read in order to form his conception of Islam: indeed we have the very manuscript he probably consulted when he read the *Risâlat al-Kindî,* Robert of Ketton's translation of the Koran, and the other works whose translations he had commissioned.[54] Peter's reading of the Koran was guided by the annotations in the margins of the manuscript, minicommentaries that guide the reader of the "diabolical Koran" by pointing out passages that would seem particularly shocking to the Christian (and especially monastic) reader. The reader is constantly told to note the "insanity," "impiety," "ridiculousness," "stupidity," "superstition," "lying," and "blasphemy" of what he is reading. When the Koran describes prophets not mentioned in the Bible, the comments of the annotator are as follows: "Note the unheard of names of prophets. Who ever heard of such prophets other than this diabolical one [meaning Muhammad]. . . . I think that these were not men but demons: they possessed this Satan, and in this way he concocted his ravings [presumably the Koran]." The annotations qualify Muslim traditions on Jesus and the Virgin as "monstrous and unheard-of fables." The origins of this Christology are diabolical: "Note how inconsistent! how changeable! What vain and contradictory things are brought together in this diabolical spirit!" "Note how he everywhere says that Christ is the son of Mary, but against the Christians and the faith says that the son of Mary is not the son of God—which is the sum of all this diabolical heresy." For the annotators, the devil and his follower Muhammad are the authors of this heresy. Numerous annotations accuse Muhammad of being too fond of women, and of playing on the Saracens' lust by promising them houris in heaven. He threatens his followers with hellfire in order to get them to follow his law and to conquer Christian lands. All this is in line with earlier heresies: "Note that he everywhere promises such a paradise of carnal delights, as other heresies had done before."[55]

These annotations, along with the *Risâlat al-Kindî* and Alfonsi's *Dialogues,* initiate Peter into a Mozarabic polemical view of Islam. Yet while these texts will teach him to see Islam through Mozarabic eyes, his own approach is different: it reflects his own peculiar concerns. Peter addresses his *Summa totius haeresis ac diabolicae sectae Saracenorum siue Hismahelitarum* to a Christian audience, as a preface to the translations of the Toledan corpus; he probably composed it shortly after his return from Spain. Peter describes the purpose of his brief tract: "It ought to be told who [Muhammad] was, and what he taught, so that those who will read that book [the Koran] may better understand what they read and know how detestable were his life and his teachings."[56]

Peter wants to dispel the false opinions that many hold about the Saracens and Muhammad, whom some wrongly identify with the heresiarch Nicholas, whose followers are condemned in Revelation (2:6). The only source of information that he explicitly cites on Muhammad's life is Anastasius Bibliothecarius's Latin translation of Theophanes's *Chronographia* (of which Cluny possessed a manuscript in the twelfth century).[57] That he should use Anastasius (and cite him) is natural: none of the texts translated in the Toledan collection provides a straightforward biography of Muhammad for the uninitiated reader. Anastasius seems to be the standard reference on the subject for writers of the early twelfth century: Hugh of Fleury incorporates parts of Anastasius's description into his *Historia ecclesiastica*.[58] Peter fills in Anastasius's account with information gleaned from *Risâlat al-Kindî* and Petrus Alfonsi's *Dialogi* (it is not always clear which, since Petrus Alfonsi himself relies heavily on the Arabic text of the *Risâla*). Peter's account of Muhammad's life and teachings is much briefer than those of either of these sources, but he adds a clear sense of where the prophet and his followers fit in the history of error: the devil works behind and through Muhammad, leading a third of the world's population into error.

Peter describes Muhammad as a poor, vile, unlettered Arab who achieved wealth and power through bloodshed, thievery, and intrigue. Finally realizing that a feigned religious vocation would serve his ambitions, he claimed that he was a prophet and usurped the authority of king. Then, at the bidding of Satan, a heretical Nestorian monk named Sergius came and joined Muhammad: together, along with several Jews, they forged a new heretical doctrine. "Muhammad, schooled in this way by the finest teachers—Jews and heretics—composed his Koran. He wove together, in his barbarous fashion, nefarious scripture from the fables of the Jews and the ditties of the heretics." All this corresponds closely to Petrus Alfonsi's description.[59] Peter goes on to describe what the Koran says about Moses and Jesus, about the torments of hell and the carnal pleasures of paradise. This mixture of truth and error inextricably woven together shows Muhammad to be the consummate heresiarch; here Peter compares Muhammad to earlier heresiarchs (not something done by either of his sources): "Vomiting forth almost all of the excrement of the old heresies (which he had drunk up as the devil poured it out), he denies the Trinity with Sabellius, with his Nestorius he rejects the divinity of Christ, with Mani he disavows the death of the Lord, though does not deny that He returned to heaven" (*Summa*, §9). Peter holds Muhammad's life—in particular his polygamy—up to opprobrium. Mixing good and evil, sublime and ridiculous, Muhammad created a monstrous cult, similar to the animal Horace described with a human head, a horse's neck, and feathers.[60]

The intention of this diabolic heresy, Peter continues, is to present Christ as a holy man, loved by God, a great prophet—but wholly human and in no way son of God. "Indeed [this heresy], long ago conceived by the plotting of the devil, first spread by Arius, then promoted by this Satan, namely Muhammad, will be completed by Antichrist, in complete accordance with the intentions of the devil" (*Summa*, §13). Peter sees three great adversaries whom the devil uses to lead Christians astray: Arius, Muhammad, and Antichrist. Each manages to trick his followers into denying Christ's divinity. It is for this reason, Peter tells us, that he composed his *Summa* and that he had the entire Toledan corpus translated: "I translated from Arabic into Latin the whole of this sect, along with the execrable life of its evil inventor, and exposed it to the scrutiny of our people, so that it be known what a filthy and frivolous heresy it is" (*Summa*, §18).

While Peter uses the works of earlier anti-Islamic polemicists, he clearly felt they were inadequate. He sets aside much of their material, apparently deeming it useless: for example the names of Muhammad's associates or the polemical descriptions of 'Alī's teachings and the birth of Shi'ism (Peter did not know enough about Islam to appreciate the importance of the latter). On the other hand, Peter finds that these earlier polemics lack a proper taxonomy of error, a sense of Islam's place in the divine plan. The devil inspired heresiarchs to lead the faithful into error; only through careful comparison with the teachings of other heresiarchs and the perusal of antiheretical works of the church fathers could this new and dangerous heresy be combated.

Peter is aware that his *Summa* is merely an introduction to the "Saracen heresy" for the Christian reader, not a refutation of it. The man he deemed most appropriate to refute Islam was Bernard of Clairvaux, to whom he sent a letter along with the Latin translation of the *Risâlat al-Kindî* in 1144. He tells Bernard that he is aware that the *Risâla* has not proved useful to the Saracens in their own language and will not become more useful to them by virtue of being translated into Latin. "Yet perhaps it will be useful to some Latins, to whom it will teach things of which they were ignorant and will show what a damnable heresy it is. It will show them that they must defend themselves against it and attack it, should they ever come across it."[61] This characterization of the defensive purpose of the translation of the *Risâlat al-Kindî* indeed could characterize the whole of the *Collectio toletana*, including Peter's own *Summa*. As an offensive tract against Islam, a real rational refutation of the Saracen heresy, the *Risâlat al-Kindî* apparently would not do; who better to compose such a refutation than Bernard: theologian, fighter of heresies, and preacher of crusade?

Bernard, however, failed to respond to the summons, and Peter himself undertook the task of refuting Islam, writing his *Contra sectam siue haeresim Saracenorum* (Against the sect or heresy of the Saracens) probably in 1155–56. The work as it survives is composed of a long prologue and two books; it may be that Peter wrote more that was subsequently lost or that he left it incomplete at his death on Christmas day, 1156. Both the structure and the strategy of the *Contra sectam siue haeresim Saracenorum* are quite different from those of the *Summa*. In the *Summa* he lambasted Muhammad from a Christian perspective; in the *Contra sectam* (after a prologue in which he justifies his polemics to Christian readers) he (in book 1) enjoins his Muslim readers to listen impartially to his arguments and tries to convince them that according to the Koran they should accept Christian scripture. In book 2 he tries to prove that Muhammad is not a prophet, by contrasting his life with those of Old Testament prophets.

In the long prologue to the *Contra sectam*, Peter justifies his enterprise by placing himself in the company of the church fathers who refuted earlier heretical doctrines, following the rule that "every error should be refuted."[62] He lists the names of ancient heresiarchs, "names monstrous to Christians," and then those of the holy men who rebutted their heresies. The need to refute Muhammad's sect is particularly urgent; its acolytes are the "worst adversaries" of the church (§1), for they dominate Asia and Africa and are present even in Europe (in Spain).

Peter then gives a rhetorical objection to this line of argument: one could say that the Saracens were pagans (*ethnici* or *pagani*) rather than heretics. For did not John define the "many Antichrists" (which, for Peter, means heresiarchs) as those who "went out from us, but they were not of us" (1 John 2:19), in other words as those who had been part of the church and had broken away from it? Peter notes that, like heretics, the followers of Muhammad adopt parts of the Christian faith and reject other parts, while they also follow some rites that seem to Peter "pagan." Like certain heretics, Peter says, Muhammad "wrote in his impious Koran" that Christ was born of the Virgin Mary, lived without sin, and performed miracles; like the Manicheans, the Saracens deny his death. Like the pagans, on the other hand, they reject baptism, the mass, and the other sacraments. Heretics or pagans, "choose whichever you like" (*Contra sectam*, §14). He asserts that pagans should also be opposed by written polemic; here, too, he lists the names of illustrious church fathers who attacked paganism in their writings. Peter himself generally prefers to consider the "Mahometan error" as a heresy.

Peter then responds to one final rhetorical objection to his tract: why compose for Muhammad's followers a treatise in Latin, a language they do not understand? Here Peter has two justifications. First of all, he hopes that someone may undertake to translate his tract into Arabic; after all, the Fathers frequently translated works useful to the church from Hebrew to Greek, Greek to Latin, Latin to Greek, and so on. Second, Peter says that his tract may prove useful to Christian readers, even if it stays untranslated (which it did). If there are any Christians who have the slightest tendency to respect or admire Islam, Peter hopes his work will quickly dissuade them. "Perhaps this tract will cure the hidden cogitations of some of our people, thoughts by which they could be led into evil if they think that there is some piety in those impious people and think that some truth is to be found with the ministers of lies" (*Contra sectam*, §20). Who are these Latin Christians who in their "hidden cogitations" might think the Saracens were pious? Peter does not say, but certainly the most likely candidates were the translators and students of Arabic science and philosophy. One such scholar, Adelard of Bath, proclaimed "I learnt from my masters, the Arabs, to follow the light of reason, while you are led by the bridle of authority; for what other word than 'bridle' can I use to describe authority?"[63] Might such preference for "Arabic reason" over "Latin authority" lead such Christian scholars into doubt, even apostasy? In this light his polemics look more like a defense of Christianity than an offensive missionary effort.

While the prologue to the *Contra sectam* is a defense of his tract to possible Christian detractors, the text itself is addressed to "the Arabs, sons of Ishmael, who serve the law of him who is called Muhammad" (*Contra sectam*, §23). He tells his readers that it is love that bids him write to them, love that Christian law enjoins on him. "I love you; loving you, I write to you; writing, I invite you to salvation" (*Contra sectam,* §26). Peter realizes, he says, that the first reaction of his Arab readers will be that they would never abandon the law given them by their prophet. He also is aware that the Koran enjoins death on those who dispute the Muslim law.[64] This, he says, astounds him, because his Arab readers are "not only rational by nature, but logical in temperament and training" they are, moreover "learned in worldly knowledge" (*Contra sectam,* §30). The injunction against debating religion flies in the face of the Arabs' propensity for learning: no rational man should accept something as true without first verifying its truth for himself.

These Arab philosophers use their reason to comprehend nature; do they not know that this nature, the highest object of the search for truth, asks Peter, the uncreated creator, the ultimate substance or essence, is God?[65] Should they not use their reason to investigate the truth concerning God? The law prohibiting religious dispute is an "infernal counsel," a law fit for irrational sheep, not rational men. Instead of reaching for your swords or stones when a Christian comes to preach the gospel, Peter says, follow rather the example of Christians who dispute with Jews, listening patiently to their arguments and responding wisely. (Peter fails to follow his own advice in his vitriolic *Against the Inveterate Stubbornness of the Jews.*) Or follow the example of King Ethelbert of Kent, who received Christian missionaries with honor and heard them out.

Peter has emphasized the rationality and learning of his Muslim audience; this is all the more striking when contrasted with his descriptions of the enemies in his *Against the Inveterate Stubbornness of the Jews,* whom he brands as beasts without reason, since they stubbornly refuse to accept the rational truth of Christianity.[66] There he contents himself with lambasting irrational Jewish beliefs for a Christian audience, showing no hope of converting Jews. Here, on the contrary, he pleads with his learned Muslim readers to hear him out, invoking the pagan king Ethelbert. Muslims, it seems, should be predisposed to recognize Christian reason; in order to prevent this, Muhammad had forbidden them under pain of death from debating matters of the faith.

Having crossed this first theoretical hurdle to gain a hearing from his rational, philosophical Muslim readership, his first and fundamental argument in favor of Christianity is not rationalistic or scientific but scriptural. While earlier polemics (including both the *Risâlat al-Kindî* and Petrus Alfonsi's *Dialogi*) often tried to prove the Trinity using various triads of philosophical concepts, Peter makes no such attempt.[67] Such argumentation is foreign to him; since exegetical argumentation is his forte, his most pressing need is to establish the validity of the Bible to his Muslim audience so he can then comfortably deploy the scriptural weapons he manipulates so well.

In order to prove the validity of the Jewish and Christian scriptures, Peter starts from the normal Christian viewpoint that Koranic stories of, say, Abraham or Noah are corrupted versions of their biblical counterparts; the marginal annotations in Robert of Ketton's translation of the Koran reflected this notion. Peter says he was amazed to find that Muhammad, in the Koran, had mixed elements from Christian and Jewish scriptures and moreover had praised those scriptures. Assuming, rather than arguing for, the primacy of Judeo-Christian scripture, he affirms that if these scriptures are divine, they should be accepted wholly, not in part; if they are not divine, they should be rejected wholly, not in part (*Contra sectam*, §57).

He knows what the Muslim objection to this argument will be: the charge that the God-given scriptures of Jews and Christians have been corrupted and that only the Koran represents the uncorrupted word of God. Here he refers to Muslim stories—gleaned from a marginal annotation to the Koran[68]—according to which the Jews lost the Torah on their way back to Israel after the Babylonian captivity. Here Peter is quite capable of ridiculing this story using his scriptural arsenal. In particular, he employs the logical arguments gleaned from the *Risâlat al-Kindî* showing how difficult it would be for Jews and Christians, dispersed over half the world, to connive together to corrupt the Torah.[69] He argues similarly against charges that Christians have corrupted the Gospel. He then concludes book 1 with the assertion that he has proved that the Bible is divine, that it is superior to the Koran, and that its authority should be accepted by all Muslims (*Contra sectam*, §88).

In book 2, Peter attempts to prove that Muhammad is not a prophet, for a prophet by definition foresees the future, whereas Muhammad did not. Here Peter is unaware that the Muslim concept of *rasûl* is quite different from the Christian notion of *propheta:* the latter by definition predicts future events, while in Islam a *rasûl* is a messenger of God, bringing the message that man must submit to God's will. In showing that Muhammad does not correspond to Peter's notion of prophethood, he is scoring a point that would carry little weight with a Muslim audience.[70] Peter uses material from the *Risâlat al-Kindî,* reshaping it to fit into his more coherent, theologically based structure. Peter narrates only the details of Muhammad's life that are necessary to show that he is not a prophet: in particular his inability to foresee his military defeats and his failure to produce miracles.[71]

Peter asserts that the last of the prophets was John the Baptist. Yet Paul foretold of the errors of false prophets: "For the time will come when they will not endure sound doctrine . . . and they shall turn away their ears from the truth, and shall be turned unto fables."[72] Just so, says Peter, were the Saracens converted to the fables of Muhammad and Jews to the fables of the Talmud. He describes the prophecies and virtuous lives of various of the Hebrew prophets and challenges his readers to produce anything analogous in order to prove that Muhammad is a prophet. This brings him back to his initial argument on the Koran; the Saracens should accept Christian scripture, reject Muhammad, and convert to Christianity (*Contra sectam*, §147–54).

Whether Peter considered his polemical work complete or whether he intended to write further, his polemical strategy, while indebted to that of his Arab and Spanish predecessors, is clearly distinct from it.[73] While effusively expressing his admiration and respect for philosophy and *ratio*, Peter is certainly not adept in the scientific-rational forms of argumentation common in the *Risâlat al-Kindî*, Petrus Alfonsi's *Dialogi*, and other such works. He is much more at home when he can marshal his formidable knowledge of scripture to refute Saracen errors.

This difference is clearly seen in the organization of the *Contra sectam*. The *Risâlat al-Kindî* opens with a defense of the Trinity based on a triad of divine attributes, an argument that apparently failed to impress Peter, since he does not reproduce it. Petrus Alfonsi opens his attack on Islam by lambasting Muhammad; since his anti-Islamic chapter is part of a debate between a Christian and a Jew, this is an understandable ploy to discredit Islam in the eyes of his Jewish interlocutor (indeed, this is the same strategy Peter adapts in his *Summa*). Peter realized that to open the *Contra sectam* by directly attacking Muhammad would only provoke the hostility of his Muslim audience. Instead, Peter uses a few well-chosen Koranic citations to try to prove that Muslims should accept Christian scriptures; once he has done that, he can return to the exegetically based polemical method that he had employed in the *Contra Petrobrusianos* and the *Aduersus Iudaeorum inveteratam duritiem*.

In this enterprise Peter saw himself as continuing the tradition of the church fathers, of scripturally based explication and refutation of heresy, just as he saw his *De miraculis* as a continuation of the traditions embodied in the writings of Gregory the Great.[74] His dissatisfaction with the earlier works of polemic that he used seems to stem from the fact that they do not resemble the works of the Fathers with which Peter was so familiar. This, perhaps, explained why these had failed to convert the Muslims: they were not proper theological tracts.

If Peter thought his polemics would be more likely to convert Muslims, he was of course badly mistaken. Peter had only a superficial bookish knowledge of Islam, nothing to compare with the more direct knowledge of Petrus Alfonsi or (especially) of the author of the *Risâlat al-Kindî*. Yet in both his works, Peter attempted to offer a defensive campaign against diabolical error: such polemics could quash the doubts of Catholic readers. For Peter, Cluny was God's citadel constantly besieged by demons. As Cluny's spiritual head, Peter was particularly well placed to repulse demonic incursions: through pastoral care of his monks, through doctrinal works such as his *De miraculis,* and through his trilogy of theological polemics against Jews, heretics, and Saracens. The three groups were increasingly linked in the twelfth and thirteenth centuries and were often seen to represent a common danger. As Dominque Iogna-Prat has shown, all three rejected the spiritual economy that Cluny embodied, where Christians through sacrifice could transform themselves and prepare themselves for the next life. This sacrifice centered around the Eucharist, reenactment of Christ's ultimate sacrifice for humanity, which was to be performed by priests who had sacrificed their sexual life in order to devote themselves to God; Christian laymen could offer up their lands to God, turning them over to monasteries like Cluny whose monks would pray to shorten their benefactors' purgatory punishments. The whole was meant to be harmoniously ordered, with the Pope at its head. Muslim, Jews, and heretics were united in their rejection of this system, clinging instead to this world in an irrational obsession with all that was physical and carnal. If these enemies could not be brought into the fold through Peter's apologetics, at least their satanically inspired errors could be dispelled from the minds of Christians, in order that the system might continue to transform humble sinners into God's elect.

Peter of Cluny's anti-Muslim polemics were to have few readers during the Middle Ages: his *Contra sectam siue haeresim Saracenorum* survives in only one manuscript. Robert's translation of the Koran survives in eighteen manuscripts, most of them from the fourteenth to sixteenth centuries.[75] The scribes of these manuscripts recognized the importance of the

Latin Koran and of other texts in the *Collectio toletana* (including Peter's *Summa*). Yet seventy years after the composition of the *Collectio toletana,* Rodrigo Jiménez de Rada, archbishop of Toledo, was apparently unaware of Robert's translation of the Koran: he induces Mark of Toledo to produce another translation (see chapter 7).

The "Heresy of Muhammad" among the Spiritual Threats to Latin Christendom

The Mozarabs, like their Eastern Christian counterparts, deployed the image of Muslim heresy as a defensive weapon. By portraying Islam as a deviant and debauched version of Christian Truth, they sought to defend their place in the *dâr al-Islâm. Reconquista* and jihad changed the confessional map of Spain, and Mozarab polemics grew more daring and more outspoken. Petrus Alfonsi brought this Mozarabic tradition north across the Pyrenees. Peter of Cluny adapted the Mozarabic defensive strategy to the spiritual needs of twelfth-century northern Europe: showing little interest in refuting Muslim doctrine or in defending Christian doctrine, he reasserted the primacy of Christian scripture over the Koran and affirmed that Muhammad was a false prophet. Other twelfth-century writers portrayed heretics in the same light. Landulf Senior, for example, writing in about 1110 (at the same time as Guibert de Nogent and Petrus Alfonsi), brands the Milanese Patarenes as "false Christs" and "false prophets" (*pseudochristi* and *pseudoprophetae*).[76]

Islam was not, for these authors, a separate religion, distinct from other spiritual rivals: it was merely one variety of heretical error. This is true for Peter of Cluny and even truer for Christian theologians who knew less about Islam than did Peter. Alan of Lille, for example, composed in about 1200 his *De fide catholica,* a four-part polemical tract directed against Cathars, Waldensians, Jews and "pagans" (*pagani*)—by which he refers to the "disciples of Mahomet." The first part, against the Cathars, is the longest: each successive section is shorter. This is a good indication of the spiritual threat that each posed, for Alan, to the Christian commonwealth: Islam is spiritual enemy number four. Alan's chapters on Islam are curious. He indeed shows a good knowledge of certain details of Muslim doctrine: Muslim belief on paradise, on Christology, Muslim marriage laws, and so on. Yet he seems to have read neither Robert of Ketton's Koran, nor

Petrus Alfonsi, nor any of the other authors I have discussed. Alan was in Catalan Montpelier and may have received this accurate (though random) information either from a Muslim or from someone who had direct contact with Muslims. Yet Alan has no coherent idea as to what Islam is; he attributes to his Muslim adversaries arguments based on the Old Testament.

At the outset of his *Contra paganos*, Alan asserts that Muhammad, inspired by the devil, established a new cult based on carnal pleasure:

> The monstrous life, more monstrous sect, and most monstrous death of Machomet is clearly found in his biography. Inspired by a malign spirit, he invented an abominable sect consonant with carnal delights, not dissonant with delights of carnal men. For this reason, many carnal men are seduced by his sect, thrown into the abyss through various errors, miserably they have perished and continue to perish. These men are in the common vernacular called pagans or Saracens.[77]

Alan has clearly culled his ideas from a hostile Christian biography of Muhammad; he later asserts that his corpse was devoured by dogs.[78] He gleaned from this reading the notion that Islam is a depraved cult based on carnal pleasure. This is the gist of most of Alan's anti-Islamic arguments: he lambasts the Muslims for asserting that God impregnated the Virgin through a material breath (*flatus materialis*).[79] They hope for carnal pleasures in heaven, interpreting literally the biblical promises of a land of milk and honey.[80] They practice ablutions thinking that water—rather than contrition and confession—can wash away sin.[81] They justify their polygamy by citing the example of the Old Testament patriarchs, when in fact they merely want to satisfy their lust.[82] The Saracens, along with the Jews, misinterpret Old Testament prohibitions against idolatry and polygamy, erroneously accusing Christians of idolatrous worship of images of the saints.[83] They follow a miscellaneous mixture of Jewish and Christian law, not led by reason (*ratione ducti*) but dragged by their own desire (*propria voluntate tracti*). Islam, for Alan, is a heretical blend of Christian and Jewish beliefs, rife with contradictions, that can be refuted through reason and authority. It is a carnal cult for a carnal people: its physical rites contrast with the spiritual sacraments of Christianity; its polygamy and celestial fornication, with the purity of the Christian priesthood. Alan seems to be unaware of the existence of the Koran; indeed he continually puts into the mouths of his Saracen adversaries citations from the Old Testament, with which they are supposed to defend their heretical doctrines.

IF TWELFTH CENTURY Latin Europe "discovered" Islam, it viewed it through its own (rather thick) lenses. Certainly, twelfth-century European Christians took Islam more seriously than they did the religious beliefs of the non-Christians such as the Wends or Lithuanians. Islam was worth studying and attacking for two reasons. First, it seemed to be another heresy of Eastern origin, like those plaguing twelfth-century Europe; as such it was less important than the Manichean error of Catharism, which indeed received more attention than Islam. The second reason for the growth of a polemical interest in Islam is the profound cultural and intellectual influence the Muslim world was exercising on Latin Europe in the twelfth century: notably through trade and through the translations of scientific and philosophical works from Arabic to Latin. Confronted with a thriving, prosperous, intellectually sophisticated Muslim world, the Christian polemicist needed to convince his readers that the "heresy of Muhammad" was a debased parody of the true religion.

It is in this context that the virulent attacks against Muhammad must be placed. Guibert de Nogent, admitting that he could only repeat what the "vulgus" said about Muhammad rather than produce a proper theological refutation of his doctrine, presented Muhammad as a clever scoundrel, a heresiarch whose life was a mocking mirror image of that of a true Christian saint, specifically in order to justify the crusaders' aggression against Muslims. Three other authors, Adelphus, Embrico, and Gautier, produced similar pictures of Muhammad. Twelfth-century authors in Spain continued the traditions of Arab Christian apologetics; Petrus Alfonsi's and Peter of Cluny's translations made these traditions available to the Latin world. Authors such as Peter of Cluny and were better informed about Islam than Guibert had been. Yet their portrayal of Islam reflects their preoccupations with heresies closer to home. The result is in no way a "dialogue" with Islam, nor even an informed monologue. Despite Peter of Cluny's pretension of addressing Muslim readers in hopes of converting them, he (like Alan of Lille) in fact attempted to defend Christianity against yet another oriental Christological heresy that had spread its tentacles westward. For all concerned, the culprit responsible for this heresy is Muhammad; the central task of the polemicist is the ridicule and denigration of the prophet of Islam.

Christian writers on Muhammad are not unique in using such tactics to denigrate a rival religion. Jesus receives similar treatment in the *Toledoth Yeshu.* Herodotus, in his *Histories,* describes the rites that the Getae (from

Thrace) devoted to their god Salmoxis. According to Herodotus, the Greeks who live on the Black Sea recounted that Salmoxis had been a slave of the Greek philosopher Pythagoras on the island of Samos; he escaped from his master and returned home to Thrace, "where he found people in great poverty and ignorance." He taught them that they would never die, but "would live in perpetual enjoyment of every blessing." In order to convince them of this, he built a secret underground chamber, where he went into hiding. The Getae thought him dead and mourned him greatly; when he reappeared three years later, he was able to convince them of their immortality and trick them into following a strange and irrational cult.[84] These descriptions offer some interesting parallels with medieval Christian portrayals of Islam. The Arabs (like the Getae) are described as poor and ignorant, in contrast with the more sophisticated Christians (or Greeks). The founder of the new religion (Muhammad or Salmoxis) is ignorant and servile, yet manages to learn the rudiments of religion from his master (Sergius/Bahira or Pythagoras). This knowledge, deformed, becomes the basis of a new and irrational cult devoted to an everlasting life of sensual pleasures, and Muhammad/Salmoxis resorts to crude tricks to dupe his ignorant followers into following him. In both cases, the reader is reassured of the superiority of his own, "normal," religious beliefs, while the rites and beliefs of the other are both explained and held up for ridicule.

Many later medieval writers reiterated the twelfth-century view of Islam as heresy. Some tried to refute Islam in theological treaties or missionary manuals. Others reproduced the hostile biography of Muhammad, having him produce bogus miracles, be devoured by pigs, and so on.[85] Gerald of Wales included in his *De principis instructione* (On the instruction of princes) a minibiography of Muhammad in which he combined elements from Hugh of Fleury's *Ecclesiastical History* (an account itself derived from Anastasius's translation of Theophanes's *Chronographica*) with the legend of his being devoured by pigs. Gerald specifically compares Muhammad's death with that of Arius, the moral being apparently that vile heresiarchs have ignoble deaths. The diversity of heresy shows the devil's ingenuity, for Gerald: he tricks the lustful inhabitants of hot climates by tempting them with Saracen polygamy, while he appeals to the avarice of chilly northern Europeans by promising them they won't have to pay any tithes if they follow the Patarene heretics.[86] In 1258 Alexandre du Pont composed a French verse *Roman de Mahomet* based on Gautier de Compiègne's *Otia.*[87] From the twelfth century onward, Muhammad the heresiarch inhabited the European imagination alongside Muhammad the golden idol: an equally powerful (if equally inaccurate) intellectual weapon with which to inculcate contempt, inspire hatred, justify conquest. In the thirteenth century, as conquest of formerly Muslim lands accelerated in Spain and as Christian princes from Lisbon to Acre affirmed their right to rule over Muslim subjects, this view of Saracen heresy became an important part of Latin Europe's ideology of power.

Part Three

❧❧

THIRTEENTH-CENTURY DREAMS
OF CONQUEST AND CONVERSION

CHRISTIAN EUROPEANS from the ninth century to the twelfth explained Islam in ways meant to reassure their Christian readers of the
superiority of Christianity. They did this in a variety of ways, but in general
they fell back on the hermeneutical and exegetical weapons that they han-
dled so well, presenting Islam as a new variety of one of the well known
and thoroughly despised enemies of old: pagan idolatry, heresy, the cult of
Antichrist, or a confused blend of all of these. Many of these traditional
Christian schema predate Islam, and many of them were adapted by the
first generations of Eastern Christians to explain away the successes of the
Muslims.

Indeed, through the twelfth century and into the thirteenth, Christian
responses to Islam were by and large defensive reactions of Christians confronted by the power and prestige of the Muslim world: embattled *dhimmis*
in Damascus or Córdoba trying to convince their correligionaries not to
convert to Islam; chroniclers in Constantinople, Jarrow, or Asturias troubled by Islam's stupendous military successes. It was the twelfth century
that saw a real awakening of interest in Islam in the Latin world: polemical lives of Muhammad, in response to the successes of Crusade and *reconquista;* celebrations of crusader victories over the idols of a supposed
Saracen paganism; the translation and adaptation of the Mozarabic anti-
Islamic polemical traditions into Latin.

In part 3, I examine how writers of the thirteenth century built upon
these traditions. The portrayal of Muhammad as a heresiarch, false prophet, and precursor of Antichrist is used to inspire and justify *reconquista* and
crusade. Chapter 7 looks at how thirteenth-century Christian kings, chroniclers, and jurists used the polemical image of Islam to affirm their rights to

conquer Muslim territories and to impose their rule over large Muslim minorities. In chapter 8 I discuss how, for a number of thirteenth-century authors, the Crusades of the thirteenth century inspired predictions of an ultimate Christian victory over Islam; many of these writers pinned their hopes on the aid of Christians from the East who would sweep away the Muslims in an apocalyptic final battle.

Other writers counted on the mass conversion of Muslims through the offices of Catholic missionaries. Indeed, the thirteenth century saw for the first time significant effort to convert Muslims to Christianity through mission—and saw a good deal of disagreement on how to do it. Chapter 9 considers how the new Franciscan order, inspired by a desire to return to the "Apostolic lifestyle," encouraged its friars to travel to Muslim lands and preach Christianity to Muslims. These Franciscans in general showed little knowledge of Islam or of the Arabic language, and for many of them the principal goal was to receive the palm of martyrdom from the Saracen adversaries, not to convert them. The Dominican order adopted a quite different strategy (see chapter 10). Dominican friars studied Arabic, pored over Koran and Hadîth, engaged Muslim scholars in theological debate, and preached to captive Muslim audiences in the mosques of the Crown of Aragon; the hope was that such argumentation would be able to prove the superiority of Christianity to the Muslim interlocutors, though by the end of the century the failure of this strategy became manifest. At the turn of the fourteenth century, Catalan Ramon Llull forged his own strategy of mission based on positive argument from shared truth (see chapter 11).

Whereas part 2 traces the *development* of polemical strategies of portraying Islam, the focus in part 3 is on the *deployment* of these strategies. In other words, I focus less on what an author says (for example) about Muhammad, and more on how he uses that portrayal of the Muslim prophet for his own ideological purposes. A great variety of uses of the polemical images of Islam occur over the course of the century. Through this variety can be traced a certain change in mood: a number of writers express optimism about the possibilities of Christian victory over Islam (through military victory, through missionary activity, or both); the optimists will at times portray Islam as only slightly different from Christianity and portray Muslims as ready to convert to Christianity given a proper mix of political allegiance and rational argumentation. This optimism grows rarer at the end of the century. Faced with the debacle of repeated crusader defeats and the recurring victories of the Mamluks (and later Ottomans), faced also with the abject failure of the missionaries' attempts to persuade

Muslims (or for that matter Mongols or Jews) to convert to Christianity, Christians Europeans in the early fourteenth century have a darker, more pessimistic view of Islam. Many fourteenth-century authors follow the lead of Dominican Riccoldo da Montecroce in portraying Muslims as illogical, invariably hostile enemies. Few by then are optimistic that Christianity can logically be shown to be superior to Islam.

Chapter 7

༺❀༻

THE MUSLIM IN THE IDEOLOGIES OF
THIRTEENTH-CENTURY CHRISTIAN SPAIN

*The Moors [Moros] are a people who believe that Muhammad was the Prophet
and Messenger of God, and for the reason that the works which he performed do
not indicate the extraordinary sanctity which belongs to such a sacred calling his
religion is, as it were, an insult to God. Wherefore, since in the preceding Title we
treated of the Jews and of the obstinacy which they display toward the true faith,
we intend to speak here of the Moors, and of their foolish belief by which they
think they will be saved. We shall show why they have this name; how many
kinds of them there are; how they should live among Christians, and what things
they are forbidden to do while they live there; how Christians should convert
them to the Faith by kind words, and not by violence or compulsion; and what
punishment those deserve who prevent them from becoming Christians, or dishonor them by word or deed after they have been converted, and also to what
penalty a Christian who becomes a Moor is liable.*

—Alfonso X "el Sabio," King of Castile and León (1252–84),
Siete partidas, 7:25

THUS DOES Alfonso X define the role of Muslims in Castilian society:
the Muslim religion is an "insult to God"; the "proof" of this is that
Muhammad did not show the "extraordinary sanctity" necessary to prove
he was a prophet.[1] This is the "foolish belief" of the Moors, a belief that,
just like the "obstinacy" of the Jews, condemns them to a subordinate role
in Christian society. Legal restrictions attempt to prevent the "pollution" of
Christians by Muslims or Jews and to facilitate their peaceful and voluntary
conversion to Christianity.

Muhammad, perceived as false prophet, is the key to the ideological justification of the subjection of Muslim Spaniards to Christian Castilian rule.

Where Guibert de Nogent used the polemical biography of Muhammad to justify the conquests of the first Crusade, Alfonso deploys the same traditions as the foundation of his own power over subject Muslims. Here is a clear example of the kind of discourse that Edward Said decried in nineteenth-century apologists for British and French empire: a derogatory portrayal of Islam as a basis for the military and political domination of Muslims.

Alfonso did not invent this ideology, of course; he wove it together of familiar strands: denigration of Islam's prophet, affirmation of Visigothic Christian rights to rule over Iberia. Over the course of the thirteenth century, the various strands begin to come together. Canon lawyers such as Catalan Dominican Ramon de Penyafort define the place of Muslims in Christian kingdoms, basing their arguments on canon law regarding Jews. Alfonso's father-in-law, Jaume I of Aragon, presents himself as a crusader and devotee of the Virgin Mary, protector of his Muslim and Jewish subjects and promoter of Dominican missions to them. Leonese Lucas de Tuy and Archbishop of Toledo Rodrigo Jiménez de Rada continue the historiographical traditions of their Asturian and Leonese forbears, chronicling the restoration of right Gothic rule and the reclamation of churches lost to the Arab invaders. The writers working in the scriptorium of Alfonso el Sabio weave these ideological strands together to form an ideology of Castilian Christian power over Muslims and Jews.

Conquest and Domination in Jaume I's Aragon

In the Crown of Aragon, the story of reconquest is marked by the crusader-king Jaume I, or James the Conqueror. Jaume's first major conquest is that of Mallorca, in the Balearics. Pope Gregory IX sends a letter to Jaume in November 1229, informing him that he is sending along men, laymen and clerics, to aid him in the conquest, and that he is "granting them that indulgence which is normally given to those who come to the aid of the Holy Land." Gregory is very clear, too, about the purpose of the Crusade: returning territory to Christendom. He says that Jaume has taken the cross, "so that, once the enemies are captured or dispersed, the land may return to the Divine Cult and the rites of the Church may expand."[2]

This justification of Jaume's conquest, as a crusade for the restoration of usurped territories to the Christian cult, is reiterated in papal documents about Jaume's later conquests, most notably that of Valencia, which he finally captured in 1238 after a long siege. Jaume staged a mass baptism of new Christian converts from Islam in front of the walls of the besieged city: a symbolically charged move meant both to discourage the Muslim defenders and to let Jaume claim the moral and religious high ground as a crusader.

Jaume consistently portrays himself as a righteous crusader in his autobiography, the *Llibre dels feyts;* he focuses on his military contests against the Muslims of the Balearics and Valencia, passing over in silence his legislative and judicial career.[3] He describes how, before making the final decisive assault on the city of Mallorca, he prayed to the Virgin, proclaiming to her that "we have come here so that Mass may be celebrated in honor of your Son." In the ensuing battle, the Aragonese troops sounded their battle cry: "Sancta Maria, Sancta Maria!" Jaume affirms that a Saracen defender later reported having seen the attack against the city led by a white knight bearing a white standard; Jaume asserts that it must have been Saint George, since "we read in histories that in other battles Christians and Saracens have seen him many times."[4] The choice of patron saint is telling: Jaume prefers George, the favorite of chroniclers of crusades to the East (as in the case of Petrus Tudebodus) rather than James or Isidore, associated with the *reconquista* of León and Castile. When Valencia surrendered and Jaume first saw his standards flying from the tops of the city's towers, he got down from his horse, faced east, knelt, and kissed the ground, shedding tears and giving prayers of thanks. Some historians hesitate to use the term "crusade" to describe Jaume's conquests, noting (correctly) that even for the king himself, a crusade to the Holy Land had a special prestige that the Iberian campaigns lacked.[5] Yet clearly Jaume uses the imagery and ideas of crusading to glorify his own exploits against Muslims closer to home. His descriptions, and indeed probably his actions, are influenced by the idealized image of the crusader. Jaume saw his successes as part of a wider confrontation between Islam and Christendom: he planned (though failed) to head East to crusade in the Holy Land, and he claims to have received letters from the Mongol khan that proposed a Mongol-Aragonese alliance against Islam.[6]

Jaume does not demonize his Saracen enemies, nor does he explicitly denigrate their religion. Indeed, he often expresses admiration for the military prowess of his adversaries. He describes in detail the negotiations with the Muslim inhabitants of towns and castles that lead to their surrender: how, for example, he carries on separate negotiations with the elders of

Uxó, Nules, and Castro so that no one might know the stipulations of the surrender treaties of the other, describing how he cleverly refused to negotiate until the Muslims had eaten, so that the food and wine might put them in a better mood and make them more apt to make concessions.[7] He prides himself in scrupulously respecting his own agreements with his Muslim subjects and presents himself as a fierce defender of their rights: when ambassadors from the Muslim community of Elx come to negotiate, Jaume tells them that if they surrender they will keep houses and possessions and be free to practice their religion (*llur llei*); the Muslims respond that they have heard that those who trust in the king can rest assured that he will keep his word.[8]

Yet Jaume can also manipulate the treaties of submission to suit his needs. He proudly describes how he exiled the Muslims of Murcia from the city and took away their mosque, bringing in Dominican friars to prove to them that the treaty permitted him to do so. When they pleaded that he leave them their mosque, since it was the best place for them to pray, he retorted that in that case he wanted it for the Christians. He had the mosque transformed into a cathedral devoted to the Virgin Mary, to whom he then prayed and shed copious tears. "In every town, however large or small, that God had permitted us to win from the Saracens, we have built a church for Our Lady Saint Mary."[9] Jaume uses the word "built" (*edificada*), it seems, to indicate either a new construction or the rededication of an appropriated mosque. Jaume earlier describes how he had seized a mosque near the castle of Murcia, affirming simply that it would not be proper for him to have to hear the call of the muezzin as he slept.[10]

In Jaume's *Llibre dels feyts* we find none of the polemical portrayals of Islam that are found, for example, in the various chronicles of the first Crusade. Jaume apparently feels no need either to demonize his enemy or to justify his own conquests. His devotion to the Virgin, and his desire to reestablish churches in her name where mass will be performed in honor of her son, are enough for Jaume. The success of his endeavor is sufficient proof that God is on his side. Yet there is nothing in the *Llibre dels feyts* to suggest that Jaume made any efforts to convert Muslims to Christianity; he insists on the protection he gives them to practice their own religion.

The image that Jaume presents of himself, the tearful devotee of the Virgin, deploying all his knightly prowess, royal authority, and strategy to restore land to her and her son, leaves no room in the *Llibre dels feyts* for the other considerable achievements of Jaume's reign: his administrative genius, his legal reforms, his patronage of Dominican missionaries; these aspects of his reign are amply documented elsewhere, as the work of Robert Burns, Pierre Guichard, and others has shown. For our purposes, it is the legal texts composed under his reign that hold the most interest, in particular as they touch upon the rights of his Muslim subjects and on their obligations to listen to the sermons of Christian missionaries.

On 12 March 1243 Jaume presided over the ecclesiastical council of Lerida. Among the subjects addressed by the council was the conversion of Muslim and Jewish subjects of the Crown of Aragon. The council issued detailed statutes on the property and inheritance rights of converts from Judaism and Islam. It also fixed fines for anyone who insulted converts. Finally, it proclaimed that "whenever an archbishop, bishop, or Dominican or Franciscan friars come to a town or place where Saracens or Jews live and wish to proffer the word of God to these same Jews or Saracens, the latter should come when convoked and should patiently listen to their preaching. And if they should be unwilling, our officials should compel them to do so and accept no excuses."[11] The same three points are reiterated in the *Fuero* of Aragon or *Vidal mayor,* named for its compiler, Vidal de Caneyas, Bishop of Huesca (d. 1252); Jaume ordered this compilation of earlier law, much of it municipal and ecclesiastical, in an attempt to regularize and codify the legal texts and customs of the kingdom of Aragon.[12] The section of the *Vidal mayor* dealing with Jews and Saracens opens with a first-person exhortation by Jaume himself, underlining the royal source of the legal authority vested in the text. It takes up the three points addressed in Lerida (inheritance rights of converts, fines for those who insult them, the obligation to listen to the sermons of missionary preachers), then adds sections on inheritance rights of Jews and Muslims, on their rights to buy and sell property, and on the problem of runaway Muslim slaves. In none of this, however, is there any sense of a need to justify or rationalize the place of subject Muslims in Jaume's kingdom. In these laws, as in the countless submission treaties contracted with the Muslim communities of his realms, the royal authority of the conquering king over his conquered Muslim subjects is invoked without any recourse to theological underpinnings. As in much civil and ecclesiastical law in this period, the legal status of Muslims is closely associated with that of Jews; here, as usual, no rationalization is offered for this association. For some historians, the role given to minority Muslims and Jews in the Christian Iberian kingdoms is simply a continuation of the *dhimmi* policies of the previous Muslim rulers; this is an association that Christian jurists for the most part avoid: Muslim law,

A Muslim being baptized by a priest in the presence of his godparents. (From the thirteenth-century Aragonese law code, the Vidal Mayor, Los Angeles, Getty Museum manuscript Ludwig XIV 6, f.242v. Reproduced with the permission of the Getty Museum.)

presented as inherently illegitimate, could scarcely be evoked as legal precedent.[13]

The Dominican and Franciscan friars whose activities Jaume encouraged in this legislation were preaching a hostile, polemical view of Islam and its prophet; but Jaume and his legislators feel no need to invoke such polemical views. There is little evidence of actual preaching to Muslim or Jewish subjects until 1263, in the aftermath of the Barcelona disputation between Dominican friar Pablo Cristiá and Rabbi Nachmanides (discussed in chapter 10). On August 26, 1263, Jaume decreed that all Jews and Muslims should attend mendicant missionary sermons and that converts should be protected from abuse and harassment.[14] On 30 August the king mollified these decrees, specifying that Jews could neither be forced to leave their neighborhoods to hear sermons nor be forced to listen against their will. An edict of 1268 limited the number of Christians who could accompany the preachers into Jewish and Muslim neighborhoods, and specified that they should be *probi homines:* the goal, it seems, was to prevent unruly mobs from harassing Muslims and Jews in their own neighborhoods.¹⁵ Jaume prohibited laymen from disputing matters of the faith publicly or privately:¹⁶ the matter could only be trusted to professionals.

In the legal texts associated with Jaume's rule, as in his *Llibre dels feyts,* no attempt is made to provide a coherent theological justification of the king's power over his conquered Muslim subjects. My point here is not to try to do justice to the complexity of the relations between Christians and Muslims in Jaume's realms, a subject studied in detail by Robert Burns and Pierre Guichard. The point is rather to underline the contrast between the works emanating from Jaume's scriptorium and those coming from that of his son-in-law Alfonso X of Castile. If Jaume shows that a polemical view of Islam and of Muhammad is not necessary to present oneself as a devout crusader bent on restoring churches to the Virgin and on protecting and restricting the social status of Muslim subjects, Alfonso will combine these elements with a polemical view of Islam to forge a coherent and powerful ideology.

Lucas de Tuy and the Affirmation of Leonese Gothic Hegemony

The kings of León and Castile are the heirs to the Asturian kingdom of the ninth century, whose carefully constructed ideology of reconquest is examined in chapter 4: the kings of Asturias were heirs to the Visigothic kingdom and were destined to restore its hegemony over the whole of the Iberian peninsula. This ideology of "Gothic revival," unlike the Catalan-Aragonese ideology of crusade, gives prime importance to ideas of political rebirth and reaffirmation, the restoration of a legitimate, Christian order. Three thirteenth-century monarchs had chronicles composed that narrated the triumphant resurgence of Gothic, Christian Spain: Berengera, Queen Mother of Castile and León, had Lucas de Tuy compose his *Chronicon mundi* between 1236 and 1242; Rodrigo Jiménez de Rada, archbishop of Toledo and close adviser to King Ferdinand III of Castile and León (San Fernando) completed his *De rebus Hispaniae* between 1243 and 1246; Alfonso X "el Sabio" (the Wise) had a team of historians compose a vast *Estoria de España* (completed under the reign of his son, Sancho IV). These three versions of a royal Leonese-Castilian historiography, though they differ in points, offer a coherent expression of the ideology of reconquest. In the previous centuries, various chroniclers (particularly those connected with León) had indeed continued to proffer the ideology of Gothic reconquest first elaborated by the Asturian chroniclers of the ninth centuries (see chapter 4). The twelfth-century sculptures of the Church of San Isidro pit Sarah and Isaac against Hagar and a turbaned archer Ishmael; they present the bishop Isidore alongside an armed soldier, as if a patron of Christian reconquest.[17] But it is the three thirteenth-century chroniclers who clearly redefine this ideology to explain and justify the conquests of the thirteenth century.

Isidore is a central character in Lucas de Tuy's version of the struggle between Christian and Moorish Spain. Lucas may have served as canon at San Isidro, the Leonese church which had received with pomp the relics of Saint Isidore in 1063; he composed a collection of Isidore's miracles.[18] What better model for Lucas than Isidore, adviser to Gothic kings, chronicler of their reigns, bishop and polymath? Lucas's Isidore faces off with twin antagonists from the Muslim world: Muhammad and Avicenna. Lucas is familiar with the brief polemical life of Muhammad that Eulogius had discovered in a Navarese monastery in 850 and incorporated into his *Liber apologeticus martyrum,* and that had subsequently been incorporated into the Asturian *Prophetic Chronicle:* Muhammad as a scoundrel and magician who invents bogus revelations to explain away his epileptic fits, who claims to be the Messiah.[19] But Lucas adds a brief but significant episode gleaned from his reading of an anonymous eleventh- or twelfth-century *Life of Isidore:* Muhammad came to Spain, debarking near Córdoba, to preach his doctrine. Isidore, returning from Rome, ordered his men to arrest Muhammad, but alas the devil warned Muhammad, who fled to Africa.[20] Lucas imagines his hero confronting the prophet of Islam and making him flee, a satisfying scene that Lucas had to include, though probably aware of its implausibility. For the Prophet's death, he relies on the polemical life of Muhammad incorporated into the ninth-century Asturian *Prophetic Chronicle:* he says that Muhammad had predicted that he would die after reigning over the Arabs for ten years and that three days after his death he would rise from the dead.[21] One of his disciples, Albimor, wishing to put Muhammad to the test, poisoned him. At his death his disciples watched his body closely for three days; seeing that he would not rise, and repulsed by the stench of his rotting corpse, they left him. Albimor later returned to find the body devoured by dogs; he took the bones and had them buried in

Medina. The denigration of Muhammad is a key element in the affirmation of Leonese hegemony; there can be no legitimacy in the rule of the Moors, followers of the heresiarch Muhammad.

Muhammad is not the only adversary of Saint Isidore. Lucas's hero is the intellectual superior of the most illustrious of the Muslim sages, Avicenna (Ibn Sînâ). After glorifying Isidore's piety and learning, Lucas explains that his successor, a shifty Greek named Teodistus, "a wolf in sheep's clothing," stole several manuscripts of Isidore's as-yet-unknown works in medicine and other sciences, then "out of hatred of the Faith, excising the truth and inserting errors, had them translated from Latin into Arabic by a certain Arab named Avicenna," who pretended the works were his own.[22] Faced with the impressive edifice of Arabic science, Lucas responds that the Arabs stole it all from the good Isidore.

Isidore predicted the fall of the Goths and their restoration, Lucas affirms.[23] As the patron saint of León, he actively aids the Leonese kings. In his *Miracles of St. Isidore,* Lucas describes the saint appearing in a vision to King Alfonso VII during the siege of Baeza (in 1147). Though the king is outnumbered and surrounded by Moorish enemies, Isidore appears to him to assure him that he will be victorious; at Isidore's side is Saint James's hand, bearing a two-edged sword.[24] Isidore (alongside Saint James and the Virgin) is a patron saint of the Spanish reconquest. On the eve of his conquest of the former caliphal capital of Córdoba, Fernando III prays to Isidore for the deliverance of the city.

For Lucas de Tuy, Muslim rule in Spain is based on violence and deceit: a deceiving pseudoprophet who urges his faithful to conquest through bogus revelations and fake miracles; shifty characters such as Teodistus and Avicenna who steal Christian Spain's intellectual property and claim it as their own. But Isidore's León is on the move, and thanks to the saint and the kings of León Christian victory is imminent.

Rodrigo Jiménez de Rada and Mark of Toledo

A more sophisticated though essentially similar view of the Muslim-Christian confrontation in Spain is found in the works of Rodrigo Jiménez de Rada, Archbishop of Toledo (1208–47) and of those working with him. Rodrigo was a principal actor in many of the events he describes: he preached crusade before the battle of Las Navas de Tolosa; he participated in Las Navas and many battles against the Almohads. He was a close adviser to Alfonso VIII, the victor at Las Navas, and to Fernando III, conqueror of Córdoba (1236) and Seville (1248). Soon after his arrival in Toledo, Rodrigo commissioned Mark, deacon of the cathedral of Toledo, to translate the Koran into Latin; he was apparently unaware of Robert of Ketton's translation. Mark completed the translation in June 1210, two years before Las Navas de Tolosa, when the Almohad presence was still a serious threat.[25] Indeed, Christian chroniclers beyond the Iberian peninsula perceived the armies of Almohad caliph al-Nasir as a menace to all Europe; for Cesarius of Heisterbach and for the anonymous author of the *Annals of Cologne,* the Cathar heretics called on the caliph to aid them against the forces of the Albigensian Crusade; for Matthew Paris, King John of England promised to convert to Islam in return for the caliph's aid against the French.[26] Writers of the twelfth century had painted Muhammad as a heresiarch, and in the thirteenth some imagine heretics, Muslims, and traitors teaming up into an anti-Christian alliance.

It is in this context that Mark presents his translation as part of the intellectual and spiritual arsenal that Christians must deploy to affirm their control over their polluted sanctuaries and to drag the Saracens back into the Christian fold. In the preface to his translation of the Koran, Mark offers a brief hostile biography of Muhammad.[27] He presents Muhammad as a skilled magician who through his travels learned the rudiments of both Judaism and Christianity and decided to urge his people to abandon their idolatry and worship the unique God. Hesitating between Judaism and Christianity, he decided that the law of the Gospel was too difficult, since it enjoined love of one's enemy and spurning the pleasures of the flesh. He opted for Judaism, yet realized that the Jews were everywhere despised because they killed Jesus Christ. For this reason he proclaimed that Jesus had not really been killed and he promulgated a new law, the Koran, mixing Jewish law, Christian law, and his own fancy. In order to foist this law on the Arabs, he called them together outside of the city of "Mecha" (which, Mark reminds the reader, means adultery), feigned an epileptic seizure, and announced to the assembled masses that Gabriel had revealed a new law to him. Mark goes on to give a fairly accurate catalog of Koranic doctrine on the unity of God, the role of Jesus as prophet, the rites of prayer and ablution, fasting and pilgrimage, and so on. Mark affirms that Muhammad established himself as a prophet and messenger of God and obtained reign over his people as had David and Solomon.

Having forged his new law, "in which he speaks as one who is delirious," Muhammad "like a magician seduced barbarous peoples through fantastic delusions," and his Saracens through war subdued the world, oppressing Christians from the north to the Mediterranean and from India to the west—to Spain, where "once many priests swore holy allegiance to God, now evil men give supplication to the execrable Muhammad, and the churches which were consecrated by the hands of bishops have now become profane temples." Mark presents the conversion of churches into mosques as a profanation or pollution; the reconquest of these places by Christian rulers, who will have them duly purified and reconsecrated by bishops, is implicitly legitimate.

Opposing the Saracens in Spain is Rodrigo Jiménez de Rada, Archbishop of Toledo. Mark tells how Rodrigo was moved to tears by seeing the Saracen oppression of his archdiocese: where priests once performed mass in honor of Christ, now the name of the "pseudoprophet" is invoked. In the towers of the churches where bells once rang, now "profane proclamations [the call of the muezzin] deafen the ears of the faithful." Rodrigo, deploring this state of affairs, making his tears his arms, urged Mark to translate the book containing the Saracens' "sacrilegious decrees and strange precepts." The point of this translation is to allow those among the orthodox who are not permitted to use arms to combat the precepts of Muslim law; in this way they can refute the "detestable decrees" of Muhammad and in so doing, "not a few Saracens may be dragged to the Catholic faith." The language here is one of force and coercion: the intellectual combat permitted through Mark's translation of the Koran is complimentary to that carried out by Christian armies. By forcibly reclaiming the Spanish churches converted into mosques, Christian princes banish the muezzin and reinstate the church bells; Christ's name, and not Muhammad's, is to be invoked. Moreover, knowledge of the Koran will provide churchmen with the intellectual weaponry needed to defeat Islamic doctrine and drag the Saracens back to the faith. It is this same desire to "expose secrets of the Moors" in order that they may be refuted that leads Mark, three years later, to translate a treatise on the unity of God by Ibn Tûmart, *mahdî* and founder of the Almohad movement.[28]

Rodrigo himself offers a similar biography of Muhammad in his *Historia Arabum,* employing, he says, "their" sources: he indeed uses Mark's translation of the Koran along with Hadîth and the *Mi'râj,* though he also uses the works of Christian chroniclers. His purpose is to "unravel that

people's slyness and ferocity," to show the reader "how, through false revelation the sly man Muhammad from his heart crafted a pestilential virus."
Rodrigo's presentation of Muhammad is much more detailed than Mark's
and more faithful to Muslim sources (though he does follow the *Chronicle
of 754* in crediting Muhammad with the conquest of Damascus). Yet the essential image is the same: a pseudoprophet who concocted bogus revelations in order to obtain power. Rodrigo stresses the *political* illegitimacy of
the rule of Muhammad and his followers: the Muslim conquests are presented as a "rebellion" against Roman power. This clearly sets the scene for
the remainder of the *Historia Arabum,* which is principally devoted to the
Muslim rulers of Spain: they, like Muhammad before them, usurped Spain
from its legitimate Gothic rulers.

This vision of history, legitimizing the Christian (re)conquest of Spain,
is clearly laid out in Rodrigo's *De rebus Hispaniae,* completed between 1243
and 1246. Where Lucas of Tuy follows and perpetuates the historiography
of Leonese *imperium,* Rodrigo is a partisan of Castile, which becomes the
main actor in the reconquest. He describes the steady progression of the
conquest as a restoration of Christian and Gothic rule, town by town. A
good example is his description of how Córdoba, "the noble city, was
purged of the filth of Muhammad."²⁹ What is of interest here is not the description of the military maneuvers that led to the capture, but rather of
the "purification" that followed it. King Fernando III enters the city and

> in the main minaret *[in turri maiori],* where the name of the perfidious
> one [Muhammad] used to be invoked, he began to exalt the wood of
> the vivifying Cross, and all began to acclaim with him, with joy and
> tears, "God help us!" Then the royal insignia *[regale uexillum]* was
> placed next to the Lord's cross, and a voice of joy and delight was heard
> coming from the tabernacle of the just, as the priests and monks in-
> toned the *Te Deum:* "God we praise you, Lord in you we trust."³⁰

The Te Deum replaces the muezzin's call; the crucified one replaces the
perfidious one. And the insignia of God's power are inextricably linked
with those of the king. Rodrigo then describes how a group of clerics

> entered into the mosque of Córdoba, which surpassed all the mosques
> of the Arabs in its size and decoration. . . . Once the filth *[spurcitia]* of
> Muhammad had been eliminated and holy water had been sprinkled

[aqua lustrationis perfusa], they transformed it into a church, erected an altar in the honor of the Blessed Virgin and solemnly celebrated mass.[31]

Fernando orders that the bells from the Cathedral of Santiago, which had been taken when al-Mansûr sacked the city in 997, be removed from the mosque and sent back to Santiago. Fernando, in harmony with his clerics, restores proper Christian order to Spain, undoing the "opprobrium" committed by al-Mansûr, cleansing Spain of "the filth of Muhammad."

For Rodrigo Jiménez de Rada, the conquest of Andalusia by Castilian armies is a *re*conquest, a restoration of proper political and ecclesiastical order. Churches return to their proper use; the proper hierarchy of priest, bishop, primate, and pope is reestablished, as is the right rule of the heir to the Gothic kings of Spain.

Alfonso X el Sabio

The ideological justification of the conquest and domination of Muslim communities in Spain had various interpretations: the concept of crusade in Jaume I's *Llibre dels Feyts*, restoration of Gothic hegemony in Lucas de Tuy and Rodrigo Jiménez de Rada, and for all these authors, the reconversion of mosques into churches.[32] It is Alfonso X of Castile and León (1252–84) who weaves these different ideological strands together into an ideology that affirms his right and duty, as "king of three religions," to rule over the entire population of the Iberian peninsula: Muslims, Christians, and Jews.

Alfonso's political struggles and his patronage of writers and translators have often been treated as separate, even opposing, tendencies. The king's intellectual hobbies are seen as so many distractions from the real work of ruling. As the Jesuit historian Juan de Mariana wrote in 1601: "While he contemplated the heavens and observed the stars, he lost his lands."[33] His futile attempt to be recognized as Roman emperor is also seen as a vain pursuit of titles made at the expense of a real exercise of power. Yet Alfonso's cultural program reflects his ideology: his vast program of translations from Arabic into Castilian Spanish reflects his desire to appropriate and to Hispanicize Arabic learning. If he often presents himself as "King of three religions," surrounded by dutiful Muslim, Christian, and Jewish subjects, it is precisely because he affirms (as had Rodrigo Jiménez de Rada) that there can be no legitimate non-Christian polity in Spain. His pursuit of the imperial title is a further attempt to bolster the legitimacy of his rule. This ideology is seen in different ways throughout the works produced under Alfonso's patronage; I focus on two of them, his national chronicle, the *Historia de España,* and his vast compendium of law, the *Siete partidas.*

Alfonso X seems to have closely supervised the creation of the *Estoria de España* (often known as the *Primera crónica general*).[34] Most of the text (or most of that part of it that was actually composed under Alfonso) deals with Roman and Visigothic history. Alfonso apparently meant it to strengthen his claim to the imperial crown; it is probably no coincidence that he abandons the *Estoria* at the same time as he gives up his claim to the title of Roman emperor.[35] The *Estoria's* vision of history justifies Alfonso's supremacy as Gothic king and Roman emperor; its objective is to trace the history of Spain "from Noah's time to our own."[36] It narrates the different dynasties that ruled Spain: Greeks, Carthaginians, Romans, Vandals, Visigoths, and Arabs. Only two of these groups are legitimate: the Romans and the Visigoths; Alfonso, king and emperor, is legitimate successor to both. The others are illegitimate interlopers—in particular the invaders from Africa, Carthaginians and Moors.[37] I examine two passages in detail: his treatment of Muhammad and his narration of the Arab conquest of Spain.

The *Estoria de España* paints Muhammad as a heresiarch, relying closely on the chronicles of Lucas de Tuy and Rodrigo Jiménez de Rada, in general preferring the more detailed and accurate narration of Rodrigo. Yet when recounting Muhammad's death, Alfonso deliberately rejects Rodrigo's account in favor of the more flamboyant (and far less reliable) legend from Lucas de Tuy: the prophet's failed resurrection, the corpse defiled by dogs. Rodrigo focused his biography of Muhammad on the implicit contrast between Muhammad and Jesus: Christ, shunning sex and worldly power; Muhammad, eagerly pursuing both. Alfonso wanted to carry this contrast farther, to their deaths: Christ's, the supreme sacrifice and glorious victory; Muhammad's, the death of an Antichrist, complete with a failed resurrection and a rotting, dog-defiled corpse. The death story, gleaned from Lucas, made dramatic and theological sense. It also made sense in the broader sweep of Alfonso's narrative, in which he describes the various groups that had ruled Spain. He privileges two groups, the Romans and the Goths: their rule is legitimate, is celebrated. Alfonso sees himself, of course, as the incarnation of both: Roman emperor and Gothic king. The Arabs, by contrast, he portrays as interlopers, never as legitimate rulers.[38] Just as Alfonso glorifies the origins of Roman and Gothic rule, he must denigrate the origins of Arab rule. What better way than by presenting their prophet and first statesman as a liar, scoundrel, and Antichrist? For Norman Daniel, the failure of medieval authors such as Alfonso and his team of scholars to stick with good, reliable, Arabic texts shows that they are unable to distinguish between reliable sources and unreliable ones. On the contrary, it shows a consummate historiographical skill: the ability to shape the past to fit a political agenda.

The same weaving together of sources to produce a new narrative is apparent in the *Estoria*'s version of the Arab invasion: the dramatic tale of the sins of the Gothic monarchy, its punitive fall to the African invaders, and its slow but steady rebirth.[39] For the *Estoria* as for Rodrigo, the evil, diabolical nature of the invaders is evident in their appearance: "their faces were as black as pitch, the most handsome among them was as black as a kettle, their eyes shone like candles." There is a long medieval tradition of associating blackness with devils and of seeing dark-skinned Muslims as semidiabolical creatures.[40] They are "the vile African people who excelled neither through strength nor through goodness, but did all with trickery and cleverness."[41] The *Estoria* describes the destruction and desolation of Spain at the hands of these barbarians, in particular their defilement of churches:

> The sanctuaries were destroyed, the churches demolished, the places where God was praised with joy [the Muslims] now blasphemed and mistreated. They expelled the crosses and altars from the churches. The chrism, the books, and all those things that were for the honor of Christianity were broken and trampled upon. The holidays and celebrations were all forgotten. The honor of the saints and the beauty of the church were turned into ugliness and vileness. The churches and towers where they used to praise God, now in the same places they called upon Mahomat.[42]

For the Alfonsine team, as for their predecessors, the lamentation over the ruin of Spain underscores the illegitimacy of Arab hegemony in Spain. The invasion prepares the scene (dramatically and ideologically) for the resurrection of Christian Spain under the Gothic kings of León and Castile. The invasions of the diabolical Africans will be righted by the reconquest by Christian kings; the perversion of churches into mosques by the restoration of mosques into churches.[43]

Alfonso's *Estoria,* like the chronicles of Lucas de Tuy and Rodrigo Jiménez de Rada, expresses this royal ideology of reconquest. The kings of León and Castile inherited the ideologically charged vision of history from their Asturian predecessors. Theirs was the only legitimate rule in the peninsula: heirs to the Goths, protectors and restorers of the church, even (for Alfonso) heir to the Roman emperors, who could deny their legitimacy? Certainly not the dynasties of foreign, African interlopers, benighted followers of an obscene, heretical pseudoprophet. This is the ideology forged by these medieval kings and their clerical chroniclers, an ideology affirmed by military success, which will thrive into later centuries and cross the Atlantic.

Alfonso affirms his right to subject Muslim and Jewish inhabitants of the peninsula to his reign in his vast program of legal texts, in particular in his *Siete partidas,* a huge compilation of law composed at Alfonso's behest. Alfonso made no attempt to implement the *Partidas* during his reign, so its provisions do not necessarily reflect real legal practice. Yet for that reason it provides a clear picture of how Alfonso envisioned his rule over his subjects and in particular (for our purposes) his Muslim subjects. For Alfonso, the struggle against Islam justifies royal control over the church: the kings have the right to ratify the election of the bishops, according to the *Partidas,* since it is the kings who defeated the Moors, transformed their mosques into churches, and replaced the name of Muhammad with that of Christ.[44]

The *Siete partidas* defines and restricts the Muslims' place in Castilian society, a place founded on their religious inferiority. *Titulo* 25 of the *Partidas,* "de los moros," defines Moors (in the passage quoted at the beginning of this chapter) as those who believe that Muhammad is God's prophet and messenger. Since Muhammad did not live a holy life worthy of a prophet, his law is an "insult to God" (*denuesto de Dios*) and "silliness" (*nescedat*); here the *Partidas* invokes the standard argument that Muhammad's failure to show the "signs of prophecy" is proof of the illegitimacy of his law. The Moors, for their "foolish belief," are explicitly given the same social and legal status as the Jews for their "obstinacy": they may live "observing their own law and not insulting ours." They may not have mosques in Christian towns and should not practice their sacrifices in front of Christians. Their mosques are royal property; hence the king may do with them what he wishes: implicitly, this includes the right to have them converted into churches or to reserve some of them for continued use as mosques.[45] Muslims coming from other kingdoms to the royal court are protected.[46] Muslims have a right to live and practice their religion, but this freedom of religion is constrained much as that of the *dhimmi* in Muslim lands, allied to an inferior social status. The Muslim (or Jew) may not own Christian slaves;[47] He may not bear witness against a Christian except in treason cases.[48]

Several of the *Partidas*'s laws involve conversion of Muslims to Christianity. Since God wishes men to be faithful to him freely and out of love, Christians must try to convert Moors gently and with words, without using constraint and without oppressing them.[49] To designate the punishment of a Christian who oppresses Muslims, the *Partidas* refers explicitly to the chapter on the Jews, further emphasizing the similarity in legal status between Jews and Muslims. While the presentation of Muhammad in the *Estoria de España* would suggest that Islam would be a heresy, the *Siete partidas,* in accordance with thirteenth-century Canon law, gives the Muslims a subordinate but tolerated status equivalent to that of Jews, while denying any legal right to practice heresy.

The *Siete partidas* also attempts to facilitate the voluntary conversion of Muslims to Christianity. No one may prevent a Muslim from converting to Christianity (law 2), or call the convert *tornadizo* (turncoat), or insult him (law 3). Fear of such insults prevents Muslims from converting to Christianity, even those who "since they possess comprehension, acknowledge the superiority our faith."[50] Conversion could produce legal problems, which the *Partidas* attempts to avoid: if cousins marry according to Muslim (or Jewish law) and then convert to Christianity, their marriage remains valid, even if it would normally be considered incestuous according to Christian law.[51] If only one member of a Muslim or Jewish couple converts to Christianity, he or she has the right to divorce, because the spouse's refusal to accept Christianity is tantamount to a "spiritual fornication."[52]

Several laws of the *Partidas* show that Islam is still considered a threat to late thirteenth-century Castilian society: not only a military threat but also a potential source of pollution through religious and sexual contamination. The ultimate pollution is apostasy: five of the ten laws involve punishments for Christians who convert to Islam. They are to lose all their property and be put to death; even if they repent and return to Christianity, they shall be unable to serve as a witness, hold public office, or be a beneficiary of another's will. Apostasy is a major preoccupation in the *Partidas*'s chapter on the Moors—much more so than in the chapter on the Jews: in the context of intermittent war with Granada and Morocco and of sporadic rebellions of Muslim subjects of Andalusia, apostasy (often accompanied by emigration and alliance with Castile's foreign adversaries) was a real worry. The *Partidas* further specifies that apostates may be accused up to five years after their death, and only those who have "rendered some great service to the Christian religion" may escape punishment. This last stipulation shows again the political context of apostasy: it allows rebels who have gone over to Castile's Muslim enemies to return to Castilian society in exchange for some "great service"—presumably either military intelligence or military service.

Sexual contamination is also a preoccupation of the *Siete partidas*. The Muslim or Jew who sleeps with a Christian virgin or widow must be stoned while his partner loses half her possessions; if she is married, both are to be put to death; if she is a prostitute, they are flogged together through the city. In all cases, the punishments for recidivists are more severe.[53] But there is no explicit prohibition of sexual relations between a Christian man and a Muslim or Jewish woman; this seems to be tacitly tolerated.

In one passage Alfonso invokes the Muslim *dhimmi* law as precedent— or at least as an example to follow. He devotes one of the *titulos* of the seventh *Partida* to those who insult (*denuestan*) "God, St. Mary, and the other saints."[54] The last of the *titulo*'s six chapters concerns Jews and Moors who proffer such insults. The chapter recalls that Jews and Moors are permitted to live in "our land" even though they do not believe in "our faith," but the condition for this permission is that they do nothing to insult Christ, his mother, or the other saints. Not only is verbal insult prohibited but also spitting on crosses, altars, or images of the saints, or striking such a holy object with hand, foot, or other object, or throwing stones at churches. "Whoever acts against this prohibition we will punish him in his body and in his possessions according to what we judge he merits for the crime that he committed." Alfonso gives the following justification for this prohibition:

> If the Moors, in all the places where they have power over the Christians, prohibit them from insulting Muhammad and from saying anything against his doctrine, and for this offense they beat them and hurt them in many ways and decapitate them, how much more appropriate it is that we prohibit them (and others who do not believe in our faith) from daring to criticize or insult our faith.[55]

If Muslims punish those who blaspheme *their* religion, we are justified in punishing those who blaspheme against Christianity, Alfonso argues.

This is the unique example, as far as I know, of a Christian legal text specifically invoking Muslim law as a legal precedent for the treatment of non-Christians. Even if the *dhimma* system was widely copied, lawyers (particularly canon lawyers) had to justify it in terms of Christian theological and legal notions.

CAN ONE FORM a coherent picture of the place of the Muslim in the different works produced in Alfonso's scriptorium? There is a tension between the association of Islam with heresy (in the *Estoria de España* and in many theological tracts and chronicles) and the attribution to Muslims of a subservient but tolerated legal status equivalent to that accorded to Jews—a status that thirteenth-century canon law accords to both Jews and Muslims but denies to heretics.

How does this fit with the prominent place given to Arabic (and, to a lesser extent, Jewish) culture in Alfonso's court? The king is patron to poets and musicians, painters and architects, scholars and translators. In the illuminations of the *Cantigas de Santa María,* the king is seen surrounded by Jewish and Muslim courtiers, scholars, and musicians; the text tells of Muslims and Jews who benefit from miracles of the Virgin Mary. And there is no more striking symbol of the fusion of Muslim and Christian traditions in Spain than the Mudejar churches built under Alfonso's reign, such as those of Santa Fe and Santiago del Arrabal, which seem to be born from a marriage between a Romanesque church and a Maghrebin mosque. On the walls of the Church of San Roman, one can still read praises of God in Latin and in Arabic.

Yet here again, the Muslim and Arabic elements of Alfonso's cultural mix are clearly subsumed into the dominant Christian Castilian framework. The Muslims and Jews who benefit from miracles in the *Cantigas de Santa María* almost invariably convert to Christianity. In the Cantigas, Alfonso sings the praises of his father, Fernando III, and his father-in-law, Jaume I, lauding them for transforming mosques into churches devoted to the Virgin.[56] Mudejar churches borrow elements from Muslim architecture, but they are emphatically Christian in form and function. The fact that prominent Muslims and Jews benefit from royal patronage serves as a symbol of their communities' subservience to Alfonso's rule—just as patronage of prominent Christians had for the caliphs of Damascus, Baghdad, or Córdoba. Alfonso's commission of a vast program of translations from Arabic to Castilian does not denote any particular respect or admiration for Islam, any more than Caliph al-Ma'mun's patronage of translators in ninth-century Baghdad was a mark of a predilection for Christianity or for Greek paganism. For both al-Ma'mun and Alfonso, translation of the intellectual riches of a rival civilization was a means of appropriation: al-Ma'mun and his court Arabize and Islamicize Greek and Persian culture and learning; Alfonso and his court Hispanicize and Christianize Jewish and Arabo-Muslim culture and learning.

In this schema, a key role is played by the affirmation of the superiority of Christianity and the denigration of Judaism and Islam. In the latter, the polemical biography of Muhammad is central: because Muhammad fails to show the signs of prophecy, because he fabricated a false religion as "an insult to God" there can be no political legitimacy under Muslim rule, and Muslims must recognize the political superiority of Christian rulers. The "proof" of this is offered not only in the biography of Muhammad in the *Estoria de España* but also in the Castilian translations of the *Mi'râj* and of the Koran, undoubtedly conceived as tools in the polemical confrontation with Islam.

Alfonso created a comprehensive and powerful ideology, weaving together various earlier arguments: the restoration of the Gothic monarchy in Spain; the affirmation of Roman imperial power; the reconversion of mosques into churches; the protection and succor of Christian subjects of Muslim rule; the illegitimacy of all Muslim rule, particularly in Spain; the appropriation and nationalization of the culture of the Muslim other. In the construction of this ideology, the denigration of Islam and the polemical biography of Muhammad play a key role. It is an ideology much more unified, developed, and coherent than any found in the court of his father-in-law, Jaume I of Aragon. This of course did not prevent Jaume from being the more effective ruler or save Alfonso from rebellion by Castilian nobles, Muslim subjects in Andalusia, and his own son Sancho. If Alfonso failed to realize the grandiose role put forward in the texts and miniatures of his scriptorium, he did, through his legal and historiographical texts, establish a blueprint for power that his successors would relentlessly pursue. Muslims and Jews of Castile would increasingly be forced into the roles given them by the king of three religions.

Chapter 8

‿⊰❋⊱∾

APOCALYPTIC FEARS AND HOPES INSPIRED BY THE
THIRTEENTH-CENTURY CRUSADES

A certain son of perdition, Muhammad the pseudo-prophet, arose. Through worldly enticements and carnal delights he seduced many people away from the truth. His perfidy has prospered until this day. Yet we trust in God, Who has already given us a good omen that the end of this beast is drawing near. The number [of the beast], according to the Apocalypse of John, is 666, of which already almost six hundred years have been completed.

Innocent III, *Quia major* (April 1213)

I N *Quia maior*, the encyclical calling the fifth Crusade, Pope Innocent III identifies Muhammad with the beast of the Apocalypse and (saying that almost 600 years of the 666 years allotted to the beast in Revelation have elapsed) predicts the ultimate defeat of the Saracens.[1] Like the author of the *Apocalypse of Pseudo-Methodius* in eighth-century Syria, or Paul Alvarus and the anonymous author of the *Prophetic Chronicle* in ninth-century Spain, Innocent makes sense of Islam by connecting it with the apocalyptic forces of evil described in the Bible. Like the earlier authors, he juggles numbers in order to find comforting prophecy of Islam's imminent demise.

Innocent and his thirteenth-century correligionaries were heirs to the Christian vision of history set forth in the works of Augustine, Isidore, and other authors. Like their predecessors, they used this schema of history to help explain the events of their own day: the Bible and exegesis were the filters through which they could best perceive the world around them, best explain new and unusual events. And the thirteenth century bore its share of events that needed explaining. From the losses to Saladin in 1187 (at Hattin and Jerusalem) to the loss of Acre in 1291, the Eastern crusading front was the scene of unmitigated disaster. Why should God will the Christians to lose to the Saracen "infidels"? The situation was further confused by the irruption onto the world scene of the Mongols: a fearful invader to be identified with the Apocalypse's barbaric peoples Gog and Magog? Or a God-sent ally ready to convert to Christianity and to help vanquish the Muslim enemy?

Just as authors in thirteenth-century Spain deployed the tools of anti-Muslim polemic to understand the victories of Christian kings over their Muslim adversaries and to justify their rule over their new Muslim subjects, other thirteenth-century writers used the same traditions to make sense of the much more confusing and disturbing events (from their standpoint) surrounding the thirteenth-century Crusades. The despair caused by Saladin's capture of Jerusalem gave way to new calls for crusade, inspiring in various authors hopes of crusader victory, of mass conversion of Muslims, or of an alliance with a Christianized Mongol empire. These hopes were regularly dashed as the news reached Europe of the failure of successive Crusades, culminating in the Mamluk capture of Acre in 1291 and the conversion to Islam of the prominent Mongol rulers. The mood at the end of the thirteenth century was decidedly bleak.

Innocent III and Lateran IV

Innocent III came to the papal throne in 1198 and was to make his mark as the most powerful and influential Pope of the Middle Ages. Innocent was anxious to recoup Christian losses in the East. Jerusalem had fallen to Saladin in 1187, and the third Crusade, led by Kings Richard the Lionhearted of England and Philip Augustus of France, was unable to wrest it back. Joachim of Fiore, the Calabrian abbot and mystic that Richard had stopped to visit on his way East, identified Muhammad and Saladin with key elements in the Apocalypse and predicted that Christendom would be devastated by an alliance between Saracen armies and Cathar heretics. This devastation would be followed by a final Christian victory to be won not by crusading armies but by humble, pious missionaries.[2] The fourth Crusade, undertaken in the sixth year of Innocent's pontificate, also went awry. The Venetians, who held its purse strings, led it to capture first the Dalmatian port of Zara, then the largest city in Christendom, Constantinople. Innocent, appalled, excommunicated the crusaders twice—but twice absolved them. The new Latin empire of Constantinople expanded the power and reach of the Catholic church, though it also created fresh problems.

Innocent's reaction (and that of many Christian Europeans) to this situation was mixed. On the one hand, euphoria and optimism fueled hopes that Muslim subjects could be converted and the frontiers of Christendom pushed ever further through fresh conquest. On the other hand, the new Muslim subject was feared: his sympathies might lie with Muslim rulers outside the Christian kingdom, and contact with Christians could lead to the latter's becoming Muslim, rather than the Muslim becoming Christian. Innocent was a lawyer and legislator, and one of his major concerns was to forge a coherent and effective policy toward non-Catholics: Greek and oriental Christians, heretics, Jews, and Muslims. In his letters to Muslim rulers, Innocent (like his predecessors) invited them to embrace the Christian faith.[3] Toward Islam, Innocent was relentless in urging a three-pronged attack: crusade against Muslim principalities, legal restrictions on Muslims living in Christian territories, and mission to Muslims everywhere.[4] This is illustrated in the canons of the fourth Lateran council (1215), which calls for a new Crusade and places legal restrictions on non-Christians.[5]

One of the major preoccupations seen in these legal restrictions is the protection of the physical and spiritual purity of Christians. The protected but subordinate role attributed to Muslims and Jews in the legal texts of Jaume I and Alfonso el Sabio reflected earlier canon law. The Christian had to be kept free from the polluting contact of the infidel subject: sexual contact was above all to be avoided. This same preoccupation is seen in the crusader kingdom of Jerusalem. The Council of Nablus (1120), for example, proclaimed harsh penalties for sexual relations between Christians and Muslims and forbade Muslims from dressing like "Franks."[6] The dress restrictions were meant to aid Christians in identifying Muslims and avoiding unnecessary contact with them. In the same spirit, the fourth Lateran council proclaimed:

> In some provinces a difference of dress distinguishes Jews or Saracens from Christians, but in certain others such confusion has developed that they are indistinguishable. Whence it sometimes happens that by mistake Christians unite with Jewish or Saracen women and Jews or Saracens with Christian women. Therefore, in order that so reprehensible and outrageous a mixing cannot for the future spread under the

cover of the excuse of an error of this kind, we decree that such people of either sex in every Christian province and at all times shall be distinguished from other people by the character of their dress in public, seeing that in addition one finds that this was enjoined upon them by Moses himself.[7]

In this canon the primary preoccupation, again, seems to be the purity and integrity of the Christian community. The prohibition of sexual relations across confessional lines is a given: such relations are "reprehensible and outrageous." The council orders that Saracens and Jews should wear distinctive clothing in order to prevent such relations, or rather in order to prevent Christians from using ignorance as an excuse for their sexual relations with non-Christians. There is no clear precedent for such legislation, though the Council of Nablus prohibited Saracens from "dressing like Franks," for the same reasons of sexual purity; the Paris Synod of 1208 ordered that Jews should wear a badge in the shape of a wheel.[8] The precedent invoked by the council itself is none other than Moses.

The fear of corruption is not merely sexual; it is also spiritual. Innocent and the council seek to protect Christians from blasphemous or sacrilegious words or acts.

On the days of Lamentation and on Passion Sunday they [Saracens and Jews] shall not appear in public at all, because some of them on such days, so we have heard, do not blush to parade in their most elegant clothes and are not afraid to ridicule the Christians, who exhibit a memorial of the most holy Passion and display signs of grief. What we most strictly forbid is for them to venture to burst out at all in derision of the Redeemer. And as we ought not to ignore the insulting of Him who atoned for our sins, we order secular rulers to inflict condign punishment upon those who so venture, to restrain them from daring at all to blaspheme Him who was crucified for us.[9]

The goal expressed is to safeguard the purity and sanctity of Christian worship: Christians should not have to endure mockery or blasphemy from infidels. To keep the rituals of Holy Week free from such contamination, the council does not hesitate to banish Muslims and Jews from public places during Holy Week, as does subsequent legislation in Spain.[10] Jews and Muslims are prohibited from holding positions of authority over Christians: "It would be too absurd for a blasphemer of Christ to be in a position of authority over Christians."[11] The council declared that converts to Christianity may not keep parts of their old rites, for they "upset by such mixing the decorum of the Christian religion." Such people must be "completely stopped by the heads of churches from observing their old rite."[12]

This legislation represents an elaboration of traditional ecclesiastical legislation limiting the place of Jews in Christian society: Jews must not have power over Christians, according to canon law. In particular, they should not own Christian slaves or hold public functions. These ideas are also extended to Muslims by subsequent legislation. The third Lateran council (1179) prohibited both Jews and Saracens from owning Christian slaves.[13] At a time when the Cathar heretics, denied any legitimate role in Christian society, are slaughtered by the troops of the Albigensian Crusade (and subsequently rooted out by papal inquisitors), Muslims, though theologically classed most often as heretics, are attributed the de facto social status of Jews. Apart from Alfonso X, no Christian legislator of the thirteenth century offers any justification for this association. But the two groups, Muslims and Jews, are increasingly lumped together in ecclesiastical and civil legislation. Muslims are granted a legitimate, subordinate role in the Christian polity, but one which will (along with that of the Jews) become more precarious in the later Middle Ages.

Muslims and Jews are also associated in their supposed hostility toward Christians. Both, for Lateran IV, are "blasphemers"; members of both groups parade around in garish clothes during Holy Week, mocking Christians who express their ritual grief at Christ's Passion. This hostility is specifically invoked to justify the prohibition from holding public office: a "blasphemer" must not be given any power over a Christian. A polemical view of Islam informs the decisions of Lateran IV: the council does not enumerate or distinguish between the different "blasphemies" of the Muslims or the Jews, but it affirms that they are sufficient to justify the exclusion of both from positions of authority.

At the same time as Lateran IV restricted the role of infidels within Christian society, it issued a detailed call for a new Crusade. Canon 71 of the council specifies how and from where the crusaders are to set forth, fixes tithes on ecclesiastical revenues to help pay for the endeavor, and prohibits merchants from selling strategic materials (arms, iron, or timber) to Muslims. Tournaments are forbidden, since they impede the business of the Crusade. Innocent apparently meant to lead the Crusade himself, though he died in 1216 before it set off.[14]

The Fifth Crusade, Prester John, and the Hopes of
a Christian Conquest of the Islamic World

The fifth Crusade was carried out under Innocent's successor, Honorius III, and chronicled by two of its clerical participants: Jacques de Vitry, bishop of Acre, and Oliver of Paderborn, canon of Köln.[15] Both authors describe the high hopes that the crusaders would conquer Egypt, hopes confirmed by the capture of Damietta, but later dashed when the crusaders, uncertain what move to make next and divided, foundered, fell into an Egyptian ambuscade, and in the subsequent negotiations for their freedom, lost all they had gained.

For Jacques de Vitry, as for such earlier writers on the Crusades as Guibert de Nogent and Adelphus,[16] the crusaders played a key role in the divine plan: the Christian reconquest and spiritual renewal of the Orient. The oriental church shone in antiquity, explains Jacques, spreading its rays to the West, but "from the time of the perfidious Muhammad until our own time" has been in decline, seduced and weakened by "the fallacious suasions of the pseudo-prophet and the dissolute wanton charms of lust." The remnant of the oriental church, surviving "like a lily among thorns," cries out like the poor widow of Lamentations: "behold, and see if there be any sorrow like unto my sorrow, which is done unto me, wherewith the Lord hath afflicted me in the day of his fierce anger" (Lam. 1:12). The (female) Orient needs, indeed tearfully begs for, the military intervention of the occidental male, submitting herself to him. In response to this cry for help, Jacques continues, many sons of the church are rushing to the aid of their mother, leaving behind wives, children, and lands in order to secure a place in heaven.[17] Jacques is confident they can succeed.

In Acre, before going to Egypt, Jacques describes how he often gazed tearfully westward across the sea, waiting with great desire for the advent of the "pilgrims"; "if we had four thousand armed men," he says, "with God's grace we would not find anyone able to resist us."[18] The Saracens are divided, he says, politically and religiously: some drink wine and eat pork in disobedience to Muhammad's law. In Acre, Saracens (many of them slaves of Christians) daily come to him for baptism, Jacques affirms; Christ and the Virgin appear to them in dreams ordering them to do so and warning them of the imminent victory of the Christians.[19] When the crusaders were besieging Damietta, Jacques says, Saracens crossed the Nile to receive baptism; more would have done so if not for the dangers of crossing the river.[20] Moreover, the Christians under Saracen rule were more numerous than the Saracens themselves: these Christians "daily wait, in tears, for aid and relief from the pilgrims."[21] When the pilgrims at last captured Damietta, Jacques saw this as a fulfillment of the Psalms: "He hath broken the gates of brass, and cut the bars of iron in sunder"; "He shall subdue the people under us, and the nations under our feet."[22]

Despite the euphoria, both Jacques and Oliver came to realize the vastness of the conquest they had launched. If Jacques had at first imagined a large but passive Eastern Christian population awaiting its Western savior, the crusaders soon began to hope for more tangible and active military allies, placing their hopes less in their own military successes than in the aid of mysterious Christians from afar. Both Jacques and Oliver tell of a book of ancient prophecy that was found in Damietta; its author, Jacques affirms, is "an astrologer whom the Saracens hold as a great prophet."[23] It foretold, among other things, the successes of the first Crusade, the recapture of Jerusalem by Saladin, and even the capture of Damietta by the current Crusade. This book then predicts the subsequent Christian conquest of all Egypt and Syria. Oliver adds that this book predicted that "a certain king of the Christian Nubians was to destroy the city of Mecca and cast out the scattered bones of Muhammad, the false prophet, and certain other things which have not yet come to pass. If they are brought about, however, they will lead to the exaltation of Christianity and the suppression of the Agarenes."[24]

The capture of Mecca and the scattering of Muhammad's bones (erroneously believed to lie in Mecca) will mark, it is hoped, the decisive victory of Christianity over Islam.[25] Jacques and Oliver refer to a second book in Arabic called the *Revelations of the Blessed Apostle Peter to his Disciple Clement, Written in One Volume* (Beati Petri apostoli a discipulo eius Clemente in uno volumine redacto). This book predicted the history of the council from its beginning to the advent of Antichrist and in particular the capture of Damietta by the Christians, which was to be followed by the arrival in Jerusalem of two kings, one from the East and one from the West, through whom, according to Jacques, "the Lord will exterminate the abominable law of impious men."[26] Oliver and Jacques pinned their hopes on conquests of Georgian Christians and of the mythic Eastern Christian king David, son of Prester John, whose reported exploits were based on those of Jenghiz Khan. Jacques lauds the exploits of "King David, a most powerful man and soldier skillful in arms, ingenious, always victorious in battle, whom the Lord brought forth in our days so that he could be a hammer against the pagans and the exterminator of the pestilential traditions and execrable law of Muhammad. It is he whom the people (*vulgus*) call Prester John."²⁷ Jacques inserts into the same letter a text, translated from Arabic, chronicling King David's conquests. The sources of these texts, he says, were Eastern merchants who gave them to the count of Tripoli; their testimony is confirmed by that of Frankish prisoners whom the Saracens had sold to King David and whom David had released.²⁸ Throughout the thirteenth century, indeed, the advances of the Mongols fueled Christian hopes that a universal victory of Christendom was imminent: missionaries were sent to the Mongols, letters exchanged proposing alliances. The Muslim world could be outflanked through the aid of this powerful new ally; Christianity would emerge victorious.

These apocalyptic scenarios also led to hopes that missions to Muslims could lead to widescale conversion. Two Christians, during the fifth Crusade, attempted to convert the Egyptian Sultan al-Kâmil: Oliver of Paderborn and Francis of Assisi.²⁹ In the concluding debacle to the Crusade, Oliver became one of the Sultan's many prisoners. After his release, in September 1221, he wrote a letter to al-Kâmil, praising him for his generosity and kindness, for acting more as a patron and benefactor than a captor.³⁰ He prays that the sultan may convert: "Kemel, may God augment the good that is in you and remove the veil of darkness from the eyes of your heart, so that you may recognize the plenitude of truth." He writes to convince the Sultan of the truth of Christianity and of the Christians' legitimate claim to dominion over Jerusalem.

Oliver notes that al-Kâmil already believes in Jesus' conception and virgin birth, his ascension into heaven, and his role as judge in the Final Judgment. Oliver seeks to convince him of the truth of the rest of Christian doctrine: the Trinity and the Incarnation, the divinity and death of Christ. You call us infidels, he says, because we worship the Trinity; you yourself unwittingly acknowledge it, he argues, when you recite David's Psalm praising God's name three times.³¹ Oliver has a fairly accurate knowledge of Islamic Christology, though he (like Alan of Lille) erroneously supposes that Muslims accept the text of the Old Testament, and that an argument based on the wording of a Psalm would carry weight with a Muslim opponent. He makes the same error later in his letter, when he defends the use of images in Christian churches by evoking Old Testament descriptions of images in the temples of Ezekiel and Solomon; the latter temple (he is referring either to the Dome of the Rock or al-Aqsa mosque) "your people frequent."³² In another letter addressed "to you, wise men and astrologers of Egypt," Oliver presents arguments "from scripture, which you cannot

negate," in favor of Christian doctrine—presenting in fact a standard collection of proof texts gleaned from the Old Testament and commonly used
in anti-Jewish tracts, but useless in arguing with Muslims.[33]

Oliver contrasts Muhammad's life and law with those of Christ. The
way to heaven, he asserts, is through chastity; your polygamy is the path to
hell. Your prophet taught you that those who were killed by their enemies
would go straight to a heaven replete with carnal delights; "our teacher"
taught us to love our enemy in hopes of attaining a purely spiritual reward
in the next life. "Your doctor," who was taught by a Jew and an apostate
monk named Sergius, ordered to conquer by the sword all who did not
recognize him.[34] Oliver proffers explanations meant to refute Muslim
objections to Christianity, defending the use of images and the doctrines
of the Trinity and the Incarnation. Oliver seems to think that little separates the Muslim from Christian truth and hopes to bring al-Kâmil to that
truth. The dream of conversion is alive and well it seems, even after the
debacle of the fifth Crusade; al-Kâmil, like a new Constantine, could be
the key to an evangelical victory for a Christian West apparently doomed to
military defeat.

Given the mixed fortunes of thirteenth-century military endeavors
against Muslims, it is no surprise that the mood of these authors swings
between euphoria and abjection. Rumors were rife that prominent infidel
rulers would convert to Christianity—or that they already had converted.
Similar things had been rumored about earlier Muslim military leaders
such as Kurbuqa or Saladin.[35] In the decades following the fifth Crusade,
similar reports circulated regarding numerous Muslim and Mongol rulers.
In 1245 the sultan of the Moroccan town of Sale announced his intention
to convert to Christianity. Innocent IV sent him an enthusiastic missive,
explaining how his realm would become a beacon of the true faith, a center
for the propagation of mission and crusade in Africa. The promised conversion never took place.[36] In 1245 Innocent addressed letters to the Mongol
khan (taken by his envoy, Franciscan John of Piano Carpini), inviting the
khan to embrace Christianity.[37] The Mongol sack of Baghdad in 1258 fueled
Christian hopes that these new allies would destroy Muslim hegemony and
usher in a new era of Christian peace.

King Louis IX, whose two Crusades affirmed his reputation for sanctity
in spite of (or perhaps because of) their military failure, hoped to convert
the Mongol khan. Jean de Joinville describes how Mongol envoys came to
Louis in Cyprus (in 1248) and proposed an alliance to help Louis conquer
Jerusalem; Louis responded by enthusiastically sending a group of Francis-

can friars, under the leadership of William of Rubruck, equipped with liturgical items, books, and a portable cloth chapel containing illustrations of key points of Christian doctrine. Through conversion, the Mongol khan, like a new Constantine, would reestablish Christian hegemony. The khan responded by demanding French submission and annual tribute: Louis, Joinville tells us, bitterly regretted that he had ever sent his envoys to the khan.[38] In 1274 envoys from the Mongol il-Khan Abaga came to the council of Lyons to negotiate an alliance with the West. The envoys accepted baptism, to the great euphoria of those present; it was said that the khan himself subsequently became Christian—this subsequently proved to be false.[39] In the year 1300, rumors spread that Jerusalem had indeed been taken by the Mongols and given back to the Christians.[40]

It was probably such false hopes that led Louis IX into the fatal debacle of his second Crusade, against Tunis. In 1269 Dominican Ramon Martí came to Paris; preparations were under way for a fresh Crusade involving both Louis and Jaume I of Aragon. Martí then was sent to Tunis (probably from November 1269 to March 1270) where he attempted to convert the Tunisian emir al-Mustansir, who had at one point, it seems, suggested that he might be willing to convert.[41] Louis set out in the spring of 1270 and landed near Tunis, apparently with the hopes of securing the conversion and allegiance of al-Mustansir. He soon found out that the promise of conversion was not to be kept, and he laid siege to the city, only to die soon after.[42]

William of Tripoli's *Notitia De Machometo* (1271) and the Anonymous *De Statu Saracenorum*

In 1270, in the aftermath of Louis IX's crusade to Tunis, several small contingents of crusaders sailed on to Acre; accompanying them was Tedaldo Visconti, Archdeacon of Liège, who upon his return to Rome in 1271 was elected Pope Gregory X. While in the East, Tedaldo met William, friar at the Dominican convent of Tripoli, who wrote for the future Pope a treatise, *Notitia de Machometo*, describing the life of Muhammad, the rise of Islam, the contents of the Koran, and the main rituals of Islam. He ridicules the Koran as a hodgepodge, calling it a little black crow dressed up in absurd multicolored feathers; it permits its followers to do whatever they want.[43] William provides a detailed description of Muslim doctrine and ritual, some of which he presents in a positive light.

In the concluding section of his *Notitia de Machometo,* William enjoins Christian theologians, "disputers," to zealously fight these errors, endorsing the Dominican missionary strategy. He concludes with a comforting prophecy of Christian ascendancy:

> It is written in their [the Saracens'] laws that the Romans or Latins shall be defeated by them, but that shortly thereafter they themselves will be defeated and destroyed; no one denies this. Thus they all predict, expect, and believe, that the age *[status]* of the Saracens must quickly end, while that of the Christians will last until the end of the world, which is coming—until the end of 7000 years, of which (according to them) much more than 6000 have already passed. Moreover, they all predict, prophesy, and believe that the Saracens will be divided into three parts: the first part will flee to the Christians, the second part will perish by the sword and the third part will perish in the desert. Amen.[44]

The optimism is even more marked in the *De statu Saracenorum* (1273), traditionally attributed to William of Tripoli, but which now appears to be an anonymous compilation that used William's *Notitia de Machometo* as its principal source.[45] This text argues that Islam is so close to Christianity that the conversion of Muslims by peaceful means should be an easy task. In order to prove this, the anonymous author presents a largely accurate (through obviously partial) description of Islamic history, doctrine, and ritual. Moreover, he makes a series of predictions of Islam's imminent demise, claiming that Muhammad himself had predicted the end of Islam when the caliphate was destroyed (which, the author says, it has recently been, in the Mongol sack of Baghdad).[46] He emphasizes similarities between Christian and Muslim beliefs on the virgin birth of Jesus, and the Koran's praise of Jesus, the Gospels, and Christians. These things, he says, "which the Saracens believe in their heart to be true" show that they "are close to the Christian faith and close to the way of salvation."[47] While he recognizes the ways in which Muslim belief differs from Christian belief, he maintains that the way to bring them into the Christian fold is through preaching, not war.

De statu begins with a history of the Saracens from Muhammad to the present day, following William of Tripoli's *Notitia de Machometo* on the rise of Islam, but going into much greater detail. William is aware of the polemical lives of Muhammad, which he reworks to present both Muhammad and the monk Bahira in a more positive light; Bahira "a simple Christian religious, of austere life,"[48] recognizes (according to *De statu Sarraceno-*

rum) in "Machometus" the fulfillment of the prediction of Genesis 16, the wild man whose hand will be against all.⁴⁹ The monk takes the young Machometus under his wing and teaches him to pray devoutly to Jesus, son of the Virgin Mary.⁵⁰ The monk's predictions are borne out by the growing power of Machometus, who becomes master of the "land of the Arabs," stretching from Carthage to Aleppo. Yet the *De statu* does not present his ascendancy in a negative light; he is still under the calming influence of the holy Bahira.⁵¹ So much so, in fact, that Machometus's companions, jealous of the influence the monk has over him, cut Bahira's throat with Machometus's sword one night after a drunken debauch; the next morning they convince Machometus that he himself killed the monk in a drunken rage. Horrified, he curses wine and prohibits it to his followers. Without the holy monk to check their malice, Machometus's followers go wild: "they run about like brigands, plunder like robbers, afflict, perturb and devastate provinces and kingdoms until the death of Machometus himself."⁵²

When the anonymous author of *De statu* turns to the Muslim conquests after Muhammad's death, however, he uses (directly or indirectly) Muslim sources and presents the conquest in a largely positive light.⁵³ He attributes the Christians' loss of Egypt to fighting between Copts and Greeks and emphasizes the generous and fair terms of submission imposed by the Muslims. (He correctly places the conquest of Egypt after the death of Muhammad, even though he had earlier said that Machometus had conquered all of North Africa as far west as Carthage.) The author describes the Muslim conquest of Syria in much the same terms: while he laments the fact that many Christians converted to Islam, he emphasizes the fairness, piety, and generosity of the conquerors.

This is most dramatically seen in *De statu*'s description of the conquest of Jerusalem by 'Umar. 'Umar comes to Sophronios, the patriarch of Jerusalem, and asks to be shown a proper place to pray to God and give thanks for his granting victory to the Muslims. Sophronios takes him to the Church of the Holy Sepulcher, but 'Umar responds that he does not want to pray there. Sophronios then shows him the temple built by Constantine, but 'Umar will not pray there either; instead, he "chose a simple place near the oratory of the Christians and prayed there." Once he completed his prayer, he explains to the patriarch why he had not wanted to pray in the Christian holy places:

If I had prayed there, the Christians would have lost those places, which would have been made oratories of my people. I did not want this to happen, but preferred that the Saracens pray in the place where I prayed. I do not want the Saracens to gather and pray to the detriment of the Christians, nor do I want one group to pray after another in the same place, for there would be too many people gathered there. I henceforth confer to this holy city this liberty, that the Saracens may not build their mosque and oratory anywhere except in the place which you assign to them."[54]

'Umar here represents Muslim tolerance of and respect for Christianity; if the Muslims are at times foes of the Christians, they are reasonable, generous, God-fearing foes.

In this way, De statu describes the Muslims' march across North Africa and into Europe, and their fights against Christian rulers in Spain, Gaul, and Italy. In these descriptions, the author seems to favor neither the Muslims nor the Christians. In the one case where he criticizes a ruler for treachery, it is the emperor Frederick II, whom he lambasts for tricking the Muslims of Sicily into accepting virtual incarceration in Lucera.[55] This calm, even laudatory description of Muslim conquest would be unsettling to the Christian reader, were it not for frequent reiteration of predictions of the imminent demise of Islam. The author repeats the prophesies found in William's Notitia, insisting that they come from Muhammad himself.[56]

After Machometus, indeed, the Arabs had forty-two leaders, who are called Caliphs (that is, successors of Machometus). Know (as the scribes and wise men of the gentiles [gentes] have prophesied) that the reign and dominion of his people after the aforesaid number of forty-two will undoubtedly be broken and finished; indeed when the forty-third arose, many thought that their prophet had lied. But since the Tartars, under the rule of their prince Hulaon [i.e., Hülägü], captured Baghdad and its Caliph (who was the forty-third) and murdered him with all his servants and relatives of the lineage of Machometus, so that no one of his lineage remained, who could succeed Machometus and be called Caliph. Thus the reign, dominion, and empire of the line of Machometus was transferred from the hand of the Arab to the hands of the Turks.[57]

The author imagines that the caliph is necessarily a direct descendant of Muhammad; the massacre by Tartars of the last remnant of his line spells the end of the caliphate, and, by extension, of Muslim might.

The author is aware that the Fatimids of Cairo also claimed the title of caliph and that they claimed to be the direct descendants of Muhammad; he notes that Saladin ended their reign. Moreover, Arab rule in the East ended once and for all: in 1250 Baybars leads a plot to murder Sultan Tu-ran-Shah, "the last king, son of kings and sultans, to descend from the lineage of the Arabs through the line of the famous Sultan Saladin"; his usurper Malik al-Mu'azzam was "the first king of the lineage of the Turks."[58] The author of *De statu* describes the violence and intrigues of the Mamluk sultans, in particular Baybars, whose cruelty he compares to that of Nero and Herod. "This Herod," he says "lest anyone of the race *[genere]* of Arabs should rise up who could be called king or sultan, extir-pated the whole royal seed, that is to say the fourteen sons that Saladin had left to be kings when he died; he murdering and suffocating them in any way he could." Baybars delights in the murder of his subjects, boasts that he is greater than Muhammad, and claims he can take on the kings of the French, English, Romans, Greeks, and Tartars, all at once.[59]

But the oppression of the Turk will not last long, the author assures his readers:

> This very year, as the wise astrologers and necromancers of the Saracens say, [Baybars] will die, and after him will arise another Turk, who will die within a year in his own dominions, and after these things should arise the dominion of Christ and the standard of the cross will be raised and borne through all Syria up to Caesarea of Cappadocia, and there will be a great commotion on earth. The true knower of these things is God.[60]

The author then reiterates his earlier predictions of the demise of the Sara-cens based on the death of the forty-third caliph at the hands of the Tartars.

This assertion of a swift and inevitable victory of Christianity over Is-lam makes his positive presentation of Islam and Muslims less problematic. There are good rulers on both sides, such as 'Umar and Saint Louis, and there are bad rulers, such as Frederick II and Baybars. Yet Muslim piety, and Muslim reverence for Christ and Mary, can be presented in an un-apologetically positive light. It is indeed only after repeated assertions that the Saracen faith is near extinction that *De statu* goes into describing it. The author says that Machometus's companions compiled the Koran fif-teen years after his death and that it does not reflect what Muhammad really taught; rather, he says, it is a mixture of Muhammad's teaching and garbled passages of Bible, philosophy, and history. Following William of Tripoli, he compares it to a small black crow adorned with fancy colored feathers, a strange and unseemly composite fit only to be laughed at.

Yet when he describes the contents of the Koran, in the following chapters of his tract, he emphasizes the common points between Christian and Muslim doctrine. He is particularly interested in the Koran's praise of Christ and the Virgin Mary; much more frequent, he says, than any praise of Machometus. This shows, he says, that Saracens in their hearts believe in the goodness of Jesus Christ, his doctrine and his Gospels, his Virgin mother, and that they are "close to the way of salvation." The author goes on to describe what he sees as the main errors in their doctrine: the belief in carnal delights in heaven and the failure to believe in the Trinity, the Incarnation, and the divinity of Christ. Yet bringing the Saracens to the truth should not prove difficult: "By virtue of the simple word of God, without philosophical arguments or military weapons, they ask for baptism of Christ and cross over into the God's sheep pen. This was said and written by one who through God has already baptized a good thousand. Amen."[61] The anonymous author claims that converting Saracens to Christianity is easy and that he himself has baptized "a good thousand." William of Tripoli concluded his *Notitia de Machometo* with dire semiapocalyptic predictions of the demise of Islam largely through military conquest: a third of the Saracens will perish by the sword, a third will perish in the desert, and a third will flee to Christianity. The anonymous author of *De statu* indeed includes this same prediction; yet he concludes his tract with the assertion that preaching the word of God will suffice to bring Saracens to the Christian truth, explicitly rejecting the twin strategies of military crusade and philosophical argument.

Perhaps even more disconcerting is an account given by pilgrim Burchard of Mount Zion, who wrote a *Description of the Holy Land* in 1283. Burchard, in the midst of describing a church devoted to Saint John the Baptist, explains that the Saracens revere John as a holy prophet. They also, he continues, believe that Jesus, born of the Virgin Mary, is the word of God but not God, "and they say that Machomet was the messenger of God and was sent by God *only to them;* I read this in the Alchoran, which is their book."[62] The emphasis here is on the fundamental compatibility of Christian and Muslim doctrine. Burchard takes the idea that Muhammad was sent specially to the Arabs (which is indeed from the Koran[63]) and transforms it into a Muslim denial of the universality of Islam: the Saracens, he implies, have a revealed religion peculiar to themselves, one for which they do not claim superiority. Burchard reinforces this impression through another passage of his *Description,* in which he presents the various nations of the Holy Land. Here the Saracens are one group among many: Latins, Greeks, Syrians, Armenians, and so on, no better or worse than the others; indeed, the Latins are the ones who are the most wicked, according to Burchard.[64] He shares with William of Tripoli and the author of *De statu Sarracenorum* the contempt of armed struggle as an evangelical tool. But whereas *De statu* sees an exhausted Islam about to fall into the arms of Christianity, Burchard sees one sect among many, neither better or worse than most of its neighbors, but one unlikely to be drawn to the cult of the violent and rapacious Latins.

Fidentius of Padua

The conquests of Baybars and his successors continued, and not all Latin observers were as dispassionate as Burchard or as optimistic as the author of *De statu.* For some, Muslims could not be converted through preaching but could only be combated through renewed crusade. Of the many pro-crusade tracts from this period, none is more impassioned than Fidentius of Padua's *Book on the Recovery of the Holy Land* (Liber de recuperatione terrae sanctae), composed between 1266 and 1291.[65] The work is a polemical tract arguing for necessity and urgency of a new crusade. Fidentius begins by tracing the history of the various peoples that have controlled the Holy Land and stressing that it should by rights belong to the Christians. He, like Jacques de Vitry, needs to denigrate the Saracens enough to show that crusade is the only viable option. Most of his tract (the final seventy-two of his ninety-four chapters) is dedicated to strategy: how to plan, execute, and secure the capture of the Holy Land.

While the anonymous author of *De statu* used history of the Holy Land, divine history, and prophecy to argue that Saracens were near to Christianity and ready to convert, Fidentius will use the same tools to argue that they are inimical to Christianity and must be attacked. Though he does not mention by name those against whom he is arguing, he complains bitterly of the Christians who—ignoring threats of excommunication—make the pilgrimage to Muslim-occupied Jerusalem, giving money to the Saracens.

There are even some Christians, he says, who "attracted by love of wealth and carnal voluptuousness, abandon the cult of Christianity and become Saracens, and then fight armed against Christians."[66]

Fidentius emphasizes the importance of the Holy Land in Judeo-Christian history, stressing the parallels between God's erstwhile chosen people, the Jews, and his new chosen people, the Christians. God promises a land of milk and honey to the Jews in exile and grants it to the followers of Abraham and Moses; yet time and again he takes it away from the Jews on account of their sins, using pagans to chastize them: Assyrians, Babylonians, Romans. Just so, God grants the promised land to his Christian faithful, but they, like the Jews of old, lose it on account of their sins. The *Liber recuperationis* is liberally spiced with passages from the Hebrew Prophets, predicting (for Fidentius) the Christian's loss of Jerusalem through their sins and their eventual (and inevitable) reconquest of it.

This is not to say that Fidentius thinks Jerusalem can be stormed by humble, pious prayers. He lists seven reasons the Christians lost Jerusalem: they are, in addition to sin, the Christians' ethnic diversity, effeminacy, indiscretion, in-fighting, defection, and dereliction. Yet, for Fidentius, all these causes fit under the rubric of sin: they all show a failure to put the interests of God above those of greed and ambition. The fact that the Saracens possess the holy places in which Christ was born, lived, and died, is a mark of shame for all Christians.

In order to prove that this is indeed shameful, and that crusade is the only possible solution, he needs to paint the Saracens in the worst possible light. He does this by giving first a brief vituperative biography of "Machometus," whom he describes as "not only . . . most false and lying, but a most atrocious plunderer, the worst spiller of human blood, and even most stinking in the sin of lust."[67] Here he repeats many of the vicious legends about Muhammad: Machometus was schooled in astrology and magic, received a religious education from the Nestorian monk Sergius, passed off his epileptic fits as visits from Gabriel. He describes the episode of Zayd and Zaynab in hostile terms and repeats Petrus Alfonsi's story of the promised and failed resurrection of Machometus.[68] Fidentius, more concerned with shock effect than veracity, finds these hostile legends useful.

If "Machomet was the father and beginning of [the Saracens'] malice," his current followers are also invariably hostile. Fidentius proffers a series of chapters on the Saracens' faults: their infidelity, lechery, cruelty, greed, cunning, stupidity, and instability. Clearly, these are not people with whom one negotiates, or to whom one sends missionary preachers; these are people whom one can only fight. In his description of "the infidelity of the Saracens," Fidentius gives a largely accurate (if extremely hostile) description of the differences between Muslim and Christian beliefs about Jesus and the Trinity. He, like William of Tripoli and the author of *De statu,* cites the Koran, in a fairly faithful Latin translation, to illustrate his points.[69] But for *De statu* the similarities were more important than the differences: they showed that the Saracens "believed in their hearts."[70] For Fidentius, these differences are crucial and irreparable: he emphasizes their hostility to Christian doctrine and to Christian ritual objects:

> These very same Saracens greatly abhor images, and they destroy pictures, and trample them, and fling them into filthy places. Indeed I heard that recently, after they captured the city of Tripoli, the Saracens dragged a crucifix on the tail of an ass, and threw all the foul things they could on the images. When indeed the Sultan Bendocar had taken the city and returned toward Damascus after his victory, I went to his army so that I might help out the captive [Christians]. And as I walking amongst the Army some Saracens called me and asked "why do you Christians adore pictures and images?" I responded to them "You are wrong, for Christians do not adore pictures or images, but they adore and venerate the saints who are in heaven, whom the pictures represent." And they were silent, not knowing what more to say.[71]

He then claims that Saracens beat their Christian prisoners so much, and promise them so many things, that they become Saracens and spit on crucifixes and icons. As in the chronicles and *Chansons* of the first Crusade, the alleged attacks on images of Christ symbolized the deep and implacable enmity of the Saracens and were meant to move the reader to anger and vengeance.[72]

For the reader who is left unconvinced, Fidentius argues that hostility to the Christian faith is not all that makes the Saracens implacable enemies. He claims that they are lecherous "from the soles of their feet to the tops of their heads"; their sodomy alone, he says, would be justification enough for Christians to fight them. He says they are cruel, greedy, crafty, and stupid. He also argues that they are untrustworthy, citing examples where various Muslim rulers, he claims, broke truces with Christians; war, rather than negotiation, is the answer, for Fidentius.

Finally, Fidentius wants to assure his reader that success is possible; like the author of *De statu Sarracenorum,* he indulges in apocalyptic predictions that promise the Holy Land to Christians. Ironically, while *De statu* used these predictions to prove that a crusade was not necessary, for Fidentius they prove that it *is* necessary. After a disclaimer that he will not prophesy since he is neither a prophet nor the son of a prophet, Fidentius tells of a book called the *Liber Clementis:* a book of prophecy containing discussions between Jesus and Peter, written in Greek, translated into Arabic, and brought to Fidentius by a Syrian monk.[73] Fidentius cites a passage from this book that, he says, predicted the fall of Antioch to the Mamluks and the suffering that this would cause the Christians. This same book, Fidentius says, contains the following prophecy of Christian victory:

> "There will come," said Christ, "a lion cub, and he will liberate the Christian people from the hands of the sons of the wolf, and he will overcome them and force their remnant into the desert from which they came, and the Christians will subjugate the sons of the wolf for forty times beyond that which the sons of the wolf subjugated the Christians.[74]

The "sons of the wolf" are of course the Saracens. The prophecy goes on to say that a succession of forty Christian kings will rule in peace and tranquility, after which Christian sins will bring on the reign of Antichrist. This new prediction fits the pattern Fidentius outlined at the outset of the *Liber recuperationis:* an alternation between peaceful rule by God's people and upheaval caused by the sins of his people. To make these parallels clearer, Fidentius gives a series of passages from the Old and New Testaments that also prophesy, he claims, God's plan to give the Holy Land back to the crusaders.

THESE THIRTEENTH-CENTURY AUTHORS, like those of previous centuries, attempted to place the tumultuous events around them into God's plan. As always, one of the most difficult things to explain was the complex net of relations between God, his chosen people, and his enemies. What was one to think of Muslims? (Or Mongols, heretics, or Jews?) How to place them in the divinely ordained march of history? Various twelfth- and thirteenth-century writers dreamed that rationalistic polemics could convert Saracens to Christianity. A sense that the days of the end were drawing near helped fuel the hopes for conversion and gave a sense of urgency for the calls to crusade: Innocent III and Saint Francis, in the early part of the century, chided Christians to take up the cross and to go on missions to Muslim lands. Over the course of the century, five major Crusades are undertaken, and scores of Franciscan and Dominican missionaries, many of them trained in Arabic, ventured to Muslim lands in Spain, North Africa, and the Levant. Yet by the end of the century these hopes were dashed. Crusade after Crusade failed, and the missionaries found that their exemplar piety and theological subtlety were not able to convince many Muslims to convert. In 1291 the Mamluk sultan al-Ashraf Khalīl took Acre, the last crusader outpost on the mainland, and in 1295 the Mongol Il-Khanid khan Ghazan converted to Islam, ending the (rather unrealistic) Christian hopes that he would convert to Christianity.

By the end of the thirteenth century and in the following centuries, as the Ottomans obtained hegemony over Anatolia and pushed their way into Europe, few Europeans were optimistic about Christian chances to defeat Islam or to wrest the Holy Land from Muslim control; the calls to crusade were in general for the defense against Ottoman advances into Europe. In this atmosphere, it is the hostile view of Islam of people like Fidentius of Padua that is to dominate European discourse on Islam, rather than the positive portrayal of *De statu Sarracenorum* or of Burchard of Mount Sion. The "beast" whose imminent demise Innocent III had predicted showed few signs of weakness or defeat; thirteenth-century Muslims proved impervious not only to Christian arms (everywhere but in Spain) but also to Christian missionaries.

Chapter 9

༺⟡༻

FRANCISCAN MISSIONARIES SEEKING
THE MARTYR'S PALM

The Lord says: "Behold, I am sending you as sheep in the midst of wolves. There-fore, be prudent as serpents and simple as doves" [Matt. 10:16]. Therefore, any brother who, by divine inspiration, desires to go among the Saracens and other nonbelievers should go with the permission of his minister and servant. And the minister should give [these brothers] permission and not oppose them, if he shall see that they are fit to be sent.

—The *Regula non bullata*, or first rule of the Franciscan order (1221)

FRANCIS OF ASSISI (1182–1226), founder of the Friars Minor, or Fran-ciscans, saw mission to infidels, and particularly to Muslims, as an inte-gral part of the renovation of Christendom, as a return to the *vita apos-tolica,* the apostolic life. By preaching to the infidel, and by accepting mar-tyrdom from him if necessary, the Franciscan friar could reenact the drama of the apostles and re-create the religious fervor of a bygone age. The friars who preached to Muslims were indeed informed by a hostile view of Islam: they often insulted the prophet Muhammad (as had the Cordovan martyrs of the ninth century) in order to obtain the palm of martyrdom. But the texts that describe these missionary martyrs have little to say about Islam, preferring to fall back on stereotypical hagiographical presentations of evil persecutors who cruelly kill God's saints. It is in the second half of the thir-teenth century, with the work of William of Rubruck and Roger of Bacon, that some Franciscans begin to develop a new strategy of mission in which rational argumentation against Islam and other religions is seen as the key to conversion of the infidel.

The Franciscan missionary activity began with Francis himself. Jacques de Vitry, chronicling the events of the fifth Crusade in Egypt, describes how

Francis "came into our army, burning with the zeal of faith, and was not afraid to cross over to the enemy army. There he preached the word of God to the Saracens but accomplished little."[1] Jacques was ambivalent about Francis and his Friars Minor: he admired their ascesis and devotion to the apostolic life, but worried about the dangers that awaited the young and inexperienced friars sent out to wander the world.[2] Jacques elaborates on Francis's mission in his *Historia occidentalis,* affirming that the mere presence of the saint transformed the Egyptian sultan from a ferocious beast into a gentle listener; he listened to Francis for days. Finally, afraid that Francis would succeed in converting his subjects, the sultan had him escorted with honor to the crusader camp, asking him, "Pray for me, that God might deign to reveal to me the law and the faith that most appeal to him." Jacques affirms that Saracens are ready everywhere to listen to the Word of God, though that they chase off the friars as soon as they insult Muhammad.[3]

Francis and his friars came to symbolize the apostolic life (*vita apostolica*) for Christians of the thirteenth century. Wandering barefoot from town to town, begging for their daily sustenance, living in community, preaching to the poor and the marginal, Francis and his followers sought in everything to follow the apostles: so much so that debates over (for example) whether the apostles had carried coin purses could rage hot; whatever the apostles had done, it seemed, the Franciscans ought to do. The apostles had been first and foremost missionaries, spreaders of the Word to infidels, and most of them had suffered martyrdom as a result of their mission. This was not lost on Francis and his followers. Francis's disciple and biographer, Thomas of Celano, says that Francis "longed to attain the height of perfection," in other words, that he was "burning intensely with the desire for holy martyrdom." For this reason he embarked in 1212 for the Holy Land, "to preach the Christian faith and penance to the Saracens and infidels."[4] Kept from reaching his goal by shipwreck, he later set out for Morocco in hopes of winning a martyr's crown there. But he fell ill in Spain and renounced the plan. Finally, in the summer of 1219, Francis sailed to Egypt, joining the forces of the fifth Crusade at Damietta in order to win the crown of martyrdom. In Thomas's version of the story, Francis was captured and beaten by the Egyptian soldiers, but the sultan (al-Kâmil) treated him kindly and listened to Francis as he defended Christianity against those who insulted it. The sultan tried to win Francis over with rich gifts, but when he saw that Francis despised them "as so much dung," he was filled with admiration for him. This admiration prevents the sultan from granting Francis the crown of martyrdom, but Thomas attributes to the sultan no particular admiration for Christianity, much less any desire to convert.[5]

Thomas commends Francis for having thrice tried (though thrice failed) to obtain the crown of martyrdom: clearly, for Thomas (and, it seems, for Francis as well), the goal of mission is as much to produce martyrs as it is to produce converts. When Francis received the news that five Franciscan missionaries had been martyred in Marrakesh in 1220, he responded, "Now I can truly say that I have five brothers!"[6] Thomas explains God's refusal to grant Francis martyrdom by saying that he had something greater in store for him, "a singular grace"—apparently referring to the stigmata.[7] Subsequently, in describing the illness that eventually kills Francis, he says that the saint described the pain as worse than any martyrdom. So, Thomas concludes, Francis really *did* suffer martyrdom, if in a somewhat unconventional way.[8] In order to present Francis as a model of the apostolic life, Thomas must find excuses for the fact that Francis did not suffer the death of an apostle—martyrdom.

The story of the first Franciscan martyrs, which is said to have inspired the conversion of Anthony of Padua, is recorded (and no doubt embellished) in several fourteenth-century Franciscan chronicles and hagiographical texts.[9] The five friars, disguised as laymen, went first to Seville (which was still Muslim); there they put on their Franciscan habits and "zealous in spirit, went to the principal mosque [*myzquitam*], which is their [the Saracens'] temple. . . . When they wished to enter, the Saracens, indignant, prevented them—with shouts, pushing and beating—from entering the mosque. For their law (*institutio*) is this: that no Christian, nor anyone else of a [non-Muslim] sect, is permitted to enter their temple." The Muslims took the friars to the "king" of Seville, whom the friars urged to convert, saying "many bad things about Muhammad and his damnable law." The king had them imprisoned in a tower, from which they continued to preach, "damning Muhammad and his followers to eternal punishment." (The chronicles do not say in which language the friars preached to the Saracens.) The king put them in the basement of the tower, then banished them to Marrakesh, where they were received by the infante Don Pedro, brother of the Portuguese king Afonso II, who was apparently serving as a mercenary for the Almohad caliph Abû Ya'qub Yûsuf al-Mustansir (1213–24). There thc friars "fervently preached to the Saracens whenever they saw them," until the "king" (*rex miramolinus,* i.e., the caliph) came across one of them preaching. Astonished that he continued preaching in his presence, the king judged that he was crazy and banished the friars, asking Don Pedro to have them escorted back to Christendom. But the friars, not so easily dissuaded from the prize of martyrdom, escaped at Ceuta and made their way back to Marrakesh, where they began preaching in a public square (*in foro*). The king had them imprisoned, without food, for twenty days, according to the hagiographical texts; when, at the urging of Christians of Marrakesh, they were freed, all were astonished to see that they had survived without food for so long. Once free, they began once again to preach, but the local Christians, fearful of the consequences, had them again taken away from Marrakesh; yet they worked their way back again, and Friar Beraldus miraculously produced a spring for the thirsty armies of Don Pedro and the *rex miramolinus* (who were together quelling a rebellion against the king). The king, furious at this miracle, had the friars arrested and brought before him; when they persisted in insulting Muhammad, he subjected them to a series of tortures, which the chronicles describe in lurid detail. He offered them the standard enticements (women, money, and worldly honors) if they would convert to Islam; when they refused, he beheaded them with his own sword. The king's arm shriveled to a gnarled stump. Don Pedro later took their bodies to Portugal (to the monastery of Sancta Cruz in Coimbra), where they duly performed miracles.

These texts reproduce the standard topoi of hagiography: the choice between worldly wealth and honors and the much more valuable crown of martyrdom, the blindness and cruelty of the "infidel" persecutor (who is duly punished by God), the patience and serenity with which the saints undergo torture and execution, the miracles, and so on. This is the same image found in the passion narratives of seventh-century Syrian martyrs, in the apologies of Eulogius and Alvarus, or in Hrotsvitha of Gandersheim's passion of Pelagius. These texts, like other contemporary Franciscan texts, have little to say about Islam, contenting themselves with a schematic, stereotypical portrayal of infidel rulers who persecute Christians.[10] Yet after accounting for hagiographical excess, there is no reason to doubt the veracity of the narrative. The five friars, close associates of Francis, wished to lead their apostolic life to its logical, glorious conclusion: martyrdom at the hands of the infidel. It took them quite an effort to obtain it. Despite repeated affronts to Muslim law (entering a mosque, preaching apostasy, insulting the Prophet and the Koran), the Almohad authorities of Seville and Marrakesh respond mildly: imprisonment, banishment. Only after repeated and deliberate provocation does the caliph finally give them what they are looking for, the crown of martyrdom. Even the hagiographical texts hint that the friars provoked the hostility of the Christian community in Marrakesh, and their relationship with Don Pedro of Portugal is ambivalent: he welcomes them but at one point keeps them under lock and key to prevent them from going out and preaching in public; in the end, it is he who takes their relics to Portugal.

The news of the five friars' deaths provoked the admiration of Francis himself and the conversion to the order of Anthony of Padua. Mission to the Saracens, for the Franciscans, was part of the *vita apostolica,* serving to bring the friars to glorious martyrdom and, incidentally, to convert unbelievers. Such mission is encouraged by the earliest extant version (1221) of the *Rule of the Friars Minor,* the so-called *Regula non bullata* (or *Regula prima*).[11] This rule is more than a simple legal document; "it is a description of a concrete way of living the Gospel"—in other words, a sort of handbook to living the apostolic life.[12] The rule enjoins mission, characteristically, with the very words Jesus (according to the Gospel of Matthew) sent the apostles to preach the word: "Behold, I send you forth as sheep in the midst of wolves: be ye therefore wise as serpents, and harmless as doves."[13] Brothers who are inspired to go on mission should seek the permission of their superiors, who in turn should not refuse them unless they are unfit to go. The rule specifies that there are two ways to live among the Saracens: either humbly, avoiding dispute and confessing to be Christians, or boldly preaching the Word in hopes of converting them. To the latter, the rule enjoins steadfastness and courage: a string of Gospel citations reminds them not to fear martyrdom.[14] In 1225 Pope Honorius III (Innocent's successor) authorized the Dominican and Franciscan missions in North Africa.[15] And Franciscans were heeding these injunctions: following the martyrs of Marrakesh in 1220 (just a year after Francis's mission to al-Kâmil), six friars were martyred in Ceuta in 1227, two in Valencia in 1228, five in Marrakesh in 1232, and Agnellus, the Bishop of Fez, in 1246; ten Franciscans were martyred in the Near East between 1265 and 1269; seven in Tripoli in 1289.[16] These martyrs no doubt inspired ambivalence: the 1220 martyrs were not canonized until 1481, when they became useful for Crusade propaganda against the Turk.[17]

Yet not all Franciscans who went to Muslim lands were in search of the martyr's palm. The *Regula non bullata* distinguished between two authorized ways of living among infidels: either humbly, avoiding dispute and confessing to be Christians, or boldly preaching the Word. The martyrs of 1220 provoked the hostility of local Christians (just as those of Córdoba had done in the ninth century). On 17 March 1226 Honorius III issued a bull that sheds light on those Franciscans who wished to live "humbly, avoiding dispute."[18] The friars are enjoined to think not only of the conversion of the infidels but also of the needs of the Christians living in Morocco. To better serve their needs, the friars should be unobtrusive, not only avoiding provoking the Muslims but also abandoning their Franciscan habit and letting their beards and hair grow, the better to circulate unnoticed and cater to the spiritual needs of the Christian community. They could even accept cash donations if circumstances did not allow begging for food. Similarly, the minister of the Franciscans and prior of the Dominicans of Tunis wrote to Pope Gregory IX asking a series of specific questions regarding confession and penance for the Christians of Tunis; in 1234, Gregory had Raymond of Penyafort respond in detail with a long missive.[19] Gregory IX himself in 1233 sent letters to three Muslim rulers, urging them to convert;[20] chronicler Matthew Paris says that letters sent by missionary preachers to Gregory exposed the "false doctrine" of Muhammad to the Christian world.[21] These Franciscans (and Dominicans) are a discreet presence in the cities of North Africa and the Near East, catering to the spiritual needs of Catholic merchants, mercenaries, adventurers, and captives. The strident provocation of those in search of martyrdom can only make their work more difficult.

This did not prevent other Franciscans from seeking martyrdom. The story of the martyrs of Ceuta (October 1227) reads very much like those of Marrakesh.[22] Friar Daniel and his companions set off first for Spain; in Tarragona they board a ship for Ceuta, where they stay in the Christian merchants' quarter, outside the city. After a night of fasting and prayer, they steal into the city and begin preaching, in Italian, to the (bemused? scandalized?) residents. They are brought before the "king" who, judging them crazy, has them imprisoned. After a week in prison, they appear again before the king, who has procured the services of a translator. They lambast Muhammad and his law and invite the king to convert; he sends them to the judge (*qâdî*), who sentences them to death. It is Don Pedro, once again, who brings their bodies to Portugal. In Ceuta in 1227, as in Marrakesh in 1220 or Córdoba in the 850s, the thirst for martyrdom pushes Christians to provoke the hostility of Muslim rulers, endangering the entente between the Muslim rulers and the Christian minority.

If the Franciscans' preaching did not produce converts, it was hoped that their martyrdom might. In 1228, the year following the Ceuta martyrs, two Franciscans, Giovanni of Perugia and Pietro of Sassoferrato, came to preach in Valencia, then under the rule of the Muslim wali Abû Zayd, who had them executed for blasphemy. Abû Zayd himself later converted to Christianity; many Christians attributed his conversion to the miraculous power of the martyrs' blood (though historians present it more plausibly as part of his attempt to ally himself with Jaume I of Aragon). Abû Zayd fought alongside Jaume in the siege of Valencia, and the place where the two Franciscans died was venerated as a holy place by generations of Valencian Christians.[23]

For Bonaventure, minister general of the Franciscan order from 1257 to 1274, the burning thirst for martyrdom was an integral part of Franciscan spirituality. It was love of the highest order: at the same time a longing to be united with God and a desire to bring the souls of the infidel to God.[24] Bonaventure's *Legenda maior,* which became the Franciscan order's official biography of its founder, insists on Francis's ardent desire for martyrdom. Bonaventure reuses and expands Thomas of Celano's account of Francis's thrice-foiled attempts to receive the martyr's crown at the hands of the Saracens. He embellishes the interview with al-Kâmil, having Francis propose an ordeal in which he and the sultan's "priests" would enter into a fire; the one who emerged unscathed would be shown to follow God's true law. When the Saracen priests refuse, Francis urges the sultan to light a fire and let Francis enter it alone; this the sultan also refuses, fearing lest this provoke a revolt among his people. When Francis rejects the gifts the sultan offers, the sultan, "filled with admiration, conceived a greater devotion for him." The sultan did not wish or did not dare to convert, Bonaventure concludes, so Francis left him.[25]

Bonaventure defines much more clearly than Thomas of Celano the place of Francis's mission to al-Kâmil in his spirituality. His description is part of his chapter on Francis's "fervor of love and desire for martyrdom." Francis, Bonaventure says, burned with a special and extreme love for God; this love encompassed the love of God's creation, through which he mounted as on a ladder toward the apprehension of God.[26] In this mystical ascent toward God, the *imitatio Christi* involves sacrificing oneself to Christ in ascesis, preaching out of a love for the souls of fellow men, and ultimately, the fervent desire for martyrdom. The height of spiritual perfection, of love for God, Bonaventure elsewhere writes, is the desire for and the achievement of martyrdom: "to long for death for Christ, to expose oneself to death for Christ, and to delight in the agony of death is an act of perfect love."[27] For Bonaventure, the desire for martyrdom is the driving force behind Franciscan missions; conversion of infidels is a laudable, but quite secondary, goal.[28] Thirteenth-century Franciscan writers show little knowledge of Islam; for them, as for the missionaries themselves, knowing the nature of the Saracen error was of little use.[29] After all, the apostles had not been schooled in pagan theology nor had they debated with pagan learned men; they had simply preached the Gospel and braved death in testimony to Christ. If God willed the infidels to convert, he would do so, most likely by producing miracles through his ministers, either before or after their death, not by having them deploy syllogistic arguments.

Franciscans were not the only missionaries to suffer martyrdom. Already in 1219 Father Richard of the Order of the Holy Trinity (an order approved by Innocent III in 1198) was put to death in Tunis, whose Christian residents (like the Cordovans more than three centuries earlier) opposed the martyrial zeal of the missionaries.[30] Yet the Friars Minor were far better known than the Order of the Holy Trinity, and European Christians knew that they modeled their lives (and deaths) on those of the apostles. Franciscans were aware, moreover, that many Muslim rulers were more obliging than al-Kâmil in offering death to aspiring martyrs: like the Cordovan martyrs of the ninth century, the friars could provoke the Muslim authorities into killing them by insulting Muhammad and the Koran. As thirteenth-century Franciscan Servasanto da Faenza explains: "If anyone, among Saracens, says anything bad about Muhammad (whom they do not believe to be God but prophet of God), they kill him without pity."[31]

These texts about the Franciscan martyrs have little to say about Islam. The polemical biography of Muhammad is indeed important, for it is by insulting the Prophet and his message that these friars obtain the death they so fervently desire. Yet the hagiographers do not report exactly what the martyrs said about Muhammad; what matters to them is that their heroes denounced anti-Christian error just as the apostles had before. The Muslim "judges" and "kings" are presented in the familiar guise of the apostles' ancient Roman persecutors: blindly killing Christ's preachers in a paroxysm of rage. There was little need to know or describe the rites and beliefs of such oppressors. When (on rare occasions) conversions were attributed to these Franciscans, it was in general through miracles worked subsequent to their martyrdom—notably in the case of the 1228 martyrs of Valencia.

William of Rubruck and Franciscan Mission beyond Islam

Other Franciscan missionaries (along with contemporary Dominicans [see chapter 10]), took a different approach to mission, seeking to use the tools of scholastic theology to prove the truth of Christianity to infidels. In the

1240s several Franciscan missionaries ventured beyond the lands of Islam, into the heart of the new Mongol empire, in order to preach Christianity and to negotiate peace: John of Piano Carpini and Benedict the Pole, sent by Pope Innocent IV, journeyed to Karakorum in 1246–47 to meet with the great khan Güyük.[32] In 1248–55, at the behest of King Louis IX of France, Franciscans William of Rubruck and Bartholomew of Cremona also traveled to Karakorum.[33] These missions represent an important change of strategy: none of these Franciscans, it seems, is keen on getting martyred. William of Rubruck, in particular, seeks to convert various Mongol rulers to Christianity not by insulting the Mongols' religious traditions but by engaging in debate with the adherents of rival religions. In discovering a world beyond the world of Islam, Muslim-Christian confrontation seems less crucial; indeed, the similarities of the two religions become all the more important when confronted by Mongol polytheism.

These missions were from the outset seen as playing a key role in the scenario of the final days. One of the traditional signs of the end of the world was the preaching of the Word of God to all non-Christians, unto the ends of the earth; this would result in the massive conversion of pagans, and then Jews, to Christianity. In 1239 Gregory IX issued the bull *Cum hora undecima,* which underlined the apocalyptic importance of the Franciscan mission:

> Since the eleventh hour has come in the day given to mankind . . . it is necessary that spiritual men possessing purity of life and the gift of intelligence should go forth with John the Baptist again to all men and all peoples of every and in every kingdom to prophesy because, according to the prophet Isaiah, the salvation of the remnant of Israel will not occur until, as St. Paul says, all of the gentiles *[plenitudo gentium]* enter first into the church.[34]

For chronicler Matthew Paris, the friars were bringing the Word to the ends of the earth; this, along with other events (such as the capture of Jerusalem by the Khwarizmians in 1244) was a sign that the final days were at hand.[35]

The Mongol invasions themselves were seen by many as harbingers of the final days. From 1236 to 1241 Ögödei khan led the Mongols in the conquest of most of Russia and parts of Poland and Hungary, inspiring fears that the Mongols might sweep across Europe; this was prevented only by the death of Ögödei khan in 1241. Latin writers like Matthew Paris portrayed the Mongols as Gog and Magog, the biblical tribes of barbaric cannibals that were destined to ravage the earth at the end of time.[36] Yet various Latin Christians pinned their hopes on a Mongol-Latin alliance to defeat the forces of Islam (see chapter 8). The Mongol sack of Baghdad in 1258 lent credence to these hopes.

It is with this mixture of hope and apprehension that William of Rubruck set out from Acre in 1248, bearing letters from Louis IX along with a portable cloth chapel embroidered with scenes from Christian history "to see if he [Louis] could draw them to our religion."[37] In his *Itinerary* (Itinerarium), William describes his voyage in detail, painting a vivid picture of the life and customs of the Mongols, describing the many religious groups within the empire, in particular Buddhists, Muslims, and Nestorian Christians. William admits that he had little success in converting non-Christians to Christianity, and he describes the native Nestorian Christians as morally corrupt and ill-educated.

Yet William is granted a unique opportunity: to participate in a religious debate with Muslims and Buddhists before Möngke khan himself.[38] As William recounts it, in preparation for the debate, he conferred with the Nestorians as to how they should best argue for Christianity. The Nestorians wanted first to debate against the Muslims, but William convinced them that it would be best to argue first against the Buddhists, since the Muslims would side with the Christians in affirming that there is only one God. He then held a mock debate with the Nestorians, William taking the Buddhist line and asking the Nestorians to prove to him that there is only one God. But, he says, "the Nestorians did not know how to prove anything, they could only repeat what the Scriptures tell. I said: 'These people do not believe in the Scriptures; if you tell them one story, they will tell you another.'" He convinced the Nestorians to let him open the debate against the Buddhists.

The day of the debate, the khan ordered, under pain of death, that no one insult or speak words of abuse to one another and that no one hinder the proceedings. At the opening of the debate, the Buddhist priests asked William if he preferred to begin with a discussion of the Creation or of the destiny of the soul after death. William affirmed that since God is the beginning and cause of all things, the debate should begin with his nature; the khan's judges agreed. William asserted that there was one God and asked the Buddhist what he believed; he responded that there were many gods: one supreme God in heaven and many lower gods. William asked him if any of these gods were omnipotent; the Buddhist sat silent for a long time, until the khan's scribes ordered him to answer, and he finally answered that no god was omnipotent. "At that, all the Saracens burst into loud laughter." William had scored a debating point for monotheism against Buddhism.

William says that he then "wanted to put forward the arguments for the Unity of the divine essence and the Trinity in the hearing of all," but that the Nestorians cut him off, wishing to have their turn to dispute with the Muslims. The Muslims responded, "We grant you that your faith is true and that whatever is in the Gospel is true, therefore we do not wish to argue on any point with you." William goes on to affirm that "in all their prayers they [the Muslims] beseech God to grant that they may die a Christian death." The Nestorians next recounted to the Uigurs the history of the world from Christ to the Last Judgment and used analogies to explain the Trinity to the Uigurs and Muslims. "They all listened without a word of contradiction, yet not one of them said, 'I believe, I wish to become a Christian.'" The debate ended with loud singing by the Christians and Muslims, and everyone went off to drink.

It is of course impossible to know to what extent this is an accurate report of the debate in Möngke khan's court. William describes himself as a skilled debater, able to parry the verbal thrusts of the Buddhist priest and to embarrass and confuse him. If William was unable to provide definitive proof of the triune nature of God, it is only because of his inept Nestorian allies who insist on taking the floor and who, since they do not know how to argue, botch the job badly. This is not implausible: as a Franciscan with a training in logic and theology, William was no doubt used to logical argumentation and verbal jousting, something that may have seemed quite foreign to the Nestorians and to others in the Mongol court. Frequently in the *Itinerary,* William expresses his frustration at his inability to express himself in the Mongol language and at the unreliability and laziness of his interpreters. Between the lines, it seems, lies the suggestion that if other Franciscan missionaries come and argue the Christian truth, they may be able to succeed where William has not.

Yet there is also a note of pessimism in William's account as he notes, to his surprise and disappointment, that his adversaries, in particular the Muslims, are uninterested in debating with the Christians. He claims that the Muslims praised the Gospels and affirmed that they believed in the truth of the Gospel and the Christian religion. They listened patiently to the Nestorians' exposition of Christian history without contradicting it. Yet, to his puzzlement, they refused to convert to Christianity. William was intellectually prepared for Muslims who would affirm the unique truth of their religion and argue with Christians; he is not prepared for a world where Muslims and Christians accept the legitimacy of each other's religions. His affirmation that Muslims pray to die as Christians is of course implausible. The stereotype that emerges from William's description of the debate is that of an Oriental other, Nestorian, Muslim, or Buddhist, who is uninterested in and impervious to the clear, rational thinking of a Western Christian. While the failure of thirteenth-century Crusades could create, in the writings of Fidentius of Padua and others, the stereotype of the barbaric Muslim endemically hostile to all things Christian, the frustration of thirteenth- and fourteenth-century missionaries would produce the stereotype of the irrational Oriental, impervious to the dictates of Christian reason.

Roger Bacon's Science of Religion

Roger Bacon was one of the most avid readers of the *Itinerary* of his fellow Franciscan William of Rubruck. Bacon attempts to turn William's debating strategy into a veritable science of religion, bent on converting the infidel through rational argumentation. It is in some ways ironic to present Roger Bacon in a chapter on Franciscan mission. Bacon had his own peculiar approach to the problems of his day, an approach that earned him the hostility of the Franciscan hierarchy and landed him in a Franciscan prison sometime between 1277 and 1279.[39] Far from diplomatic, Bacon was a vocal critic of many of the intellectual and political tendencies in the church: notably the Crusades and the missionary strategies of his fellow friars. He develops his ideas in his various works, particularly the *Opus maius,* which he composed at the bidding of pope Clement IV in 1266–68. For Bacon, the fruits of centuries of crusade and mission were scant: "there are few Christians; the whole breadth of the world is occupied by unbelievers, and there is no one to show them the truth."[40] No one, that is, until Roger Bacon came along. War does not win converts; it kills infidels and sends them to hell, making the survivors all the more hostile to Christianity.[41] More often than not, crusades fail to meet their military goals, as the expedition of Louis IX so painfully illustrated. Bacon is not a complete pacifist; military defense of the Holy Land is legitimate, and he even suggests the use of high-tech mirrors to create fires in the enemy camp.[42] But it is preaching and philosophical argument, not war, that will win converts to Christianity.

Bacon acknowledges that many preachers set out to convert infidels, braving danger, preaching with difficulty through interpreters, and often reaping a harvest of conversions. How much more could they do if they had a proper education in their audiences' languages and in philosophical argumentation![43] Bacon's ambition is to create a science of religion: a rational basis for Christian truth and a scientific way of understanding the different religions of the world. He affirms that the only two ways to bring infidels to the faith are through miracles or through human reason; since we cannot count on miracles, rational argumentation is the only real alternative. He acknowledges that Gregory the Great had affirmed that "Faith to which reason affords a proof has no merit"; this means, Bacon affirms, that Christians should accept the authority of Scripture as superior to human reason; it does not mean that one cannot use reason to bring the infidel to the faith.[44] One of the keys to this scientific approach to religion was astrology, which explained the differences in the world's various religions and which predicted the ultimate victory of Christianity. His emphasis on scientific and linguistic learning made him dismissive of scholasticism and hostile to Parisian bishop Stephen Tempier's condemnation of Aristotle in 1277. It is no accident that it was soon thereafter that Bacon landed in jail.

While Bacon's reliance on astrology may strike modern readers as quirky and pathetic, for Bacon astrology was the most rational of sciences, one, moreover, capable of uniting the mathematical sciences with the (hitherto) uncertain truths of history and theology. At any rate, it allowed Bacon to take a fresh approach to the problem of infidels. He classifies all of world religions into six fundamental groupings: Saracens, Tartars, pagans, idolaters, Jews, and Christians, affirming that the seventh will be that of Antichrist.[45] The differences in these religions are related to the influence of the planets: the Tartars, under the influence of Mars, "burn with the desire to dominate." The Saracens, under the influence of Venus, "are plunged in the passions of lust."[46]

The association between the Saracen religion and the cult of Venus is evident elsewhere (in Petrus Alfonsi and other writers); more generally, the portrayal of Saracen libidinousness is commonplace. Predictably, Bacon has little good to say about Muhammad or the Koran. Muhammad "feigned" prophecy, producing false miracles "by fraud and deception"; he led a "most vile" life as an adulterer who "took every beautiful woman away from her men and raped her."[47] Even the most malicious of earlier Christian authors, in their hostile distortions of Muhammad's polygamy, do not accuse him of indiscriminate rape.

Despite this, Bacon, unlike so many earlier Christian authors, does not describe Muhammad as inspired by the devil; Satan seems to play no part in Bacon's science of religion. No reference, either, is made to Ishmael as the ancestor of the Saracens. These absences are significant. Bacon bases his theory of religion not on biblical history but on Greco-Arabic scientific and philosophical works, and on the descriptions of rival religions that he has gleaned from his own reading (including the *Itinerary* of William Rubruck). Adherents of rival religions are not blind or evil; they are simply at different stages in the progression toward God. "The rational soul was born to know and to love," Bacon affirms; "Truth however can be perceived in a sect to the extent in which that sect contains knowledge of God in whatever way, because all sects refer to God."[48] Each religion reflects the soul's knowledge of God, even if that knowledge is at times imperfect, leading to religious error. Such error can be imputed to ignorance, and when infidels are properly instructed (following Bacon's own method), they should be able to recognize the truth of Christianity. Islam (like other religions) is not antithetical to Christianity: it is merely a garbled and imperfect form of it.

Here, then, is Bacon's argument for Christian truth. He starts with the existence of God, for which he proposes two proofs. The first is the universal agreement of humanity: all six religions agree that God exists. The second form of proof is through creation. Bacon equates God with Aristotle's first cause: since every effect has a cause, and there cannot be an infinite number of causes going back to eternity, there must be one first cause, to which nothing is prior: this is God. Since there is only *one* first cause, this proves that there is only one God: wise men, among Saracens, Jews, Tartars, and Christians, all recognize God's unity, and they have little trouble refuting the pagans and idolaters in disputations, Bacon affirms, referring to William Rubruck's debate in the court of the Mongol khan. The Tartars, while not polytheist, practice pagan rites such as fire-worship and lack philosophical sophistication.[49]

This leaves three rivals in the field: "Three other [sects] are very rational: the sects of the Jews, the Saracens, and the Christians"[50] Having "proven" the existence and unity of God, Bacon affirms that man's role is to serve God as best he is able, and that for this God saw fit to reveal his law to man: Jews, Saracens, and Christians all agree on this. He cites al-Fârâbî and Avicenna (significantly, rather than the Bible or Augustine) on the necessity of revelation. Just as there is only one God, Bacon affirms, there can only be one revelation, one law.[51]

Philosophy provides the key to proving the superiority of Christianity, for Bacon, (as it had for twelfth-century apologist Petrus Alfonsi). Mathematics reveal the arcane truths of Trinity, Christology, and the rest of

Christian doctrine.⁵² "Moreover, the philosophers not only show the way to the Christian sect, they destroy the other two sects."⁵³ The "irrationality" of Judaism was already shown by Seneca, Bacon affirms, and it is manifest in the "horrible and filthy" animal sacrifices enjoined in the Old Testament.⁵⁴ As for the irrationality of the "sect of the Saracens," Bacon repeatedly invokes Avicenna himself, who (he claims) criticizes Muhammad for promising carnal pleasures (and not spiritual ones) in heaven.⁵⁵ Indeed, he says, "Avicenna and other philosophers contradict [the Saracens'] people and priests"; Avicenna was in search of "another Law, which would promise glory not only of bodies, but rather of souls."⁵⁶ Bacon was right that Avicenna rejected the more literalist interpretations of the sensual pleasures the Koran ascribes to paradise; he is wrong in thinking that this led Avicenna and other "Saracen" philosophers to reject Islam and seek a better law, any more than Bacon's embrace of science (which was subsequently to put him in prison) entailed a rejection of Christianity. It is tempting to think that, as he sat in his Franciscan prison cell, Bacon felt a certain solidarity with Avicenna (as he imagined him): both rejecting the certainties of their contemporaries in search of higher truths, both misunderstood and persecuted by an ignorant cadre of clerical purists.

Bacon, like the anonymous author of *De statu Sarracenorum*, thought the Saracens could be brought to the Christian truth through preaching—though Bacon underpinned his missionary strategy with supposedly foolproof philosophical argumentation (explicitly rejected in *De statu*). Both authors provide comforting predictions of the imminent demise of Islam, supposedly gleaned from the works of Muslim writers. While the author of *De statu* claims to have found these prophecies in the Saracens' holy books, Bacon prefers to ground his in the "hard science" of astrology:

And they [the Saracens] speak beautifully and with certitude about the destruction of the law of Muhammad. For according to what [ninth-century astronomer] Abû Ma'shar said in the seventh chapter of his second book, the law of Muhammad cannot last beyond 693 years. But it can and will last that long unless it is shortened by some coinciding cause (as has been said); this shortening can be greater or longer for different reasons. And now it is the year of the Arabs 665 from the time of Muhammad [1267 C.E.] and therefore it will soon be destroyed by the grace of God, and this will be a great relief for Christians. For this let us praise God, Who gave the light of reason to the philosophers, light by which the faith is confirmed and strengthened and by which we can perceive how we should destroy the enemies of the faith. And these predictions correspond with the thirteenth chapter of the Apocalypse. For it says that the number of the beast is 663, which is thirty years less than the above number. But scripture in many places subtracts something from a complete number, because this is the custom of Scripture, as Bede says. And thus, perhaps, God wished it, that the things expressed in the Apocalypse not be expressed completely, but that they be somewhat concealed. Thus, before the end *[tempus ultimum]* which is determined for this sect, according to its principal cause (as Abû Ma'shar calculated it), perhaps the Saracens will be destroyed either by Tartars or by Christians. And already most of the Saracens have been destroyed by the Tartars, as has their former capital, Baghdad, and the Caliph who was as their Pope. All this happened twelve years ago.[57]

For Bacon, the current situation was dire: a divided, apathetic, unphilosophical Christendom was surrounded by numerous infidel peoples, against which it sent ineffectual crusading armies and poorly prepared missionaries. Yet there was cause for hope: the predictions of the Apocalypse, confirmed by the scientific calculations of Saracen astrologers and by the Mongol sack of Baghdad, showed that Islam had at most thirty years ahead of it. The need to educate Franciscan missionaries in Bacon's intellectual system was urgent, but the hopes for success were good.

It is hard to know what impression this message left on Clement IV and his entourage. It certainly found a cold reception among Bacon's fellow Franciscans, as Bacon's imprisonment dramatized. Bacon's work left little mark on later writers on Islam. His thought was too quirky, too marginal, too suspect. There were other authors better informed about Islam than Bacon, authors who had firsthand experience with Muslims and with Muslim texts.

Reactions to Franciscan Mission to Islam: New Horizons, Criticisms

Bacon criticized his fellow Franciscans who actively sought out the palm of martyrdom, a goal more important to them than the conversion of infidels. The two goals were not necessarily incompatible: martyrs, it was believed, produced miracles, which could in turn soften the hearts of the infidels. This was shown dramatically in the case of the Valencian emir Abû

Zayd, who had two Franciscan missionaries put to death and whose subsequent conversion to Christianity was attributed to the miraculous power of the new martyrs. The Franciscan archbishop of Canterbury, John Pecham, suggested that in response to the fall of Acre Christendom send out missionaries, "spiritual warriors," to preach the Word; if their sermons did not convert the Muslims, he suggests, perhaps the spectacle of their martyrdom would. Just as Christian Cordovans of the ninth century sought out martyrdom through public blasphemy, so did fourteenth-century Franciscans, such as the missionaries to Tana who were sentenced to death after telling their Muslim judge (*qâdî*), "In no way is [Muhammad] a prophet, but rather a diabolical man who carried out the ministry of the devil."[58]

For those who were more interested in preaching the Gospel than in becoming martyrs, the lands east of Islam became attractive. It was primarily Franciscan missionaries that Pope Innocent IV and the French king Louis IX sent to negotiate with and preach to the Mongols in the mid-thirteenth century: one of them was William of Rubruck, whose relation of his mission Bacon put to good use. In 1289 Nicolas IV sent John of Monte Corvino to China; Franciscans continued to voyage east in the following centuries—and west as well, founding missions on the coast of California in the eighteenth century. But few of their missions were to Muslims.

Some thirteenth-century authors looked askance at the Franciscan missionaries' rush to embrace martyrdom. Thomas of Chobham criticized the Franciscan approach in his *Summa de arte praedicandi*, which he probably wrote while master in theology in Paris between 1222 and 1228.[59] In the third chapter of this preacher's manual, Thomas defines the appropriate audiences for the preacher's sermons. He acknowledges that according to the Gospel, preachers must be sent to infidels everywhere to preach the Word without regard for danger to their own lives. Yet the Gospel's injunctions referred to missions to the Roman pagans; today's Saracens are different:

> It seems that the Universal Church sins when it does not send its preachers to such places [infidel lands], and it may not excuse itself by saying that in these places it has been proclaimed that the preachers who preach Christ are to be put to death. For the Lord said: "Behold, I am sending you as sheep in the midst of wolves. Therefore, be prudent as serpents and simple as doves" [Matt. 10:16], as if to say "I send you to preach to those who will kill you as wolves devour sheep." . . . It therefore seems that preachers should not hesitate to go preach where they

know they will be killed, as long as it is the authority of the Church that sends them. But to this some say that things are different with the Saracens than they once were with the Gentiles. For the Gentiles listened to the preaching of the apostles and others and argued with them, and many of them were converted by them. They did not kill the preachers as long as any hope remained that they might pervert them to their idolatry. But now it has been decreed among the Saracens that if anyone come as a preacher, as soon as he names Christ, he should immediately be killed without being heard out. And so they say that to go to such people is not to go to preaching, but rather to go to death without preaching. Nor are they certain that God will produce miracles through them when they die; and they go rather to tempt God than to preach. However, we read in many stories *[legenda]* of the saints that many rushed to be martyred in the places where they saw the swords ready on the necks of the martyrs; these people did not preach but died, and God nevertheless performed miracles through them.[60]

In scholastic style, Thomas is giving both sides of the argument; his testimony shows that the Franciscan missions provoked criticism in Paris in the 1220s: the argument centers around the interpretation of Matthew 10:16, which the *Regula non bullata* (quoted at the beginning of this chapter) cited to justify Franciscan mission. Thomas affirms that the Saracens kill any preacher who mentions Christ. The stories of the Moroccan martyrs of 1220 and 1227 show, on the contrary, how difficult it often was for preachers to obtain the martyrdom they so fervently desired. But for Thomas these missionaries, killed before being heard out, were not fulfilling the Gospel injunction to preach to all everywhere; rather they were going to their deaths without preaching. Unsure that God will produce miracles through them, were they not provoking him? Thomas does indeed cite a counterargument: after all, he says, we read of saints of old who rushed to be martyred by the oppressor's sword without preaching, and God produced miracles through them.

For Thomas, the Franciscan missions, whether or not one approved of them, had less to do with preaching than with the desire to rush out and meet the oppressor's sword in order to win the crown of martyrdom. Why do the Saracens not allow the Christians to preach in their lands? Thomas says that, in peace negotiations between Christians and Saracens, the Christians ask the Saracens to grant them permission to send preachers in Muslim lands. To which, Thomas says, the Saracens reply that they will gladly do so, if Saracen preachers may safely preach in Christian churches. Since the church will not allow this, Christian preachers cannot preach to the Saracens.[61] This closes the topic for Thomas: pursuit of martyrdom, laudable or not, has little to do with the injunction to preach to infidels. The political situation makes it impossible to preach to Saracens.

Thomas has a more practical suggestion for those who wish to fulfill the evangelical injunction to preach to infidels: why not preach to the Jews? After all, he says, Christian princes can force Jews to listen to the preachers' sermons, and one could hope that a few of them might convert. Some respond, he says, that one should not cast pearls before swine and that there is little hope to convert the "incorrigible and obstinate" Jews. But Thomas says that Jews regularly convert, and that missionary activity toward them should be encouraged.[62] Here again the preacher bends to practical political consideration: to preach to infidels, one needs the help of a Christian prince who can compel them to listen (though conversion itself remains entirely voluntary, for Thomas).

In the newly (re)conquered areas of Spain, of course, not only Jews but also Muslims were numerous. They indeed provided a large captive audience for those who were more interested in converting the infidels than in winning the palm of martyrdom. Thomas's strategy will be applied to these "captive" Jews and Muslims by the Dominicans in the Crown of Aragon.

Chapter 10

⌖

The Dominican Missionary Strategy

THOMAS OF CHOBHAM'S pragmatic approach to preaching to infidels was adopted by Dominican preachers in the second half of the thirteenth century. The Dominican order had been from its outset a missionary order, whose initial purpose was to bring Cathars back into the Catholic fold. Dominican missionaries, moved more by a desire to convert (or perhaps less of a desire to meet a martyr's end) soon found it expedient to focus their efforts on the Muslim and Jewish subjects of Christian rulers: even if the latter's active support could not be secured, they certainly wouldn't put the missionaries to death. Here—particularly in Aragon under King Jaume I—crusade and mission were closely linked.

Jaume I's Aragon became a veritable testing ground for the new Dominican missionary strategy to convert Jews and Muslims: Dominicans learned Hebrew and Arabic, studied the Bible, Talmud, and Koran, and (with the help of royal coercion) forced Jews and Muslims to debate with them and to listen to their sermons. Ramon Martí, in particular, sought to deploy the tools of logic and scholastic theology to decimate the rival religions and prove the truth of Christianity. Yet the missionary efforts of Martí and his associates had only limited success, and increasingly, Christian theologians, like Dominican Thomas Aquinas, affirmed that it was impossible to prove the truth of Christianity through reason alone. Yet when missionary Riccoldo da Montecroce failed to convert Muslims of Baghdad, he attributed his failure to the irrationality of the Muslims. At the end of the thirteenth century, the hopes of converting the Muslim to Christianity dwindled, and (as in some Franciscan texts), the irrational, oriental Muslims were blamed.

The Forging of a Dominican Missionary Strategy:
Ramon Penyafort and Ramon Martí

The two prominent figures in the inauguration of this missionary effort were Catalan friars Ramon de Penyafort (d. 1275) and Ramon Martí (d. 1285). Ramon de Penyafort studied law in Bologna (from 1210 to 1219) where he met Dominic; he became a Dominican in 1222. Ramon served as confessor and chaplain to Pope Gregory IX from 1230 to 1238, then served as master general of the Dominicans from 1238 to 1240. Most of the rest of his life he spent in Barcelona, where, as spiritual adviser to Jaume I, he convinced the king to establish an inquisition in Aragon and to give his backing to the evangelical activities of his team of Dominican missionaries.[1] In the last thirty-five years of his life, Ramon rallied royal and papal support for the establishment of language schools for missionaries, for the obligatory attendance of Muslims and Jews at the friars' missionary sermons.[2]

The most prolific of Ramon Penyafort's missionary disciples was Ramon Martí, who by 1250 was part of the team of Dominicans missionaries under Penyafort's guidance.[3] In that year the Dominican provincial chapter of Toledo established a school of Arabic for eight of its friars, including Ramon Martí.[4] Martí was not only educated in Arabic and Hebrew but also studied the Talmud and works of Arabic philosophy: al-Ghazâlî, Ibn Sînâ, al-Razi, and others.[5]

Most of Martí's missionary efforts were directed toward Jews, and he shows the same strategy in his works of polemic against both religions: he attempts to attack the religion at its base by showing how its own scriptures invalidate its precepts. This line of attack was not new: Petrus Alfonsi, for example, ridiculed the Koran and the Talmud, showing supposed contradictions in them. Yet the Dominican missionaries pursued this tactic with a zeal and perseverance never seen before: they schooled themselves in Hebrew, Aramaic, and Arabic, pored over the Talmud and Koran, produced massive tracts for the use of their missionaries, and (with the aid of King Jaume) forced Jewish and Muslim scholars to debate with them.

A number of such debates between Christians and Muslims of Aragon are attested in documents from both sides. The most famous and best documented such debate, however, was between a Jew and a Christian: Rabbi Moses ben Nachman (Nachmanides) and the Dominican convert from Judaism Pablo Cristiá. The disputation took place in Barcelona in July 1263, in the presence of Jaume himself, and of Ramon Penyafort; it is quite possible that Martí was present as well. Pablo Cristiá tried to show, using carefully chosen passages of the Talmud, that the Messiah had already come; Nachmanides parried Pablo's attacks by asserting that he had misinterpreted the passages in question, and by presenting alternate (generally nonmessianic) interpretations. The result of the debate is what might have been expected: neither side succeeded in convincing the other, but each side claimed to have out-debated the other. Two accounts of the debate were subsequently composed, one in Latin and one in Hebrew, and of course they differ widely.[6]

It is clear that the Dominicans were not pleased with the outcome of the Barcelona disputation and that they felt that the problem was neither with the premises nor the method of debate, but with its execution. This is why Martí composed (probably with a team of helpers) his *Pugio fidei* (Dagger of the faith), a handbook for future debates between Dominican missionaries and Jews.[7] He organizes his work along the general lines taken by Pablo Cristiá, specifically trying to parry the objections made by Nachmanides and giving a much more thorough exposition of the Talmud passages in question. He cites Jewish texts in Hebrew and Aramaic, providing a Latin translation. The aggressive purpose of the *Dagger* is clear: the Dominican missionaries are to seek out the Jews, force them into debate, and attack the heart of their doctrine.

If the 1263 debate was the best-documented confrontation, it was not the only one: there is evidence for numerous debates between Christian clerics (usually Dominicans) and Jews or Muslims.[8] There is some evidence of debate from the Muslim side. Two Muslim prisoners in Christian Europe, 'Abd Allâh al-Asîr (fl. 1267) and Muhammad al-Qaysî (fl. 1309), composed works of anti-Christian polemics; al-Qaysî says that during his captivity he had been accosted by an "impudent monk" (probably a friar) with whom he debated the faith in the presence of the (unnamed) Christian king. Al-Qaysî's *Kitâb miftâh al-dîn* gives his version of that debate. These works represent a new defensive stage in anti-Christian polemics in the Muslim west; along with other similar works of the period, they represent a clear reaction to the military success and missionary activity of Christian Europe.[9]

The Dominicans never produced a *Pugio fidei* directed against Islam: no encyclopedic work for the use of missionaries. Martí, like other Catalan polemicists and missionaries of his day, seemed principally concerned with converting Jews, and secondarily Muslims, though the two projects are inseparable: he cites the Koran in his anti-Jewish polemic and discusses Jewish practice in his attacks on Islam.

Martí did produce a diptych of texts for the evangelization of Muslims: *De seta Machometi* (composed before 1257) and the *Explanatio symboli apostolorum* (written in 1257).[10] The differences between the two texts reflect the two phases of mission, according to the Dominican strategy: the *De seta Machometi* furnishes missionaries with arguments with which to attack Islam; and the *Explanatio symboli apostolorum,* with an explication of the truth of Christianity. First destroy error, then expound truth. Martí may have composed one or both works while in Tunis, and the *Explanatio* may also be meant to serve an apologetical purpose among the Christian community of Tunis: to expound to Christians their own religion, explaining away Muslim objections to Christian doctrine.

Martí meant the first of the two texts, the *De seta Machometi,* to be a practical guide for Christians in theological disputes; he gives his readers responses to key Muslim arguments against Christianity, such as the charge of falsification of the Gospels; in this it is similar in purpose to his *Pugio fidei.*[11] But while the *Pugio fidei* was an immense encyclopedia of anti-Jewish argument, Martí's *De seta Machometi* is a brief text focused almost exclusively on the life and deeds of Muhammad. His strategy is to make the Prophet a scapegoat: it is the Prophet and his false law that he attacks, not the wisdom of subsequent Muslims. He will try to bring the Arab philosophers into the Christian camp by using their philosophical arguments against Muhammad: he cites Averroes to prove that a true prophet must produce miracles (*De seta,* 16). Muhammad becomes Martí's sole (if formidable) adversary: reason, natural law, philosophy, and even much of Muslim doctrine, he tries to show, are on the Christians' side.

As in the *Pugio fidei,* Ramon is scrupulous about the use and citation of his sources. As he uses only Arab sources, gone is the ridiculous, the vicious, the flamboyant: no trained bulls or vultures, no death by pigs, no floating coffins. Instead, he narrates Muhammad's life as gleaned from the Koran and from writings of Muslim authors Ibn Ishâq, al-Bukhâri, and Muslim b. al-Hajjâj[12]; he is also indebted to the *Risâlat al-Kindî.,* which he cites by name.[13]

Muhammad is not a true prophet, affirms Martí; rather, he is one of the false prophets that Jesus announced in Matthew 7:15: "Beware of false prophets, which come to you in sheep's clothing, but inwardly they are ravening wolves." Martí organizes his entire tract around this central premise. The "fruits" mentioned by Matthew are the signs of prophecy, which are four: that he be truthful, that he be virtuous, that he perform miracles, and that he come with a true law. Martí's "quadruple refutation" attempts to show that Muhammad meets none of these four tests.

First Martí concedes that in some things Muhammad was truthful: here he gives a (now-familiar) list of Koranic precepts that are in agreement with Christian doctrine: the unity of God, the Virgin birth, the praise of Jesus and the Gospel, and so on. "Yet many of his words were false"[14]: the Koran claims that the Virgin Mary was the sister of Aaron, that Jesus announced the arrival of Muhammad, and that Jesus was not really crucified. Here, too, under the rubric of Muhammad's "lies," Martí presents the Muslim paradise, full of the pleasures of eating and love-making, and contrasts it with the pure and austere heaven of Paul and the Gospels. Martí also gleans some sayings attributed to Muhammad in the Hadîth collections of al-Bukhâri and Muslim b. al-Hajjâj: that flies wings' contain poison and that the day of judgement would come within one hundred years of Muhammad. The choice of passages clearly shows the polemical purpose; by pouncing on whatever he finds to be shocking or ridiculous, he can conclude, "all these things seem to be the words of a stupid man or a scoffer rather than a prophet or messenger of God." (*De seta,* 32). The purpose is not to understand Islam but to vilify it. While this could no doubt evoke nods of approbation from fellow Dominican missionaries, it is hard to imagine Muslims being convinced through such an arbitrary and hostile selection of Hadîth passages.

The second fruit of prophecy, for Martí, is purity and sanctity. "We will show by the deeds and sayings of Muhammad and through his books that he was not clean, but rather filthy and a sinner."[15] This "filthiness" is all sexual: Martí goes through the familiar litany of the Muhammad's polygamy and the Koranic laws of marriage. Here again, is the standard argument that Muhammad's sex life is proof positive that he is not a true prophet, a theme that is found in both Christian and Jewish writers (such as Maimonides) against Islam.[16]

The third fruit of prophecy, in Martí's definition, is miracles. He cites the stories (from Ibn Ishâq and the Koran) of the Meccans challenging Muhammad to perform miracles and of Muhammad's refusal.[17] The miracle of splitting the moon, Martí says, is not attested in the Koran. Moreover, he says, citing the *Risâlat al-Kindî,* such a miracle would be physically impossible, given the size of the moon; had it happened, there would have been many witnesses to attest to it.

Martí's fourth fruit of prophecy is that the prophet bring a good and holy law; here he tries to show that Muslim law goes against both divine law (as mandated by Scripture) and natural law (as mandated by reason). Of the eleven precepts that Martí here condemns as transgressions of divine and natural law, seven involve sex and marriage: polygamy is "against divine mandate, against natural law and against reason."[18] He similarly condemns what he presents as Muslim law regarding divorce, nonvaginal intercourse, concubinage, coitus interruptus, and homosexuality.[19] Acknowledging that homosexuality is in fact illegal in Islam, he nonetheless claims that since four witnesses are needed to convict homosexuals, Muhammad thus "gave cause and opportunity to his followers so that many of them perpetrate this shameful act almost without shame and fear."[20]

For Ramon Martí, missionary friar under a vow of celibacy, the most false and shocking thing about Muhammad and his followers is their sexual practices: polygamy, homosexuality, even sex in heaven! This gulf of incomprehension flavors Martí's portrayal of Muhammad's death. Earlier polemicists related horrendous fables about Muhammad's shameful murder and the defilement of his corpse by pigs or dogs. The Muslim story of his death, by contrast, shows him surrounded by his loved ones, peacefully dying with his head in the lap of his beloved wife 'A'isha. For Muslims, this touching scene emphasizes Muhammad's humanity (just as, for Christians, the birth and death of Christ emphasize his humanity). Yet Martí is unable to see anything other than filth in this scene: "When he died he had his head between 'A'isha's breast and her chin, and she mixed her saliva with that of Muhammad. In this way the death or end of Muhammad was vile, unclean, and abominable. And such a death is in no way appropriate for a prophet or a messenger of God."[21] In a standard Christian deathbed scene, an attentive priest would hear confession and administer communion and extreme unction, and the dying man would prepare his soul to meet its maker. Instead of the Body of Christ, Martí seems to be implying, Muhammad's last solace was the saliva of profane kisses; instead of the anointing hand of a priest, he is caressed by the breasts of a woman; instead of confessing and turning away from sin, he is clinging desperately to it.[22]

Martí, unlike most earlier Latin polemicists, has sketched a biography of Muhammad that Muslims would recognize as true in most of its details, gleaned as they are from Arab (and principally Muslim) sources. Yet the selection and presentation of these sources shows an unshakeable hostility. Of the wide range of material available in the Koran, Ibn Ishâq, al-Bukhâri, and Muslim b. al-Hajjâj, Martí focuses on what will shock a Christian clerical audience: the sex life of the Muslim prophet and Muslim laws regarding sex and marriage. Throughout, he contrasts Muslim law and belief with injunctions from the Gospels.

Martí means his tract to be used in arguments with Muslims (though whether in formal disputations, missions, or merely in defensive arguments is unclear). Since most Martí's arguments are based on acceptance of the Bible, a Muslim could respond simply that the text of the Bible has been falsified. In the final section of *De seta Machometi* Martí argues against the charge of falsification.[23] He bases his argument almost exclusively on the Koran, citing at length Koranic praise for the Torah and Gospels. To the charge that the Scriptures were falsified after the composition of the Koran, Martí argues that this would be impossible: Jews and Christians of different languages all over the world agree on the text of the Torah; how could they have contrived, he asks (echoing the *Risâlat al-Kindî*), to delete the name of Muhammad from their text? The same argument applies to charges of Christians' wilful corruption of the Gospels. Here Martí uses an analogy with the Koran: just as Muslims recognize the incorruptness of the Koran and the impossibility for anyone to change the text without it being known, so too is it impossible to imagine the wilful changing of the text of the Gospels.

Martí's *Explanatio symboli Apostolorum* (1257) comes at the same issues from a different perspective. It is an exposition of the Christian credo, divided into twelve articles (each of which is attributed to one of the apostles). Before explaining the twelve articles of the credo, Martí needs to establish the authority of Scripture: he does so by refuting the Muslim charge of falsification of the scriptures (*tahrîf*) in an expanded version of his treatment of the subject in *De seta Machometi*.[24] He can then go on to instruct his readers in the basic tenets of Christianity; for each of the twelve articles, he provides standard biblical proof texts (from both the Old and New Testaments), which the Saracen is now supposed to accept. Martí at times refers to the Koran, either to use it in support of Christian doctrine or to refute it where it opposes Christian doctrine. The work could thus be used either to instruct a convert from Islam in the basic tenets of Christianity or to educate those who are already Christians and inoculate them against Muslim anti-Christian arguments. If Martí composed the work in Tunis, he may well have done so with both these goals in mind. If we are to believe Ramon Llull, Martí wrote an Arabic version of the *Explanatio*, which he presented to the "King of Tunis" in a failed attempt to convert him to Christianity.[25]

The *Explanatio* is thus an apologetical (pro-Christian) text rather than a polemical (anti-Muslim) one. I will not here delve into the details of the biblical citations and rationalistic arguments that he gives to "prove" the Trinity, Incarnation, and other Christian doctrines. What is of interest here is how Martí uses his studies in Greek and Arabic philosophy to portray Muslim doctrine as irrational where it differs from Christian doctrine. For example, in a long passage on marriage, he affirms that reason and natural law permit marriage only between one man and one woman; he concludes that therefore the Saracens' marriage law permitting polygamy "is not a law of rational and honest humans, but rather of pimps and whores."[26] Saracen law is opposed to natural law, opposed to reason.

He develops this idea in greater length in his discussion of the carnal pleasures that the Koran promises in heaven. He presents the standard Catholic doctrine that the body will be resurrected at the end of time, to share the soul's punishment in hell or glory in heaven. There will, however, be no eating or drinking in heaven, contrary to what "Muhammad's fables" promise.

> For he led the Saracen wise men into error, so that they do not believe in the resurrection of bodies as it is portrayed in the Koran. For there it says that after resurrection they will have bodily delights, such as delight in food, drink, and sex. These things, if they indeed existed in the next life, would prevent the intellect from contemplating and delighting in the Supreme Good. Therefore, since they could see that this is improper (as in fact it is), they denied the resurrection of bodies, placing man's beatitude in the soul, not understanding that the human body could live without food.[27]

He goes on to cite Avicenna, who showed that divine and spiritual pleasures were superior to those of the body.[28] He cites al-Fârâbî and al-Ghazâlî to make the same point: the highest pleasures are those of the intellect, incomparably sweeter than those of the bodily senses.[29] The message is clear: the learned among the Saracens reject Muhammad's irrational "fables" of banquets, wine, and sex in heaven. Christian ideas of beatitude, in contrast, are in accordance with philosophical truth.

Peter the Venerable lambasted Jews for their stubborn refusal to recognize Jesus as the Messiah, which showed, he affirmed, that they were irrational, subhuman beasts. At the same time, he praised the Saracens for their rationality and learning; clearly, they must be ripe to convert, once

Christian doctrine is rationally explained to them. Yet Muslims were no more apt than Jews to be converted by Christians' supposedly rational arguments. Hence Martí (and other thirteenth-century authors) classify the Muslims as irrational: it is far easier to lambast one's opponents as irrational, subhuman beasts than to call into question the rational basis of one's own system of beliefs. The Latin Christian worldview, carefully constructed over the centuries and increasingly buttressed by philosophy, could not allow itself to be undermined by infidel objections. If many of the most acute philosophical minds of the Middle Ages belonged to Saracens, they must be somehow crypto-Christians, or they must at least secretly reject the law of Muhammad. Like his contemporary Roger Bacon, Martí plays up intellectual division within Islam to make Avicenna and al-Fârâbî into free-thinking rationalists who rejected the Koran.

RAMON PENYAFORT and Ramon Martí did not limit their missionary efforts to Jaume's territories: they were also active in North Africa, especially Tunis. Already in 1234, Ramon de Penyafort, at the time confessor to Pope Gregory IX, wrote a long missive to the prior of the Dominicans and the minister of the Franciscans in Tunis, answering, in the Pope's name, a long series of questions that they had sent, though at the time the friars in Tunis seemed more preoccupied with ministering to the Latin Christian community of Tunis than with mission to the Muslims.

The aggressive Dominican approach to mission, embodied in the work of Martí, had the backing of two powerful crusading kings, and it could boast some dramatic successes. Its proponents bragged of those successes: according to a biography of Ramon Penyafort written in the first half of the fourteenth century, Friar Ramon and his Dominican associates had converted more than ten thousand Muslim souls to Christ.[30] These figures are certainly exaggerated, and the Dominican missions had also hardened the resistance of many Jews and Muslims: what easier way to offend them than to directly attack their holy writings and to tell them they have been interpreting them wrong for centuries? The Franciscan approach to mission was different; instead of engaging bookish confrontation between religious scholars, the barefoot Franciscan Friars preached to the assembled masses, at times provoking the Muslim rulers to martyr them.[31] Franciscan mission, "of the heart more than of the head," gained the respect of Muslims, even if it won few converts;[32] the Dominican methods led to spirited intellectual defense of Islam. The Dominican approach involved largely *negative* reasoning: reason could be used to attack the Koran and to defend

Christianity from various kinds of arguments, but not to prove the truth of Christianity.

Rejecting the Idea That Christian Truth Can Be Proven by Reason: Thomas Aquinas

The Dominican missionary strategy was in line with developing thirteenth-century doctrine, which increasingly affirmed that the truth of Christianity could not rationally be proven, for if it could, there would be no merit in faith (in the oft-evoked words of Pope Gregory I). Reason was an arm that could be used offensively to prove the "irrationality" of rival creeds or defensively to defend Christianity against the charge of irrationality, but it could not prove the Christian truth, for faith was indispensable. This affirmation is to be understood in the context not only of polemics against Judaism, Islam, and heresy but also of the controversy caused by the growing impact of Greco-Arabic philosophy on the study of theology: in 1231 Gregory IX had reiterated an earlier prohibition against teaching the scientific works of Aristotle in Paris.

Thomas Aquinas justifies the use of reason to complement faith in his *Summa contra gentiles*. Thomas and Ramon Martí had together been students of Albert the Great, and it is apparently Martí who transmits (in 1269?) the request from Ramon de Penyafort, that Thomas compose a *Summa* to serve as another weapon in the Dominican arsenal of philosophical polemics and apologetics against Islam.[33] Aquinas incorporates into his *Summa,* arguments from Martí's *Capistrum Iudaeorum* (1267); Martí, in turn, employs arguments from the *Summa contra gentiles* in his *Pugio fidei* (composed in 1278).[34] There is some debate over whether Thomas's "gentile" adversaries are meant to be Muslims, generic non-Christian philosophers, or even Averroists in Paris; indeed Thomas may have thought his work appropriate to all three groups.

Little in the *Summa contra gentiles* addresses Islam specifically. In one brief passage, Thomas does show that he has a general (and of course, quite negative) idea of who Muhammad was. In *Summa contra gentiles* 1:6, Thomas invokes the miracles performed by Christ as proof of the truth of Christianity; to this he contrasts Muhammad who produced no miracles:

> Those who introduced the errors of the sects proceeded in contrary fashion, as instanced by Muhammad, who enticed peoples with the

promise of carnal pleasures, to the desire of which the concupiscence of the flesh instigates. He also delivered commandments in keeping with his promises, by giving the reins to carnal pleasure, wherein it is easy for carnal men to obey: and the lessons of truth which he inculcated were only such as can be easily known to any man of average wisdom by his natural powers: yea, rather the truths which he taught were mingled by him with many fables and most false doctrines. Nor did he add any signs of supernatural agency, which alone are a fitting witness to divine inspiration, since a visible work that can be from God alone, proves the teacher of truth to be invisibly inspired: but he asserted that he was sent in the power of arms, a sign that is not lacking even to robbers and tyrants. Again, those who believed in him from the outset were not wise men practiced in things divine and human, but beastlike men who dwelt in the wilds, utterly ignorant of all divine teaching; and it was by a multitude of such men and the force of arms that he compelled others to submit to his law. Lastly, no divine oracles or prophets in a previous age bore witness to him; rather did he corrupt almost all the teaching of the Old and New Testaments by a narrative replete with fables, as one may see by a perusal of his law. Hence by a cunning device, he did not commit the reading of the Old and New Testament Books to his followers, lest he should thereby be convicted of falsehood. Thus it is evident that those who believe his words believe lightly.[35]

This is the *Summa*'s one brief rebuttal of Muhammad and his doctrine. Thomas's knowledge of Islam is sparse; despite the reference to a "perusal of his law," there is no evidence that Thomas had ever seen a Latin translation of the Koran or that he had read any major Latin polemical text against Islam. Yet his portrayal, if a brief caricature, is similar to that of the Dominican missionaries, and it is tempting to see a discussion with Ramon Martí or Ramon Penyafort as the source of his slight knowledge of Islam. Clearly, Thomas is completely unaware of Muslim counterarguments to his arguments, and he does not consider Muslim doctrine to be theologically sophisticated enough to merit thorough perusal and refutation. This is all the more surprising because Thomas read (and incorporated into his theology) the works of a number of important Muslim philosophers and theologians. He nevertheless brands Muhammad's followers as "carnal," "beastlike," irrational men. Does he (like Ramon Martí) consider that "rational" men like al-Fârâbî or Avicenna must ipso facto reject (at least in private) the "irrational" law of Muhammad? Thomas does not address the question directly, but we find the same charge (heard perhaps from the lips of Martí) that Muhammad discouraged his followers from studying the Bible.

Shortly after he finished his *Summa contra gentiles,* Thomas composed a brief tract, *Reasons for the Faith against the Muslims,* for the cantor of Antioch, who had asked him to provide arguments to defend the faith against the objections of Muslims and Eastern Christians. The Muslim objections to Christian doctrine (as reported by the Cantor) are the standard ones: God can have no son because he has no wife; it is "insane" to profess three persons in one God; Christ was not crucified in order to save mankind; it is ridiculous to believe Christians eat God on the altar or to believe that man's fate is not predetermined by divinely ordained destiny. To each of these Muslim objections, Thomas gives a long reply to show how Christian doctrine is consistent with (though not provable by) reason. These Muslim objections, for Thomas, far from reflecting any irrationality (or nonrationality) of Christian doctrine, reflect the irrational, "carnal" nature of the Muslims. In response to the objection that God can have no son because he has no wife, Thomas comments: "Since [the Muslims] are carnal, they can think only of what is flesh and blood," and they thus cannot understand the Christian doctrine of spiritual generation of the Son by the Father.[36]

Thomas is clear about the limits of the defensive arguments he provides:

First of all I wish to warn you that in the disputations with unbelievers about articles of the faith, you should not try to prove the Faith by necessary reasons. This would belittle the sublimity of the Faith, whose truth exceeds not only human minds but also those of angels; we believe in them only because they are revealed by God.

Yet whatever comes from the Supreme Truth cannot be false, and what is not false cannot be repudiated by any necessary reason. Just as our Faith cannot be proved by necessary reasons, because it exceeds the human mind, so because of its truth it cannot be refuted by any necessary reason. So any Christian disputing about the articles of the Faith should not try to prove the Faith, but defend the Faith. Thus blessed Peter [1 Pet. 3:15] did not say "Always have your proof," but "your answer ready," so that reason can show that what the Catholic Faith holds is not false.[37]

This is a clear definition of the Dominican polemical strategy: reason can be used to destroy rival creeds and defend one's own doctrines from the charge of irrationality but not to prove the truth of Christianity. The idea that reason is insufficient to prove the faith would be bitterly disputed by various thirteenth-century theologians, in particular Roger Bacon and Ramon Llull. At the same time that Christian theologians began to admit that they were unable to prove their doctrines through reason, in part in reaction to the works of Muslim and Jewish philosophers, they increasingly lambasted Muslims (and Jews) as "carnal" and "irrational." This tendency is nowhere more blatant than in the works of Dominican missionary Riccoldo da Montecroce.

Riccoldo da Montecroce

It is perhaps with a feeling of optimism similar to William of Tripoli's that a Florentine Dominican, Riccoldo da Montecroce, set out for the Levant in 1288. Riccoldo had entered the Dominican order in 1267, after having received an education in letters.[38] Now, after twenty-one years in the order, he had obtained permission from Muño de Zamora, master general of the order, to make a pilgrimage to Jerusalem and to preach as a missionary to Mongols and Muslims. He describes his voyage in his *Liber peregrinationis* (c. 1300), in which he combines a narration of his pilgrimage to the holy sites with an ethnographical sketch of the different peoples he encountered on his travels (paying particular attention to their religious beliefs and practices). He sailed to Acre in 1288 and traveled inland to visit the holy sites of Galilee, Jerusalem, the Jordan River. He describes how at each of the holy places he and his companions performed mass, reading (or singing) the relevant Gospel passages. But Riccoldo was not simply on a pilgrimage: he continued east, eventually reaching Tabriz (in Iran), capital of the Mongol Ilkhan Khanate, where he preached through an interpreter.[39] He eventually made his way to Baghdad, where he studied Arabic and read the Koran. He spent "many years" in the East, as he himself says; it was in Baghdad that he received the news of the fall of Acre to the Mamluks in 1291; he was still there, apparently, when the Ilkhan Ghazan converted from Buddhism to Islam, sparking destruction of churches, synagogues, and Buddhist temples.

It may be at this time of persecution that Riccoldo fled Baghdad only to be accosted by two Muslim Mongols who beat him, tried to make him convert to Islam, "to preach Muhammad and his perfidious law"; they stripped him of his Dominican habit and obliged him to make a living as a camel driver.[40] Riccoldo was still in the East when he wrote his *Five Letters on the*

Fall of Acre (see the introduction), expressing his astonishment and despair that God should allow the Saracens to vanquish the Christians and kill friars. Riccoldo returned to Italy around 1300, in order, it seems, to answer at the papal curia charges that he had recklessly classified certain Eastern Christian sects as heretical. It may be upon his return that he completed his *Liber peregrinationis;* he subsequently composed a polemical work against the Koran, the *Contra legem Sarracenorum* (Against the law of the Saracens), in which he makes use of earlier Latin and Arabic anti-Muslim polemics (in particular the twelfth-century Arabic *Liber denudationis*). His final work, the *Libellus ad nationes orientales* (Treatise on the oriental nations), describes the different Christian sects of the Orient; ironically, Riccoldo, who had lived for a dozen years in the East, here slavishly follows the classifications of Thomas Aquinas, who had never set foot in the East. It may be that Riccoldo, under scrutiny for too rashly expressing his own views about oriental Christians, wished in his final two works to confine himself to the compilation of impeccable authorities.[41]

Throughout these works one senses the disillusionment of the missionary as he comes to realize that his grand project is doomed to failure. Riccoldo addresses the first of his *Five Letters on the Fall of Acre* to God, expressing his astonishment that he should allow such misfortune to befall Christendom, that he should give such power and glory to the Saracens. The Saracens, Jews, and Tartars mock us, asking, "Where is the God of Christians?" taunting Christians who thought that Jesus son of Mary was God and that he would help them. Riccoldo himself saw in Baghdad the sad procession of Christian prisoners bound for the slave markets, including nuns, sanctified virgins, now bound for infidels' beds. He saw liturgical items and Latin books sold in the markets (where he bought a manuscript of Gregory the Great's *Moralia in Job*). He also found, to his horror, a Dominican habit, torn and bloody where the sword had killed his fellow friar; is it just for the holy Dominican and Franciscan friars to perish so? How, Riccoldo asks God, can you allow this "cruel beast" to dishonor your name, deflower your sanctified virgins, violate your churches? Riccoldo chides himself for having been so presumptuous as to think he could "defeat him [Muhammad] through Your force and destroy his perfidious law"; had not far better men attempted to slay this "beast" and failed, notably Francis and Dominic? Had not great kings and barons, including "Louis, Saint, King of France," attempted to destroy it by force, only to suffer humiliating defeats that discouraged other Christians? Riccoldo had come as a Dominican missionary to bring Mongols and Muslims into the Christian fold: now Acre had fallen, its inhabitants sold into slavery or massacred; Mongols were converting to Islam; and Christians in Baghdad faced threats and violence.

What troubled Riccoldo most is that God should permit (even seem to condone) the "blasphemies" of the Koran. "As You know, frequently, as I read the Koran in Arabic, with great grief and impatience in my heart, I would place this book on Your altar, before the image of You and your holy mother and say: 'Read! Read what Muhammad says!' And it seemed to me that You did not want to read."[42] The "blasphemies" that shock him so, are, among others, that Jesus is man, not God; that he was in fact a Muslim who never claimed to be God; that the apostles, Abraham, and other biblical figures were Muslim. These are by and large the same ideas that shocked the anonymous annotator of Robert of Ketton's Latin translation of the Koran. Yet to Riccoldo, overwhelmed by Muslim victories and mocked by non-Christians in Baghdad, these "blasphemies" are all the more perplexing. Can it be true, he asks Jesus, that you are, as the Saracens say, one of them? That would indeed explain why you favor them. He addresses the same question to the apostles.

In the final two of the five letters on the fall of Acre, Riccoldo accepts the inscrutable justice of God's ways. No longer viewing the massacre of Acre's friars as unjust, he now presents it as the glorious conferral of the crown of martyrdom. His final letter is his description of the "response" he received from God to his first four letters. He was reading Gregory the Great's *Moralia in Job* and prayed to Gregory, asking why he had received no reply to his letters and insistent prayers. He then heard a voice in his heart saying "Take it and read!";[43] in obedience to this voice, he opened Gregory's book and placed his finger on a random passage. Here he read that God does not directly answer the doubts and prayers of each individual, because he has answered them once and for all in Scripture. Riccoldo thanks God for this clear response, yet admits that a doubt remains: he has read in the Bible that sometimes God chastises people as "friends," in order to make them repent; others he crushes as enemies, as if to begin their eternal punishment in this life. Which is the case, he asks, of the oriental Christians? Are they your friends, receiving a particularly bitter lesson? If so, when will you liberate them from their Saracen oppressors? Or are the oriental Christians rather your enemies?

Riccoldo expresses the same ambivalence—toward oriental Christians, Mongols, and Saracens—in his *Liber peregrinationis*. In this work Riccoldo describes his travels from Acre to Baghdad, taking care to describe the customs and beliefs of the various religious communities he encounters; I concentrate on his portrayal of Saracens, which he places after his arrival in Baghdad:

> This city, Baghdad, is the center and capital of the Saracens, both in terms of their education and religion and in terms of their political power. . . . There the Saracens have their greatest universities [*maxima studia*] and their great teachers. There are many Saracen clerics [*religiosi*] there. Their different sects convene there. There one finds the great monasteries of the Saracens, called *mujarrad,* which means contemplatives. When I wanted to eliminate the perfidy of Muhammad, seeking to assault them in their capital and in the place of their university, I needed to converse with them at times; they received me as if I were an angel of God—in their schools, classrooms, monasteries, churches or synagogues, and in their homes. And I payed close attention to their law and their works; I was astounded at how, in such a perfidious law, one could find works of such great perfection.[44]

This passage conveys Riccoldo's ambivalence, his blend of admiration and contempt for the Muslims of Baghdad. He is indeed awed by what he sees in Baghdad, by the elaborate organization of Islamic learning and charity and by the zeal and piety of the Muslims. He describes in detail Baghdad's madrasas, which he compares favorably to European monasteries as centers for ascesis, contemplation, and study. These Saracens study assiduously, show the utmost respect in their mosques (they enter barefoot; they pray and study quietly). He praises their scrupulous respect for the rituals of ablution and prayer; he lauds their generous alms-giving, their profound respect for God's name. He affirms that he was received with such warmth and hospitality that he might have been at home among his own Dominican friars; his Muslim hosts always greeted him by praising Christ's name. Moreover, he affirms, brotherly love reigns amongst the Saracens; they rarely fight among themselves, but valiantly unite against those whom they consider the enemies of their faith. This praise probably reflects Riccoldo's own experience in Baghdad, although it is exaggerated. The point, as Riccoldo makes clear, is to shame his Christian reader into better moral conduct: "We have not told these things so much in order to praise the Saracens, but rather to lambast certain Christians who are unwilling to do for the law of life what the damned do for the law of death."[45] For despite his warm praise of the Saracens' piety and good works, he affirms that they are damned, that their law is "the law of death." After ten pages (in the modern edition) of praise for the Saracens' piety, Riccoldo launches into fifteen pages of attack against the "law of the Saracens," which he lambasts as "profuse, confused, obscure, mendacious, irrational, and violent."[46]

In calling it "profuse" *[larga],* Riccoldo means to contrast Islam with the Christian way: "narrow is the way which leadeth unto life," as the Gospel says; in contrast, the Saracens follow the broad way "that leadeth to destruction" (Matt. 7:13–14). He claims that Saracens believe that all they need to do to assure their place in heaven is to profess the Shahâda: "There is no God but God and Muhammad is his prophet." Thus the Saracens can sin as much as they please, firm in the belief that if they profess the Shahâda they will get into heaven. The Saracens' law is also "confused": the Koran, he claims, is jumbled, following neither a logical nor a chronological order. It is also "obscure": the Saracens themselves affirm that no one, except God, can fully understand the Koran. It is "mendacious," says Riccoldo, because it contains many lies: here he reiterates several of the standard Christian ideas of Muslim errors: Mary as the sister of Aaron and Moses, the false miracle of the splitting of the moon.

Yet the core of Riccoldo's criticism of the Koran is that it is supposedly *irrational.* Muslim divorce law is contrary to reason and to natural law. Riccoldo affirms (erroneously following the *Liber denudationis*) that the Koran permits sodomy, which reason prohibits. Equally irrational and ridiculous, for Riccoldo, are the carnal delights the Saracens await in heaven; here he again follows the *Liber denudationis,* claiming that the Saracens believe that heavenly penises will be "as long as a fresh horse can run in one day before becoming tired." This law is so manifestly irrational, says Riccoldo, that

> Their wise men began to execrate the perversity of their law. Since this law could be eliminated either through the books of the prophets, by the law of Moses, or even by the veracious books of the philosophers, therefore the Caliph of Baghdad ordered that nothing should be studied in Baghdad except the Koran. For this reason, we find that they know very little about the truth of theology or the subtlety of philosophy. Nevertheless, their wise men put no faith in the sayings of the Koran, but deride it in secret. In public, though, they honor it, on account of their fear of others.[47]

Yet the Saracen masses are deceived by this ruse, Riccoldo affirms, and by an equally necessary ruse, which is to accuse the Christians and Jews of having falsified their scriptures, even though the Koran itself praises the Torah and Gospel. Here Riccoldo expounds at length the well-worn arguments of the *Risâlat al-Kindî* (which he found in the *Liber denudationis*), arguing that it would be impossible for the many bickering Jews and Christians to plot together to alter Scripture.

Since neither reason nor miracles are on the Saracens's side, continues Riccoldo, they have had to spread their law by the sword: "Sixth and final point: it should be known that the law of the Saracens is violent and that it was introduced through violence. Hence they themselves know quite well that this law will last only as long among them as their victories by the sword."[48] Every Friday, he continues, the Saracens assemble for prayer; the preacher begins by unsheathing a sword and placing it where all can see it; this is the sign that their law began by the sword and will finish by the sword. (In his *Contra legem Sarracenorum* he repeats this charge, contrasting the Saracen preacher raising his sword with the Christian preacher raising the cross).[49] The Koran enjoins the Saracens to kill infidels, since Muhammad, unable to produce miracles, could not spread his law in any other way. He acknowledges that modern Saracen ascetics seem to produce miracles: living naked in the cold of Anatolia, or (in Baghdad) putting out fires with their bare feet or eating live snakes and scorpions. But such miracles, he affirms, unlike useful miracles such as cures, are signs of the Antichrist, not of divine favor.[50]

Riccoldo shows the same kind of admiration for Muslim piety that is in the *De statu Sarracenorum*, yet Riccoldo is far more pessimistic about the chances of converting Muslims to Christianity. *De statu* was written at a time when Acre was still in Latin hands, and hopes were high that the Mongols would convert to Christianity. It was still possible to imagine the pious, intelligent Saracens seeing the light and peacefully converting to Christianity. Riccoldo has been disillusioned: Acre has fallen; the Mongols are turning to Islam; and his years of mission in the Orient have produced few converts. Though he frankly admires the Muslims' learning, culture, piety, and hospitality, he shows little hope that they will convert peacefully. Their law will perish by the sword, but it seems unlikely that this will happen any time soon. In order to explain his own failures as a missionary (and the failures of others like him or better than him—for example, Dominic and Francis, whose missionary efforts he evokes in his *Letters*), he must blame the stubborn irrationality of the Saracens. Riccoldo profusely praises their learning and erudition, yet later claims they are prohibited from studying philosophy since the caliphs know it would disprove their "irrational" religion. Riccoldo apparently says this without irony; it is in fact Paris, rather than Baghdad, that sees repeated prohibitions against studying Aristotle's philosophical and scientific works in the thirteenth century. In the mid-twelfth century, Peter the Venerable lauds the Arab audience of his *Contra sectam siue haeresim Saracenorum* as the epitome of rationality; this rationality, he naively hopes, will lead them to accept the truth of Christianity. The bitter experience of thirteenth-century missionaries was that the Saracens were unimpressed by their "rational" arguments; increasingly, they will conclude (as Peter the Venerable did for the Jews) that these Saracens must be irrational. This will indeed become the predominant stereotype in the fourteenth and fifteenth centuries. Riccoldo is torn both ways: he admires the learning and sophistication of his Muslim hosts, yet he is rankled by their resistance to his "rational proofs" against their religion; surely, they cannot be all that rational?

RICCOLDO EXPOUNDS the same vision of Islam in greater detail in his *Contra legem Sarracenorum.* His goal is to comprehensively refute the Koran; he makes extensive use of earlier polemical tracts, especially the *Liber denudationis,* but also Peter the Venerable (and the *Corpus toletanus*) and Ramon Martí.[51] He follows Peter the Venerable in portraying Islam as the sum of all previous heresies: "the excrement of all the ancient heresies, which the Devil had sparsely sprinkled in each, Muhammad revomited it all together."[52] He compares the various tenets of Muhammad's law with those of ancient Christian heresiarchs.

In the second chapter of the *Contra legem,* Riccoldo explains how to argue with Saracens. They are curious and willing to discuss religion. "And since they excel in reason and have sharp intellects, they do not want to believe anything they cannot understand."[53] The first thing to do in arguing with them is not to expound Christian law, for that would be casting pearls before swine, as they will only deride our doctrines.

> Rather, first and principally one must insist on showing how vain their law is. For one cannot inculcate virtues before extirpating vice. And this method should be chosen since it is simpler; for it is easier to show that their faith is frivolous than to prove that our faith is true, because faith is an invisible gift from God. Whereas our faith has existence without appearance, theirs has appearance without existence. We do not have arguments *[rationes]* for proving the Trinity and the other things of our faith, for if we did faith would not be faith, and it would not be merito-

rious. But we have the authority of the Gospel, as even the Koran testifies, and we have miracles.[54]

Riccoldo affirms that reason cannot be used to prove the Trinity or other Christian doctrines, but it can be used to attack Islam. This is of course the standard Dominican strategy, which Ramon Llull bitterly objected to: using reason to denigrate and destroy rather than to build from commonly accepted truths. Since the Koran itself testifies to the authority of the Gospel, Riccoldo continues, Scripture too can be used to disprove the Koran: "one must concentrate on the refutation of such a perfidious law and show that it is not a law of God, and that the Saracens ought to accept the authority of the Gospels and the Old Testaments. We can prove this using the Koran itself, just as Goliath was killed with his own sword."[55] The strategy he is describing is essentially that of Peter the Venerable: use the Koran to prove the superior authority of the Bible, then use the Bible to attack Muhammad and the Koran and to prove the truth of Christianity. In the more than 150 years since Peter's *Contra sectam*, despite the work of scores of Dominican missionaries, despite schooling in Arabic and in Muslim philosophy and theology, the strategy is the same, and the results will be the same: the Dominican missions to Islam are a failure.

I will not describe in detail the polemics of Riccoldo's *Contra legem*; throughout, Riccoldo expands the arguments he made in his *Liber peregrinationis*, adding arguments culled from his readings. As in his earlier work, he reproaches the Koran for being confusing, contradictory, unorganized, violent—in a word *irrational*. While Muslims claim that the beauty of the Koran's Arabic proves its divine origins, Riccoldo affirms the contrary: the Koran is in verse, when everybody knows that God speaks to prophets clearly, *in prose*.[56] He derides the Muslim legends of the *Mi'râj*.[57] The real author of the Koran is the devil.[58] He repeats and expands upon the notion that the Muslim elite is secretly Christian: he tells of a caliph of Baghdad who supposedly was Christian; when he died he was found to be wearing a crucifix.[59] Moreover, the study of philosophy leads wise Muslims away from their erroneous faith.

There arose against both groups [Sunnis and Shiites] certain Saracens expert in philosophy. They started to read the books of Aristotle and Plato and started to despise all the sects of the Saracens and the Koran itself.

When someone warned the Caliph of Baghdad, named [name left blank in manuscript] about this, he built in Baghdad two very prestigious schools, Nizamiyya and Mustansiriyya . He reformed the study of the Koran and ordered that whoever came from the provinces to study the Koran in Baghdad, these students would have rooms and stipends for their needs. He also ordered that the Saracens and those studying the Koran should in no way study philosophy. And they do not consider those who study philosophy to be good Saracens, because they all despise the Koran.[60]

Here Riccoldo has combined (and elaborated upon) two ideas from his *Peregrinatio,* where he praised Baghdad's madrasas in his section on the positive portrayal of Saracen mores, only to lambast the anti-intellectual policies of Baghdad's caliphs in his anti-Islamic section. Here he resolves this apparent contradiction by bringing two elements together, making the founding of madrasas into a clever anti-intellectual ploy: the point of having government-funded educational institutes, he tries to make his reader believe, is precisely to squelch philosophical reading and speculation by assuring that only the Koran is read and taught, not any philosophical texts that will contradict it.

Riccoldo affirms that Muhammad, in the Koran, professes Christian truth without understanding it: Riccoldo produces the standard arguments for the Trinity based on the Koran's use of plural nouns to refer to God; he also produces Koranic passages that, he claims, prove the existence of the Holy Spirit and of Christ as the Word of God. He notes that the Koran praises the Torah and Gospel and asks why in that case the Muslims do not study them? The answer, he says, is that they would soon discover their error; in order to prevent this, they prohibit the study of the Bible (just as they prohibit the study of philosophy for the same reason). Indeed, he says, the Saracens have four "remedies" to prevent their error from being revealed: they kill anyone who attacks the Koran; they prohibit religious disputation; they warn Saracens not to believe what non-Saracens say; and they proclaim, "your law is for you, mine is for me."[61] Yet it is amazing, says Riccoldo, that the Saracens prefer the Koran to the Gospel; the reason, once again must be their irrationality, to which there is only one remedy: "Consequently, when certain doubts arise in the Koran and certain questions which the Saracens cannot answer, they should not only be invited but be *compelled* into the Banquet of the Truth."[62] Since the Saracens are unconvinced by our rational arguments, Riccoldo seems to be saying, they ought to be compelled to join the church. Where dialogue fails, Riccoldo recommends force. Riccoldo's work is to become one of the most widely read anti-Islamic tracts from the fourteenth century to the sixteenth; his image of the Saracens as violent and irrational zealots who are impervious to reason and can only be countered by force has a long life ahead of it.

Alfonso Buenhombre

The efforts of Ramon Penyafort, Ramon Martí, and other Dominicans had launched a large and complex missionary machine, producing voluminous, erudite works. Yet they produced few converts; Jews and Muslims were unimpressed with the rationalistic attack on their beliefs and their holy texts.[63] Ramon Llull was right in his critique of their ineffectiveness, though Llull's own method proved even less fruitful.

In the midst of such discouragement, one Dominican missionary sounded an optimistic note—or so he would have his readers believe. Alfonso Buenhombre, a Spanish Dominican who traveled in North Africa and was active in missions to Jews and Muslims, became bishop of Marrakesh in 1343. Educated in Paris, fluent in Arabic, he was the epitome of the Dominican missionary ideal, which sought to prove the superiority of Christianity over Judaism and Islam through rational argumentation and the careful exegesis of the adversaries' scripture.

Among Alfonso's works is a Latin translation of the *Disputation of the Saracen Abû Tâlib and the Jew Samuel*. Alfonso tells us that he found an Arabic manuscript of the work, which he translated into Latin while imprisoned in Marrakesh. The *Disputation* takes the form of an exchange of seven letters between two learned friends: Abû Tâlib and Samuel. The two, living in Marrakesh, decided that together they would study both the Torah and the Koran, to see which of their two religions was better. Samuel later moved to Toledo, and they subsequently continued their discussion in the letters that make up the *Disputation*. In these letters, each disputant uses the other's scripture to raise doubts about his religious doctrine. In fact, each disputant proves unable to defend his own religion and ends up affirming the truth of Christianity: Samuel, using the Koran, tries to prove that Muhammad not only considered that Jesus was a great prophet, but was also the Messiah; Abû Tâlib uses the Torah to prove that the Messiah has come in the person of Jesus and to prove the Incarnation and the Trinity. In the final letter, Abû Tâlib confesses that the Muslims have a secret book that reveals that Muhammad, on his deathbed, bade his disciples to receive baptism and to follow Christ, that this was the only way to be freed from sin. He concludes with a promise that he would come to Toledo, where both he and Samuel may receive the gift of baptism.[64]

To find such a text, of course, is a Dominican missionary's dream. If a learned Jew and Muslim can through careful study come to realize the superiority of Christianity, there is hope for the Dominican missionary effort. Argument and disputation, based not on philosophical proofs (*rationes necessariae*) but on careful study of Koran, Hadîth, Torah, and Talmud, can indeed bear fruit. Such a find seemed too good to be true as indeed it was: it was a pious hoax that a learned Christian (probably Alfonso Buenhombre himself) foisted on his Latin readers, a hoax not brought to light until 1992.[65] The sources of the *Disputation* are not only the Koran and Torah but also the chronicles of Lucas de Tuy and Rodrigo Jiménez de Rada and Latin anti-Muslim texts such as those of Ramon Martí. Is this pious fraud meant to be a tool for Dominican missionaries in the line of action? Is it meant to cheer them on in their often daunting and thankless endeavor? Or is it a desperate attempt to justify Dominican mission to a skeptical audience of Parisian theologians? At any rate, Alfonso seemed to like this strategy: he also produced an anti-Jewish text that he claimed was written by a Jewish rabbi and that he also "found" in Morocco.[66]

Alfonso Buenhombre's hoax epitomizes the failure of the Dominican ambition to convert the Jewish and Muslim worlds to Christianity through disputation. Late thirteenth- and fourteenth-century theologians increasingly denied that it was possible to prove the faith through reasoned argument: reason can be used to defend the faith, for Thomas Aquinas, but not to prove it. Both the Franciscan and Dominican approaches turned out to be failures. One of their sharpest critics, Ramon Llull, forged his own idiosyncratic strategy for converting Muslims.

Chapter 11

⌖

FROM VERDANT GROVE TO DARK PRISON:
REALMS OF MISSION IN RAMON LLULL

RAMON LLULL criticized sharply—though obliquely—the Dominican missionary strategy. On no less than five separate occasions in his writings, he refers to Ramon Martí's mission to the king of Tunis as a failure, without ever mentioning Martí by name.[1] As Llull tells the story, Martí went to Tunis and logically proved to the king that the religion of Muhammad was false, so that he was ready to abandon it. If the good friar would prove to him the truth of Christianity, the king and all his people would convert. The friar responded that "the faith of the Christians is so transcendent that it cannot be proved by necessary reasons; it is only to be believed, nothing else. Here is the *Symbol* written in Arabic [probably an Arabic translation of Martí's *Explanatio simboli Apostolorum*]. Believe it and you will be saved."[2] The king rebuked the friar for having used reason to destroy his faith without being able to prove Christianity; he banished him from his kingdom. Llull laments that if only the friar had been properly educated in logic and philosophy he could have proved the truth of Christianity to the king. While Dominicans like Martí and Thomas Aquinas affirmed that one could not prove Christian truth through "necessary reasons," Llull devoted his life to trying to do precisely that.

Llull rejects the Dominican strategy, forging his own approach, an idiosyncratic fusion of Dominican rationalism and thoroughness with Franciscan mysticism and pathos. For Llull, the superiority of Christianity to Islam can be demonstrated rationally, if through the rather abstruse and idiosyncratic tool of Llull's *Art*. For Llull (as for many earlier authors) Muhammad lacks the signs of prophecy, and the Koran is full of contradictions. He asserts that learned Muslims themselves are aware of this and do not believe that Muhammad was a prophet.[3] They are (like Peter the Venerable's imagined Muslim audience a century and a half earlier) an audience ripe for conversion, if only Christians can properly attend to the task.

Llull on Llull: The *Vita Coaetanea*

Near the end of his life, in August 1311, Llull narrated his life to "friends," apparently Carthusian monks of the Parisian monastery of Vauvert, one of whom transcribed it as the *Vita coaetanea*. The text, while at times misleading and containing considerable gaps in chronology, is a precious testimony showing us how Llull, at the age of about eighty, saw his life and mission in retrospect.[4]

The *Vita coaetanea* tells how the young Ramon, seneschal to the future king Jaume II of Mallorca, one day sat composing a poem for a woman he was in love with; he was interrupted by a vision: he saw before him Christ in agony on the cross. This vision came to him repeatedly over the next few days before he concluded that he must abandon the world and serve only Christ. Asking how he might best do this, he decided that the finest service he could offer to Christ would be to convert the Saracens. He resolved to do three things: to preach conversion to the Saracens, giving up his life for Christ if necessary; to write "a book, the best in the world, against the errors of unbelievers [*infidelium*]"; and to convince the Pope and the Christian princes to establish monasteries where Christians could learn Arabic and the languages of other infidels.[5] Subsequently, on the feast of Saint Francis, he heard a sermon telling how

> Saint Francis had abandoned and rejected everything so as to be firmly united to Christ and to Christ alone, etc. Ramon, incited by the example of Saint Francis, soon sold his possessions, reserving a small portion for the support of his wife and children; and, in order to ask the Lord and His saints for guidance in the three things the Lord had placed in his heart, he set out for the shrines of Saint Mary of Rocamadour, Saint James, and other holy places, intending never to return.[6]

This is of course the elderly Llull describing his youthful conversion, describing it, moreover, using the topoi of hagiography, in particular of monastic conversion stories. The difference is that Ramon, instead of joining (or forming) a religious order, set out to devote his life to the conversion of the Saracens, via the three ideas that he would champion throughout his life. Notably absent from his list of three projects is the Crusade, which Llull repeatedly advocated after the fall of Acre in 1291. Here the elderly Llull accurately describes his early ideas, in which crusading is largely rejected.

The young Llull decided to set out for Paris, to receive an education in arts and theology. But he met up with Ramon de Penyafort, who convinced him to return instead to Mallorca, where he could learn Arabic. He bought a Muslim slave who taught him Arabic for nine years. One day he heard that his Muslim slave had blasphemed Christ's name; Llull, "impelled by a great zeal for the Faith, hit the Saracen on the mouth, on the forehead, and on the face."[7] The slave later attacked his master with a knife and wounded him; Ramon and the other members of the household subdued him and had him imprisoned. Ramon prayed to the Virgin for guidance: should he have the man who had taught him Arabic killed, or should he let him live and risk being attacked again? His prayers were answered in a singular way; he discovered that the slave had hanged himself in his prison cell. This incident provides several interesting clues about Llull's personality, his curious mix of fanaticism and tolerance: Llull cannot bear to hear harsh, blasphemous language, nor can he bear the thought of killing his slave. Yet the rejection of his own ideas (by Muslims, as here, or by Christians), inspires in him a righteous rage.

Immediately following the death of the slave, in the *Vita coaetanea,* is a revelation: "After this, Ramon went up a certain mountain [Mount Randa] not far from his home, in order to contemplate God in greater tranquility. When he had been there scarcely a full week, it happened that one day while he was gazing intently heavenward the Lord suddenly illuminated his mind, giving him the form and method for writing the aforementioned book against the errors of the unbelievers."[8] Llull receives a revelation on the mountain, like some new Moses or Muhammad (though the text makes no such direct comparison): God exposes to him a new book, which can be used to bring the infidels to understand Christian truth. Llull would also have in mind the more recent examples of Francis, who is supposed to have climbed Mount Alverne and received his stigmata, and Bonaventure, who on the same mountain composed the *Itinerarium mentis in Deum.*[9] After his eight days on the mountain, Llull descended to the monastery of Santa Maria de la Real and wrote down the book revealed to him, his *Ars major* (or *Ars generalis*). The *Vita* is certainly making grandiose claims for Llull's *Art:* revealed by God, it is a logical, surefire method for bringing infidels to the faith through rational argumentation; it is, as Llull would claim in other works, a sort of key to all knowledge. When Llull finished formulating his *Art,* the *Vita* continues, he returned to Mount Randa and built a hermitage "on the very spot where he had stood when God had shown him the method of the Art."[10] There he was visited by an angelic shepherd who revealed new secrets about God and the angels and who in reverence kissed the books Llull had written. In many ways all Llull's later works follow from this initial inspiration: they are explanations or commentaries of his *Art:* he is endlessly applying it to specific disciplines, haranguing reluctant readers to take it seriously, adapting its arguments to the specific exigencies of apologetics and polemics. He was now a man with a peculiar, God-given mission, and he would spend the rest of his life trying to put it into action. The vision on mount Randa is traditionally dated to 1274; by 1276 he was in Mallorca at the court of the new king, Jaume II, whom he convinced to establish a monastery at Miramar, on the northern coast of Mallorca, to educate Franciscan missionaries in Arabic.

The *Vita* briefly describes some of Llull's numerous trips to Paris and Rome: Paris, where he attempted to convince scholars to take his *Art* seriously (and upbraided them as obfuscating Averroists when they did not), and Rome, where he constantly urged Popes and curia to establish monasteries, modeled on Miramar, for the linguistic and scholarly training of monk-missionaries (he lambasted their worldliness and corruption when they did not heed his calls). Having little success in either endeavor, Llull went to Genoa, with the intention of embarking for North Africa and testing his new missionary method directly upon Muslims. Suddenly confronted by the real possibility of death at the hands of Muslims, he became frightened and did not board a ship leaving for "Saracen lands" and subsequently suffered deep doubt and depression at his failure. He eventually boarded a Genoese ship bound for Tunis where he tried his argumentation on prominent Muslims.

The *Vita* describes how Llull, upon arriving in Tunis, announced that he was prepared to convert to the "sect of Muhammad" if the Saracens were able to prove that it was superior to Christianity; this attracted a number of Saracen wise men who attempted to convert him. Ramon "was easily able to answer their arguments" asserting that the Christian doctrines of the Trinity and Incarnation were provable through recourse to the divine dignities, the attributes that Muslims and Christians alike ascribe to God. Ramon affirmed that he could "clearly prove" Christian doctrine, "using clear arguments based on a certain Art divinely revealed, as it is believed, to a Christian hermit not long ago, if you would care to discuss these things calmly with me for a few days."[11] As the *Vita coaetanea* tells the story, Ramon's method was bearing fruit; the "infidels" were gradually coming to see the truth, until one day a Saracen warned the king that Ramon would subvert and destroy the law of Muhammad if the king did not have him quickly beheaded. The king seemed inclined to kill Ramon, but one of his counselors advised that it would be dishonorable to kill such a wise and prudent man; besides, he added, if we kill him then the Christians will not allow Saracen preachers into their lands. The king decided to let Llull live but to expel him from his kingdom. Similarly, when the *Vita* narrates his disputation with the Saracen "bishop" of Bougie, the "bishop" responds to Llull's irrefutable Trinitarian argument with stunned silence and harsh imprisonment; a courtier warns against letting him speak before the court since no one will be able to argue against him; and finally the king orders his expulsion.

Llull's autobiographical portrait reflects his sense of mission and his unshakable confidence in his God-given method. He has a surefire means for proving the truth of Christianity, revealed to him by God on Mount Randa. If he fails to convert Muslims, it can only be because of the violent hostility of a few powerful Saracen leaders; if Popes, cardinals and kings fail to acknowledge the divinely inspired nature of his strategy, they must be evil as well, blinded by their lust for power and mundane delights. Yet this is the voice of an elderly, embittered Llull. Llull's strategy emerges in his early works and undergoes significant changes over the course of his life.

Llull's Strategy of Positive Argumentation (*Mediante Fide*)

Llull wrote more than 250 works, in Catalan, Latin, and Arabic, and most of them deal in one way or another with strategies for converting Muslims and Jews to Christianity. His emphasis differs and, indeed, changes over time, and it would be rash, in this brief chapter, to hazard broad generalizations concerning Llull's opus or to pretend to offer a thorough analysis of his writings on Islam. Yet the general bent of his strategy is clear, and it differs from that of the Dominicans. The goal, as he explained in various of his works, is to argue to infidels "not against the faith, but through the faith."[12] He sought, in other words, to bring Muslims (and Jews) to the Christian faith by positive argument, based on what they *already* believe, rather than by attacking that belief. In his early works Llull accordingly showed little enthusiasm for crusade. In one of his earliest works, the *Llibre de contemplació en Déu*, Llull rejects crusade for what sounds like a very Franciscan idea of mission.

I see many knights who go to the Holy Land beyond the sea, wanting to conquer it by force of arms, and in the end they are all brought to naught without obtaining their aim. Therefore it seems to me, O Lord, that the conquest of that Holy Land should not be done but in the manner in which You and Your apostles have conquered it: by love and prayers and the shedding of tears and blood.

As it seems, O Lord, that the Holy Sepulcher and the Holy Land beyond the sea should preferably be conquered by preaching rather than by force of arms, the Holy monk-knights should go forward, O Lord, buttress themselves with the sign of the cross, fill themselves with the grace of the Holy Spirit, and go preach to the infidels the truth of Your Passion, and shed for Your love all the water of their eyes and all the blood of their bodies, just as You have done out of love for them!

So many knights and noble princes had gone to the land beyond the sea, O Lord, to conquer it, that if this manner would have pleased You, surely they would have wrested it from the Saracens who hold it against our will. This indicates, O Lord, to the holy monks that You hope every day that they do out of love for You what You did out of love for them; and they can be sure and certain that should they throw themselves into martyrdom out of love for You, You shall hear them out in all they want to accomplish in this world in order to give praise to You.[13]

Here Llull seems very close to the Franciscan martyrs: it is by following the example of Christ and the apostles that the missionary can hope to convert the infidel. The missionary martyr can convert through the shedding of his own tears and blood, through his love and prayers. Yet in this same work, Llull gives coercion an important place: Christians should use the power they have over Saracen and Jewish captives to teach them by force the tenets of Christianity, with the hope that they may (voluntarily) convert and then become missionaries to their own people.[14]

Llull's ambivalence about crusading has been aptly described by Benjamin Kedar as "the many opinions of Ramon Llull."[15] In his novel *Blaquerna*, Llull has the sultan of Egypt send an envoy to Rome to lambast the Pope: the Christians, claims the sultan, must be the *real* followers of "Mafumet," since they are trying to spread their religion by the sword. God does not wish the Christians to possess the Holy Land because they are unwilling to follow the example of the apostles. Elsewhere in *Blaquerna* Llull seems to endorse crusade, presenting it as a necessary corollary to missionary activity.

Yet coercion and force are advocated essentially as a means to achieve an audience for the application of Llull's logical polemics. The key to providing the rational argumentation for these confrontations is Llull's *Art*. The *Art*, an arcane matrix of interwoven concepts, presented in a complex system of geometrical figures and tree diagrams, has daunted and discouraged many of Llull's readers from the thirteenth century to the present. Llull himself was aware of this problem, to which he responded by simplifying and streamlining his system and by creating mnemonic devices to help the reader memorize it.[16]

For our purposes what matters most about the *Art* is that Llull presents it as a practical and comprehensive means of obtaining knowledge. Since all knowledge emanates from and participates in divine wisdom, all truths are connected, and all truth leads inexorably to the great truths of Christianity. The key is provided by nine "dignities," Llull's version of the divine attributes that had long played an important role in Jewish, Christian, and Muslim theology and in Christian attempts to prove the doctrine of the Trinity. Llull's deployment of the dignities is different from that of earlier authors, who tended to pick three of the attributes and to identify them with the three persons of the Trinity. Over the course of his life, Llull came to distinguish, for each of the nine dignities, between principles of actor, recipient, and action. Thus God's goodness (*bonitas*) is not static but dynamic: it involves an actor who does good (*bonificans*, which Llull equates with the Father), a recipient of the good (*bonificatum*, the Son), and the action of transmitting goodness (*bonificare*, the Holy Spirit). The same "proof" of the Trinity can be made from the dynamic relationship implied in the eight other dignities (greatness, duration, power, wisdom, will, virtue, truth, and glory). By combining the nine dignities with a series of corresponding relative principles and subjects of knowledge in a multiplicity of possible combinations, all knowledge can be shown to be connected, and all in accordance with Christian truth. Llull devoted his life to refining, explaining, and promoting his *Art*, convinced that he had found the key to the unification of knowledge and the conversion of infidels.

Along with this structured approach to knowledge, Llull articulates a scheme of history involving three successive ages: an age of ignorance, an age of belief, and an age of understanding.[17] While structurally similar to the scheme of three ages (*status*) conceived by Joachim of Fiore (and subsequently embraced by spiritual Franciscans), the content and purpose of Llull's structure of history are his own. In the age of ignorance or age of the gentile, the idolater, trapped in the material world, worships physical objects as gods and benefits from no revealed religious law. In the age of belief, God reveals his laws to mankind and shows the truth of his law through miracles, such as those performed by Moses or by Christ and the apostles. In the age of understanding, there is no longer any need for miracles, as man through "necessary reasons" can come to comprehend the truth through his own power. This scheme of history, which Llull develops over the course of his various works, sets him apart from the Dominicans and Franciscans whose works he criticized. The Jews and Muslims were stuck in the age of belief, for Llull, whose strategy was to bring them to Christian truth through understanding; the Dominicans' denial that *rationes necessariae* could prove the truth of Christianity showed that the Dominicans, too, Llull implies (though he does not say so in so many words) were stuck in the age of belief and could have little luck in converting infidels; instead of guiding them from mere belief to true understanding, Dominicans like Martí were asking infidels to exchange one set of beliefs for another. The Franciscans could be said to be stuck in the age of belief in a different way: in wishing to re-create an apostolic age of martyrs and miracles, they were resorting to the tactics of a bygone age; far better to teach and preach Llull's *Art*.

Book of the Gentile and the Three Wise Men

One of the most important of Llull's early works designed to help convert infidels is *Book of the Gentile and the Three Wise Men* (Libre del gentil e los tres savis), which he composed in Mallorca between 1271 and 1276.[18] In his prologue, Llull presents a learned, aged, gentile philosopher meditating on death, in tearful melancholy because he knows he will die and that there is no life after death. Llull's gentile, like Theodore Abû Qurrah's outsider from a remote mountainous region or Peter Abelard's gentile philosopher, is meant to be an intelligent neutral observer, neither Jew, Christian, nor Muslim.[19] He wanders far from his land, into a forest. At the edge of this forest, three wise men (a Jew, a Christian, and a Muslim) meet at the gates of a great city; they decide to walk together in the forest. They come to a clearing, at the center of which are five trees surrounding a fountain; there, they see a beautiful woman on horseback, her horse drinking at the fountain: she is Lady Intelligence. She explains to them that inscribed on the flowers of the five trees are combinations of the different virtues and vices. By contemplating the concord between these virtues (and the opposition of the virtues to the vices), the wise can be led to spiritual truth.

At this point, Lady Intelligence takes leave of the three sages. One of them (Llull does not say which one) laments:

> "Ah! What a great good fortune it would be if, by means of these trees, we could all—every man on earth—be under one religion and belief, so that there would be no more rancor or ill will among men, who hate each other because of diversity and contrariness of beliefs and of sects! And just as there is only one God, Father, Creator, and Lord of everything that exists, so all peoples could unite and become one people, and that people be on the path to salvation, under one faith and one religion, giving glory and praise to our Lord God."
>
> "Think, gentlemen," the wise man said to his companions, "of the harm that comes from men not belonging to a single sect, and of the good that would come from everyone being beneath one faith and one religion. This being the case, do you not think it would be a good idea for us to sit beneath these trees, beside this lovely fountain, and discuss what we believe, according to what the flowers and conditions of these trees signify? And since we cannot agree by means of authorities, let us try to come to some agreement by means of demonstrative and necessary reasons [raons necessàries]."[20]

The sage, whose religious affiliation is deliberately not mentioned, speaks for all three: just as there is only one God, there can only be one true religion. If we could discover it rationally, using "necessary reasons," war and strife could be eliminated and mankind would be united under the banner of true religion.[21] At this point the gentile arrives, weeping over his mortality, and explains his plight to the sages. They affirm that he need not be sad and that there is a life after death, in which the evil are punished and the good are rewarded. The gentile, intrigued, asks them to prove this to him; this proof occupies the first of the four books of the Libre del gentil.

This first book, then, is devoted to proving the truths that are generally accepted by all three monotheistic religions: the existence of God, the creation of the universe ex nihilo, the resurrection of the body, and the eternal punishment or reward of men and women, based on their acts during life. The three sages collaborate to prove these ideas and Llull (again) significantly keeps them anonymous, saying "a sage" and "another sage" rather than "the Jew" or "the Christian." While I will not enter into the details of the supposedly rational "proofs" of Llull's arguments, they are to a large extent conventional in content, even if couched in Llull's idiosyncratic arboreal allegory. His arguments for the existence of God are in the tradition of Anselm of Canterbury and quite similar (in content, if not in form) to those of Llull's contemporary Thomas Aquinas. Once the three sages have proved these truths to the gentile, he asks to be initiated into their religion; he learns to his surprise that they have three different religions and are unable to agree about which one is the true one. He then proposes that each of the three sages present in turn his religion, and that he (the gentile) should be able to ask questions, but that the other two sages should remain silent during their companion's presentation.

Since the Jew's religion is the oldest of the three, the gentile asks him to begin. He presents Judaism (in book 2) in eight essential doctrines, which he attempts to prove through reference to the different flowers; the gentile at times listens in silence, at times asks questions or voices objections. Then it is the turn of the Christian, who (in book 3) similarly presents his religion in fourteen articles. Finally (in book 4) the Saracen expounds twelve articles of Islam. In the epilogue, the gentile reiterates the three sages' words, showing them that he has perfectly understood their arguments. He then offers a profuse prayer of praise and thanks to God for bringing him to the truth, for he now understands which religion will permit him, through God's grace, to reach paradise. He warmly thanks the three sages, who congratulate him and prepare to leave him. Wait, he says, don't you want to know which of your religions I chose? No, they respond; each of us is convinced you chose his religion, and we prefer to keep it this way. If we know which religion you chose, that will only prejudice our own discussion. The three sages leave him to return to the city. Before they leave each other they decide that they will meet regularly for discussions, until they have come to agreement on which law is true; then they will go forth and preach this law to the world. They beg each other's pardon for anything they might have said to offend each other's faith and each returns to his duties of teaching and preaching his respective religion.

The *Libre del gentil* is indeed an exceptional work, seen in the context of medieval Christian texts about Islam (or Judaism): four wise men calmly discussing religion in a verdant grove. There are no attacks on Muhammad or the Koran, no charges of Jewish deicide or of the Talmud as blasphemous. Such texts of religious disputation almost invariably end in conversion: yet here the reader does not even learn which religion the gentile has chosen, and none of the three sages converts at all (though they all agree that they wish to find the one true law).[22] While such tracts commonly present gross caricatures of the opponents' religions, Llull, scrupulous in his use of authentic Jewish and Muslim sources, presents a remarkably fair and accurate portrayal of each of the three religions. Llull's tract stands out as an irenic island is a sea of tempestuous disputation and polemic.

Yet the serene tone and apparent evenhandedness do not stand up to close scrutiny: they comprise, for Llull as for Theodore Abû Qurrah, a strategic posture for the defense of Christianity against its rivals. The four characters in the *Libre del gentil* all accept without question that only *one* of the three religions can lead to eternal bliss, that the adherents of the two erroneous religions are bound for hell. And while Llull never explicitly announces which religion the gentile chooses, the dialogue clearly indicates that it is Christianity. When (for example) in book 2, the Jew explains that his people have been in captivity for the past twelve hundred years, the gentile responds that perhaps it is because the Jews have unwittingly sinned against God, a clear reference to the Christian notion that the destruction of the temple and the subjugation of the Jews was punishment for the killing of Christ. The gentile later exclaims that he would in no way wish to become a Jew if that meant he would have to suffer servitude with the Jews on account of their sins. Clearly, Judaism will not be the religion the gentile chooses at the end of the debate.[23]

Similarly, in book 4 the gentile rejects a number of the Saracen's arguments. When the Saracen tries to prove that Muhammad was a prophet, the gentile first expresses his astonishment that God would send a prophet to the Arabs, but not to the gentile's people; he then affirms that God could not send a prophet to contradict another prophet, so that if (as the Koran affirms) Moses and Jesus were prophets, Muhammad cannot be one. The gentile makes other objections to Muslim doctrine. The Saracen gives a long description of the sensual pleasures that await the Muslim in paradise; to this the gentile voices a number of reservations. If eating, drinking, and sex occur in heaven, he objects, there will be the resultant "filth"; the Saracen affirms that while this is true in this world, God has willed it to be otherwise in the next. The gentile then argues that the ultimate purpose for which man was created is to have his glory in God, not in material things; the Saracen responds that man's happiness would be incomplete without both physical and spiritual pleasures. The gentile then objects that since the Muslim man is promised a large number of wives in heaven if he has been good in this life, then a good woman should have a large number of husbands; the Saracen responds that God honors man more than woman in this life and in the next. Then the gentile asks if *all* the Saracens believe in the heaven that he has described. The Saracen replies:

> It is true that among us there are differing beliefs with respect to the glory of Paradise, for some believe it will be as I said, and this they take from a literal interpretation of the Koran, which is our law, of the Proverbs of Muhammad [the Hadîth], and of commentators' glosses on the Koran and the Proverbs. But there are others among us who take this glory morally and interpret it spiritually, saying that Muhammad was speaking metaphorically to people who were backward and without understanding; and in order to inspire them with a love of God he recounted the above-mentioned glory. And therefore those who believe this say that in Paradise there will be no glory of eating or of lying with women, nor of the other things mentioned above. And these men are natural philosophers and great scholars, yet they are men who in some ways do not follow too well the dictates of our religion, and this is why we consider them as heretics, who have arrived at their heresy by studying logic and natural science. And therefore it has been established among us that no man dare teach logic or natural science publicly.[24]

Llull here places into the mouth of his supposedly Muslim character what is meant to be a harsh condemnation of Islam. The whole project of the *Libre del gentil* is to reach spiritual truth through the logical use of "necessary reasons"; the underlying idea is that all truths concord and that no knowledge contradicts the ultimate truth. Yet here Llull's Saracen frankly admits that logic and natural philosophy contradict Islam and that Muslims subsequently ban them. Despite all the polite language of respect, we find the same charge that we found in Ramon Martí and Riccoldo da Montecroce: that Islam is fundamentally irrational.[25]

Llull himself, in several later works, affirms this interpretation of his *Libre del gentil*. In his *Liber de fine*, for example, Llull recommends it for those wishing to convert the Tartars: "Concerning theology, my above-mentioned books are very good, in particular the *Book of the Gentile*, in which a Christian, a Saracen and a Jew debate concerning the truth in the presence of a certain gentile. And in this book readers can discover, if they wish, that the holy Catholic faith corresponds to the truth and the Jews and Saracens are in error."[26]

Liber de Fine

The youthful Llull may have been naively optimistic that his logical argumentation *mediante fide,* employing his *Art,* could convert the Saracen and Jewish masses. In his *Vita coaetanea,* Llull came to realize that his task would not be so easy, and he was quick to blame the rich and powerful (among Saracens and Christians) who, out of spite and worldly ambition, failed to be convinced by his methods. Llull finally embraced crusade following the fall of Acre in 1291. There was indeed still some hope of an alliance with the Mongols. In 1300 Ilkhan Mahmud Ghazan took Damascus from the Mamluks; Jaume II of Aragon wrote to congratulate him; and Llull himself set out for the East in hopes of converting him to Christianity, though he was not able to reach the sultan. Ghazan in 1302 wrote to Pope Boniface VIII proposing an anti-Muslim alliance, but in 1303 he was defeated by the Mamluks. Llull learned that the khan had converted to Islam, not Christianity.[27] Christendom would have to make practical plans for crusade without counting on Eastern allies. He wrote a series of tracts arguing for the necessity of an expedition to recovery the Holy Land—a crusade to be accompanied by missionaries trained in Arabic and in Llull's *Art.* The most complete espousal of these themes is to be found in his *Liber de fine.*

Llull was more than seventy years old when he composed, in Montpellier, his *Liber de fine* (1305). It is at once a summation of his life's works, a bitter rumination over the failure of his ideas, and a last desperate plea that the Pope, cardinals, secular rulers, *someone* take heed of what he is saying: "He that hath ears to hear, let him hear" (Matt. 11:15), he pleads three times.[28] The world is in bad straits, laments Llull at the beginning of *De fine:* infidels far outnumber Christians; they attack us, take away our lands, blaspheme against the Trinity and the Incarnation. Meanwhile the Christians, apathetic, "do not wish to remedy this iniquitous and unjust state of affairs." He describes his own efforts to remedy this situation: "For this a certain man gave up everything he had and then labored long, wandering over the entire earth so that he could convince the pope, the lord cardinals and the other princes of this world to give aid and remedy to such a great and vile evil."[29] He describes how he tried to persuade these powerful men to found monasteries dedicated to the training of missionaries: "But I, this man, could obtain nothing. And I could not do so because the public good has no friends. . . . For in this affair I could do no more, since I was almost alone in acting, and I was able in no way to find anyone who would help me."[30] Now, Llull says, he wishes to write to the Pope, cardinals, and princes and explain clearly to them how they can convert the infidels and heretics to the Catholic church and take back the Holy Land. If no one listens to me, sniffs Llull, at least *I* will be able to face the supreme judge with a clear conscience, knowing that I have done all in my power.

The first of the three books of *De fine* is entitled "On Disputation with Infidels." Llull affirms that the Pope should appoint a cardinal whose sole duty is the conversion of infidels. He would supervise the construction of four monasteries specialized in the education of missionaries: one monastery for missionaries to the Saracens, one for missionaries to the Jews, one for those to the "schismatics," one for those to the Tartars and other pagans. Devout and learned clerks unafraid of sacrificing their lives to Christ would enter the monasteries, learn the appropriate infidel language, and study the scriptures and doctrines of the infidel religion. When finished with this course of study, the clerics would go off in pairs to preach conversion to the infidels; for each pair who left the monastery, two more would be admitted. Llull acknowledges that there are indeed many devout clerics who do go off and preach to infidels: yet, since they lack specialized education in disputation, they are ineffectual.[31] Moreover, not knowing the language, they resort to unreliable interpreters, and hence receive only the scorn of more educated infidels.[32]

Llull devotes a chapter to specific strategies for converting Saracens. He first briefly summarizes the Muslim doctrines in accordance with Christianity, then the main areas of disagreement (concerning himself only with doctrine, not with rites). The two sticking points are the Incarnation and the Trinity, which the Saracens misunderstand (they believe, he says, that we worship three gods). The preacher must patiently explain these two key doctrines, proving the Trinity through

> forceful reasons *[cogentes rationes],* against which no man can argue the contrary. I already wrote these reasons for you and I declared them in my many books in Arabic and Latin, which confirm that one should believe in the Blessed Trinity. And among those Saracens who are most learned, few believe in Muhammad (since they well know that this man was a sinner and that in their law he placed many ridiculous things). And thus some learned Arabs are Christians—among which I could number myself. Once the better Saracens are converted the lesser ones can be converted by the better ones.[33]

The Saracens, Llull says, claim that they benefit from one miracle: the Koran, so perfect that it can only be the work of God. "What they say, that it is a miracle, can easily be destroyed and annulled by reason," says Llull: though the Koran is indeed "very ornate," it also contains many false things and many descriptions of lascivious acts.[34]

The differences between Llull's characterization of Islam in the *Libre del gentil* and in the *Liber de fine* are striking. True, one finds in both the idea of positive arguments based on shared philosophical truths to prove key doctrines, the Incarnation and the Trinity. But in the later work Llull, who lambasts the negative argument used by the Dominicans, indulges in the same strategies: attacks against Muhammad and the Koran, portrayed as irrational, lascivious, filled with "absurdities" (*trufas*).

Next in *De fine* are similar sections on how to conduct missions to Jews, schismatics (which he subdivides into Greeks, Jacobites, and Nestorians), and Tartars (and other pagans). In each of these section he gives rational "proofs" of the superiority of Catholic doctrine, referring to his own previous works (such as the *Libre del gentil*, in the passage quoted above). The heresies or divisions among Christians are not only damaging to Christianity but also prevent Christians from converting infidels: it is told, says Llull, that a Saracen, convinced that Christianity was better than Islam, came to a Christian land. But there he saw, in disgust, that Christians could not agree among themselves, and not knowing whether to become a Nestorian, Jacobite, Greek, or Latin Christian, he left without converting.[35] Similarly, when "Cassanus, emperor of the Tartars" (i.e., Ilkhan Mahmud Ghazan) professed his willingness to convert to Christianity if anyone could make him certain of its truth, he found no Christian able to do so, and so converted to Islam.[36]

Yet preaching is not the only way to combat error: When the apostles said to Jesus "behold, here are two swords," he responded, "It is enough" (Luke 22:38). This means "that you should fight with preaching and with weapons against infidels."[37] Llull devotes the second book of *De fine* to a grand strategy for reconquering the Holy Land. He compares the pomp and luxury he found around the altar of Saint Peter in Rome with the poverty surrounding the altar of the holy sepulcher in Jerusalem, where there are only two lamps, and one is broken; the holy city itself is nearly abandoned; it has become the abode of snakes.[38] Christians who fear the judgment day must strive to return Jerusalem to glory. First, he says, a cardinal must be appointed whose sole duty is to aid in the recovery of the Holy Land. Next a son of a king must be chosen to become the "warrior king" (*rex bellator*): he will be king of Jerusalem (if he can take it back), and meanwhile king over whatever lands he can capture from the infidels. Llull may have in mind Jaume II of Mallorca as the most likely candidate for *rex bellator*.[39] Llull explains how the conquest should be financed (through tithes) and how the clergy of the new kingdom should be organized. The existing military orders (Templars, Hospitalers, Santiago, Teutonic Knights, etc.) must be combined into one, called *De militia;* let anyone who refuses this fusion contemplate the hellfire that surely awaits him.[40]

How, then, should this king go about (re)conquering the Holy Land? Llull gives five possible itineraries: first, overland through the Byzantine empire and the lands of the Turks; second, by sea to the island of Rashid in Egypt, from which the conquest of Alexandria could be undertaken; third, to Cyprus, which then could be used as a base for mainland conquests; fourth, to Tunis by sea and then across Africa by land. But Llull prefers the fifth option: first the conquest of the Arab kingdom of Granada, then across the straits of Gibraltar to Ceuta, then a gradual conquest that would push east to Tunis, Egypt, and finally Jerusalem.[41]

I will not go into the details of the different military strategies (by land and by sea) that Llull recommends. I note, however, that in his chapter "De Almirallia" he advocates the prohibition of all maritime trade with Muslim lands; the admiral of the crusading king's fleet is to capture any Genoese, Catalan, or other Christian ship that attempts to brave this interdict. Moreover, the crusading fleet is to conduct raids all along the North African coast, capturing castles, sacking towns, and so on, thus destabilizing the region, making the coast uninhabitable. The author of the irenic dialogue of the *Libre del gentil* has become the advocate of Christian piracy.

Not that Llull ever neglects the intellectual side of this campaign: the military order is to have preachers trained in Arabic who can carry on theological disputations with Saracen prisoners. The captives will also be forced to read the works of Christian polemicists in Arabic: the *Risâlat al-Kindî,* the *Liber denudationis,* and Llull's own *Libre del gentil*.[42] Llull optimistically predicts that many prisoners will be converted in this way; they should then be released, provided with gifts to cover their needs, and be sent back home to preach conversion to their compatriots. The preachers will also go to the various Saracen princes, explaining the Christian faith to them and promising them that they can keep their castles and lands if they will convert.

Llull's *Liber de fine* represents a change of missionary strategy. Indeed, he still claims that his necessary reasons can prove the superiority of Chris-

tianity, but he now seems to realize that irenic, philosophically based debate alone will not suffice. Military force must be used to conquer territory
from Saracen rulers and to force them to open their lands to the preaching
of Christian missionaries;[43] while conversion is voluntary, it is to be encouraged by the compulsory Christian education of prisoners. The captives
will be obliged to read not only Llull's own *Libre del gentil* but also two traditional works of anti-Muslim polemic, implicitly acknowledging that his
own approach needs to be supplemented by two standard strategies for
which he had long criticized Ramon Martí and the Dominicans: attacking
the beliefs of the infidels (particularly regarding Muhammad's status as
prophet) and using key passages from the Koran (or Torah, in arguing with
Jews) to prove Christian truth.[44]

Llull put this modified strategy into practice in a work he composed a
few months later, his *Liber de predicatione contra Iudaeos.*[45] Llull himself
had preached to Catalan Jews and Muslims compelled by royal legislation
to listen to his sermons; in 1294 King Charles IV of Naples granted him
permission to preach to the Muslims of Lucera and to Muslim prisoners in
the Castel d'Ovo.[46] He now advocated imposing the same system on the
rest of the Muslim world. Llull's brief *Liber de participatione Christianorum
et Sarracenorum* (1312) also reflects the application of his new strategy.[47] As
he tells it:

> Ramon proposed to come to the most noble and virtuous lord Frederic,
> king of Sicily, so that he . . . negotiate with the honored and mighty
> king of Tunis, in order that learned Christians conversant in Arabic go
> to Tunis in order to show the truth concerning the faith, and that
> learned Saracens come to the kingdom of Sicily to dispute with Chris-
> tians about their faith. And perhaps in this way there can be peace be-
> tween Christians and Saracens, if they can adopt this custom every-
> where, rather than having Christians go in order to destroy Saracens, or
> Saracens to destroy Christians.[48]

Here again, peaceful disputation is presented as an alternative to war, in apparent contradiction with his *Liber de fine,* perhaps because of the entente
between Frederick III and Ibn al-Lihiqnî, the new sultan of Tunis.[49] The
Liber de participatione proposes two arguments meant to clinch the debate
for the Christians. First, Llull presents the Koranic verse "God does not
beget, is not begotten, nor does he have any equal" (112:2-4), attempting to
show that this is true in a physical sense but not in a spiritual sense. When

properly understood, this passage does not contradict the Trinity, which Llull subsequently tries to prove through syllogistic arguments based on the "dignities"; these arguments, he concludes, the Saracens cannot rationally deny. Llull bases his argument for the Incarnation not only on the same type of syllogism, but also on the common Islamic portrayal of Jesus as "spirit" and "word" of God. He thus adapts the standard Dominican strategy of using the Koran to prove the truth of Christian doctrine to his own system of argumentation based on the *Art*. He claims that "This way of proving is easy, thorough, and beyond doubt."[50] Frederick III apparently showed little enthusiasm for Llull's proposed exchange of scholars between Tunis and Sicily.[51]

LLULL'S LATER WORKS reflect both his continuing efforts to adapt his missionary strategy to a changing world and a mounting sense that his work is unappreciated and hence ultimately futile. He laments in *De fine*, "I cannot make the above-mentioned *Arts* take root in this world, rather for this I am neglected, since all rush to acquire pompous or lucrative knowledge. And I languish for the public good which I see in the *Arts,* and I live in sadness in pain, wandering over the world."[52] In 1311 Llull composed his *Phantasticus:* he presents himself on his way to the council of Vienne, which he would try to convince to adopt a modified version of the plan laid out in *De fine*.[53] On his way he meets a successful, worldly archdeacon who, upon learning who his traveling companion is, exclaims: "Ramon, I have often heard about you; they say you are really crazy *[phantasticus]*."[54] In particular, the cleric accuses Llull of being crazy for teaching that there is an *Ars generalis* that applies to all knowledge and that the Christian faith is provable.[55] In the debate that follows, Llull attempts to prove that the worldly, ambitious cleric is the real *phantasticus,* not Llull who has devoted his life to the conversion of infidels. Significantly, Llull is unable to convince the cleric and each leaves convinced that the other is the real *phantasticus.*

It would be easy to write off Llull, this *phantasticus,* as a quirky footnote in the development of Christian images of Islam: Llull, despite occasional success at getting the ear of a Pope or king, is largely a lonely outsider, while Dominicans such as Penyafort, Martí, and Aquinas are among the key shapers of church policy and orthodox theology. Llull's works indeed attracted a small and devoted group of followers, "Llullists," over the following centuries, most notably among fourteenth-century Parisian academics and fifteenth-century Italian humanists. Yet these readers in general were interested in Llull's systematic approach to knowledge and not directly in Islam. Conversely, those who were interested in Islam did not read Llull, preferring works such as Petrus Alfonsi's *Dialogues,* Riccoldo's *Libellus contra legem Saracenorum,* or Robert of Ketton's translation of the Koran.

Yet Llull's long itinerary and stubborn perseverance are instructive. Llull's knowledge of Muslim philosophy matched that of Ramon Martí or Riccoldo da Montecroce, and his sympathetic understanding of Muslim piety was deeper than theirs. Islam, for the young Llull, was something positive, and Muslims' piety and learning would lead them (with the help of Llull's *Art*) to abandon their errors and embrace the doctrines of the Trinity and Incarnation. Llull pushes admiration and appreciation of the religious other to its limits. For neither Llull nor any other thirteenth-century author (Muslim, Jew, or Christian) could simply conclude that a rival faith was as valid and salutary as his own. There can be only one true religion. Llull's genteel philosophical politeness begins to fray as the Jewish and Muslim infidels refuse to be convinced by his arguments. He advocates compulsory Christian education for them, advocates war of conquest to force them to listen to Christian missionaries. The theater of religious debate was no longer a verdant grove, as it had been for the young Llull when he composed the *Libre del gentil;* it had become a dark prison.[56]

CONCLUSION

I N 1542, as the armies of Sulayman the Magnificent prepared to invade Hungary, a Swiss publisher named Johann Herbst found himself in jail in Basel. The crime he had committed, along with his accomplice Theodor Buchman, was to publish the Koran in Robert of Ketton's Latin translation of the 1140s, along with Riccoldo da Montecroce's *Contra legem Sarracenorum* and other medieval polemical works against Islam. The Basel municipal council judged that it was dangerous to publish the "fables and heresies" of the Koran. Help came to the embattled humanists in the form of a letter to the council from none other than Martin Luther himself, who declared his support for the project, saying that there was no better way to injure Muhammad and the Turks than to publish their "lies and fables" for all to see.[1] Earlier the same year Luther himself had completed his German translation of Riccoldo's *Contra legem Sarracenorum*. When Martin Luther and his contemporaries sought to comprehend Islam and to engage in polemics against it, they turned naturally to translations and texts produced between the twelfth and the early fourteenth centuries.

The ideological responses to Islam that I examine in this book were redeployed countless times in medieval and modern Europe. Europeans would not again expend the same intellectual effort against Islam as did their forbears to explain, refute, convert. Rather, the intellectual weapons forged in the twelfth and thirteenth centuries were reused, anthologized, translated, published. Petrus Alfonsi's attack on Islam found its way into the encyclopedic *Speculum historiale* of Vincent of Beauvais; thirteenth-century Dominican minister general Humbert of Romans recommended it as required reading for those who preached the Crusades, and numerous fourteenth- and fifteenth-century authors reused it.[2] Chroniclers repeated and reworked the standard hostile polemical bibliographies of Muhammad the heresiarch. Riccoldo da Montecroce's polemics were reused in the fourteenth century by Petrus du Pennis, Fazio degli Uberti, and other authors; his *Liber peregrinationis* was translated into French and Italian.[3] Jean Germain, bishop of Chalons, arguing in favor of a new Crusade, produced (c. 1450) a vast compilation and French translation of a number of the works examined in this book. Little truly new was written about Islam between 1300 and the Enlightenment. There were occasional exceptions, the best known being that of Juan de Segovia, whose grand project was a trilingual Koran: the Arab text alongside new translations into Latin and Spanish.[4] Yet for the most part the humanists turned their back on Islam: Arab and Muslim culture were parts of the "Gothic" accretion that they wished to shed in order to return to a pure, antique wisdom. The old stereotypes of barbaric invaders, now couched in the vocabulary of humanism, flowed easily from their pens: gone was any sense that Islam could be a serious intellectual or theological adversary.[5]

The portrayals of Islam presented in this book found their first expression in the defensive ruminations of Christian *dhimmis* subjected to a vigorous new Muslim empire. The earliest Christian authors to describe the Muslim conquest and dominion of the Christian Roman empire reiterated the standard topoi used since the Hebrew prophets to explain their subjugation: the Muslim invader was a scourge sent by God to punish his wayward flock. As Christians got to know Islam better, and as they saw with growing alarm that their correligionaries were converting to Islam, they portrayed the rival faith as a Christological heresy, a worldly religion cleverly crafted by the cunning heresiarch Muhammad to dupe an uncouth and lascivious people into following him. In keeping with Edward Said's characterization of "resistance culture," the subjected *dhimmis* rejected the triumphalist historiography of the ruling Muslims and countered with their own subversive reading of Muslim history.

Far from these communities of *dhimmis,* Christians of northern Europe and of Byzantium could imagine their Saracen enemies as idolaters who practiced the discredited and colorful rites of the ancient pagans, devoting sacrifices and prayers to a pantheon of idols that included Jupiter, Apollo, Priapus, and their special god Muhammad. This image of Saracen idolatry provided a useful caricature with which the Christian author could justify and glorify the killing of Muslims and the conquest of Muslim territories. By creating a largely imaginary enemy outside the bounds of Christian Europe, the *Chansons de Geste* could revel in the knightly violence that was in reality more often directed at internal Christian enemies.

This caricature of Saracen paganism was untenable for those with even a rudimentary familiarity with Islam, many of whom portrayed Islam as a Christian heresy. For Guibert de Nogent, chronicling the first Crusade, Muhammad was merely the latest and most nefarious of a long line of oriental heresiarchs: the success of Islam was proof of the oriental penchant for heresy, calling for the intervention of vigorous and stolid Latins. The image of Islam as heresy, an image forged by *dhimmis* in the Near East and Spain, came to northern Europe at a time when Latin Christians were increasingly in contact with Muslims and when they were increasingly preoccupied with the supposedly nefarious influence of other non-Christians, Jews and heretics. The association between these various enemies of the faith is crucial for understanding the Christian perceptions of Muslims (or, for that matter, of Jews or heretics) in the following centuries. Petrus Alfonsi included an anti-Muslim chapter in his *Dialogues against the Jews;* Peter of Cluny composed a polemical triptych against Jews, Muslims, and Petrobrusian heretics; Alain de Lille, a treatise against Cathars, Waldensians, Jews and Muslims.

The development of scholastic theology in the twelfth and thirteenth centuries went hand in hand with the new forms of argumentation used against infidels. If Catholic doctrine was based on reason, it should be possible to prove it to Jews, heretics, and Muslims through logical exposition and argumentation. For various Christian writers, from Petrus Alfonsi to Roger Bacon and Ramon Llull, logical "necessary reasons" (*rationes necessariae*) could prove the faith to the infidel. Others did not go so far: Thomas Aquinas affirmed that the faith could be shown not to be contradicted by reason but could not be proven by rational arguments. Fellow Dominicans such as Ramon Martí and Riccoldo da Montecroce accordingly used rational argumentation and textual criticism to attack the beliefs, rites, and sacred writings of Jews, heretics, and Muslims but did not try to prove the articles of the Christian faith to them.

The widespread failure of the missionary movements had become clear by the early fourteenth century, as the fall of Acre and the conversion of the Mongols to Islam made manifest. If the infidels were impervious to the subtle reasoning and clear arguments of the missionaries, the fault must lie with the infidels themselves: the obstinate Jews, lascivious Saracens, and barbarous Mongols, all too obsessed with the literal and carnal to understand the intellectual or the spiritual. Peter of Cluny contrasted the learned, logical Arabs with the obdurate Jews whose failure to accept Christian reason led him to wonder whether they really could be rational humans, rather than insensate beasts. Increasingly, as Muslims proved as impervious to "rational" polemics as Jews, the two groups were lumped together as stubborn and irrational infidels. Missionaries such as William of Rubruck and Riccoldo da Montecroce painted the Oriental, Muslim or not, as a foreign, lethargic being unfit for rational argumentation. Because of this irrationality, it was entirely appropriate to use coercion and force with these infidels: to treat them forcefully, as one would treat children or animals, compelling them to submit to Catholic authority, to listen quietly to missionary sermons, and so on.

This phenomenon of lumping together the enemies of the Catholic faith should not be exaggerated. It was one thing to be forced to listen to a Dominican sermon in one's Barcelona mosque or synagogue, something else entirely to be massacred as a Cathar by the Albigensian crusaders. The same authors who associated Jews, Muslims, and heretics as the devil's minions could distinguish their different social and legal statuses. There is a fundamental distinction between violence aimed at the eradication of a deviant group (the Cathar heretics) and coercion aimed at enforcing and maintaining the inferior social status of accepted groups (such as Jews and Muslims).

Accompanying the polemical association between Jews and Muslims was an increasing judicial association. There was indeed, from the thirteenth century onward, a growing volume of law restricting the legal status of Jews and Muslims and limiting the "polluting" contacts between Catholics and infidels. Over the course of the twelfth and thirteenth centuries, Church legislation and legal commentaries tended to confirm this trend: for juridical purposes, Muslims were treated as Jews (rather than as pagans or heretics). The principal aim of this legislation was to prevent "contamination" of Christendom through contact with the infidel: sexual contact, social ties, religious contamination through the syncretistic rites of recidivist converts, and so on. The Muslim or Jew, like the leper, needed to be marked, isolated, quarantined, in order to protect the Christian. The twin (and seemingly contradictory) concerns were to keep the Christian community safe from all "contamination" from the infidel (living in the same house with him, being subjected to his power) and to convert the infidel (or at least to remove social and economic impediments to his conversion). Yet there was a growing amount of legislation about just about *everything* in this period, and it is often difficult to distinguish between an increase in persecution and an increase in documentation. The sticky problem of the link between law on the one hand and social interaction on the other is beyond the scope of this book; it has been studied by many.[6]

It is not always clear what the relationship is between the ideological or textual denigration of Muslims, Jews, and others and the legal and social restrictions and violence imposed on them. Does an increasingly intolerant ideology cause increasing persecution? Or does the reality of social subjugation call for an ideology to justify it? Or are the two independent phenomena with little direct connection? From a perusal of work by modern historians, one could suppose that the latter was the case: social historians, legal historians, and historians of religious polemic have for the most part avoided the thorny problem of the connection between ideology and social practice.

Others have suggested a link between the growing association between the various enemies of Christendom (or of those who were perceived as such) and the increasing violence and repression exercised against them. Many historians of Judaism in northern Europe have seen the anti-Jewish violence of the first Crusade as a watershed between the early Middle Ages, when Jews were accepted in Christian society, and the later Middle Ages, when they were subject to increasing persecution. For Jeremy Cohen, it is the missionary efforts of the thirteenth-century mendicant friars that marks the rise of intolerance, leading to an intensification of violence against Jews and to a sharp decline in their legal and social status; for him the "Muslim connection," the increasing link between the anti-Muslim and anti-Jewish polemics of mendicants and others, may be in part responsible for this change.[7] For Robert Moore, it was the twelfth century that saw the emergence of a "persecuting society," a clerical elite bent on defining doctrinal and social orthodoxy and exercising repression and coercion against those who were outside this orthodoxy: Jews, heretics, lepers, homosexuals, prostitutes (curiously, Moore does not mention Muslims). "Reason," for Moore, became in the twelfth and thirteenth centuries the "flag" of this clerical elite, justifying its power over Christian society. Those who opposed that power, from inside or out, were branded as irrational.[8]

Yet such historiographical models of an increasingly intolerant Europe are at times driven by anachronistic teleological considerations.[9] We now know, for example, that 1391 brought anti-Jewish pogroms to Spain, leading to widespread conversions; 1492 saw the expulsion of Jews from Spain; Muslims were subsequently (from 1499 to 1526) banned from the different Spanish kingdoms; the Moriscos (descendants of Muslim converts to Christianity) were expelled from Spain between 1609 and 1614; the sixteenth and seventeenth centuries were marked by confrontation between the Ottoman empire and parts of Christian Europe; the nineteenth and twentieth centuries saw the French and British conquer large parts of the Muslim world; and the twentieth saw the Holocaust. The roots of these events are sought in the Middle Ages—to some extent, legitimately so. Yet we risk seriously misunderstanding the medieval actors in these events if we see every piece of anti-Jewish legislation or every act of violence against a Jew as a sort of precursor to the Holocaust. Whatever one thinks of the French and British conquests of large parts of the Muslim world, they are not merely the reenactment of the timeless Western greed embodied in the Crusades, as some have claimed.[10] To catalog the anti-Muslim sentiments from the writings of medieval Latin authors and expose them to the disapproving gaze of the presumably enlightened Anglophone reader of the twentieth century, as Norman Daniel has done, is little help in understanding what drove those authors to write what they wrote.

In my introduction I set two goals for this book: first, to examine these various Christian writings about Islam on their own terms, placing them in their particular (and multiple) contexts, rather than on a time line showing, say, the inexorable rise of orientalism or of ideologies justifying colonial expansion; second, to present a number of examples of the social and ideological uses of denigration and contempt, examples that should be of interest to nonmedievalists: historians, anthropologists, sociologists, and others.

I have undertaken this contextualization in dialogue with a number of important works in the field, notably Edward Said's *Orientalism* and *Culture and Imperialism*. Said's presentation of the political and social implications of nineteenth- and twentieth-century discourse on the Orient is fascinating and often compelling, yet underlying it, at times, seems to be the notion of an eternal and immutable Occident with an essentially unchanging view of the Orient from Herodotus via Dante to Ernest Renan and Jane Austen. What little Said has to say about the Middle Ages lacks context, as if medieval authors who wrote about Islam lived in a social and political void. Medieval orientalism is at once timeless and immature; an "adolescent" orientalism, waiting for the political and social context of modern European Empires.[11] Said's Occident, bereft of its historical and cultural variety, shorn of the individual motivations of its writers (particularly the pre-nineteenth-century writers), risks becoming every bit as much a caricature as the inscrutable Orient of the nineteenth-century romantics. The fact is that throughout the Middle Ages, on both sides of the Muslim-Christian divide, writers used the intellectual tools at their disposal, in particular the twin tools of reason and revelation, to affirm their own religious and intellectual superiority and political hegemony over the other—but also at times to explain their own (embarrassing) subjection to the other.

This book examines these processes primarily from the European Christian side of the equation (with comparative references to Muslim practices, particularly in chapter 2). The goal, rather than to dole out posthumous prizes for "tolerance" or castigations for intolerance, is to understand what motivated individual writers to portray Saracens as pagan idolaters or to paint Muhammad as a debauched heresiarch—or, on the contrary, to argue that Islam was as legitimate (or nearly so) as Christianity. I have sought to accomplish on a broad scale the careful contextualization that a number of scholars have performed for specific periods and authors: Sydney Griffith for seventh-century Palestine, Thomas Burman for eleventh- and twelfth-century al-Andalus, Dominique Iogna-Prat for the writings of Peter of Cluny, David Nirenberg for fourteenth-century Catalonia, and so on. Only by carefully examining the specific contexts in which medieval authors worked can we understand what motivated them to portray Islam as they did. Among the various motivations exposed are the desire to justify a war against or an alliance with a Muslim state, an attempt to dissuade Christians from converting to Islam, and a need to justify the rule of Christian princes over Muslim subjects. Only by paying close attention to the contexts and motivations of individual writers can we understand what they say about Islam, not by attempting to string them together to produce a narrative of growing intolerance.

This is not to deny that these writings form textual traditions, and individual writers were reacting to these textual traditions, as well as to their particular historical contexts. Moreover, these traditions continued well beyond the thirteenth century—indeed in some respects until the twentieth: the orientalism in the writings of William of Rubruck, Fidentius of Padua, or Riccoldo da Montecroce finds an echo in some of the nineteenth- and twentieth-century texts discussed by Edward Said in *Orientalism;* debates about how "Spanish" or how "Arab" was medieval Iberia rage hot in nineteenth- and twentieth-century Spain.[12]

Kathleen Biddick has offered "an invitation to medievalists to bring the European Middle Ages out of disciplinary exile and to engage complex temporalities of postcolonial histories."[13] The invitation is accepted, and I hope this book has made some contribution to that process. The portrayal of Muslims in medieval Europe has not received the same attention as that of Jews and heretics in the historiography of the late twentieth century. The existence and development of Jewish and heretical communities posed a number of key political, social, historiographical, and eschatological problems for medieval Latin writers; these problems (and their implications for European social and intellectual history) have been studied and debated in depth and with sophistication: comparative models from other periods of history, from anthropology, and from other disciplines have been put to good use to understand the dynamics of Christian-Jewish and Catholic-heretical interactions. The problems posed by Islam have not received the same scrutiny, as if a new revealed religion whose adherents succeeded in dominating most of the formerly Christian world, turning it into a flourishing empire, did not pose problems of the same magnitude. Even cursory attention to the ideological underpinnings of colonization and of anticolonial "resistance culture" can shed light on the medieval European responses to Islam and underline their importance in the forging of European historiographical and political identities.

I in turn extend an invitation to those who work on the ideologies of colonialism, anticolonialism, and postcolonialism to deepen their historical understanding of these problems through the comparative study of earlier ideological constructs of the other, whether that other is portrayed as the intruding "colonist" or the subjected "colonized." The European colonial enterprise of the modern era began in many respects in the Middle Ages, and the texts analyzed in this book provide key theoretical underpinnings for European Christian hegemony over those who are non-Christian (or in the case of Irish, Byzantines, and others can somehow be presented as "less" Christian than their conquerors).[14] Moreover, while the colonial empires of the nineteenth and twentieth centuries are unprecedented in scope, conquerors since the Sumerians have forged ideologies that justified and celebrated their subjection of other peoples, while the conquered have constructed their own ideologies of resistance. Cross-cultural comparison, with depth in time as well as breadth in space, can only help our understanding of these processes.

The anti-Muslim ideology of the twelfth and thirteenth centuries lives on, in various forms. The animosity of a pseudo-Methodius in the seventh century, a Paul Alvarus in the ninth, or for that matter, of Luther in the sixteenth can be explained as a hostility born of fear: all three saw Islam engulfing the Christian world. Yet this image persisted in twelfth- and thirteenth-century Europe, among writers who were not subject *dhimmis* and could have no reasonable fear of Muslim conquest. For François de Medeiros, European Christians of the thirteenth century abandoned the universalism of the Gospel and of the early church in order to portray themselves as a new chosen people, whom God preferred over the Nations: physically, morally, and intellectually superior to Africans and Asians, whom they branded as pagans, heretics, and schismatics.[15] Perhaps it would be more accurate to say that the two visions—universalist and exclusivist—coexisted in European culture throughout the Middle Ages and beyond. Through mission and crusade, Europeans sought to bring their universal religion (and their culture, which for them was inseparable from it) to the wayward Saracens, Tartars, and others. Yet the religious and social order that (for them) would invariably accompany adhesion to Christianity was a European one, with the Pope at Rome as leader. The portrayal of Islam as a debauched heresy, the defensive ideology of "colonized" *dhimmis*, had been transformed into an aggressive ideology of cultural superiority justifying European conquest and hegemony over the benighted other.

Perhaps indeed European denigration of the other is the back side of Christian universalism. As European Christian ideology crystalized and hardened in the twelfth and thirteenth centuries, there was less and less room for dissent. The increasing use of reason to justify this ideology aggravated the situation: those who refused to listen to Christian reason must be irrational: the blind Jew, the stubborn heretic, the flesh- bound Saracen. Well into the thirteenth century, the Saracen indeed had a better reputation than the non-Christians closer to home. The Saracen was reputed for his learning, seen as eminently rational; he (like the Jew) became the object of philosophical polemics and impassioned preaching. When, toward the end of the thirteenth century, it became clear that the Saracen was (like the Jew) impermeable to such "rational" argument, he was relegated to the subrational world of carnal, semibeastly humans. The Saracen (and more generally the non-Christian, be he Jew or Cathar or, in the centuries that followed, an African animist or an Inca priest) was different, was inferior, precisely because he refused the universal and rational message of Christianity.

Notes

꿎꾸뉸

Introduction: Riccoldo's Predicament or, How to Explain Away
the Successes of a Flourishing Rival Civilization

1. Two exceptions are William of Tripoli, *Notitia de Machometo*, in Wilhelm von Tripolis, *Notitia de Machometo; De statu Sarracenorum*, ed. Peter Engels (Würzburg: Corpus Islamo-Christianum, 1992), §6, p. 216; Petrus Alfonsi, *Dialogi contra Iudaeos* (*Diálogo contra los Judíos*), Latin edition by Klaus-Peter Mieth with Spanish translation by Esperanza Ducay (Zaragoza: Instituto de Estudios Altoaragoneses, 1996), §5, p. 94. In English, *Moslim* is first attested in 1615; *Islam*, in 1613 (*Compact Edition of the Oxford English Dictionary* [Oxford: Oxford University Press, 1971 and 1985], 1:1856, 1489). In French, *Mussulman* is used for the first time in the sixteenth century; *Islam*, in 1697 (according to Alain Rey, *Le Robert: Dictionnaire historique de la langue française* [Paris: Dictionnaires le Robert, 1992 and 1998], 1886, 2328).

2. There have been several useful short studies more limited in scope or period: Phillipe Sénac, *L'Image de l'autre: L'Occident médiéval face à l'Islam* (1983); Jacques Waardenburg, *Islam et occident face à face: Regards de l'histoire des religions* (Geneva, 1998); and Georges Anawati, *Islam e Cristianesmo: L'incontro tra due culture nell'Occidente médiévale* (Milan, 1994). Many more-specialized studies are noted in the bibliography and notes to the following chapters.

3. See David Blanks, "Western Views of Islam in the Premodern Period: A Brief History of Past Approaches," in Michael Frasetto and David Blanks, eds., *Western Views of Islam in Medieval and Early Modern Europe: Perception of the Other* (New York: St. Martin's Press, 1999), 11-54, esp. 24-29.

4. See, for example, Edward Said, *Covering Islam: How the Media Experts Determine How We See the Rest of the World* (New York: Random House, 1981).

5. "Le plus bel éloge de la colonisation française," René Grousset, *Histoire des Croisades et du royaume franc de Jérusalem*, 2 vols. (Paris, 1934), 2:754, commenting on Ibn Jubayr, *Rihla* (trans. R. Broadhurst, *The Travels of Ibn Jubayr* [London, 1952], 316–17); on this passage, see Benjamin Kedar, "The Subjected Muslims of the Frankish Levant," in James Powell, ed., *Muslims Under Latin Rule, 1100–1300* (Princeton: Princeton University Press, 1990), 135–74 (esp. 167).

6. Carole Hillenbrand, *The Crusades: Islamic Perspectives* (Edinburgh: University of Edinburgh Press, 1999).

7. Said, *Orientalism* (New York: Random House, 1978), 3.

8. Theophanes, *Chronographia*, ed. Carolus de Boor, 2 vols. (Leipzig, 1883; reprint Hildesheim, 1963), 339; *The Chronicle of Theophanes the Confessor*, trans. (into English) Cyril Mango and Roger Scott (Oxford: Clarendon Press, 1997), 471; Dan. 9:27, 11:31, 12:11; cf. Matt. 24:15, 1 Macc. 1:54, 6:7.

1. God and History in the Christian West c. 600

1. J. Fernández Catón in 1966 listed 967 manuscripts of the *Etymologies;* see Jocelyn Hillgarth, "The Position of Isidorian Studies: A Critical Review of the Literature, 1936–1975," *Studi Medievali* 24 (1983):817–905, here 827.

2. Here I can hardly do better than to echo the words of Jacques Fontaine, who says that Isidore's *Etymologies* show his "inlassable effort pour organiser tout le savoir et toute l'activité de son temps, qui est peut-être le principe d'unité plus profond de son oeuvre et de sa vie"; Fontaine, *Isidore de Séville et la culture classique dans l'Espagne wisigothique* (Paris: Etudes augustiniennes, 1983), 11.

3. See Bernard Guenée, *Histoire et culture historique dans l'Occident médiéval* (Paris: Aubier-Montaigne, 1980), 20–23; Mircea Eliade, *Myth of the Eternal Return, or Cosmos and History,* W. Trask, trans. (Princeton, 1954), 111.

4. See Arnaldo Momigliano, "Pagan and Christian Historiography in the Fourth Century A.D.," in Momigliano, ed., *The Conflict between Paganism and Christianity in the Fourth Century* (Oxford: Oxford University Press, 1963), 79–99.

5. See Guenée, *Histoire et culture historique,* 148–54; R. Schmidt, "Aetates mundi: Die Weltalter als Gliederungsprinzip der Geschichte," *Zeitschrit für Kirchengeschichte* 67 (1955–56):288–317 (esp. 306–8); Momigliano, "Pagan and Christian Historiography"; Wallace-Hadrill, "The Eusebian Chronicle"; Paul Bassett, "The Use of History in the *Chronicon* of Isidore of Seville," *History and Theory* 15 (1976):278–92; Jocelyn Hillgarth, "Historiography in Visigothic Spain," 291.

6. Eusebius, in contrast, started his *Chronica* with Abraham. See Bassett, "Use of History," 280, 285.

7. For a comparison of these periods with those used by other early medieval chroniclers, see Guenée, *Histoire et culture historique,* 150–52. On Isidore's *Chronica maiora,* see Luis Vázquez de Parga, "Notas sobre la obra histórica de San Isidoro," in Díaz y Díaz, *Isidoriana,* 99–107; Hillgarth, "Position," 834–36; Hillgarth, "Historiography in Visigothic Spain," *Settimane* 17 (1970) *La storiografia altomedievale,* 261–311, 345–52. Isidore includes a much-abridged version (referred to as the *Chronica minora*) in *Etymologies* (Etymologiarum sive originum libri 20), ed. W. M. Lindsay, (Oxford, 1911), 5.39.

8. Isidore, *Chronica majora,* ed. Theodor Mommsen, MGH AA 11:2, 391–506, §417; Mommsen gives the variant readings of other manuscripts, dated from eleven or sixteen years later, corresponding perhaps to later reworkings (or at least recopyings) of the text.

9. Isidore, *Chronica majora,* §418, citing Acts 1:7; Isidore goes on to cite a similar passage, Matt. 24:36.

10. Isidore, *Chronica majora,* §408.

11. The same is true in the *Chronicle* of Isidore's elder contemporary, John of Biclaro, for whom "Byzantium is still incomparably the greatest of Christian powers" (Hillgarth, "Historiography," 268).

12. John of Biclaro, *Chronicle,* in Julio Campos, ed., *Juan de Biclaro, obispo de Gerona, su vida y obra* (Madrid: Concejo Superior de Investigaciones Científicas, 1960), §91–92; for an English translation see Kenneth Wolf, *Conquerors and Chroniclers of Medieval Spain* (Liverpool: Liverpool University Press, 1990), 61–80.

13. *De origine Gothorum* is the work's proper title, though it is frequently referred to as *Historia Gothorum* (History of the Goths). See Fontaine, "Cohérence et originalité de l'étymologie isidorienne," in Fontaine, *Tradition et actualité chez Isidore de Séville* (London: Variorum, 1988), 138; Isidore, *Las Historias de los Godos, Vandalos y Suevos de Isidoro de Sevilla* (León: Centro des Estudios y Investigación San Isidro, 1975), introduction by the translator C. Rodriguez Alonso, 24–26. For analyses of the *De origine Gothorum,* see Marc Reydellet, *La royauté dans la littérature latine, de Sidoine Apollinaire à Isidore de Séville* (Rome: École Française de Rome, 1981), 505–54; Wolf, *Conquerors,* 12–27.

14. Gregory the Great, *Dialogues* 3:38 (PL 77:316); cited in Bernard McGinn, *Antichrist: Two Thousand Years of the Human Fascination with Evil* (San Francisco: Harper, 1994), 80; see Claude Dagens, "La fin des temps et l'Église selon Grégoire le Grand," *Recherches en Sciences Religieuses* 58 (1970):273–88.

15. McGinn, *Antichrist,* 77.

16. *Etymologies,* 3:11:20–22. Isidore paints a similar picture of the Antichrist in his *Sententiae;* see Pierre Cazier, *Isidore de Séville et la naissance de l'Espagne catholique* (Paris : Beauchesne, 1994), 147–49.

17. John 2:22; on this passage, see McGinn, *Antichrist,* 55.

18. Mark 13:1–37; Matt. 24:1–25:46; Luke 21:5–38. See McGinn, *Antichrist,* 38–41.

19. McGinn, *Antichrist,* 45ff.

20. Hilary of Poitiers, *De Trinitate* 6.42 (PL 10:191).

21. For the theme of false prophets, see also Matt. 7:15, 24:11, 24:24.

22. Isidore seems to have used Pliny's *Natural History* indirectly, by way of Solinus's third-century *Collectanea rerum memorabilia.* See Gregory Guzman, "Reports of Mongol Cannibalism in the Thirteenth-Century Latin Sources: Oriental Fact or Western Fiction?" in Scott Westrem, ed., *Discovering New Worlds: Essays on Medieval Exploration and Imagination* (New York: Garland, 1991), 31–68 (47).

23. On the structure of *Etymologies,* 9, see Isidore, *Etymologies,* 11, critical edition, French translation, and commentary by Marc Reydellet (Paris: Belles Lettres, 1984), intro., 1–26; on Isidore's treatment of the origins of Goths and Hispani in this section of the *Etymologies,* see Helena de Carlos Villamarín, *Las antigüedades de Hispania* (Spoleto: Centro italiano di studi sull'Alto medioevo, 1996), 111–52.

24. *Chronica maiora,* §7; cf. *Etymologies,* 9:2:3.

25. *Etymologies,* 9:2:6. Cf. *Chronica maiora,* §13: "Abraham annorum c. genuit Isaac, ex Sara libera. Nam primum ex ancilla Agar genuerat Ismael, a quo Ismaelitarum gens qui postea Agareni, ad ultimum Saraceni sunt dicti." Isidore seems to be taking this identification from Jerome, who in his *Commentarii in Ezechielem* writes "madianaeos, ismaelitas et agarenos—qui nunc saraceni appellantur, assumentes sibi falso nomen sarae quo scilicet de ingenua et domina uideantur esse generati," CCSL 75:25.

Isidore elsewhere gives a fuller entry for Saracens: "Saracens *[Saraceni]* are so called, either because they claim to be born from Sarah or because (as the pagans say) they are of Syrian origin, like the Syrigenes *[Syriginae].* They live in a vast desert. They are also called the Ishmaelites, as Genesis teaches, because they are from Ishmael. Or [they are called] Cedar from the name of Ishmael's son. They are also called Hagarens *[Agareni]* from Hagar. They are, as we said, erroneously called Saracens, because they falsely pride themselves on being descendants of Sarah" (*Etymologies,* 9:2:57).

Modern etymologists do not agree on the origins of the term "Saracen"; see Irfad Shahîd, *Rome and the Arabs: A Prolegomenon to the Study of Byzantium and the Arabs* (Washington: Dumbarton Oaks, 1984), 123–41. For an overview of early medieval Latin texts that discuss the term "Saracen," see Ekkehart Rotter, *Abendland und Sarazenen: Das okzidentale Araberbild und seine Entstehung im Frühmittelalter* (Berlin: Walter de Gruyter, 1986), 68–77.

26. Shahîd, *Rome and the Arabs,* 100–101: the first-century authors are Josephus and Polyhistor.

27. *Etymologies,* 9:2:13–14, using Gen. 10:6–7, and Virgil, *Georgics* 2, 117. See Shahîd, *Rome and the Arabs,* 104 n. 62; Rotter, *Abendland und Sarazenen,* 77–82.

28. *Etymologies,* 19:23:7 and 8:5:59. Earlier writers associated Arabs with Christological heresies. Eusebius, in his *Historia ecclesiastica,* portrays Arabia as a hotbed of such heresies; see Shahîd, *Rome and the Arabs,* 107–8. John of Skythopolis, writing in the early sixth century, says that Arabia contained many heretics; see John Lamoreaux, "Early Eastern Christian Responses to Islam," in John Tolan, ed., *Medieval Christian Perceptions of Islam: A Book of Essays* (New York: Garland, 1996), 3–31 (11).

29. Shahîd, *Rome and the Arabs,* 99; Lamoreaux, "Eastern Christian Responses," 9–11.

30. Shahîd, *Rome and the Arabs,* 98, 101.

31. *Antonini Placentini itinerarium* 38:2–6 (CCSL 175 [1965]); see Rotter, *Abendland und Sarazenen,* 12–31.

32. Eusebius refers to the "robbers of Arabia" in his *Praeparatio evangelica,* citing Diodorus Siculus; see Shahîd, *Rome and the Arabs,* 98. Similar sentiments are found in Ammianus Marcellinus, *Res gestae;* Julian the Apostate, *Orationes;* and Cyril of Scythopolis, *Life of Euthymius,* according to Lamoreaux, "Early Eastern Christian Responses," 9–10. In the Eusebius/Jerome chronicle Isidore would have read this description of Saracens as potential aggressors of Christians: "Saraceni in monasterium beati antonii inruentes sarmatam interficiunt" (*Eusebii Caesariensis Chronicon. Hieronymi continuatio,* CCSL 616c A, p. 240).

33. Françoise Thelamon, *Païens et Chrétiens au IVème siècle: L'apport de l'*Histoire ecclésiastique *de Rufin d'Aquilée* (Paris: Études augustiniennes, 1981), 123–47.

34. Isidore, *Chronica majora*, §24.

35. He explains, following Lactantius, that "Quos pagani deos asserunt, homines olim fuisse produntur, et pro uniuscuiusque vita vel meritis coli apud suos post mortem coeperunt," Isidore, *Etymologies*, 8:11:1. For a detailed analysis of *Etymologies*, 8:11, and its sources, see Katherine MacFarlane, *Isidore of Seville on the Pagan Gods (Origines VIII.11)* (Philadelphia: American Philosophical Association, 1980). She notes that Isidore bases the passage quoted primarily on Lactantius, *Institutiones divinae*, though he would have found similar ideas in his reading of Augustine, Tertullian, and others (11).

36. *Etymologies*, 8:9:4. Isidore found the idea of the "solace of contemplating images" in Lactantius, combining it with the idea of the demonic nature of idols, gleaned from his reading of Augustine's *City of God*. See MacFarlane, *Isidore of Seville on the Pagan Gods*, 12.

37. Isidore, *Etymologies*, 8:11:7–8).

38. MacFarlane, *Isidore of Seville on the Pagan Gods*, 13.

39. This is one of the midrashic explanations of Gen. 21:9, where Sarah sees Ishmael "playing" (*mesaheq*, which the Vulgate translates as *ludentum*). In Midrash Genesis Rabba 53.11 according to Rabbi Akiba this expression refers, variously, to worship of idols (cf. Exod. 32:6), to sexual misconduct (Gen. 39:17), or violent games that lead to bloodshed (2 Sam. 2:14). According to the Midrash, Ishmael shot arrows in Isaac's direction supposedly "in play," but in fact with the intention of killing him. See Louis Ginzberg, *Legends of the Jews*, 7 vols. (Philadelphia: Jewish Publication Society of America, 1968) 1:237–40, 263–69; 5:230–33, 246–47. Thanks to Alan Corre for these references.

40. See Hillgarth, "Historiography in Visigothic Spain," 293–96.

41. Simon is mentioned in Acts 8:9–24, but Isidore's version of his life is based on one of the apocryphal Gospel accounts. One of the oldest and most widely known versions was that of the apocryphal *Actus Petri cum Simone*, in R. A. Lipisius and M. Bonnet, eds., *Acta Apostolorum Apocrypha* (Leipzig, 1891), 1:45–103; English translation with introduction and bibliography by J. K. Elliot, *The Apocryphal New Testament* (Oxford, 1993), 390–430. On the medieval legends regarding Simon and on his role as "father of the heresiarchs," see Alberto Ferreiro, "Jerome's Polemic against Priscillian in His *Letter to Ctesiphon*," *Revue des études augustiniennes* 39 (1993):309–32; Valerie Flint, *The Rise of Magic in Early Medieval Europe* (Princeton, 1991), 338–44.

42. On the use of typological figuration in early hagiography, see Derek Krueger, "Typological Figuration in Theodoret of Cyrrhus's *Religious History* and the Art of Postbiblical Narrative," *Journal of Early Christian Studies* 5 (1997):393–419; Marc Van Uytfanghe, "L'Empreinte biblique sur la plus ancienne hagiographie occidentale," in Fontaine and Pietri, eds., *Le monde latin antique et la Bible*, vol. 2 of *La Bible de tous les temps* (Paris: Beauchesne, 1985); James Earl, "Typology and Iconographic Style in Early Medieval Hagiography," *Studies in the Literary Imagination* 8 (1975):15–46.

43. Brian Stock, *The Implications of Literacy: Written Language and Models of Interpretation in the Eleventh and Twelfth Centuries* (Princeton: Princeton University Press, 1983), 119 (in regard to the eleventh-century heretics of Orleans).

44. "Constantinus autem in extremo vitae suae ab Eusebio Nicomediensi episcopo

baptizatus in Arrianum dogma convertitur. Heu pro dolor! Bono usus principio et fine malo," *Chronica majora,* §334. Constantine was an ambiguous figure for early medieval authors (e.g., Jerome and Gregory of Tours): the first Christian emperor yet baptized an Arian heretic; see Ian Wood, "Gregory of Tours and Clovis," *Revue belge de philologie et d'histoire* 63 (1985):249–72 (251).

45. "Constans Arrianus effectus catholicos toto orbe persequitur," *Chronica majora,* §336.

46. "Iste Acefalorum haeresim suscepit atque in proscriptionem synodi Calchedonensis omnes in regno suo episcopos tria capitula damnare conpellit," *Chronica majora,* §397. See Hillgarth, "Historiography," 295–97.

47. "Fridigernus Ataricum Valentis auxilio . . . ex catholico Arrianus cum omni gente Gothorum effectus est," *Chronica majora,* §349.

48. See Hillgarth, "Historiography"; Suzanne Teillet, *Des Goths à la nation gothique: Essai sur les origines de l'idée de la nation* (Paris: Belles Lettres, 1984), 463–501.

49. On the theme of Constantine and Christian peace in the works of Eusebius and Lactantius, see Teillet, *Des Goths à la nation gothique,* 68–69.

50. *Etymologies,* 8:1:1, taken from Leander of Seville, *Sermon on the Triumph of the Church for the Conversion of the Goths* (Homilia de triumpho Ecclesiae ob conversionem Gothorum), trans. in Barlow, *The Fathers of the Church: Iberian Fathers,* 2 vols. (Washington, D.C.: Catholic University of America, 1969), 1:229–35; passage cited p. 230. Isidore gives the same definition of heresy in his *Sentences,* 1:16:6–7; Cazier, *Isidore,* 116.

51. Braulio of Saragossa describes it thus: "contra Judaeos, postulante Florentia germana sua proposito virgine, libros duos in quibus omnia quae fides catholica credit, ex legis et prophetarum testimoniis approbavit" (PL 82:67). Bat-Sheva Albert (*"De fide catholica contra Judaeos* d'Isidore de Séville: La polémique anti-judaïque dans l'Espagne du VIIᵉ siècle," *Revue des Études Juives* 141 (1982):289–316; here 313) concludes that Isidore wrote it as a sort of theological primer for Christian clerics.

52. Isidore, *Against the Jews* (De fide Catholica ex veteri et novo testamento contra Iudaeos ad Florentinam sororem suam) (PL 83:449–538) 2:28.

53. Isidore, *Against the Jews,* 2:5.

54. Albert, *"De fide catholica."*

55. See Isidore, *Against the Jews,* 2:17; Albert, *"De fide catholica,"* 294–95.

56. Albert, *"De fide catholica,"* 296–97.

57. Isidore, *Against the Jews,* 1:5.

58. *Lex Visigothorum,* MGH leges sectio 1 (1902), 12:2:12–13.

59. *Lex Visigothorum,* 12:2:3–11; E. A. Thompson, *The Goths in Spain* (Oxford: Oxford University Press, 1969), 111.

60. *Lex Visigothorum,* 12:2:16; trans. Hillgarth, *Christianity and Paganism,* 108.

61. *Lex Visigothorum,* 12:2:13–14.

62. "At the beginning of his reign he [Sisebut] forced the Jews into the Christian faith, indeed acting with zeal, 'but not according to knowledge' [Rom. 10:2], for he compelled by force those who should have been called to the faith through reason," Isidore, *On the Origin of the Goths,* §60; trans. Wolf, *Conquerors,* 106.

63. Albert, "Isidore," 209.

64. "One way of protecting ritual from scepticism is to suppose that an enemy, within or without the community, is continually undoing its good effect. On these lines responsibility may be given to amoral demons or to witches and sorcerers," Mary Douglas, *Purity and Danger: An Analysis of Concepts of Pollution and Taboo* (London: Routledge, 1966), 174.

65. Daniel Sperber, "Min," *Encyclopaedia Judaica* 16 vols.(Jerusalem, 1971–72), 12:1–3; Salo Baron, *A Social and Religious History of the Jews,* 18 vols. (New York, 1952–83), 2:130–35; William Green, "Otherness Within: Towards a Theory of Difference in Rabbinic Judaism," in J. Neusner and E. Frerichs, eds., *To See Ourselves as Others See Us: Christians, Jews, and "Others" in Late Antiquity* (Chico: Scholar's Press, 1985), 49–69 (esp. 58–59).

66. Talmud, Sanhedrin 107b; see Jean-Pierre Osier, *L'Evangile du ghetto: La légende juive de Jésus du IIe au Xe siècle* (Paris: Berg, 1984), 141.

67. Talmud, Gittin 56b–57a; see Osier, *L'évangile du ghetto,* 151.

68. Talmud, Sanhedrin 43a; Deut. 13:6–9; see Osier, *L'évangile du ghetto,* 148.

69. For an example from the twelfth century, see Petrus Alfonsi, *Dialogi contra Iudaeos* (Pedro Alfonso de Huesca, *Diálogo contra los Judío,* Latin text edited by Klaus-Peter Mieth with Spanish translation by Esperanza Ducay [Zaragoza: Instituto de Estudios Altoaragoneses, 1996], §10, p.160; for similar statements in the thirteenth-century *Milhemet Mizvah,* see Robert Chazan, *Daggers of Faith: Thirteenth-Century Christian Missionizing and Jewish Response* (Berkeley: University of California Press, 1989), 41–42, 55–56.

70. The summary that follows includes the key narrative elements common to most of the medieval versions of the *Toledoth;* see Osier, *L'Evangile du ghetto.*

71. *Toledoth Yeshu,* trans. (into English) Hugh Schonfield, *According to the Hebrews: A New Translation of the Jewish Life of Jesus (the Toledoth Jeshu), with an Inquiry into the Nature of Its Sources and Special Relationship to the Lost Gospel According to the Hebrews* (London: Duckworth, 1937), 53. For French translations of the varying versions of the text, see Osier, *L'évangile du ghetto.*

72. John Tolan, "Un cadavre mutilé: Le déchirement polémique de Mahomet," *Le Moyen Âge* 104 (1998):53–72.

73. Douglas, *Purity and Danger,* 104–5.

74. Albert, *"De fide,"* 296 n. 38.

75. See Osier, *L'évangile du Ghetto,* 18–19; for later medieval examples of Jewish anti-Christian legends and iconography, see Marc Epstein, *Dreams of Subversion in Medieval Jewish Art and Literature* (University Park: Pennsylvania State University Pres, 1997).

76. This is Green's characterization of the rabbinic reaction to the *minim* (Green, "Otherness Within," 58). As Jonathan Smith remarks, "The radically 'other' is merely 'other'; the proximate 'other' is problematic, and hence, of supreme interest" (Jonathan Smith, "What a Difference a Difference Makes," in Neusner and Frerichs, eds., *To See Ourselves as Others See Us,* 3–48 [here 5]).

77. On Columbus's struggles to fit his discoveries into the concepts of his inadequate vocabulary, see Smith, "What a Difference," 32–36.

78. See Jacques Fontaine and C. Pellistrandi, eds., *L'Europe héritère de l'Espagne wisigothique* (*Collection de la Casa de Velázquez* 35) Madrid: Casa de Velázquez, 1992.

79. Gen. 16:12, discussed above; the notion that Ishmael had invented black magic is found in the Babylonian Talmud, Sanhedrin 91a.

2. Islamic Dominion and the Religious Other

1. Citations from the Koran are from the translation by N. Dawood (London: Penguin, 1956).

2. 'Abd al-Malik Ibn Hisham, *The Life of Muhammad* (Sîrat rasûl Allâh), trans. A. Guillaume (Oxford: Oxford University Press, 1955), 181–87. On the *Mir'âj*, see B. W. Robinson, "Mir'âdj," EI² 7:99–106.

3. Ibn Hisham, *Life of Muhammad*; J. Jones, "Ibn Ishâk, Muhammad b. Ishâk b. Yasâr b. Khiyâr," EI² 3:834–35; M. Watt, "Ibn Hishâm," Abû Muhammad 'Abd al-Malik," EI² 3:824.

4. Ibn Hisham, *Life of Muhammad*, 72.

5. A. Abel, "Bahîrâ," EI² 1:922–23.

6. One such verse is: "Have We [God] not lifted up your [Muhammad's] heart and relieved you of the burden which weighed down your back?" Koran 94:1–3. This seems to refer to the spiritual anxieties Muhammad felt before his call, though later texts made this the source of the legend that the angels cut open his breast, took his heart out, and cleansed it of sin. See Fazlur Rahman, *Islam*, 2d edition (Chicago: University of Chicago Press, 1979), 16.

7. For example, see al-Bukhârî 66:2:2; Muslim, 43:15, pp.88–89 (references from Thomas Burman, *Religious Polemic and the Intellectual History of the Mozarabs* [Leiden: Brill, 1994], 265, 267]).

8. Ibn Hisham, *The Life of Muhammad*; J. Jones, "Ibn Ishâk, Muhammad b. Ishâk b. Yasâr b. Khiyâr," EI² 3:834–35; Watt, "Ibn Hishâm," Abû Muhammad 'Abd al-Malik," EI² 3:824.

9. Ibn Hisham, *Life of Muhammad*, 105–6; see Montgomery Watt, *Muhammad at Mecca* (Oxford: Oxford University Press, 1953), 39–52.

10. Ibn Hisham, *Life of Muhammad*, 106–7; see Watt, *Muhammad at Mecca*, 50–52.

11. Koran 16:103. It is unclear who is meant here; several Muslim commentators on the Koran suggest that it may refer to Salmân al-Fârisi, although he apparently became a companion of the prophet in Medina and would on that account not be referred to in this earlier (Meccan) Sûra.

12. These miracle stories may be a reaction to the needs of Christian converts to Islam. "Que peut-on déduire de cet intérêt accordé aux prophéties et aux miracles sinon que l'originalité de l'Islam est ici battue en brèche par ceux-là mêmes qui la défendaient, parce qu'ils s'étaient vus contraints sous l'effet de la conscience mythique

dominante à rechercher des racines dans le fonds biblique disponible afin de mieux as-
seoir ce qu'ils considéraient comme les attributs indispensables de tout prophète et, à
plus forte raison, du dernier et du plus illustre à leurs yeux." Abdelmajid Charfi, "La
fonction historique de la polémique islamochrétienne à l'époque abbasside," in Samir
Khalil Samir and Jørgen S. Nielsen, eds., *Christian Arabic Apologetics during the Abbasid
Period (750–1258)* (Leiden: Brill, 1994), 44–56 (here 52).

13. On the many such references in the Koran, see Faruq Sherif, *A Guide to the Contents of the Qur'an* (London: Ithaca Press, 1985), 40–41.

14. It seems unlikely that the merchant Muhammad was in fact illiterate; early
Hadîth describe him drawing up legal documents. For Goldfield, the Koranic *um-
miyyûn* (plural of *ummi*) refers to those peoples who have not yet received divine scriptures; Muhammad was *ummi*, therefore, because he belonged to a people who had
benefited from no previous revelation of scripture. However, from the third Muslim
century onward, the predominant Muslim tradition is that *ummi* means illiterate. See I.
Goldfeld, "The Illiterate Prophet (Nabî Ummî): An Inquiry into the Development of a
Dogma," *Der Islam* 57 (1980):58–67; Annemarie Schimmel, *And Muhammad Is His Messenger: The Veneration of the Prophet in Islamic Piety* (Chapel Hill: University of North
Carolina Press, 1985), 71–2.

15. Ibn Hisham, *Life of Muhammad,* 165–66; see Watt, *Muhammad at Mecca,* 101–9.

16. Koran 53:23; Ibn Hisham, *Life of Muhammad,* 166; Watt, *Muhammad at Mecca,*
102.

17. Cf. Koran 5:68, 6:33–35; see Rahman, *Islam,* 16–18.

18. Rahman, *Islam,* 37–40; Hava Lararus-Yafeh, *Intertwined Worlds: Medieval Islam
and Bible Criticism* (Princeton: Princeton University Press, 1992), 35.

19. Most of these regulations are in Sûras 4, 24, and 65. See Rahman, *Islam,* 38;
Sherif, *Guide to the Contents of the Qur'an,* 126–30.

20. Koran 2:143–49; see Abdulaziz Sachedina, "Islamic Theology of Christian-
Muslim Relations," *Islam and Christian Muslim Relations* 8 (1997):27–38; Rahman, *Islam,*
19–20, 26–28.

21. Watt, *Muhammad at Medina* (Oxford: Oxford University Press, 1956), 205, 303–4;
Watt, "Hanîf," EI² 3:168–70.

22. As Rahman says, "Western critics . . . [are] so addicted . . . to pathetic tales of
sorrow, failure, frustration, and crucifixion that the very idea of success in this sphere
seems abhorrent," *Islam,* 19.

23. Ibn Hisham, *Life of Muhammad,* 652–58; Watt, *Muhammad at Medina,* 345–47.

24. Ibn Hisham, *Life of Muhammad,* 682.

25. The succession crisis provoked by Muhammad's death is discussed by Ibn
Hisham, *Life of Muhammad,* 682–90.

26. See Fred M. Donner, *The Early Islamic Conquests* (Princeton: Princeton University Press, 1981), 91–96; Shahîd, *Rome and the Arabs;* Fergus Millar, "Hagar, Ishmael,
Josephus, and the Origins of Islam," *Journal of Jewish Studies* 44 (1993):23–45.

27. For detailed studies of the conquest see Donner, *Early Islamic Conquests;* Walter

Kaegi, *Byzantium and the Early Islamic Conquests* (Cambridge: Cambridge University Press, 1992).

28. Sophronius, *Sermon on the Theophany,* cited by Christoph von Schönborn, *Sophrone de Jérusalem: Vie monastique et confession dogmatique* (Paris, 1972), 90–91; see below, chap. 3.

29. Watt, *Muhammad at Medina,* 309–15.

30. Vajda, "Ahl al-Kitâb," EI² 1:272–74; Jacques Waardenburg, "Jugements musulmans sur les religions non-islamiques à l'époque médiévale," in *La signification du bas Moyen Age dans l'histoire et la culture du monde musulman: Actes du 8ᵉ congrès de l'Union Européenne des Arabisants et Islamisants* (Aix en Provence, 1976), 323–41; Waardenburg, "World Religions as Seen in the Light of Islam," in A. Welch and P. Cachia, eds., *Islam: Past Influence and Present Challenge* (Edinburgh, 1979), 245–75.

31. Koran 2:111–13, 2:62; Sachedina,"Islamic Theology of Christian-Muslim Relations," 110

32. Koran 4:46–48; Watt, *Muhammad at Medina,* 204–8.

33. Koran 62:5; Lararus-Yafeh, *Intertwined Worlds,* 146.

34. Koran 2:75, 7:175; Robert Caspar and J. M. Gaudel, "Textes de la tradition musulmane concernant le tahrîf (falsification) des Écritures," *Islamochristiana* 6 (1980):61–104; Lararus-Yafeh, *Intertwined Worlds,* 19–35, 77–79. For an example of a ninth-century polemical letter accusing Jews and Christians of falsifying scripture, see Gaudel's translation of the letter attributed to 'Umar II (Gaudel, "The Correspondence between Leo and 'Umar: 'Umar's Letter Re-discovered?" *Islamochristiana* 10 [1984]:109–57, here 134–36).

35. Watt, *Muhammad at Medina,* 315–20.

36. On the Koranic passages that refer to Jesus and to Christian doctrine, see Sherif, *Guide to the Contents of the Qur'an,* 60–64, 89–90; Sahas, "Arab Character," 199 n. 72.

37. Koran 4:156.

38. Ibn Hisham, *Life of Muhammad,* 239ff; Lazarus-Yafeh, *Intertwined Worlds,* 77–78; J. Schacht, "Ahmad," EI² 1:267. Another eighth-century Muslim author makes the same claim: see Gaudel's translation of the letter attributed to 'Umar II (Gaudel, "The Correspondence," 138).

39. On this curious charge, and its later place in Muslim-Jewish polemics, see Lazarus-Yafeh, *Intertwined Worlds,* 50–74.

40. Watt, *Muhammad at Medina,* 319; Sachedina, "Islamic Theology of Christian-Muslim Relations," 118–20.

41. Claude Cahen, "Dhimma," EI² 2:234–38.

42. Charfi, "La fonction historique de la polémique islamochrétienne," 55.

43. Sarah Strousma, "The Signs of Prophecy: The Emergence and Early Development of a Theme in Arabic Theological Literature," *Harvard Theological Review* 78 (1985):101–14 (esp. 106–7).

44. "For a Muslim polemical theologian . . . the claim that Jesus Christ had been crucified was merely *wrong,* whereas the claim that he was the Son of God and one of a

triplicity in the godhead was *blasphemous*"; Mark Swanson, "The Cross of Christ in the Earliest Arabic Melkite Apologies," in Samir and Nielsen, *Christian Arabic Apologetics,* 113–45; quotation at 118.

45. See the passage quoted above, Koran 9:29–35. The Arabic term "associator" (*mushrikūn*) is a common derogatory epithet given to Christians (see below, chap. 3).

46. Andrew Palmer, Sebastian Brock, and Robert Hoyland, eds. and trans., *The Seventh Century in the West-Syrian Chronicles* (Liverpool: Liverpool University Press, 1993), xxi.

47. Gaudel, "The Correspondence," and below, chap. 3.

48. Gaudel, "The Correspondence" ; the response attributed to Leo is discussed below, chap. 3.

49. Gaudel, "The Correspondence," 155–56.

50. Oleg Grabar, "Kubbat al-Sakhra," EI² 5:297–99; Grabar, "The Meaning of the Dome of the Rock," in D. Hopwood, ed., *Studies in Arab History: The Antonius Lectures, 1978–1987* (London, 1990), 151–63; K. Creswell, *Early Muslim Architecture,* 2 vols. (Oxford: Oxford University Press, 1940; reprint New York, 1979) 1:65–129; C. Kessler, " 'Abd al-Malik's Inscription," *Journal of the Royal Asiatic Society* (1970):2–14; Nassar Rabbat, "The Dome of the Rock Revisited: Some Remarks on al-Wasiti's Accounts," *Muqarnas* 10 (1993):66–75; Rabbat, "The Meaning of the Umayyad Dome of the Rock," *Muqarnas* 6 (1989):12-21; Amikam Elad, "Why Did 'Abd al-Malik Build the Dome of the Rock?" in J. Raby, and J. Johns, eds., *Bayt al-Maqdis: 'Abd al-Malik's Jerusalem* (Oxford: Oxford University Press, 1992), 33–58; Josef van Ess, " 'Abd al-Malik and the Dome of the Rock," in Raby and Johns, eds., *Bayt al-Maqdis,* 89–104; Carolanne Mekeel-Matteson, "The Meaning of the Dome of the Rock," *Islamic Quarterly* 43 (1999):149–85.

51. Scholars have traditionally assumed that the date of 692 referred to the Dome's completion, but Sheila Blair argues plausibly that 'Abd al-Malik ordered the mosque "in the first half of 692 on his victorious return from Iraq as part of a major buildup of Damascus and Jerusalem," Blair, "What Is the Date of the Dome of the Rock?" in Raby and Johns, eds., *Bayt al-Maqdis,* 59–85, quotation at 84.

52. Grabar, "The Meaning of the Dome of the Rock," 157.

53. "The aim was to offer a program that would explain the legitimacy of the Umayyad dynasty's rule," M. Almagro et al., *Qusayr 'Amra: Residencia y baños omeyas en le desierto de Jordanía* (Madrid, 1975), 120. For the description of these paintings, see 55–57.

54. These are the estimates of Bulliet, *Conversion to Islam in the Medieval Period: An Essay in Quantitative History* (Cambridge, Mass.: Harvard University Press, 1979), 44, 82, 97, 109. Others scholars have questioned Bulliet's figures; for an overview of this debate, see Michael Morony, "The Age of Conversions: A Reassessment," in M. Gervers and R. Bikhazi, eds., *Conversion and Continuity: Indigenous Christian Communities in Islamic Lands, Eighth to Eighteenth Centuries* (Toronto: Pontifical Institute of Medieval Studies, 1990), 135–50. For the debate regarding conversion to Islam in Spain, see below, chap. 4.

55. Bulliet, "Conversion Stories in Early Islam," in Gervers and Bikhazi, eds., *Conversion and Continuity,* 123–33.

3. Early Eastern Christian Reactions to Islam

1. *Chronicon ad A.C. 1234 pertinens,* trans. in Palmer et al., *The Seventh Century,* 141. For an analysis of this passage and similar sentiments by other Syrian Christian authors, see S. Brock, "Syriac Views of Emergent Islam." *Studies in the First Century of Islamic Society,* ed. G. H. A. Juynboll (Carbondale, Ill., 1982), 9–21 (esp. 10–11).

2. A number of Greek texts attribute the defense of Constantinople against the onslaughts of its successive attackers to the intervention of the saints; in particular to the Virgin, who protected it with her robe (which was one of the city's prize relics). See Norman Baynes, "The Supernatural Defenders of Constantinople," *Analecta Bollandiana* 67 (1949):165–77.

3. Brock, "Syriac Views," 14–15.

4. For the example of seventh-century Egyptian bishop John of Nikiu, see John Moorhead, "The Earliest Christian Theological Responses to Islam." *Religion* 11 (1981): 265–74 (esp. 268).

5. Sophronios, *Christmas Sermon;* trans. Walter Kaegi, "Initial Byzantine Reactions to the Arab Conquest," *Church History* 38 (1969):139–49. On Sophronius (c. 560–638; Patriarch 634–38), see von Schönborn, *Sophrone de Jérusalem,* who gives references (103 n. 18) to the various editions of the Greek text as well as to the incomplete Latin translation in PG 87:3201–12.

6. This refers to the Philistine occupation of Bethlehem in 1 Chron. 11:16–19, 2 Sam. 23:14–17.

7. Sophronios, *Christmas Sermon;* trans. Kaegi, "Initial Byzantine Reactions," 141.

8. He gives a similar view of the invasions as chastisement for Christians' sins in his *Synodal Letter* (PG 87:3146–200, at 3197D); see von Schönborn, *Sophrone,* 89–90, 100.

9. Sophronios, *Sermon on the Theophany,* cited by von Schönborn, *Sophrone,* 90–91.

10. Trans. John Lamoreaux, "Early Eastern Christian Responses to Islam," in John Tolan, ed., *Medieval Christian Perceptions of Islam: A Book of Essays* (New York: Garland, 1996), 3–31 (here 14–15), from PG 91:540.

11. B. Flusin, "Démons et Sarrasins: L'auteur et le propos des *Diègèmata Stèriktiká* d'Anastaste le Sinaïte," *Travaux et mémoires* 11 (1991):381–409; Sydney Griffith, "Anastasios of Sinai, the *Hodegos,* and the Muslims," *Greek Orthodox Theological Review* 32 (1987):341–58.

12. Griffith, "Anastasios of Sinai."

13. Bernard Flusin has announced his forthcoming critical edition of this text (see Flusin, "Démons et Sarrasins").

14. Flusin, "Démons et Sarrasins," 385.

15. Flusin, "Démons et Sarrasins," 386.

16. Flusin, "Démons et Sarrasins," 387, 404–5.

17. Edition of Greek text and French translation of text in Flusin, "L'esplanade du Temple à l'arrivée des Arabes," in Raby and Johns, eds., *Bayt al-Maqdis,* 17–31 (here 25–26); see also Flusin, "Démons et Sarrasins," 386, 393, 408.

18. Alain Ducellier, *Chrétiens d'Orient et Islam au Moyen Age,* 161–62; Nicetas seems to be deforming (willfully or no) a passage of John of Damascus discussed below (n. 54, this chapter).

19. Alain Ducellier, *Chrétiens d'Orient et Islam au Moyen Age* (Paris: Armand Colin, 1996), 161–64; PG 110:873. For other Greek texts about Koubar, see John Meyendorff, "Byzantine Views of Islam." *Dumbarton Oaks Papers* 18 (1964):115–32 (esp. 118–19).

20. *Doctrine of Jacob Recently Baptized* (Doctrina Jacobi nuper baptizati), trans. Kaegi, "Initial Byzantine Reactions," 141.

21. *Doctrine of Jacob Recently Baptized,* trans. Kaegi, "Initial Byzantine Reactions," 141.

22. Quoted by Lamoreaux, "Early Eastern Christian Responses to Islam," 19; see also Ducellier, *Chrétiens d'Orient et Islam au Moyen Age,* 27–35; Moorhead, "Earliest Christian Theological Responses," 265–66.

23. I quote this Nestorian chronicler of c. 670 as translated in Claude Cahen, "Note sur l'accueil des chrétiens d'Orient à l'Islam," *Revue de l'histoire des religions* 166 (1964):51–58 (quotation at 52–53); see also Moorhead,"Earliest Christian Theological Responses," 266–67. The *Secrets of Rabbi Simon Ben Yohay,* a Jewish apocalypse of the mid-eighth century, presents the Arab invasions as a positive event in the eschatological drama; see Nehemia Levtzion, "Conversion to Islam in Syria and Palestine and the Survival of Christian Communities," in Gervers and Bikhazi, eds., *Conversion and Continuity,* 289–311.

24. Norman Roth, *Jews, Visigoths and Muslims in Medieval Spain* (Leiden: Brill, 1994), 206.

25. *Apocalypse of Pseudo-Methodius,* ed. and trans. Francisco J. Martinez, in "Eastern Christian Apocalyptic in the Early Muslim Period: Pseudo-Methodius and Pseudo-Athanasius," (Dissertation, Catholic University of America, 1985), 58–201; G. J. Reinink, "Pseudo-Methodius: A Concept of History in Response to the Rise of Islam," in Averil Cameron and Lawrence Conrad, eds., *The Byzantine and Early Islamic Near East* (Princeton: Princeton University Press, 1992), 1:149–87; Brock, "Syriac Views," 17–20. Reinink (p. 185) concludes that "the hypothesis that the *Apocalypse* of ps.-Methodius was composed in reaction to 'Abd al-Malik's foundation of the Dome of the Rock on the site of the Jewish Temple is very attractive."

26. *Apocalypse of Pseudo-Methodius,* preface, 122.

27. See chap. 1.

28. *Apocalypse of Pseudo-Methodius,* §1, p. 140.

29. *Apocalypse of Pseudo-Methodius,* §2, p. 124.

30. *Apocalypse of Pseudo-Methodius,* §5, p. 128. The author is describing the Madianite wars narrated in Judg. 6–8; the identification of the Madianites with the Ishmaelites is found in Judges 8:24.

31. *Apocalypse of Pseudo-Methodius,* §11, p. 144–45.

32. This text provides strong evidence that large-scale conversions now were perceived as a threat by Christians such as the pseudo-Methodius; this piece of evidence seems to have been overlooked in the debates over the demography of conversion from Christianity to Islam (see chap. 2). Of course it is impossible to translate the subjective perception of "mass" conversions into even approximate numbers.

33. 1 Tim. 4:1.

34. *Apocalypse of Pseudo-Methodius*, §13, pp. 147–48; Heb. 12:8

35. *Apocalypse of Pseudo-Methodius*, §5, p. 130; §10, p. 139.

36. Brock ("Syriac Views," 19) argues for a date between 690 and 692; Reinink ("Pseudo-Methodius," 178–83) argues that the author may be reacting to (among other things) the construction of the Dome of the Rock in 691 and hence posits 692 as the date of composition. (See above, n. 25.)

37. *Apocalypse of Pseudo-Methodius*, §13, p. 149, paraphrasing Ps. 78:65.

38. *Apocalypse of Pseudo-Methodius*, §13, p. 150.

39. *Apocalypse of Pseudo-Methodius*, §13, p. 150.

40. *Apocalypse of Pseudo-Methodius*, §13, p. 151; these northern barbarians are described earlier, when Alexander locks them up behind the Gate of the North (§13, pp. 132–34).

41. On John of Damascus, see Daniel Sahas, *John of Damascus on Islam: The "Heresy of the Ishmaelites"* (Leiden: Brill, 1972); Sahas, "John of Damascus on Islam, Revisited," *Abr-Nahrain* 23 (1984–85):104–18; Sahas, "The Arab Character of the Christian Disputation with Islam: The Case of John of Damascus (ca. 655–ca. 749)," in B. Lewis and F. Niewohner, eds., *Religionsgespräche im Mittelalter* (Wiesbaden: Otto Harrassowitz, 1992), 185–205; Ducellier, *Chrétiens d'Orient et Islam au Moyen Age*, 103–20; Le Coz, intro. to his translation of Jean Damascène [John of Damascus], *Écrits sur l'Islam* (Paris: Cerf, 1992), esp. chap. 2, 41–65; Meyendorff, "Byzantine Views of Islam," 117–18; Armand Abel, "La polémique damascénienne et son influence sur les origines de la théologie musulmane," in *L'Élaboration de l'Islam: Colloque de Strasbourg* (Paris, 1961), 61–85; Rachid Haddad, *La Trinité divine chez les théologiens arabes (750–1050)* (Paris: Beauchesne, 1985).

42. Sahas, "Arab Character," 188, 190.

43. Sahas, "John of Damascus on Islam, Revisited," 110–12; Sahas, "Arab Character," 202–4.

44. Sahas, *John of Damascus*, 43–45; Sahas, "Arab Character," 194.

45. See chap. 2; Bulliet, *Conversion*; Levtzion, "Conversion to Islam."

46. "In mind and in heart John still lives in Byzantium. The fact that the Byzantine emperor—whose victorious return to the Middle East he is hopefully expecting—has actually fallen into the iconoclastic heresy is, for him, a matter of greater concern than are the beliefs of the Arab conquerors" (Meyendorff, "Byzantine Views," 118).

47. On the dating of the *Fount*, see Le Coz, intro. to Jean Damascène, *Écrits sur l'Islam*, 62.

48. Sahas, *John of Damascus*, 51–58.

49. Abel, "Polémique damascénienne," 74.

50. Chapter 100 takes up eight pages of the forty-nine total in Kotter's edition of

Liber de haeresibus (John of Damascus, *Liber de haeresibus*, in P. Bonifatius Kotter, ed., *Die Schriften des Johannes von Damaskos*, 5 vols. [Berlin, 1969–81], 4:19–67). In other words, this one chapter comprises 16 percent of the text; it is sixteen times the size of the average chapter. One other chapter is as long, chap. 80, on the Massalianoi.

51. John of Damascus, *Liber de haeresibus*, in *Works* 4:60. On this passage, see Sahas, "Arab Character," 192 n. 37.

52. Σαρακηνοὺς δὲ αὐτοὺς καλοῦσιν, ὡς ἐκ τῆς Σάρρας κευοὺς, διὰ τὸ εἰρῆσΘαι ὑπὸ τῇ Ἄγαρ τῷ ἀγγέλῳ · Σάρρα κενήν με ἀπέλυσευ. John of Damascus, *Liber de haeresibus*, in *Die Schriften des Johannes von Damaskos*, 4:60; Sahas, *John of Damascus*, 132–33.

53. John of Damascus, *Liber de haeresibus*, in *Die Schriften des Johannes von Damaskos* 4:60; Sahas, *John of Damascus*, 133. This confusion between the name Habar (or Koubar) and the word *akbar* becomes the basis for later Byzantine writers to accuse Muslims of idolatry; see chap. 5; Meyendorff, 118–19; Ducellier, *Chrétiens d'Orient*, 161–64.

54. On his association of Islam with Arian Christology, see Sahas, "John of Damascus on Islam, Revisited," 108–9.

55. John of Damascus, *Liber de haeresibus*, in *Die Schriften des Johannes von Damaskos* 4:60–61; Sahas, *John of Damascus*, 132–33.

56. John of Damascus, *Liber de haeresibus*, in *Die Schriften des Johannes von Damaskos* 4:61; Sahas, *John of Damascus*, 134–35.

57. John of Damascus, *Liber de haeresibus*, in *Die Schriften des Johannes von Damaskos* 4:62; Sahas, *John of Damascus*, 134–35.

58. John of Damascus, *Liber de haeresibus*, in *Die Schriften des Johannes von Damaskos* 4:63; Sahas, *John of Damascus*, 134–39. The word translated as *Associators,* Ἑται'- ιριασταὶ, corresponds to the Arabic *mushrikūn,* a common derogatory epithet given to Christians.

59. John of Damascus, *Liber de haeresibus*, in *Die Schriften des Johannes von Damaskos* 4:63–64; Sahas, *John of Damascus*, 136–37.

60. Haddad, *Trinité divine*, 87.

61. John of Damascus, *Liber de haeresibus*, in *Die Schriften des Johannes von Damaskos* 4:64; Sahas, *John of Damascus*, 136–37.

62. John of Damascus, *Liber de haeresibus*, in *Die Schriften des Johannes von Damaskos* 4:64; Sahas, *John of Damascus*, 136–37. "John of Damascus' account of the *jahiliyyah* is almost identical to that of Ibn al-Kalbi, who derived his information from his father, Muhammad b. Al-Said al-Kalbi (d. 763), a contemporary to John of Damascus. Both present *jahiliyyah* as the Abrahamic tradition which, however, deteriorated into a crude polytheism and litholatry" (Sahas, "Arab Character," 197–98).

63. John of Damascus, *Liber de haeresibus*, in *Die Schriften des Johannes von Damaskos* 4:64; Sahas, *John of Damascus*, 136–37.

64. John of Damascus, *Disputatio Christiani et Saraceni*, in *Die Schriften des Johannes von Damaskos* 4:432; Sahas, *John of Damascus*, 148–49.

65. John of Damascus, *Disputatio Christiani et Saraceni*, in *Die Schriften des Johannes von Damaskos* 4:438; Sahas, *John of Damascus*, 154–55.

66. Sahas, "Arab Character," 198–99.

67. Sahas, "Arab Character," 197.

68. Brock, "Syriac Views of Emergent Islam," 19; Meyendorff, "Byzantine Views," 117–18.

69. Muslims may pass from being a minority to a majority around 825 for Iran, 900 for Egypt, Syria, and Iraq; see chap. 2; Bulliet, *Conversion*, 82, 97, 109.

70. *Passion of Anthony Ruwah*, ed. and trans. Ignace Dick, "La passion arabe de S. Antoine Ruwah néo-martyr de Damas (+ 25 déc. 799)," *Le Muséon* 74 (1961):109–33; see Lamoreaux, "Early Eastern Christian Responses," 22–24.

71. Lamoreaux, "Early Eastern Christian Responses," 23.

72. Meyendorff, "Byzantine Views," 129–30; Sidney Griffith, "The View of Islam from the Monasteries of Palestine in the Early 'Abbâsid Period: Theodore Abû Qurrah and the *Summa Theologiae Arabica*," *Islam and Christian-Muslim Relations* 7 (1996):9–28 (22). Anastasius the Sinaite tells such a story of a certain Georges the Black; Flusin, "Démons et Sarrasins," 387 (récit C 13).

73. Theophanes refers to him as Peter of Maiouma. Theophanes, *Chronographia* 642–43; trans. (into English) Mango and Scott, 577–79; P. Peeters, "La Passion de s. Pierre de Capitolias († 13 janvier 715)," *Analecta Bollandiana* 57 (1939):299–333; Moorhead, "Earliest Christian Theological Responses," 268; Sahas, "Arab Character," 192 n. 38.

74. Griffith, "The View of Islam," 22; Ducellier, *Chrétiens d'Orient*, 81–86, 100–103; P. Peeters, "La Passion de s. Michel le sabaïte," *Analecta Bollandiana* 48 (1930):65–98; Peeters, "S. Romain le néomartyr († 1 mai 780) d'après un document géorgien," *Analecta Bollandiana* 30 (1911):393–427.

75. Lamoreaux, "Early Eastern Christian Responses," 23; Griffith, "The View of Islam," 22; Sidney H. Griffith, "The Arabic Account of 'Abd al-Masîh an-Nağrânî al-Ghassânî," *Le Muséon* 98 (1985):331–74; K. Schultze, "Das Martyrium des heiligen Abo von Tiflis." *Texte und Untersuchungen*, n.s. 13.4 (1905).

76. " Ἀμερουμνῆς Συρίας," Gregory of Dekapolis, *Sermo* (PG 100:1201–16); on Gregory, see *Oxford Dictionary of Byzantium* (Oxford: Oxford University Press, 1991), 880.

77. On Theodore Abû Qurrah, see Griffith, "Faith and Reason in Christian Kalâm: Theodore Abû Qurrah on Discerning the True Religion," in Samir and Nielsen, *Christian Arabic Apologetics*, 1–43; Ignace Dick, "Un continuateur arabe de saint Jean Damascène: Théodore Abuqurra, évêque melkite de Harran. La personne et son milieu," *Proche Orient chrétien* 12 (1962):209–23, 319–32; 13 (1963):114–29; Ducellier, *Chrétiens d'Orient*, 91–95, 103–10, 119–24; Abel, "Polémique damascienne"; Meyendorff, "Byzantine Views," 120–21; Haddad, *Trinité divine*.

78. Robert Caspar, "Les versions arabes du dialogue entre le Catholicos Timothée et le Calife al-Mahdi," *Islamochristiana* 3 (1977):107–75; Haddad, *Trinité divine*, 30–31.

79. Sahas, *John of Damascus*, 157–59; on the common charge of abrogation (*naskh*) see J. Burton, "Naskh," EI², 7:1009.

80. Griffith, "Theodore Abû Qurrah's Arabic Tract on the Christian Practice of Venerating Images," *Journal of the American Oriental Society* 105 (1985):66–67.

81. Haddad, *Trinité divine*, 39.

82. On this text, see Griffith, "Faith and Reason." The treatise as it survives has no title; the full descriptive title, *Treatise on the Existence of the Creator and the True Religion*, was given by its first modern editor, Louis Cheikho.

83. Griffith, "Faith and Reason," 40.

84. His argument for the Trinity is based on an analogy with Adam. Adam has the gift of generation (he begets his own kind) and of emanation (Eve came from his rib). Since God the creator must exhibit all the attributes of his creation in the highest degree, he too must generate: "from what the intellect deduces from the similitudes of Adam's nature, God is three persons: one generating, and one being generated, and one emanating" (trans. Griffith, "Faith and Reason," 17). This is an analogy rather than a "proof" it seems, for he elsewhere asserts that man cannot hope to understand the Trinity, a mystery even beyond the comprehension of the angels (Haddad, *Trinité divine*, 88).

85. This same line of argumentation is taken by the anonymous author of an earlier Arabic apology for Christianity; see Samir, "Earliest Arab Apology for Christianity," in Samir and Nielsen, *Christian Arabic Apologetics*, 103.

86. Samir, "Earliest Arab Apology."

87. This analogy comes from an anonymous ninth-century Arab Christian text cited by Haddad, *Trinité divine*, 89.

88. Haddad, *Trinité divine*, 98–115 (on biblical Trinitarian arguments), 115–27 (on Trinitarian analogies), and 130–245 (on philosophical/theological arguments based on divine attributes).

89. Haddad, *Trinité divine*, 232–33, diagrams nineteen different divine triads presented by Christian theologians between 750 and 1050.

90. See chaps. 6 and 7.

91. Theophanes, *Chronographia*, 399, trans. Mango and Scott, 550. On this correspondence, see Gaudel, "The Correspondence" ; Arthur Jeffrey, "Ghevond's Text of the Correspondence between 'Umar II and Leo III," *Harvard Theological Review* 37 (1944): 269–332. According to the chronicler Sebêos, the caliph Mu'âwiya sent a letter inviting Emperor Constantine IV to convert (Ducellier, *Chrétiens d'Orient*, 30).

92. Gaudel, "The Correspondence," 113.

93. Gaudel, "The Correspondence." The letter attributed to 'Umar is discussed in chap. 2.

94. Jeffery, "Ghevond's Text," 273–76. Jeffery notes that there are two versions of this exchange: Ghevond's Armenian text, which contains interpolations clearly later than the eighth century; and an abbreviated Latin text, which seems to have no direct relation to Ghevond. For Jeffery, the most likely solution is that both versions are based on a (now lost) Greek text, which may or may not be by Leo III.

95. Not to be confused with the scientist Abû Yûsuf Ya'qûb b. Ishâq al-Kindî; the first writer to name the two correspondents was al-Bîrûni (d. 1048) (F. Rosenthal, "Al-Kindî, 'Abd al-Masîh b. Ishâk," EI² 5:123–24).

96. "L'examen attentif de l'ensemble révélera qu'il est sorti d'une seule plume et que le Hashémite anonyme que l'on nous présente n'est qu'un 'bon diable' destiné plus à préparer et à introduire les arguments du Kindite, qu'à défendre l'Islam et à assurer la défaite de l'argumentation du Chrétien" (Armand Abel, "L'Apologie d'al-Kindi et sa place dans la polémique islamo-chrétienne," *Atti del covegno internazionale sul tema: L'oriente cristiano nella storia della civiltà* [Rome: Accademia Nazionale dei Lincei, 1964], 501–23, quotation at 502). "On remarquera que le musulman n'a développé aucun des points de la théologie islamique qui confirme, à l'aide de textes ou d'arguments de fait, la véracité de la mission du Prophète, qu'il n'a pas attaqué sérieusement la dogmatique chrétienne, et qu'il n'a présenté, comme aspects de l'Islam, que ceux que les Chrétiens attaquaient avec le plus de violence: la sensualité et l'hédonisme de l'Islam, le Paradis charnel et voluptueux, la guerre sainte avec ses profits temporels, la conversion avec ses avantages mondains. La réplique se trouvera ainsi préparée: l'esprit du lecteur, mis en éveil sur les aspects les moins reluisants de l'Islam, sera mûr pour lire avec profit et plaisir la longue 'réfutation' chrétienne" (ibid., 502–3).

Georges Tartar, in his introduction to his French translation of the *Risâlat al-Kindî* (Dialogue islamo-chrétien sous le Calife al-Ma'mûn, 813–834: Les épîtres d'al-Hashimî et d'al-Kindî [Paris: Nouvelles Éditions Latines, 1985], 45–61), asserts that the first letter is indeed by a Muslim. His arguments are naive and unconvincing, linked, it seems, with his own efforts to evangelize Muslims. Samir Khalil Samir, rejecting Tartar's arguments, notes that the *Risâlat* borrows a section verbatim from the early ninth-century apologist Abû Râ'itah al-Takrîtî (Samir, "Earliest Arab Apology for Christianity," 57–114; 111 n. 237); this same conclusion is reached independently by Haddad, *Trinité divine*, 43.

97. *Risâlat al-Kindî*, Tartar trans., 86–87, 120–21.

98. *Risâlat al-Kindî*, Tartar trans., 133–34; Koran 4:169–71.

99. *Risâlat al-Kindî*, Tartar trans., 129–33.

100. *Risâlat al-Kindî*, Tartar trans., 125–27; on this passage see Abel, "L'Apologie d'al-Kindî," 504.

101. *Risâlat al-Kindî*, Tartar trans., 137–53; see Abel, "L'Apologie d'al-Kindî," 506–7.

102. *Risâlat al-Kindî*, Tartar trans., 148–53.

103. *Risâlat al-Kindî*, Tartar trans., 152–53.

104. *Risâlat al-Kindî*, Tartar trans., 153. The "signs of prophecy" were an important theme of early Christian and Jewish polemic against Islam: "signs" were described by which one could "objectively" ascertain whether or not someone was a prophet; unsurprisingly, Muhammad always fails these tests. See Strousma, "Signs of Prophecy."

105. *Risâlat al-Kindî*, Tartar trans., 153–66; Koran 17:59–61.

106. *Risâlat al-Kindî*, Tartar trans., 166.

107. *Risâlat al-Kindî*, Tartar trans., 175–206.

108. *Risâlat al-Kindî*, Tartar trans., 207–8; Matt. 15:1–2; 23:25–28.

109. This argument is a common defense against charges of *tahrîf* among Arab Christian apologists; see Strousma, "Signs of Prophecy," 111.

110. *Risâlat al-Kindî*, Tartar trans., 238–82.

111. Theophanes, *Chronographia* 333–34, trans. Mango and Scott, 464–65. Theo-

phanes's sources of information about Muhammad are not clear. His description is similar to that of Bartholomew of Edessa; since the latter's text is undated, it is unclear which author (if either) used the other (Anne Proudfoot, "The Sources of Theophanes for the Heraclian Period," *Byzantion* 44 [1974]:367–439; 386).

112. Theophanes, *Chronographia* 333, trans. Mango and Scott, 464.

113. Theophanes, *Chronographia* 334, trans. Mango and Scott, 464. Theophanes is the first author to charge Muhammad with being an epileptic, an accusation that will be repeated by many later polemicists; see Astérios Argyriou, "Éléments biographiques concernant le prophète Muhammad dans la littérature grecque des trois premiers siècles de l'Hégire," in Toufic Fahd, ed., *La vie du prophète Mahomet: Colloque de Strasbourg (octobre 1980)* (Paris, 1983), 160–82 (168); Ducellier, *Chrétiens d'Orient*, 127.

114. Theophanes, *Chronographia* 334, trans. Mango and Scott, 464–65.

115. Theophanes, *Chronographia* 428, trans. Mango and Scott, 592.

116. Theophanes, *Chronographia* 335–36, trans. Mango and Scott, 466.

117. Theophanes, *Chronographia* 336, trans. Mango and Scott, 467.

118. Theophanes, *Chronographia* 339, trans. Mango and Scott, 471; Dan. 9:27, 11:31, 12:11; cf. Matt. 24:15, 1 Macc. 1:54, 6:7.

119. Jenny Ferber, "Theophanes' Account of the Reign of Heraclius," in E. Jeffreys, M. Jeffreys, and A. Moffatt, eds., *Byzantine Papers: Proceedings of the First Australian Byzantine Studies Conference* (Canberra: Humanities Research Center of the Australian National University, 1981), 32–42.

120. Theophanes, *Chronographia* 329–30, trans. Mango and Scott, 460–61; Ferber, "Theophanes' Account," 38.

121. Theophanes, *Chronographia* 332, trans. Mango and Scott, 462.

122. Amalek is the biblical name of a nomadic desert people who on several occasions attack the people of Israel (see Exod. 17:8–13; Num. 14:45; Deut. 25.17–19; Judg, 6:3; 1 Sam. 150).

123. Kaegi suggests this in "Initial Byzantine Reactions," 149.

124. See bibliography, under the heading "Eastern Christian Reactions to Islam," in particular the works of Ducellier and Khoury.

125. Hawkes, *Shakespeare's Talking Animals* (London: Edward Arnold, 1973), 211, cited by Smith, "What a Difference," 38; italics are Hawkes's.

4. Western Christian Responses to Islam (Eighth–Ninth Centuries)

1. I have explored this comparison in Tolan, "Réactions chrétiennes aux conquêtes musulmanes: Etude comparée des auteurs chrétiens de Syrie et d'Espagne (VIIᵉ–IXᵉ siècles)," *Cahiers de civilisation médiévale* (forthcoming).

2. J. M. Wallace-Hadrill, "Bede's Europe," in Wallace-Hadrill, *Early Medieval History* (Oxford: Oxford University Press, 1975), 60–75.

3. Wallace-Hadrill, "Bede's Europe," 65–67; Ekkehart Rotter, *Abendland und Sarazenen: Das okzidentale Araberbild und seine Entstehung im Frühmittelalter* (Berlin: Walter de Gruyter, 1986), 31–42.

4. Bede complained that Adamnan wrote *lacinioso sermone;* for this reason, he reworked it in better style combining it with descriptions from *ueterum libris.* See Plummer's notes to Bede, *Ecclesiastical History of the English People* (Historia ecclesiastica gentis Anglorum), ed. Carolus Plummer, 2 vols. (Oxford: Oxford University Press, 1896, 1975), 2:303–4; there is no firm date for Bede's work (*Ecclesiastical History,* 1:cli). Bede's text has been translated by L. Sherley-Price, *Ecclesiastical History of the English People* (London: Penguin, 1955, 1990).

5. Rotter, *Abendland und Sarazenen,* 73n, 86–88.

6. "Vbi dum Christiani sancti baptistae iohannis ecclesiam frequentant, saracenorum rex cum sua sibi gente aliam instituit atque sacrauit," Bede, *De locis sanctis,* ed. J. Fraipont, CCSL 175 (1965), 251–80, §17. Compare the following passage from another text of Bede: "Damascus: nobilis urbs Foenicis quae et quondam in omni Syria tenuit principatum et nunc Sarracenorum metropolis esse perhibetur, unde et rex eorum Mauuias famosam in ea sibi suae que genti basilicam dicauit, Christianis in circuitu ciuibus beati baptistae Iohannis ecclesiam frequentantibus" (Bede, *Nomina regionum atque locorum de actibus apostolorum,* ed. M. L. W. Laistner, CCSL 121 [1983], 167–78).

7. Adamnan, *De locis sanctis libri tres,* CCSL 175:220; Rotter, *Abendland und Sarazenen,* 39.

8. On Mavia (Μαυία, Mâwîya), see Françoise Thelamon, *Païens et Chrétiens au IVème siècle: L'apport de l'Histoire ecclésiastique de Rufin d'Aquilée* (Paris, 1981), 130–36.

9. "In inferiore uero parte urbis, ubi templum in uicinia muri ab oriente locatum ipsi que urbi transitu peruio ponte mediante fuerat coniunctum, nunc ibi saraceni quadratam domum subrectis tabulis et magnis trabibus super quasdam ruinarum reliquias uili opere construentes oratione frequentant, quae tria milia hominum capere uidetur" (Bede, *De locis sanctis,* §2).

10. Bede, *De locis sanctis,* §10; trans. Wallace-Hadrill, "Bede's Europe," 66.

11. A Maronite chronicler describes Mu'âwiya praying at the various Christian holy sites in Jerusalem; see Ducellier, *Chrétiens d'Orient,* 75.

12. "Sidus dei uestri, quod hebraice dicitur chocab, id est luciferi, quem saraceni hucusque uenerantur" (Jerome, *In Amos,* 2:5, CCSL 76:589). "Luciferum, cuius cultui saracenorum natio dedita est" (Jerome, *Vita sancti Hilarionis,* CCSL 75:108). Bede's source for this seems to be Pliny, *Natural History,* 2:6; Rotter, *Abendland und Sarazenen,* 247–49.

13. Bede, *Interpretatio nominum Hebraeorum* PL 93:1102; Rotter, *Abendland und Sarazenen,* 98.

14. Bede, *Ecclesiastical History of the English People,* 1:25, 3:30, 2:13; trans. L. Sherley-Price, 74–76, 200—201, 129. After the kingdom of Kent relapses into paganism, King Earconbert also orders the destruction of idols (*Ecclesiastical History of the English People,* 3:8; trans., 155).

15. Bede, *Ecclesiastical History of the English People,* 5:23, trans. L. Sherley-Price, 323.

16. On this identification, see Plummer's notes to Bede, *Ecclesiastical History of the English People,* 2:338–39, trans. L. Sherley-Price, 375n.

17. On Bede's use of *perfidia,* see Plummer's notes to Bede, *Ecclesiastical History of the English People,* 2:18–19.

18. Bede, *De schematis et tropibus,* cited by Ernst R. Curtius, *European Literature and the Latin Middle Ages,* trans. W. Trask (Princeton: Princeton University Press, 1973), 47.

19. "Significat semen eius habitaturum in eremo, id est saracenos uagos, incertis que sedibus. Qui uniuersas gentes quibus desertum ex latere iungitur incursant, et expugnantur ab omnibus. Sed haec antiquitus. Nunc autem in tantum manus eius contra omnes, et manus sunt omnium contra eum, ut africam totam in longitudine sua ditione premant, sed et asiae maximam partem, et europae nonnullam omnibus exosi et contrarii teneant" (Bede, *In principium Genesis usque ad natiuitatem Isaac,* 4:16, CCSL 118A).

20. Bede, *De temporum ratione,* 66 (CCSL 123B). His principal (but perhaps not sole) source here seems to be the *Liber pontificalis.* See Wallace-Hadrill 67ff; Rotter, *Abendland und Sarazenen,* 202–8.

21. Bede, *De temporum ratione,* 66 (CCSL 123B).

22. Bede, *De temporum ratione,* 66 (CCSL 123B). See Wallace-Hadrill, "Bede's Europe," 68.

23. *The Fourth Book of the Chronicle of Fredegar and Its Continuators,* ed. and trans. J. M. Wallace-Hadrill, (London, 1960), 53–55.

24. Rotter, *Abendland und Sarazenen,* 156–57.

25. *Chronologia regum* Gothorum (PL 83:1115–18, esp 1118); *Chronicon moissiacense* (MGH SS 1:282–313; 2:257–59) 1:290; see Georges Martin, "La Chute du Royaume Visigothique d'Espagne dans l'historiographie chrétienne des VIIIe et IXe siècles," *Cahiers de Linguistique Hispanique médiévale* 9 (1984):210–33.

26. On the chronicles regarding the sack of Benevento, see James Waltz, "Western European Attitudes toward Muslims before the Crusades," Ph.D. diss., University of Michigan, 1963, 47. On the portrayal of the battle of Poitiers, see Rotter, *Abendland und Sarazenen,* 217–30.

27. Liudprand, *Anapodosis,* cited by Waltz, "Western European Attitudes," 114–16.

28. "Illam aecclesiam christiani homines sepe conparabant ad paganis Sarracinis, qui illi volebant eam destruere," Hugeburc, *Vita Sancti Willibaldi* MGH SS 15:95; Rotter, *Abendland und Sarazenen,* 43–65.

29. "Sicut aliis gentibus Hispaniae et Provinciae et Burgundionum populis contigit; quae sic a Deo recedentes fornicatae sunt, donec iudex omnipotens talium criminum ultrices poenas per ignorantiam legis Dei et per Sarracenos venire et saevire permisit," MGH epistola 3:343; Waltz, "Western European Attitudes," 134; Rotter, *Abendland und Sarazenen,* 230, 257–58.

30. "Tribulatio . . . Saracinorum, Saxonum et Fresonum," Zacharias, *Epistola ad Bonifatium* MGH ep. Sel 1:123; Rotter, *Abendland und Sarazenen,* 258.

31. *Chronicle of 741,* also known as the *Chronica byzantia-arabica,* is in CSM 7–14. On this text see César Dubler, "Sobre la crónica arábigo-bizantina en la península ibérica," *Al-Andalus* 11 (1946):283–349.

All references to the *Chronicle of 754* refer to the 1980 edition by J. López Pereira (*Crónica mozárabe de 754* [Zaragoza: Anubar], 1980) and to the translation by Wolf, *Conquerors and Chroniclers,* 111–58, who provides an analysis at 28–45. Two other modern editions of this chronicle are that of T. Mommsen (*Continuatio isidoriana hispana anni DCCLIV,* in MGH Auct. ant. 11) and that of J. Gil, (*Chronica muzarabica,* in CSM

15–54). On this text, see José Eduardo López Pereira, *Estudio crítico sobre la crónica mozárabe de 754* (Zaragoza: Anubar, 1980); Roger Collins, *The Arab Conquest of Spain, 710–797* (Oxford: Oxford University Press, 1989), esp. chap. 3, "The Tenacity of a Tradition" (52–80); Carmen Cardelle de Hartmann, "The Textual Transmission of the Mozarabic Chronicle of 754," *Early Medieval Europe* 8 (1999):13–29.

32. Wolf, *Conquerors and Chroniclers*, 28.

33. *Chronicle of 741 (Chronica byzantia-arabica)*, §16, CSM 9.

34. *Chronicle of 741 (Chronica byzantia-arabica)*, §13, CSM 9.

35. *Chronicle of 754 (Chronica muzarabica)*, §6, trans. Wolf, *Conquerors and Chroniclers*, 113.

36. *Chronicle of 754*, §8, trans. Wolf, *Conquerors and Chroniclers*, 113–14.

37. *Chronicle of 741 (Chronica byzantia-arabica)*, §36, CSM 13.

38. *Chronicle of 754*, §41, trans. Wolf, *Conquerors and Chroniclers*, 127.

39. *Chronicle of 754*, §41, trans. Wolf, *Conquerors and Chroniclers*, 127.

40. *Chronicle of 754*, §51, trans. Wolf, *Conquerors and Chroniclers*, 130; cf. *Chronicle of 741 (Chronica byzantia-arabica)*, §36, CSM 13.

41. *Chronicle of 754*, §52, trans. Wolf, *Conquerors and Chroniclers*, 130–31.

42. *Chronicle of 754*, §55, trans. Wolf, *Conquerors and Chroniclers*, 132–33; Collins, *Arab Conquest*, 63.

43. *Chronicle of 754*, §54, trans. Wolf, *Conquerors and Chroniclers*, 132.

44. *Chronicle of 754* §53, trans. Wolf, *Conquerors and Chroniclers*, 131.

45. The passage describing the battle in the *Chronicle of 754* may be a later interpolation, as Collins notes (*Arab Conquest*, 54).

46. Collins, arguing from the Arabic sources, concludes that October 734 is the most likely date; see Collins, *Arab Conquest*, 90–91.

47. *Chronicle of 754*, §80, trans. Wolf, *Conquerors and Chroniclers*, 143–44.

48. *Chronicle of 754*, §81, trans. Wolf, *Conquerors and Chroniclers*, 145 (and analysis at 41).

49. See Wolf, *Conquerors and Chroniclers*, 39–43, 87–90.

50. See Collins, *Early Medieval Spain: Unity in Diversity* (New York: St. Martin's, 1983), 189.

51. On the meaning (and pitfalls) of the term *mozarab*, see Burman, *Religious Polemic*, 7–9; Mikel de Epalza, "Mozarabs: An Emblematic Christian Minority in al-Andalus," in S. K. Jayyusi, ed., *The Legacy of Muslim Spain* (Leiden: Brill, 1992), 149–70; Pedro Chalmeta, "Mozarab" EI² 7:246.

52. For references to eighth-century Spain, see Wolf, "Christian Views of Islam in Early Medieval Spain," in Tolan, ed., *Medieval Christian Perceptions of Islam*, 85–108; on parallel Eastern Christian attitudes, see chap. 3.

53. The demography of conversion to Islam has been a subject of much dispute among historians (see chap. 2). For the debate concerning the rate of conversion to Islam in Spain, see Bulliet, *Conversion*, 44, 50–51; David Wasserstein, *The Rise and Fall of the Party Kings: Politics and Society in Islamic Spain, 1002–1086* (Princeton: Princeton University Press, 1985), 168, 237–38; Morony, "Age of Conversions," 136; Epalza, "Mozarabs: An Emblematic Christian Minority," 158–62.

54. Epalza, "Falta de obispos y conversión al Islam de los Cristianos de al-Ándalus," *Al-Qantara* 15 (1994):386–400.

55. There has been much speculation on the supposed Islamic influences on the so-called heresy of adoptionism in eighth-century Spain. Historians have been too quick to accept at face value the accusations of Islamic influence leveled by the enemies (notably Alcuin) of the adoptionist Spanish churchmen. The main issues in fact seem to have been Spanish efforts to assert their traditional independence against papal hegemony, as McWilliam shows (J. McWilliam, "The Context of Spanish Adoptionism: A Review," in Gervers and Bikhazi, eds., *Conversion and Continuity,* 75–88.). Epalza attempts to resuscitate the idea of an "occulted" Islamic influence on supposed adoptionist doctrines, but his arguments are unconvincing (Epalza, "Influences islamiques dans la théologie chrétienne médiévale: L'adoptionisme espagnole," *Islamochristiana* 18 [1992]:55–72).

56. Alcuin refers to a *Disputatio Felix cum sarraceno* in one of his letters to Charlemagne, MGH *Epistolae Karolini aevi* 2 (1895):284. See Wolf, "Christian Views," 93.

57. Jessica Coope, *The Martyrs of Córdoba: Community and Family Conflict in an Age of Mass Conversion* (Lincoln: University of Nebraska Press, 1995), 7.

58. Vincent Lagardère, *Histoire et société en occident musulman au moyen âge: Analyse du Mi'yar d'al-Wanšarîsî* (Madrid: Casa de Velázquez, 1995), 476.

59. Eulogius, *Memoriale sanctorum,* 2:1:1, CSM 397–98, trans. Edward Colbert, *The Martyrs of Córdoba, 850–859: A Study of the Sources* (Washington: Catholic University of America, 1962), 194; Coope, *Martyrs,* 7.

60. Paulus Alvarus, *Indiculus luminosus,* §35, CSM 314–15, trans. Richard Southern, *Western Views of Islam in the Middle Ages* (Cambridge, Mass.: Harvard University Press, 1962), 21; on this passage, see Coope, *Martyrs,* 8; Carleton Sage, *Paul Albar of Córdoba: Studies on His Life and Writings* (Washington: Catholic University of America, 1943), x; Colbert, *Martyrs,* 300.

61. Eulogius includes a fragment of the (now lost) work in his *Memoriale sanctorum* 1:7, CSM 375–76; see Wolf, "Christian Views," 97, 106 n. 41; Wolf, *Christian Martyrs in Muslim Spain* (Cambridge: Cambridge University Press, 1988), 52–53. On his lives of the two martyrs Joannes and Adulphus, see Wolf, *Christian Martyrs,* 63; Eulogius, *Memoriale sanctorum,* 2:8, CSM 412.

62. The bibliography on the martyrs of Córdoba is immense; for a survey of scholarship from the sixteenth century to 1970, see Wolf, *Christian Martyrs,* 36–47. More recent works on the martyrs include: Wolf, "Christian Views"; Dominique Millet Gérard, *Chrétiens mozarabes et culture islamique dans l'Espagne des VIIIᵉ–IXᵉ siècles* (Paris: Études Augustiniennes, 1984); Coope, *The Martyrs of Córdoba*; Tolan, "Mahomet et L'Antéchrist dans l'Espagne du IXᵉᵐᵉ siècle," *Orient und Okzident in der Kultur des Mittelalters; Monde oriental et monde occidental dans la culture médiévale, Wodan: Greifswalder Beiträge zum Mittelalter* 68 (1997):167–80; Daniel, "Spanish Christian Sources of Information about Islam," *Al-Qantara* 15 (1994):365–84. One final article should be used with caution, as the author accepts at face value many of the polemical assertions of the Christian defenders of the martyrs: Clayton Drees, "Sainthood and Suicide: The Motives of the Martyrs of Cordoba," *Journal of Medieval and Renaissance*

Studies 20 (1990):59–89. The Latin texts in defense of the martyrs are edited by Juan Gil in CSM.

63. Eulogius, *Memoriale sanctorum*, 2:1:2, CSM 398.

64. Alvarus gives roughly the same version of these events; he may well be using the *Memoriale sanctorum* (Alvarus, *Indiculus luminosus*, §3, CSM 275–76).

65. Coope, *Martyrs*, xv–xvi.

66. Eulogius, *Memoriale sanctorum*, 2:4:3, CSM 403–4; Wolf, *Christian Martyrs*, 25.

67. Edward Said, *Culture and Imperialism* (New York: Vintage, 1993); Tolan, "Mahomet et L'Antéchrist."

68. Paulus Alvarus, *Vita Eulogii*, §4, CSM 332; Wolf, *Christian Martyrs*, 15–16, 123 n. 56.

69. Alvarus, *Vita Eulogii*, §4–7, CSM 332–34.

70. Alvarus, *Indiculus luminosus*, §19, CSM 291. On the use of pejorative diminutives in the works of Alvarus and Eulogius, see Millet-Gérard, *Chrétiens mozarabes*, 97.

71. Alvarus, *Vita Eulogii*, §6, CSM 333; see Coope, *Martyrs*, 61.

72. Millet-Gérard, *Chrétiens mozarabes*, 30; J. Fernández Alonso, "Espagne," DHGE 15:909–11; F. Perez, "Cordoue," DHGE, 13:844–46.

73. Coope, *Martyrs*, 55–69.

74. "In ipso die, quo sceptrum regni adeptus est, Christianos abdicari palatio iussit, dignitate priuauit, honore destituit, multa postmodum in nos mala irrogari disponens, si regni felicitate et prosperis potiretur euentibus," Eulogius, *Memoriale sanctorum*, 2:16:2; on Muhammad's purge of Christian courtiers, see Wolf, *Christian Martyrs*, 16; Coope, *Martyrs*, 32–33.

75. Wolf, *Christian Martyrs*, 2.

76. Eulogius, *Liber apologeticus martyrum*, §12, CSM 481; on this passage, see Wolf, "Christian Views," 96. Norman Daniel misunderstands the clear fact that Eulogius's and Alvarus's harsh anti-Muslim sentiments are not shared by the majority of Mozarabs; for him their writings show that "[a]ll the Christians held the Arabs and their civilization in contempt" ("Spanish Christian Sources," 367). Clearly, for Eulogius and Alvarus, the problem is that *far too few* Christians feel such contempt.

77. Alvarus, *Indiculus luminosus*, preface, CSM 271.

78. Isa. 56:10; Alvarus, *Indiculus luminosus*, §10, CSM 282–83.

79. Alvarus, *Indiculus luminosus*, §3, CSM 275.

80. Eulogius, *Liber apologeticus martyrum*, §12, CSM 484.

81. 2 Thess. 2:10–11; Rom. 1:18, 1:21–32; 2 Pet. 119–23; Eulogius, *Liber apologeticus martyrum*, §12–13, CSM 482—83. He later draws the same conclusions from Gal. 1:9, 1 John 4:1, Hos. 8:4, and Matt. 24:11; Eulogius, *Liber apologeticus martyrum*, §18, CSM 486.

82. Alvarus, *Indiculus luminosus*, §21–35, CSM 293–315. He uses, in particular, Jerome, *Commentarium in Danielem* (PL 25:491–584), and Grégoire le Grand, *Moralia in Job* (PL 75:527–1162, 76:1–782).

83. Alvarus, *Indiculus luminosus*, §21, CSM 293–95. On this passage, see Southern, *Western Views of Islam*, 23; Wolf, *Christian Martyrs*, 91–95.

84. John 2:22; see chap. 1, and Millet-Gérard, *Chrétiens mozarabes*, 109.

85. Alvarus, *Indiculus luminosus,* §21, CSM 294–95. Jerome identifies *tempus, tempora et dimidium temporis* as a period of three and a half years, at the end of time, during which "sancti potestati Antichristi permittendi sunt, ut condemnentur Judaei, qui non credentes veritati, susceperunt mendacium," Jerome, *Commentarii in Danielem,* 2:7, CCSL 75A.

86. Eulogius, *Liber apologeticus martyrum,* §20, CSM 487–88; Millet-Gérard, *Chrétiens mozarabes,* 47.

87. Eulogius, *Epistola* 3:9, CSM 500; Fontaine, "Mozarabie hispanique et monde carolingien," 25–26.

88. Eulogius, *Liber apologeticus martyrum,* §14–15, CSM 483; the biography is in §16, CSM 483–86. Millet-Gérard provides an analysis and French translation of this text (*Chrétiens mozarabes,* 125–37; translation on 126–27); English translations may be found in Wolf, "The Earliest Latin Lives of Muhammad," in M. Gervers and R. Bikhazi, eds., *Conversion and Continuity,* 89–101, and Colbert, *Martyrs,* 336–38. On the dates of Eulogius's trip to Pamplona, see Colbert, 181–86.

Manuel Diaz y Diaz ("La circulation des manuscrits dans le Péninsule ibérique du VIIIᵉ au XIᵉ siècle," *Cahiers de civilisation médiévale* 12 [1969]:219–41, 383–92; here 229) observes that Eulogius could be claiming to have found the text in Navarre in order to avoid inculpating Christians closer to home. The author of the biography seems originally to have lived in the region around Seville in the eighth or early ninth century (Wolf, "Christian Views," 93ff.; Wolf, "The Earliest Latin Lives of Muhammad," esp. 90–91).

89. *Historia de Mahometh pseudopropheta,* cited here from the translation by Wolf in "The Earliest Latin Lives of Muhammad," 97–99.

90. See Tolan, "Un cadavre mutilé."

91. Coope, *Martyrs,* x.

92. 2 Kings 9:22, 33–37.

93. "Taceam sacrilegum . . . de beatissima uirgine mundi regina, sancta et uenerabili Domini et Saluatoris nostri genitrice Maria canis impuris [Muhammad] dicere ausus est. Protestatus enim est . . . quod eius foret in saeculo uenturo ab se uiolanda uirginitas," Eulogius *Memoriale sanctorum,* 1:7, CSM 376.

94. Eulogius, *Documentum martyriale,* §4, CSM 464. In the same work, Eulogius later remarks how Flora had shown him her neck, wounded from a lashing by Muslim authorities, "touching it gently with my hand—because I did not think I ought to caress the wound with kisses—I departed from you and for a long time I sighed thinking about it." (21, CSM 472, trans. Wolf, *Christian Martyrs,* 66). All this suggests an element of twisted sexual fantasy behind the imagined rape of Flora. On this passage see Daniel, "Spanish Christian Sources," 371.

95. Rape and forced prostitution are among the topoi borrowed from antique martyrologies, as Coope shows (*Martyrs,* 42). Drees, astonishingly, accepts Eulogius's polemical accusation at face value, showing a credulity that mars his article in other places as well (Drees, "Sainthood and Suicide").

96. Eulogius, *Liber apologeticus,* §16, CSM 484, trans. Wolf, "Earliest Latin Lives," 98.

97. Lam. 5:2–8; Eulogius, *Documentum martyriale,* §18, CSM 470.

98. Eulogius, *Liber apologeticus martyrum,* §22–23, CSM 488–90.

99. Millet-Gérard, *Chrétiens mozarabes,* 95–122, 145–48.

100. Even if, as Coope says, there are "isolated reports of voluntary martyrdoms in al-Andalus after Eulogius' death" (*Martyrs,* 33), nothing rivals the troubles of 851–59. On the emigration of Mozarabic clerics to Asturias under the reign of Alfonso III, see Dominique Urvoy, "La pensée religieuse des Mozarabes face à l'Islam," *Traditio* 39 (1983):419–32 (here 420).

101. Raguel, *Vita vel passio S. Pelagii,* in Enrique Florez, *España sagrada: Teatro geográfico-histórico de la iglésia de España,* 54 vols. (Madrid, 1754–59), 23:230–35; Wolf, *Christian Martyrs,* 34. Hrotsvitha of Gandersheim's *Passio S. Pelagii* is discussed in chap. 5.

102. Wolf, *Christian Martyrs,* 34–35.

103. Wolf, *Christian Martyrs,* 34–35, 116.

104. Alvarus, *Vita Eulogii,* §10, CSM 336; Coope, *Martyrs,* 52–53; Epalza, "Falta," 397–99.

105. Wolf, *Christian Martyrs,* 107–8.

106. See Coope, *Martyrs,* chap. 4, "Christians as the Enemy," 55–69.

107. Alvarus, *Epistola* 13, CSM 224–26; Coope, *Martyrs,* 61

108. Alvarus, *Epistola* 13, CSM 224–26.

109. Samson, *Apologeticus,* 2:preface, CSM 547–55.

110. Samson, *Apologeticus,* 2:preface, CSM 547–55; see Coope, *Martyrs,* 56–60.

111. Samson, *Apologeticus,* 2:preface:3, CSM 550.

112. Alvarus, *Indiculus luminosus,* §35, CSM 313. Circumcision became a major issue among Muslim and Christian Andalusians; see Coope, *Martyrs,* 58, 82–83.

113. Samson, *Apologeticus,* 2:preface:5, CSM 551.

114. Samson, *Apologeticus,* 2:preface:2, CSM 548–50.

115. Charles Burnett, "The Translating Activity in Medieval Spain," in Jayussi, ed., *The Legacy of Muslim Spain,* 1036–58 (here 1037).

116. Samson, *Apologeticus,* 2:7:2, CSM 569–70, part of this passage is translated by Coope, *Martyrs,* 59.

117. Epalza ("Mozarabs," 155–56) notes that it may be in part thanks to Ostegesis's efforts that Málaga is one of the few Andalusian cities with a documented Christian population into the twelfth century; see also Epalza, "Falta de obispos," 396–99; Epalza, "Les Mozarabes, état de la question," *Revue du monde musulman et de la Méditerranée* 63–64 (1992):39–50 (esp. 43).

118. Epalza, "Mozarabs," 159–62. Bulliet also asserts that "most converts were passive" in the early Islamic centuries (Bulliet, "Conversion Stories," 132).

119. Fragments of the *Book of Fifty-Seven Questions* survive in al-Qurtubî's *Al-I'lâm,* a thirteenth-century work of anti-Christian polemic. On Hafs ibn Albar, see van Koningsveld, "Christian Arabic Literature from Medieval Spain: An Attempt at Periodization," in Samir and Nielsen, *Christian Arabic Apologetics,* 203–24, esp. 206–12; Hafs Ibn Albar, *Le Psautier mozarabe de Hafs le Goth,* ed. and trans. Marie-Thérèse Urvoy (Toul-

ouse: Presses Universitaires du Mirail, 1994); D. Dunlop, "Hafs ibn Albar, the Last of the Goths?" *Journal of the Royal Asiatic Society* (1954):136–51; Dunlop, "Sobre Hafs ibn Albar al-Qûtî al-Qurtubî," *Al-Andalus* 20 (1955):211–13. On al-Qurtubî's use of Hafs ibn Albar, see Burman, *Religious Polemic,* 158–60.

120. This distinction between polemics and apologetics corresponds to the one drawn by Millet-Gérard between "polémique fermée" and "polémique ouverte" (*Chrétiens mozarabes,* 173).

121. CSM 143–44, 363; Diaz y Diaz, "Circulation de manuscrits"; Sage, *Paul Albar,* 221–23.

122. Liudprand de Crémone, *Antapodosis,* ed. Joseph Becker, in MGH SS *in usum scholarum* (1915):1–158; Coope, *Martyrs,* 66–68; Helmut G. Walther, "Der gescheiterte Dialog: Das ottonische Reich und der Islam," in A. Zimmerman and I. Craemer-Ruegenberg, eds., *Orientalische Kultur und europäisches Mittelalter* (Berlin and New York: Walter de Gruyter, 1985), 20–44.

123. See *Chroniques Asturiennes (fin IXe siècle),* ed. and trans. (into French) Yves Bonnaz (Paris: CNRS, 1987), lvi, 30–31, 106; Diaz y Diaz, "Circulation des manuscrits," 224. Florez (*España sagrada* 10:457) cites the following passage from the *Breviario antiguo* of Oviedo: "Cum anno Domini 883 vigesimum quartum post martyrium SS. Eulogij et Leocritiae, Magnus Adephonsus Oveti Rex quemdam Presbyterum, Dulcidium nomine, Cordubam, ut coram Mahomat Cordubae Regem nonnulla ad utriusque pertinentia tractanda statum, dimitteret; Presbyter Dulcidius cum esset in urbe, quomodo ipsorum corpora Sanctorum Eulogij et Leocritiae Martyrum in suam pervenire potestatem posset, curavit . . . et dispositis negotiis Dulcidius Adephonsum de sacris reliquiis certiorem fecit, qui cum Hermengildo episcopo ovetensi, et clero, solemni processione ordinata, illis extra urbem Ovetum obviam fuit. Quibus receptis, et in capsam cypressinam translatis, et in Capella S. Leocadiae sub arae tabula conditis, Regis et Procerum devotio occupavit laetitiam. Quae translatio facta fuit die IX. Januarii, quo sacra corpora pervenerunt Ovetum."

124. On the composition and dates of these chronicles, see Bonnaz's introduction to *Chroniques Asturiennes;* Wolf, *Conquerors and Chroniclers,* 46–60; Peter Linehan, *History and Historians of Medieval Spain* (Oxford: Oxford University Press, 1993), 95–127; Martin, "La Chute."

125. *Prophetic Chronicle* 2.2, in *Chroniques asturiennes,* 3.

126. *Prophetic Chronicle* 2.1, in *Chroniques asturiennes,* 3.

127. "Quia non fuit in illis pro suis delictis digna paenitentia, et quia dereliquerunt praecepta Domini et sacrorum canonum instituta, dereliquit illos Dominus ne possiderent desiderabilem terram," *Prophetic Chronicle,* §5, in *Chroniques asturiennes,* 7.

128. *Prophetic Chronicle,* §7–8, in *Chroniques asturiennes,* 8–9, 66–67.

129. There are two versions of this chronicle: the Roda version (Bonnaz's "version primitive") and the Oviedo version ("version erudite"). The latter is prefaced by a letter from Alfonso III to Sebastian: "Adefonsus Rex Sebastiano nostro salutem. Notum tibi sit de historia Gothorum, pro qua nobis per Dulcidium presbyterum notauisti pigritiaque ueteres scribere noluerunt sed silentio occultauerunt. Et quia Gothorum Chronica

usque ad tempora gloriosi Wambani regis Isodorus, Hispalensis sedis episcopus, plenissime edocuit, et nos quidem ex eo tempore, sicut ab antiquis et a praedecessoribus nostris audiuimus, et uera esse cognouimus, tibi breuiter intimabimus" (*Choniques asturiennes*, 31).

This seems to indicate that Dulcidius assembled the documentation, perhaps largely from manuscripts that he himself had brought to Oviedo from Toledo and Córdoba. This may (as Bonnaz speculates) make him the author of the Roda version, which is then reworked by Sebastian before being given royal approval by its official *auctor*, Alfonso. See *Choniques asturiennes*, xlvi–lxv. Quotations are from Wolf's translation of the Roda version, except where indicated.

130. *Chronicle of Alfonso III*, §4/5, *Choniques Asturiennes* 36, trans. Wolf, *Conquerors*, 162–63.

131. The earliest extant text to mention Pelagius, it seems, is a prologue to a *Testamentum* of Alfonso II, dated 16 November 812 (Martin, "La Chute").

132. *Chronicle of Alfonso III*, §9, in *Choniques Asturiennes*, 47–48, trans. Wolf, *Conquerors*, 166–67. See Linehan, *History and Historians*, 102–5.

133. *Choniques Asturiennes*, lxxii–lxxiv.

134. The following section is based in part on Tolan, "Reliques et païens: La naturalisation des martyrs de Cordoue à St. Germain (IXème siècle)," in Philippe Sénac, ed., *Aquitaine-Espagne (VIIIe–XIIIe siècle)* (Poitiers: Centre Supérieur d'Études de Civilisation Médiévale, 2001), 39–55 which contains full references to secondary works on Aimoin's text. Aimoin, *Translatio sanctorum martyrum Georgii monachi, Aurelii et Nathaliae*, AASS (July), 6:459–69, PL 115:939–60.

135. Eulogius, *Memoriale sanctorum*, 1:12, CSM 379; *Liber apologeticus martyrum*, 7, CSM 479–80; see Wolf, *Christian Martyrs*, 77–85.

136. Usuard, *Le martyrologe d'Usuard: Texte et commentaire*, ed. Jacques Dubois, Société des Bollandistes: Subsidia hagiographica 40 (1965): 62; B. Gaiffier, "Les notices hispaniques dans le martyrologe d'Usuard," *Analecta Bollandiana* 55 (1937):275–76. Usuard composed his *Martyrologe* after returning from Spain in 858 but before learning of Eulogius's death; he adds Eulogius to the *Martyrologe* at the date of 30 September, not on the day of his death (11 March 859). As Dubois says, "Cette date arbitraire ne peut s'expliquer que par l'utilisation d'une place rendue vide par le déplacement de saint Eustache. Usuard évita de mettre *natalis*. Il est probable qu'il avait appris la mort de son ami sans précision de jour" (Dubois, "Les Martyrologes du moyen âge latin," *Typologie* 26 [1978]:48 n. 96).

137. "Eodem die, natalis sanctorum Georgii diaconi, Aurelii, Felicis, Nathaliae et Liliosae, quorum primus, mirae abstinentiae monachus, ab Ierosolimis Cordubam adveniens, cum reliquis ex eadem urbe claro germine ortis diu optatum sibique a Domino praemonstratum meruit assequi martyrium," Usuard, *Martyrologe*, p. 291, VI. KL. Sept. [27 August], entry no. 3).

138. Paschasius Radbertus, *Expositio in Matheum*, in Benjamin Kedar, *Crusade and Mission: European Approaches toward the Muslims* (Princeton: Princeton University Press, 1984), 30–31, 205.

139. Rafael Jimenez Pedrajas, "San Eulogio de Córdoba, autor de la Pasion francesa de los mártires cordobeses Jorge, Aurelio y Natalia," *Antologica annua* 17 (1970):465–571 (esp. 474–79), describes seven medieval manuscripts, three of which date from the ninth and tenth centuries (and so might be read by the hypothetical reader of 1000).

140. On this translation, see Guzman, "Reports of Mongol Cannibalism."

141. Anastasius's translation is included in Boor's edition of Theophanes, *Chronographia*; see Kedar, *Crusade and Mission*, 33–34, 206–7.

142. Kedar, *Crusade and Mission*, 35.

5. Saracens as Pagans

1. *Chanson de Roland*, ed. Ian Short (Paris: Livre de Poche [Lettres gothiques], 1990), ll. 2580–91; trans. Gerard J. Braut, *The Song of Roland* (University Park: Pennsylvania State University Press, 1978). I have (here and in subsequent citations) slightly modified Braut's translation.

2. See Michael Camille, *The Gothic Idol: Ideology and Image-Making in Medieval Art* (Cambridge: University of Cambridge Press, 1989), esp. 129–64.

3. Norman Daniel, *Heroes and Saracens: An Interpretation of the Chansons de Geste* (Edinburgh: Edinburgh University Press, 1984). Numerous critics have rejected Daniel's view; see for example Jean Flori, "La caricature de l'Islam dans l'occident médiéval: Origine et signification de quelques stéréotypes concernant l'Islam," *Aevum* 2 (1992): 245–56 (251).

4. Hrotsvitha of Gandersheim, "Pelagius," in H. Homeyer, ed., *Opera* (Munich: MGH, 1970), 130–46, ll. 55–60. Pelagius was put to death in 925; see Homeyer's introduction to "Pelagius," 123–29; Wolf, *Christian Martyrs*, 34; Celso Rodríguez Fernández, *La Pasión de San Pelayo* (Santiago de Compostela: Universidad de Santiago de Compostela, 1991). On this passage see Kedar, *Crusade and Mission*, 10.

5. Hrotsvitha, "Pelagius," 63–67; Isidore, *Etymologies*, 9:2:49, 14:3:15.

6. Hrotsvitha, "Pelagius," 243–49.

7. Hrotsvitha, "Pelagius," 179–83.

8. On the portrayal of eastern European pagan ritual, see Robert Bartlett, "Reflections on Paganism and Christianity in Medieval Europe," *Proceedings of the British Academy* 101 (1999):55–76.

9. The following analysis of crusading chronicles is adapted from Tolan, "Muslims as Pagan Idolaters in Chronicles of the First Crusade," in M. Frassetto and D. Blanks, eds., *Western Attitudes towards Islam* (New York: St. Martin's Press, 1999), 97–117. On these chronicles and their ideologies see also Flori, *Pierre l'ermite et la première croisade* (Paris: Fayard, 1999), particularly chaps. 3 and 4; Cipollone, *Cristianità-Islam: Cattività e liberazione in nome di dio* (Rome: Pontifica Università Gregoriana, 1992) 73–83; Flori, "En marge de l'idée de guerre sainte: L'image des Musulmans dans la mentalité populaire en Occident (XIème–XIIème siècles)," in *L'occident musulman et l'occident chrétiens au Moyen Age* (Rabat: Publications de l'Université Mohammed V, 1995), 209–21; Flori, " 'Oriens horribilis': Tares et défauts de l'Orient dans les sources relatives à la première

croisade," *Wodan: Greifswalder Beiträge zum Mittelalter* 68 (1997):45–56; Flori, "Radiographie d'un stéréotype: sens et contre-sens," in *Maroc-Europe: Histoires, économies, sociétés* 3 (1992), 91–109; Svetlana Loutchitskaja, "*Barbarae nationes:* Les peuples musulmans dans les chroniques de la Première croisade," in Michel Balard, ed., *Autour de la première croisade* (Paris, 1996), 99–107; Loutchitskaja, "L'image des musulmans dans les chroniques des croisades," *Le Moyen Age* 105 (1999):717–35.

10. The Crusade of 1101, launched to support and defend the new crusader states in the Levant, was an unmitigated failure. Welf, Thiemo, and their men were ambushed by the Seljuks near Ereghli. Many died; many (including Thiemo) were taken captive; Welf managed to escape. See Jonathan Riley-Smith, *The First Crusade and the Idea of Crusading* (Philadelphia: University of Pennsylvania Press, 1986), 120–34.

11. *Passio Thiemonis archiepiscopi* (MGH SS 11:51–62), §11, p. 58; see Karl Morrison, *Understanding Conversion* (Charlottesville: University Press of Virginia, 1992), 137–38.

12. Such confrontation is a common trope in texts about conversion of pagans to Christianity. In some cases missionaries destroy idols, in others the new converts destroy their former idols; most dramatic are stories in which divine power (at times invoked by missionaries) causes the idols to crumble and fall. See Camille, *Gothic Idol,* especially the discussion of Saracen idols, 129–64.

13. *Passio Thiemonis*, §15, p. 61.

14. The *Martyrologium*, which in the early Middle Ages had been a simple calendar of saints' feast days, by the eleventh century often contains brief narratives of the passions of the various martyrs; these were to be read daily. See Bernard Gaiffier, "De l'usage et de la lecture du martyrologe," *Analecta Bollandiana* 79 (1961):40–59; Gaiffier, "A propos des légendiers latins," *Analecta Bollandiana* 97 (1979):57–68; Philipart, *Les Légendiers latins* (*Typologie* 24–25, 1977); Dubois, *Les Martyrologes du moyen âge latin* (*Typologie* 26, 1978).

15. Otto of Freising, *The Two Cities: A Chronicle of Universal History to the Year 1146 A.D.*, Charles Mierow, trans. (New York, 1928), §7:7, 411–21.

16. The term occurs six times in Raoul de Caen's *Gesta Tancredi* (RHC occ 3:620, 670, 679, 691, 698, 705). The anonymous *Tudebodus imitatus et continuatus* contains the term "machumicolae" twice (RHC occ. 3:220, 227).

17. The bibliography on the first Crusade is vast. For a good introduction to both the events of the Crusade and cultural and social forces that shaped it, see Flori, *La première croisade*; Flori, *Pierre l'ermite et la première croisade*. See also John France, *Victory in the East: A Military History of the First Crusade* (Cambridge: Cambridge University Press, 1994); the best introduction to the subject in English remains that of Jonathan Reilly-Smith, *The First Crusade*. For an extensive bibliography on the Crusades, see Kenneth Setton, gen. ed., *History of the Crusades*, 6.

18. Raymond d'Aguilers, *Liber*, John H. Hill and Laurita L. Hill, eds. (Paris: Librairie orientaliste Paul Geuthner, 1969), 145.

19. The relations between these texts, and the scholarly disputes surrounding them, are too complex for me to do justice to them here. The best introduction to the subject is Flori, *Pierre l'ermite et la première croisade*, chaps. 3 and 4. See also Flori, "Des

chroniques à l'épopée . . . ou bien l'inverse?" *Perspectives médiévales* 20 (1994):36–43; Reilly-Smith, *First Crusade*, 135–52; Suzanne Duparc-Quioc, *La Chanson d'Antioche: Étude critique* (Paris: Librairie orientaliste Paul Geuthner, 1978); J. Hill and L. Hill's introduction to their edition of Petrus Tudebodus, *Historia de Hierosolymitano itinere* (Paris: Librairie orientaliste Paul Geuthner, 1977); France, *Victory in the East*, 374–82.

20. *Gesta Francorum et aliorum Hierosolimitanorum*, ed. and trans. (into French) Louis Bréhier, *Histoire anonyme de la première croisade* (Paris: Honoré Champion, 1924), 118, 216.

21. Raymond d'Aguilers, *Liber*, 35.

22. Raoul de Caen, *Gesta Tancredi*, preface (RHC occ. 3:603).

23. Petrus Tudebodus erroneously gives 1097.

24. Petrus Tudebodus, *Historia*, 31.

25. CSM 2:374.

26. Both Robert the Monk and Guibert of Nogent also saw the Crusades as literal fulfillments of biblical prophecies that had previously been understood in the spiritual or allegorical senses; see Reilly-Smith, *First Crusade*, 142–43. The passage (along with many others, some of which I draw attention to in the notes) is almost identical to *Gesta Francorum*, 2. This could mean that Petrus Tudebodus is using the *Gesta* or vice versa, or that they have a common source (now lost) that they both employ. For the scholarly debate on the primacy of these various sources, see this chapter, note 8.

27. Petrus Tudebodus, *Historia*, 32.

28. Petrus Tudebodus, *Historia*, 32.

29. On the idea of martyrdom in the chronicles of the first Crusade, see Flori, "Mort et martyre des guerriers vers 1100," *Cahiers de Civilization Médiévale* 34 (1991):121–39; Reilly-Smith, *First Crusade*, 151–52; H. Cowdrey, "Martyrdom and the First Crusade," in P. Edbury, ed., *Crusade and Settlement* (Cardiff: University College of Cardiff, 1985), 46–56; Colin Morris, "Martyrs on the Field of Battle before and during the First Crusade," *Studies in Church History* 30 (1993):93–104. The idea that warriors fallen in battle could be considered martyrs was abhorrent to the Byzantine church, according to Ducellier, *Chrétiens d'Orient et Islam*, 193–94.

30. Petrus Tudebodus, *Historia*, 35; Matt. 10:28.

31. Petrus Tudebodus, *Historia*, 35–36. According to J.Hill and L. Hill (see their notes to the text, 35–36) Tudebodus is here using language from martyrologies.

32. For example, see Petrus Tudebodus, *Historia*, 50, 75, in addition to the passages discussed below.

33. Petrus Tudebodus, *Historia*, 51.

34. Petrus Tudebodus, *Historia*, 128. The "Publicans" may refer to Paulician heretics, associated with Muslims in several Byzantine texts; see Ducellier, *Chrétiens d'Orient et Islam au Moyen Age*, 137, 166; Loutchitskaja, "Barbarae nationes," 105.

35. Babylon, conveniently, is the name not only of the city on the Euphrates identified with Antichrist but also of an important fortress outside of Cairo; hence the ruler of the Egyptians, in many crusader chronicles is referred to as the King of Babylon. See Petrus Tudebodus, 73, 77, 148; Raymond d'Aguilers, 58, 110. Corosana, mentioned in

Matt. 11:21 and Luke 10:13, is associated in crusader chronicles with the Turks. See Petrus Tudebodus 36, 37, 49, 73, 89, 91, 92, 113; Raymond d'Aguilers, 56, 87; *Chanson d'Antioche* ll. 4790, 5080, 9379, 9387. On the association of these places with the Antichrist, see *Libellus de Antichristo* (PL 101:1293). Both Raymond d'Aguilers and Ekkehard of Aura use "Hispania" to refer to the areas under Saracen control; this suggests that they saw a close parallel between the fight against the Saracens in both East and West. See Raymond d'Aguilers, *Liber*, introduction by John and Laurita Hill, 13, and their note at 50.

36. Petrus Tudebodus, *Historia*, 76; almost identical is the description in *Gesta Francorum*, 94.

37. Petrus Tudebodus, *Historia*, 79–80. Rainaldus Porchetus's martyrdom is also described in the *Chanson d'Antioche*, ll. 3972–4038; see Duparc-Quioc, *La Chanson d'Antioche: Étude critique*, 198–99, 212–14. Riley-Smith (*The First Crusade*, 115), takes these descriptions of Rainaldus's martyrdom, it seems, at face value.

38. See Tolan, "Le Baptême du Roi 'Païen' dans les Épopées de la Croisade," *Revue de l'Histoire des Religions* 216 (2000):707–31.

39. Petrus Tudebodus, *Historia*, 100. This vision is also described in the *Gesta* (128–30), but their is no mention made of the martyrs; Christ merely promises a "magnum adiutorium."

40. Petrus Tudebodus, *Historia*, 112. This is almost identical to the passage in the *Gesta*, 154, though there, there was no mention of the fallen crusader/martyrs participating in the vengeance.

41. Petrus Tudebodus, *Historia*, 134.

42. Raymond d'Aguilers has celestial warriors lead Christians into battle (45) and says that many people saw Ademar of Puy lead the Crusaders into Jerusalem (151). Ademar, papal legate and leader of the Crusade, had died in Antioch (of disease). Saint George also leads celestial armies into battle in the *Gesta* (155), Robert the Monk (RHC occ. 3:832), and *Chanson d'Antioche*, ll. 2179 and 9063.

In the Muslim sources, it is often Muhammad who leads the celestial troops to victory. Kamal al-Din, for example, has a Christian captive swear that he was captured by a larger-than-life celestial warrior (translated in Francesco Gabrieli, *Arab Historians of the Crusades* [Berkeley: University of California Press, 1969], 38).

43. Petrus Tudebodus, *Historia*, 91.

44. Petrus Tudebodus, *Historia*, 92. This same language is used in the later abridgement of his chronicle (the so-called *Tudebodus abbreviatus*) at RHC occ. 3:194.

45. Petrus Tudebodus, *Historia*, 93.

46. Ps. 79:6 (Vulgate 78:6); Petrus Tudebodus, *Historia*, 94.

47. Petrus Tudebodus, *Historia*, 94.

48. Petrus Tudebodus, *Historia*, 95–96.

49. The interview between Kurbuqa and his mother is described in almost identical terms in the *Gesta*, 118–24.

50. Petrus Tudebodus, *Historia*, 137.

51. Petrus Tudebodus *Historia*, 147–48; cf. the *Tudebodus abbreviatus* (RHC occ. 3:163).

52. The parallels between the crusading army and the army of the Israelites is made by other chroniclers of the first Crusade, including Robert the Monk, Baldric of Dole, and Guibert of Nogent; see Reilly-Smith, *First Crusade*, 140–42.

53. Raymond d'Aguilers, 58.

54. Raymond d'Aguilers, 103. Robert the Monk and Guibert of Nogent also refer to the Franks as God's chosen people; see Reilly-Smith, *First Crusade*, 147–48.

55. Raymond d'Aguilers, 145. Earlier, during the siege of Marra, Raymond says, the Saracens, "ut maxime nos provocarent, cruces super muros ponentes multis inuriis eas afficiebant" (94).

56. See Gavin Langmuir, *History, Religion, and Antisemitism* (Berkeley: University of California Press, 1990), 298–303; Langmuir, *Toward a Definition of Antisemitism* (Berkeley: University of California Press, 1990), chaps. 9, 11, 12; Joshua Trachtenberg, *The Devil and the Jews: A Medieval Conception of the Jews and Its Relation to Modern Antisemitism* (Philadelphia: University of Pennsylvania Press, 1983); R. Po-Chia Hsia, *The Myth of Ritual Murder: Jews and Magic in Reformation Germany* (New Haven: Yale University Press, 1988).

57. Raymond D'Aguilers, 150–51.

58. Anna Comnena, *Alexiad*, E. Sewter, trans. (London: Penguin, 1969), 211–12, 309–10.

59. See chap. 3; Ducellier, *Chrétiens d'Orient et Islam au Moyen Age*, 161–64.

60. Robertus Monachus, chap. 21 (RHC occ. 3:878); cf. the similar treatment in the chronicle by Baudri of Dole, who has the Amiravissus swear by "per Machomet et per omnia deorum nomina" (RHC occ. 4:110). In the *Historia et Gesta ducis Gotfridi* (RHC occ. 5:501), it is the "miraldus Babilonis" who gives a long lament on hearing of the fall of Jerusalem; he invokes Machomet not as a god but as "praeceptor noster et patrone"; see Flori, "Oriens horribilis," 47.

61. On Raoul and his *Gesta Tancredi*, see Jean Charles Payen, "L'hégémonie normande dans la *Chanson de Roland* et les *Gesta Tancredi*: De la Neustrie à la chrétienté, ou Turold est-il nationaliste?" in Hans-Erich Keller, ed., *Romance Epic: Essays on a Medieval Literary Genre* (Kalamazoo, 1987), 73–90; Payen, "L'image du grec dans la chronique normande: sur un passage de Raoul de Caen," in *Images et signes de l'Orient dans l'Occident Médiéval* (Aix-en-Provence, 1982), 267–80.

62. Raoul de Caen, chap. 129 (RHC occ. 3:695–696); on this passage see Camille, *Gothic Idol*, 142–45.

63. For example: "Hoc templum dominicum in veneratione magna cuncti Sarraceni habuerant, ubi precationes suas lege sua libentius quam alibi faciebant, quamvis idolo in nomine Mahumet facto eas vastarent, in quod etiam nullum ingredi Christianum permittebant. Alterum templum, quod dicitur Salomonis, magnum est et mirabile," Fulcher of Chartres, *Historia Iherosolymitana* chap. 26 (RHC occ. 3:357) He later says: "Tancredus autem Templum dominicum festino cursu ingressus, multum auri et argenti, lapidesque pertionsos arripuit. Sed hoc restaurans, eadem cuncta vel eis appretiata loco sacrosancto remisit, licet in eo nihil tunc deicum ageretur, quum Sarraceni legem suam idolatria supersitioso ritu exercerent, qui etiam Christianum nullum in id

ingredi sinebant," (chap. 28, pp. 359–60). See Penny J. Cole, " 'O God, the Heathen Have Come into Your Inheritance' (Ps. 78.1): The Theme of Religious Pollution in Crusade Documents, 1095–1188," in Maya Schatzmiller, ed., *Crusades and Muslims in Twelfth-Century Syria* (Leiden: Brill, 1993), 90–91.

The chronicle known as *Tudebodus imitatus et continuatus* says that Tancred entered the temple, where he saw a huge silver statue of Mahomet enthroned. Comparing the statue to a crucifix, he proclaimed that this was not Christ but Antichrist and ordered his men to destroy it and put the silver to good use, *Tudebodus imitatus et continuatus,* chap.124 (RHC occ. 3:222–23).

64. RHC occ. 3:3, 727; Cole, " 'O God,'" 95.

65. Cole, " 'O God,'" 101–2. When Saladin "reconquered" Jerusalem in 1187, he had the Muslim holy sites ritually washed in rose water to cleanse them of Frankish "pollution," *Continuation des histoires des Croisades de Guillaume de Tyr,* ed. Brière (Paris, 1824), 138; 'Imâd al-Din, *al-Fath al-qussi fil-fath al-Qudsi,* trans. in Gabrieli, *Arab Historians of the Crusades,* 171–72. See Tolan, *Les Relations des pays d'Islam avec le monde latin du milieu du Xème siècle au milieu du XIIIème siècle* (Paris: Bréal, 2000), 161–64.

66. The *Chanson d'Antioche* was perhaps composed in the early years of the twelfth century by a crusader, Richard the Pilgrim, though the surviving version is a late twelfth-century reworking attributed to Graindor de Douai. Suzanne Duparc-Quioc argues for the traditional attribution to Richard le Pèlerin and Graindor and attempts to distinguish between the two versions (Duparc-Quioc, *La Chanson d'Antioche: Étude critique*). Robert F. Cook argues against it in *"Chanson d'Antioche," chanson de geste: Le cycle de la croisade est-il épique?* (Amsterdam: Benjamins 1980), 15–27. The attribution has subsequently been defended by Lewis Sumberg and Hermann Kleber: Sumberg, "Au confluent de l'histoire et du mythe: La *Chanson d'Antioche,* chronique en vers de la première croisade," in Karl-Heinz Bender, ed., *Les Épopées de la croisade* (Stuttgart, 1987), 58–65; Kleber, "Graindor de Douai: Remanieur-auteur-mécène?" in Bender, ed., *Les Épopées de la croisade,* 66–75. See also Flori, *Pierre l'ermite et la première croisade,* 56–63; Flori, "Des chroniques à l'épopée."

67. *Chanson d'Antioche,* ed. Suzanne Duparc-Quioc (Paris: Librairie orientaliste Paul Geuthner, 1977), ll. 205–11 (pp. 27–28).

68. Robert Chazan, *European Jewry and the First Crusade* (Berkeley: University of California Press, 1987).

69. *Chanson d'Antioche* (ll. 218–248, pp.28–29) identifies the destruction of Jerusalem by Titus and Vespasian as vengeance for the Crucifixion; this is standard Christian interpretation of the destruction of the temple of Jerusalem and the subsequent Jewish diaspora. What is far from standard, however, is that the *Chanson* presents Titus and Vespasian as *Christians*. For the association between the porch at Moissac and the Arch of Titus, see Linda Seidel, "Images of the Crusades in Western Art: Models as Metaphors," in Vladimir Goss and Chrsitine V. Bornstein, eds., *The Meeting of Two Worlds: Cultural Exchange between East and West during the Period of the Crusades* (Kalamazoo: Medieval Institute, 1986), 377–91.

70. *Chanson d'Antioche,* ll. 4891ff. This passage is discussed by Alexandre Eckhardt,

"Le Cercueil flottant de Mahomet," *Mélanges de philologie romane et de littérature médiévale offerts à E. Hoepffner: Publications de la Faculté des Lettres de l'Université de Strasbourg,* fasc. 113 (1949), 77–88. Eckhardt (78–82) finds earlier legends of pagan statues held in the air by means of magnets, dating from the description of a floating idol of Serapis that, according to Rufinus de Aquilea, was in the Serapion of Alexandria. On this legend, see Tolan, "Un cadavre mutilé."

71. *Chanson d'Antioche,* ll. 4968–70. Earlier in the epic, the poet expressed the same prophecy in a slightly different form (ll. 3447–50).

72. *Chanson d'Antioche,* ll. 9242–48, p. 454. In the *Chanson de Jérusalem,* Godfrey of Bouillon swears that he will conquer Mecca and take the golden candelabra that stand before the idol of Mahon (*La Chanson de Jérusalem.* ed. Nigel Thorpe, *The Old French Crusade Cycle,* vol. 6. [Tuscaloosa: University of Alabama Press, 1992], ll. 7276–87)

73. The similarities between this section of the *Chanson* and sections of *Passion of Thiemo* may indicate that the author of the *Passion* was familiar with the *Chanson* or vice versa. This section is probably one of the passages added by Graindor de Douai in the late twelfth century (Duparc-Quioc, 105). Later writers, including Marco Polo, also tell of the legendary three brother-kings (see *Chanson d'Antioche,* 269n).

74. *Chanson d'Antioche,* ll. 5310–12.

75. *Chanson d'Antioche,* ll. 5323–47.

76. *Chanson d'Antioche,* ll. 6620–21.

77. She appears three times in the *Chanson d'Antioche,* where her name is Calabre: ll. 766–73, 5252–68, 6838–956. Duparc-Quioc (105–6) says the first episode is an addition by Graindor de Douai, whereas the second was probably part of the original by Richard le Pelerin.

78. *Chanson d'Antioche,* ll. 9111–16, p. 448.

79. Duparc-Quioc, 57 n. 48.

80. RHC occ. 4:14, 137; Cole, " 'O God' "; Reilly-Smith, *First Crusade,* 146.

81. One anonymous chronicler of the second Crusade says that Muslims worship Mahumet; the patriarch of Jerusalem in 1204 asserts that the Saracens adore their god "Magometh" (Kedar, *Crusade and Mission,* 88–90).

82. *Chronica minorita Erphordiensis,* cited by Golubovich, *Biblioteca bio- bibliografica* 1:261.

83. Trans. Craig Hanson, "Manuel I Comnenus and the 'God of Muhammad': A Study in Byzantine Ecclesiastical Politics," in Tolan, ed., *Medieval Christian Perceptions of Islam,* 55–82 (translation at 55); Greek text given at 78 n. 31.

84. On the sources of this misinterpretation, see Hanson, "Manuel I Comnenus."

85. Ducellier, *Chrétiens d'Orient et Islam au Moyen Age,* 251.

86. Ducellier, *Chrétiens d'Orient et Islam au Moyen Age,* 306–7.

87. Ducellier, *Chrétiens d'Orient et Islam au Moyen Age,* 415.

88. Ducellier, *Chrétiens d'Orient et Islam au Moyen Age,* 298–313.

89. The bibliography on the *Chanson de Roland* is immense. On the image of the Saracens in the *Chanson,* see Jean Dufournet, "Notes sur les noms des Sarrasins dans la

Chanson de Roland," *Revue des langues romanes* 91 (1987):91–105; Flori, "Pur eshalcier sainte crestiënté: Croisade, guerre sainte et guerre juste dans les anciennes chansons de geste françaises," *Le Moyen Age* 97 (1991):171–87; Carole Bervoc-Huard,"L'Exclusion du sarrasin dans la *Chanson de Roland:* Vocabulaire et idéologie," in *Exclus et systèmes d'exclusion dans la littérature et la civilisation médiévales* (Paris: Honoré Champion, 1978), 345–61; Payen, "Une poétique de génocide joyeux: Devoir de violence et plaisir de tuer dans la *Chanson de Roland,*" *Olifant* 6 (1979):226–36.

On the ideology of the *Chanson de Roland,* see Peter Haidu, *The Subject of Violence: The Song of Roland and the Birth of the State* (Bloomington: University of Indiana Press, 1993); Erich Köhler, *Ideal und Wirklichkeit in der höfischen Epik: Studien zur Form der Frühen Artus- und Graldichtung* (Tübingen: M. Niemeyer, 1956, 1970); John Benton, "'Nostre Franceis n'unt talent de fuïr': The *Song of Roland* and the Enculturation of a Warrior Class," *Olifant* 6 (1979):237–58; Morrissey, *L'empereur à la barbe fleurie: Charlemagne dans la mythologie et l'histoire de France* (Paris: Gallimard, 1997), 71–123. On later Spanish uses of the Roncevaux legend, see Tolan, "The Battle of Roncesvalles as Nationalist Polemic: 1050–1624," in Marina Pérez de Mendiola, ed., *Bridging the Atlantic: Toward a Reassessment of Iberian and Latin American Cultural Ties* (Albany: State University of New York Press, 1996), 15–29.

90. Dedavant sei fait porter sun dragon
   E l'estandart Tervagan e Mahum
   E un'ymagene Apolin le Felun.

(Chanson de Roland, ll. 3266–68)

91. Dufournet, "Notes sur les noms des Sarrasins dans la Chanson de Roland"; Bercovici-Huard, "L'Exclusion du sarrasin."

92. Paul Bancourt, *Les Musulmans dans les chansons de geste du Cycle du roi,* 2 vols. Ph.D. diss., l'Université de Provence, Aix-en-Provence, 1982; Daniel, *Heroes and Saracens;* Jacoby, "La littérature française dans les états latins de la Méditerranée à l'époque des croisades, diffusion et création," *Essor et fortune de la Chanson de geste dans l'Europe et l'Orient latin: Actes du 9ᵉ congrès international de la Société Rencesvals* 2 (Modena, 1984):617–46.

The following collections contain articles on the image of the Saracens in medieval epic and romance: Keller, ed., *Romance Epic: Essays on a Medieval Literary Genre* (Kalamazoo: Medieval Institute, 1987); Buschinger and Spiewok, eds., *Orient und Okzident in der Kultur des Mittelalters; Monde oriental et monde occidental dans la culture médiévale, Wodan: Greifswalder Beiträge zum Mittelalter* 68 (1997); and the following issues of *Senefiance* 11 (1982); 20–21 (1987); and 25 (1988).

93. Daniel, *Heroes and Saracens.*

94. See E. Langlois, *Table de noms propres de toute nature dans les Chansons de geste* (Paris, 1904), 413–18.

95. Camille, *Gothic Idol,* 135ff., 171.

96. According to the council of Vienna (1311–12), "Sarraceni conveniunt ut ibidem

[in their mosques] adorent Mochometum" (*Conciliorum Oecumenicorum Decreta* [Bologna, 1973], 380).

97. Michael Paull, "Figure of Mahomet in Middle English Literature," Ph.D. diss., University of North Carolina, 1969; Jennifer Bray, "The Mahometan and Idolatry," *Studies in Church History* 21 (1984):89–98.

98. Camille, *Gothic Idol*, 156.

99. *Le Roman d'Alexandre,* ed. E. Armstrong, with modern French translation by L. Harf-Lancner (Paris: Livre de Poche, 1994), branche 3, ll. 940–44, 6152, 6203.

100. Ranulph Higden, *Polychronicon Together with the English Translations of John of Trevisa,* ed. J. R. Lumby, 6 vols. (London, 1876), 6:25; see Dorothee Metlitzki, *The Matter of Araby in Medieval England* (New Haven: Yale University Press, 1977), 206.

101. "Pluis de xx et vi ans fu li rois Sarrazins," cited by Bancourt, *Les Musulmans dans les chansons de geste,* 341.

102. *Gormont et Isembart: Fragment de Chanson de Geste du XIIᵉ siècle,* ed. Alphonse Bayot (Paris, 1931), ll. 193, 186, 204, 507; reference from D. Evans in *Notes and Queries* 230 (1985):159; see *Dictionnaire des lettres françaises,* ed. Geniviève Hasenohr and Michel Zink (Paris: Fayard, 1992), 554–55.

103. See Rodinson, *La fascination de l'Islam* (Paris: Maspero, 1989), 171.

104. Azo, *Summa Aurea,* cited by Kedar, "De Iudeis et Sarracenis: On the Categorization of Muslims in Medieval Canon Law, " in R. Castillo Lara, ed., *Studia in honorem eminentissimi cardinalis Alphonsi M. Stickler* (Rome: LAS, 1992), 207–13, reprinted in Kedar, *The Franks in the Levant, Eleventh to Fourteenth Centuries* (Aldershot: Variorum, 1993), quotation at 210; see also Kedar, *Crusade and Mission,* 88.

105. Peter Abelard, *Dialogus philosophi cum Iudeo et Christiano,* Cristina Trovo, ed. and trans. (into Italian), *Pietro Abelardo, Dialogo tra un filosofo, un giudeo e un cristiano* (Milan: Rizzoli, 1992); trans. (into English) P. Payer, *Dialogue of a Philosopher with a Jew and a Christian* (Toronto, 1979); on this text, see Peter Von Moos, "Les collations d'Abélard et la 'question juive' au XIIᵉᵐᵉ siècle", *Journal des Savants* (1999):449–89.

106. *Estoire del saint graal,* ed. Jean-Paul Ponceau (Paris: Honoré Champion, 1997), §62, p. 42. On this text, see Michelle Szkilnik, *L'archipel du graal: Étude de l'Estoire del saint graal* (Geneva: Droz, 1991). Thanks to Michelle Szkilnik for bringing this passage to my attention.

107. Firmin le Ver, *Dictionnaire Latin-Français de Firmin le Ver,* Brian Merrilees and William Edwards, eds., CCCM series in 4° I (1994), 444, 331.

108. For example, Embrico of Mainz, *Vita Mahumeti,* ed. Guy Cambier, *Collection Latomus* 52 (Brussels, 1961); Humbert of Romans (see Kedar, *Crusade and Mission,* 89). Servasanto da Faenza, a thirteenth-century Franciscan wrote: "Nam si quis inter Sarracenos malum de Matometo diceret, quem tamen deum esse non credunt, sed prophetam dei, sine ulla miseratione eum occiderent" (from a sermon in British Library MS Harley 3221, f.197v; thanks to David D'Avray for providing this reference for me). For other examples see chap. 6.

109. Jean Bodel, *Jeu de Saint Nicolas,* ed. Albert Henry (Geneva: Droz, 1981); Jean Dufournet, "Du double a l'unité: Les Sarrasins dans Le Jeu de saint Nicolas," in R. Pick-

ens, ed., *Studies in Honor of Hans-Erich Keller: Medieval French and Occitan Literature and Romance Linguistics* (Kalamazoo: Medieval Institute, 1993), 261–74; Camille, *Gothic Idol*, 129–35; *Dictionnaire des lettres françaises*, 748–51.

110. The idea of leaving the world of epic and entering that of hagiography is noted by Dufournet in "Du double a l'unité."

111. Paull, "Figure of Mahomet," 207.

112. Paull, "Figure of Mahomet," 209–10.

113. Paull, "Figure of Mahomet," 218; on the iconography of this common theme of the fall of the idols during the flight into Egypt, see Camille, *Gothic Idol*, 1–9.

114. Quoted from Paull, "Figure of Mahomet," 213.

115. Paull, "Figure of Mahomet," 220–27.

116. Paull, "Figure of Mahomet," 242–50.

117. Paull, "Figure of Mahomet," 157–67.

118. Paull, "Figure of Mahomet," 163.

119. Paull, "Figure of Mahomet," 165.

120. Baltimore, Walters Art Gallery MS 10137, f.1r, reproduced (and discussed) by Camille, *Gothic Idol*, 136.

121. Cole, " 'O God,'" 86–88.

122. The mosque of Toledo is described in the royal charter authorizing the consecration of the former mosque as a cathedral; transcription edited by J. F. Rivera Recio, *La iglesia de Toledo en el siglo XI (1086–1208)* (Rome, 1996), 1:70 n. 17, as cited by Patrick Henriet, "Hagiographie et historiographie en péninsule ibérique (XIᵉ–XIIIᵉ siècles): Quelques remarques," *Cahiers de linguistique hispanique médiévale* 23 (2000):53-85 (citation at 71 n. 73).

123. Guenée, *Histoire et culture historique*, 305.

124. *Die Chronik von Karl dem Grossen und Roland: Der lateinische Pseudo-Turpin in den Handschriften aus Aachen und Andernach*, ed. Hans-Wilhelm Klein (Munich: W. Fink, 1986), chap. 12 (p. 62), chap. 17 (p. 80), chap. 4 (p. 44); this last passage is reproduced by Ranulf Higden in his *Polychronicon*, 6:29.

125. Marlène Albert-Llorca and Jean-Pierre Albert, "Mahomet, la Vierge, et la frontière," *Annales HSS* 50 (1995):855–86. Ethnologists and local residents affirm that the Mahoma expresses local tradition and identity more than any hostility toward Islam.

6. Muhammad, Heresiarch (Twelfth Century)

1. Guibert de Nogent, *Dei gesta per Francos I*, ed. R. B. C. Huygens, CCCM 127A (1996), 100; trans. (into English) Robert Levine, *The Deeds of God through the Franks* (Woodbridge: Boydell Press, 1997); Levine's translation is faulty here (36).

2. Tolan, "Anti-Hagiography: Embrico of Mainz's *Vita Mahumeti*," *Journal of Medieval History* 22 (1996):25–41.

3. Adelphus, *Vita Machometi*, in B. Bischoff, ed., "Ein Leben Mohammeds (Adelphus?) (Zwölftes Jahrhundert)," *Anecdota Novissima: Texte des vierten bis sechzenten Jahrhundert* (1984):106–22 (113).

4. Adelphus, *Vita Machometi*, 122.

5. Guibert de Nogent, *Dei gesta per Francos I*, p. 94; trans. Levine, *Deeds of God*, 32. See Cole, " 'O God,'" 97–98; Flori, "La caricature de l'Islam dans l'Occident médiéval," 253–54. Embrico of Mainz says nothing about what his sources on Islam are.

6. According to the *Risâlat al-Kindî*, the monk Sergius changed his name to Nestorius (Nastûr) because he wished to spread the Nestorian heresy. *Risâlat al-Kindî*, Tartar trans., 181; see above, chap. 3.

7. Guibert de Nogent, *Dei gesta per Francos* 1, p. 95; trans. Levine, *Deeds of God*, 36.

8. Embrico of Mainz, *Vita Mahumeti*, ll. 255–76.

9. Theophanes, *Chronographia* 334, trans. Mango and Scott, 464; see above, chap. 3.

10. Adelphus, 209–12.

11. Adelphus, 246–57; Guibert, *Dei gesta*, 97–98. Embrico has his Mammutius train a bull for a different purpose: the Magus announces that whoever can tame the bull will become the king of Lybia, and of course only Mammutius can do so (Embrico, *Vita Mahumeti*, 359–86, 601–80). See Guy Cambier, "L'épisode des taureaux dans *La légende de Mahomet* (ms. 50, Bibliothèque du Séminaire de Pise)," *Hommage à Léon Herrmann*, *Collection Latomus* 44 (1960):228–36.

12. Adelphus, ll. 89–91, citing Horace, *Epod.* 5.67.

13. See above, chap. 1; Tolan, "Un cadavre mutilé."

14. Guibert, *Dei gesta* 1: 99; trans. Levine, *Deeds of God*, 33; on this passage, see Levine, "Satiric Vulgarity in Guibert de Nogent's *Gesta Dei per Francos*," *Rhetorica* 7 (1989):261–73 (esp. 269–70).

15. Guibert, *Dei gesta*, 1:100; trans. Levine, *Deeds of God*, 36.

16. See Tolan, "Un cadavre mutilé."

17. Guibert, *Dei Gesta*, 89-90; trans. Levine, *Deeds of God*, 30.

18. Guibert, *Dei Gesta*, 1:91-93; trans. Levine, *Deeds of God*, 30–32.

19. Guibert, *Dei Gesta*, 1:98; trans. Levine, *Deeds of God*, 34.

20. In the *Gesta Pontificum Cenomannensium*, quoted by Moore in *Origins of European Dissent* (Oxford: Basil Blackwell, 1978, 1985), 86–87.

21. "Unde deum Machomen reputabant atque per illas partes illius nomen erat celebre," Guibert, *Otia*, 1053–54. "Hoc ubi uiderunt stulti, Mahumet coluerunt," Embrico, *Vita Mahumeti*, 1145. He earlier asserts, "Hic si queratur qui sit quem sic ueneratur: Nomen habet Mahumet; quo duce fisa tumet," 67–68.

22. See above, chap. 5; Cole, " 'O God,'" 86–88.

23. See P. Sjoerd van Koningsveld, "La Apología de Al-Kindî en la España del siglo XII: Huellas toledanas de un 'animal disputax,'" in *Estudios Sobre Alfonso VI y la reconquista de Toledo: Actas del II congreso internacional de estudios mozárabes* (Toledo: Instituto de Estudios Visigotico-Mozarabes, 1989):107–29.

24. Al-Khazrajî includes the letter of "the Goth" (*al-Qûtî*) in his own tract, the *Maqâmi' as-sulbân* (*Mallets for Hammering the Crosses*). This letter seems to have been reworked by its Muslim redactor; see Burman, *Religious Polemic*, 62–70.

25. Burman, *Religious Polemic*, 70–84; Burman, "*Tathlîth al-wahdânîyah* and the

Twelfth-Century Andalusian-Christian Approach to Islam," in Tolan, ed., *Medieval Christian Perceptions of Islam,* 109–28.

26. Burman provides an English translation of this text in *Religious Polemic,* 215–385. This text is sometimes referred to as the *Contrarietas alfolica.*

27. For the first four texts, see Burman, *Religious Polemic.* For Petrus Alfonsi's *Dialogi,* see Tolan, *Petrus Alfonsi and His Medieval Readers* (Gainesville: University Press of Florida, 1993), 27–33.

28. It is possible, as d'Alverny and Daniel have suggested, that the author is not a convert, but a Mozarab Christian with a fairly good knowledge of Islam; for them his claim to be a convert is a mere literary artifice. I find their arguments unconvincing. Burman notes that, given the lack of evidence, the author could plausibly be a Mozarab, a convert from Islam, or a convert from Judaism (since Hebrew words appear at one point in the text). The mention of conversion (artifice or no), along with the blatantly hostile portrait of Muhammad, suggests that the text was written in Christian-controlled territory, as Burman reasonably notes, though he is too quick to identify Toledo as the possible locus of production. There are plenty of other towns in Christian Spain where such a text could have been produced (Marie-Thérèse d'Alverny, "Marc de Tolède," in *Estudios sobre Alfonso VI y la reconquista de Toledo,* 3 vols. (Toledo: Instituto de Estudios Visigótico-Mozárabes, 1986–92), 3:25–59 (here p. 47); Daniel, *Islam and the West,* 30; Burman, *Religious Polemic,* 51–56, 335).

29. Burman, *Religious Polemic,* 157–89.

30. Petrus Alfonsi, *Dialogi contra Iudaeos,* 94.

31. Petrus Alfonsi, *Dialogi contra Iudaeos,* 97. For the *Risâlat al-Kindî,* there were two signs of prophecy: revelation of things unknown (past and future) and performance of miracles. See above, chap. 3; *Risâlat al-Kindî,* Tartar trans., 153, 173; Strousma, "Signs of Prophecy."

32. Petrus Alfonsi, *Dialogi contra Iudaeos,* 97.

33. *Risâlat al-Kindî,* Tartar trans., 149; Koran 33:37–38.

34. *Liber denudationis,* §7:11, ed. Burman, *Religious Polemic,* 288–91; see Burman's commentary at 105–6.

35. Petrus Alfonsi, *Dialogi contra Iudaeos,* 102–3; *Risâlat al-Kindî,* Tartar trans., 166; on this passage see Tolan, "Un cadavre mutilé," 61–62.

36. Petrus Alfonsi, *Dialogi contra Iudaeos,* 95; see Tolan, *Petrus Alfonsi,* 29.

37. *Liber denudationis,* §11:2.

38. Petrus Alfonsi, *Dialogi contra Iudaeos,* 99; see Tolan, *Petrus Alfonsi,* 30–31.

39. Burman, *Religious Polemic,* 122–23; *Risâlat al-Kindî,* Tartar trans., 153–66; Koran 17:59–61; *Liber denudationis,* §4:6, 12:1–8; Petrus Alfonsi, *Dialogi contra Iudaeos,* 96–97.

40. *Liber denudationis,* 9:11–16.

41. *Liber denudationis,* 7:1–10.

42. See Burman, *Religious Polemic,* 106–7.

43. *Liber denudationis,* 9:20.

44. *Liber denudationis,* 3:4; *Risâlat al-Kindî,* Tartar trans., 251; Burman, *Religious*

Polemic, 108–9; on Tahrîf and Eastern Christian defense from this charge, see above, chaps. 2 and 3.

45. Koran 4:164, 20:8.

46. Burman, *Religious Polemic,* 115–20, discusses these passages and their probable Eastern sources.

47. Petrus Alfonsi, *Dialogi contra Iudaeos,* 104–5; see Tolan, *Petrus Alfonsi,* 36–37.48. Petrus Alfonsi, *Dialogi contra Iudaeos,* 105.

49. Burman, "*Tathlîth al-wahdânîyah.*"

50. Tolan, *Petrus Alfonsi,* 108–110.

51. This section has been developed at greater length in Tolan, "Peter the Venerable on the 'Diabolical Heresy of the Saracens,'" in Alberto Ferreiro, ed., *The Devil, Heresy, and Witchcraft in the Middle Ages: Essays in Honor of Jeffrey B. Russell* (Leiden: Brill, 1998), 345–67; see also Dominique Iogna-Prat, *Ordonner et exclure: Cluny et la société chrétienne face à l'hérésie, au judaïsme et à l'Islam* (Paris: Aubier, 1998), English trans. *Order and Exclusion* (Ithaca: Cornell University Press, 2001). These two works contain references to the huge bibliography on Peter of Cluny.

52. See Tolan, *Petrus Alfonsi,* 116–17.

53. See Thomas Burman, "*Tafsīr* and Translation: Robert of Ketton, Mark of Toledo, and Traditional Arabic Qur'ān Exegesis," *Speculum* 73 (1998):703–32.

54. The original manuscript of the *Collectio toletana,* used by Peter of Cluny as he composed his own anti-Islamic works, is conserved in the Bibliothèque de l'Arsenal (MS n° 1162); see d'Alverny, "Deux traductions latines du Coran au Moyen-Age," *Archives d'histoire doctrinale et littéraire du Moyen Age* 16 (1947–48):69–131, reprinted in d'Alverny, *Connaissance de l'Islam dans l'Occident médiévale* (London: Variorum, 1994); Tolan, "Peter the Venerable."

55. Tolan, "Peter the Venerable," 355–56.

56. Peter of Cluny, *Summa totius haeresis Saracenorum,* in *Schriften zum Islam,* ed. and trans. (into German) Reinhold Glei, Corpus Islamo-Christianum, series latina 1 (Alternberg: CIS-Verlag, 1985), §3.

57. Kedar, *Crusade and Mission,* 90n.

58. Kedar, *Crusade and Mission,* 87, 208–10.

59. Petrus Alfonsi, *Dialogi,* §5, 94–95; the same material is in the Latin translation of the *Risâlat al-Kindî* (Latin translation, 401–2, 413–14). Peter seems to be following Alfonsi's narration of these events rather than that of the *Risâlat,* though he does correct Alfonsi, who identified Sergius as a Jacobite monk [*Dialogi,* 95]; Peter, (following the *Risâlat al-Kindî,* Latin translation, 413) identifies Sergius as a Nestorian (Peter of Cluny, *Summa,* 206).

60. Peter of Cluny, *Summa,* §10; Horace, *Ars poetica,* 1:1–2.

61. Peter of Cluny, *Letter,* §111, p. 295. Another version of this letter is edited by James Kritzeck, *Peter the Venerable and Islam* (Princeton: Princeton University Press, 1964), 212–14; the latter version does not contain Peter's criticisms of the *Risâlat al-Kindî.* Several passages of the text are also common to the *Summa.* For the relationship between these three texts, see Constable 2:275–84; d'Alverny, "Deux traductions," 72–76; Kritzeck, *Peter the Venerable and Islam,* 27–30.

62. *Contra sectam* (*Liber contra secta, sive haeresim Saracenorum*) in *Schriften zum Islam,* here §9.

63. Adelard, *Questiones naturales,* in *Beiträge zur Geschichte der Philosophie und Theologie des Mittelalters* 31, pt. 2; see p. 11. See Charles Burnett, "Adelard of Bath and the Arabs," *Rencontres de cultures dans la philosophie médiévale: Traductions et traducteurs de l'antiquité tardive au XIVe siècle* (Louvain la Neuve: Université Catholique de Louvain, 1990), 89–107. For other examples of similar statements by twelfth-century Latin writers, see Tolan, *Les relations entre le monde arabo-musulman et le monde latin* (*milieu du Xe–milieu du XIIIe siècle*) (Paris: Bréal, 2000), 175–79.

64. Peter of Cluny, *Contra sectam,* §29; he quotes the Koranic injunctions at §35. On this, see Kedar, *Crusade and Mission,* 99–104.

65. "Quae uero est natura haec, que substantia, uel essentia? None illa, quae communi uniuersarum gentium more, iuxta proprietatem uniuscuiusque linguae Deus creditur, Deus dicitur? Est igitur natura illa, Deus ille, qui solus increatus est, qui solus creator est" (*Contra sectam,* §32). Peter may have taken the identification of *substantia* with God the creator from Petrus Alfonsi, who identifies the creator with God the Father and with *substantia.* Petrus Alfonsi, *Dialogi contra Iudaeos,* §6, pp. 104–5; see Tolan, *Petrus Alfonsi,* 36–37.

66. Petrus Venerabilis, *Adversus Iudeorum inveteratam duritiem,* ed. Yvonne Friedman, CCCM 58 (1985); Iogna-Prat, *Ordonner et exclure,* chap. 10, "Les Juifs appartiennent-ils à l'espèce humaine?"

67. *Risâlat al-Kindî,* Tartar trans., 125–27; Petrus Alfonsi, *Dialogi,* §6, pp. 105–6 (see Tolan, *Petrus Alfonsi,* 36–39). For other examples of this common ploy, see Burman, *Religious Polemic,* 72–73, 81–82, 163ff; Daniel, *Islam and the West,* 200–209.

68. MS A, 28v; Peter of Cluny, *Contra sectam,* §64–65; see Kritzeck, *Peter the Venerable and Islam,* 177–78.

69. Peter of Cluny, *Contra sectam,* §66–67; *Risâlat al-Kindî,* Tartar trans., 251–53.

70. Peter of Cluny, *Contra sectam,* §97–154; a similar argument is found in the *Risâlat al-Kindî,* Tartar trans., 137–73

71. *Risâlat al-Kindî,* Tartar trans., 137–53; Peter of Cluny, *Contra sectam,* §117, 119.

72. 2 Tim. 4:3–4; Peter of Cluny, *Contra sectam,* §138.

73. For Kritzeck, the text is complete as is (*Peter the Venerable and Islam,* 155–56). Torrell and Bouthillier think he had planned on writing more: J. Torrell and D. Bouthillier, *Pierre le vénérable et sa vision du monde* (Louvain, 1986), 182. For Iogna-Prat, the text is probably complete (*Ordonner et exclure,* 343–44).

74. Torrell and Bouthillier, *Pierre le Vénérable et sa vision du monde, passim* (see index, p. 441, "Grégoire le Grand").

75. 1 MS from the twelfth century, 4 from the thirteenth, 6 from the fourteenth, 3 from the fifteenth, 4 from the sixteenth, according to d'Alverny, "Deux traductions," 108–13.

76. Stock, *Implications of Literacy,* 177.

77. Alan of Lille, *Contra paganos,* (pt. 4 of *De fide catholica*), in d'Alverny, ed., *Cahiers de Fanjeaux* 18 (1983):325–50 (here 331–32).

78. Alan of Lille, *Contra paganos,* 347.

79. Alan of Lille, *Contra paganos*, 332–36; d'Alverny, "Alain de Lille et l'Islam," *Cahiers de Fanjeaux* 18 (1983):301–24, notes that this is in fact a veritable, if rather obscure, Muslim interpretation of certain passages of the Koran.

80. Alan of Lille, *Contra paganos*, 338–39.

81. Alan of Lille, *Contra paganos*, 341–43.

82. Alan of Lille, *Contra paganos*, 340–41.

83. Alan of Lille, *Contra paganos*, 344–46.

84. Herodotus, *Histories* 4:94–95 (trans. Aubrey de Sélincourt [London: Penguin, 1954]); François Hartog, *Le miroir d'Hérodote: Essai sur la représentation de l'autre* (Paris: Gallimard, 1980), 102–25. Herodotus, it should be noted, finds the explanation given by the Greeks of the Black Sea improbable; this does not of course alter its ability to explain the Getan other for the Greeks who told it.

85. John Lydgate, in his *Fall of Princes*, recounts the standard litany of Muhammad's bogus miracles, followed by epileptic fits and death at the hands (or rather snouts) of pigs (Paull, "Figure of Mahomet in Middle English Literature," 191–95). Other texts tell essentially the same story: William Langland's *Piers Plowman* and Ranulph Higden's *Polychronicon*, 6:14–51 (a world chronicle of early fourteenth century, translated into English by Trevisa in the late fourteenth century; see Metlitzki, *Matter of Araby in Medieval England*, 198–99, 205–6). Even the fourteenth-century Hebrew anti-Christian work the *Nizzahon vetus* says that the Muslims worship Muhammad and that Muhammad died by falling drunk onto a garbage heap and being devoured by pigs (*Nizzahon vetus*, ed. David Berger, *The Jewish-Christian Debate in the High Middle Ages* [Philadelphia: Jewish Publication Society of America, 1979], 110, 217). For further examples see Tolan, "Un cadavre mutilé"; Daniel, *Islam and the West*, 100–30.

86. Gerald of Wales, *De principis instructione*, in J. Brewer, ed., *Opera* (*Rolls Series* 21): 8:68–71.

87. Alexandre du Pont, *Le Roman de Mahomet;* see Marie-Geneviève Grossel, "L'Orient en miroir inverse: Le *Roman de Mahomet* d'Alexandre du Pont," *Wodan: Greifswalder Beiträge zum Mittelalter* 68 (1997):73–86.

7. The Muslim in the Ideologies of Thirteenth-Century Christian Spain

1. Alfonso el Sabio, *Las siete partidas* (Madrid: Real Academia de la Historia, 1807, 1972). Juan Antonio Arias Bonet has produced an edition of the *Primera partida* based on London, British Library MS 20787 (Valladolid, 1975). The English translations are taken (with occasional modifications) from *Siete partidas*, Samuel Scott, trans. (Chicago: American Bar Association, 1931).

2. Letter in F. Balme et al., eds., *Raymundiana seu documenta quae pertinent ad S. Raymundi de Pennaforti vitam et scripta*, 4 vols. (Rome: Domo generalitia ordinis praedicatorum, 1898–1901), 4:2, 12–13.

3. Robert I. Burns, "The Spiritual Life of Jaume the Conqueror King of Arago-Catalonia, 1208–1276: Portrait and Self-Portrait," in *Jaime I y su Época* (Zaragoza: Cometa, 1980), 323–57.

4. Jaume I, *Llibre dels feyts*, ed. Ferran Soldevila (Barcelona: Edicions 62, 1982), §84.

5. Pierre Guichard, *Les Musulmans de Valence et la reconquête (XIᵉ–XIIIᵉᵐᵉ siècles)*, 2 vols. (Damascus: Institut Français de Damas, 1990–91), 397. On Jaume's abortive plans for a crusade to the Holy Land, see Jaume I, *Llibre dels feyts*, §473–93; Burns, "Spiritual Life of Jaume the Conqueror," 343.

6. Burns, "Spiritual Life"; on the proposed alliance with the Mongol khan, see Jaume, *Llibre dels feyts*, §481.

7. Jaume I, *Llibre dels feyts*, §249–53; see André Bazzana, Patrice Cressier, and Pierre Guichard, *Les châteaux ruraux d'al-Andalus: Histoire et archéologie des husûn du sud-est de l'Espagne* (Madrid: Casa de Velázquez, 1988), 157–58, 172.

8. Jaume I, *Llibre dels feyts*, §416–17; on this and other examples see Burns, "Spiritual Life of Jaume the Conqueror," 344–45.

9. Jaume I, *Llibre dels feyts*, §447–50.

10. Jaume I, *Llibre dels feyts*, §445.

11. *Cortes de los antiguos reinos de Aragón y de Valencia y Principado de Cataluña* (Madrid, 1896), 1:217–18, as cited by Jaume Riera i Sans, "Les Llicències reials per predicar als Jueus i als Sarraïns (segles XIII–XIV)," *Calls* 2 (1987):113–43 (quotation at 127 n. 4).

12. The Latin text, composed between 1247 and 1252, survives only in a late thirteenth-century Navarro-Aragonese translation, in a lavishly illustrated manuscript in the Getty Museum, Los Angeles (MS Ludwig XIV 6, 83 MQ 165); *Vidal mayor*, facsimile edition, Huesca: Diputación Provincial, 1989. The section on Jews and Saracens is at ff. 242v–45v. On this text, see Gwendollyn Gout Grautoff, "*Vidal mayor*: A Visualisation of the Juridical Miniature," *Medieval History Journal* 3 (2000):67–89.

13. See Burns, "Muslims in the Thirteenth-Century Realms of Aragon: Interaction and Reaction," in Powell, ed., *Muslims Under Latin Rule*, 70; Kedar, "De Iudeis et Sarracenis: On the Categorization of Muslims in Medieval Canon Law"; Henri Gilles, "Législation et doctrine canoniques sur les Sarrasins," in *Cahiers de Fanjeaux* 18 (1983), *Islam et Chrétiens du Midi*, 195–213; Emilio Bussi, "La condizione giuridica dei musulmani nel diritto canonico," *Rivista di storia del diritto italiano* 8 (1935):459–94; Peter Herde, "Christians and Saracens at the Time of the Crusades: Some Comments of Contemporary Medieval Canonists," *Studia Gratiana* 12 (1967):361–76.

14. Riera i Sans, "Llicències reials," 116–17; Burns, "Journey from Islam," 352.

15. Mark Johnston, "Ramon Lull and the Compulsory Evangelization of Jews and Muslims," in Larry Simon, ed., *Iberia and the Mediterranean World of the Middle Ages: Studies in Honor of Robert I. Burns* (Leiden, 1995), 3–37 (esp. 9–11); Robert Chazan, *Daggers of Faith: Thirteenth-Century Christian Missionizing and Jewish Response* (Berkeley: University of California Press, 1989), 38–48.

16. Robert Burns, *Muslims, Christians, and Jews in the Crusader Kingdom of Valencia* (Cambridge: Cambridge University Press, 1984), 91.

17. John Williams, "Generationes Abrahae: Reconquest Iconography in Leon," *Gesta* 16 (1977):3–14.

18. Patrick Henriet, "Hagiographie et Politique à León au début du XIIIᵉ siècle: Les chanoines réguliers de Saint-Isidore et la prise de Baeza," *Revue Mabillon*, n.s. 8 (1997):

53–82 (here 54). On Lucas, see Georges Martin, *Les juges de Castille: Mentalités et discours historique dan l'Espagne médiévale. Annexes des Cahiers de linguistique hispanique médiévale* (Paris: Klincksieck, 1992), 6:201–49; Linehan, *History and Historians of Medieval Spain,* 357–58; Henriet, "Hagiographie léonaise et pédagogie de la foi: Les miracles d'Isidore de Séville et la lutte Contre l'hérésie (XIe–XIIIe siècles)," *Melanges de la Casa de Velazquez* (2000); thanks to Emma Falque for letting me see her critical edition of Lucas's *Chronicon* in progress.

19. Lucas de Tuy, *Chronicon mundi,* in A. Schott, ed., *Hispaniae illustratae* 4 (1608): 1–119 (here 53–54); on the ninth-century sources, see above, chap. 4.

20. Lucas de Tuy, *Chronicon mundi,* 54; Henriet, "Hagiographie léonaise et pédagogie de la foi."

21. See above, chap. 4.

22. Lucas de Tuy, *Chronicon mundi,* 53.

23. Lucas de Tuy, *Chronicon mundi,* 52–53.

24. This text is edited by Henriet, "Hagiographie et Politique à León au début du XIIIe siècle," 77–82 (and discussed at 63–76).

25. See Thomas Burman, "*Tafsīr* and Translation," 703–32; d'Alverny, "Deux traductions," 69–131; d'Alverny, "Marc de Tolède," 3:25–59; d'Alverny and Georges Vajda, "Marc de Tolède, traducteur d'Ibn Tumart," *Al-Andalus* 16 (1951):99–140, 259–307. These three articles are reprinted in d'Alverny, *Connaissance de l'Islam.*

26. Salimbene of Adam, *Chronica* (MGH SS 32), 28; Cesarius of Heisterbach, *Annales colonienses* (MGH SS 17), 826; Matthew Paris, *Chronica maior,* ed. H. R. Luard, *Rerum britannicarum medii aevi* no. 57, 7 vols. (London, 1872–83), 2:559–66. See Martín Alvira Cabrer, "La imagen del *Miramolín* al-Nasir (1199—1213) en las fuentes christianas des siglo XIII," *Anuario de Estudios medievales* 26 (1996):1003–28; Jacques Berlioz, "*Tuezles tous, Dieu reconnaîtra les siens*": La croisade contre les Albigeois vue par Césaire de Heisterbach (Portet sur Garonne: Loubatières, 1994), 18–19, 54–57.

27. This preface is edited in d'Alverny and Vajda, "Marc de Tolède, traducteur d'Ibn Tumart," 260–68.

28. This text is edited in d'Alverny and Vajda, "Marc de Tolède, traducteur d'Ibn Tumart," 268–69 (preface), 269–79 (*Tractatus de unione dei*).

29. Rodericus Ximenius de Rada, *Historia de rebus Hispanie siue historia gothica,* CCCM 72 (1987), §9:16:297–99. On Rodrigo and his chronicle, see Linehan, *History and Historians of Medieval Spain.*

30. Rodericus Ximenius de Rada, *Historia de rebus Hispanie,* 9:16:297–99.

31. Rodericus Ximenius de Rada, *Historia de rebus Hispanie,* 9:17:299–300.

32. On the conversion of mosques into churches, see Pascal Buresi, "Les conversions d'églises et de mosquées en Espagne aux XIème–XIIIème siècles," in *Villes et religion: Mélanges offerts à Jean-Louis Biget par ses élèves* (Paris: Publications de la Sorbonne, 2000), 333–50; Julie Harris, "Mosque to Church Conversions in the Reconquest," *Medieval Encounters* 3 (1997):158–72; Amy Remensnyder, "The Colonization of Sacred Architecture: The Virgin Mary, Mosques, and Temples in Medieval Spain and Early Sixteenth-Century Mexico," in *Monks and Nuns, Saints and Outcasts: Religion in Medieval*

Society: Essays in Honor of Lester K. Little (Ithaca: Cornell University Press, 2000), 189–219.

33. Cited by Manuel González Jiménez, *Alfonso X el Sabio, 1252–1284* (Palencia: La Omeda, 1993), 255.

34. For the text of Alfonso's *Estoria de España,* I have used the version known as the *Primera crónica general de España,* ed. Ramón Menéndez Pidal (Madrid, 1955). On the portrayal of Islam in the *Estoria,* see Tolan, "Rhetoric, Polemics, and the Art of Hostile Biography: Portraying Muhammad in Thirteenth-Century Christian Spain," in *Pensamiento hispano medieval: Homenaje a Horacio Santiago Otero,* ed. José María Soto Rábanos (Madrid: Consejo Superior de Investigaciones Científicas, 1998), 1497–1511; Tolan, "Alphonse X le Sage, roi des trois religions," *Wodan: Greifswalder Beiträge zum Mittelalter* 74 (1997):123–36. On the differing versions, the composition, and the authorship of the *Estoria de España,* see Gonzalo Menéndez Pidal, "Cómo trabajaron las escuelas alfonsíes," *Nueva revista de filología hispánica* 5 (1951):363–80; Diego Catalán, "El taller historiográfico alfonsí: Métodos y problemas en el trabajo compilatorio," *Romania* 84 (1963):354–75; this and other studies on Alfonso's historiography are reprinted in his *La estoria de España de Alfonso X: Creación y evolución* (Madrid: Universidad Autónoma, 1992); Ines Fernandez-Ordonez, "La *Estoria de España,* la *General estoria* y los diferentes criterios compilatorios," *Revista de Literatura* 50 (1988):15–35. See also Charles Fraker, "Alfonso X, the Empire, and the *Primera crónica,*" *Bulletin of Hispanic Studies* 55 (1978):95–102; Anthony J. Cárdenas, "Alfonso's Scriptorium and Chancery: Role of the Prologue in Bonding the *Translatio Studii* to the *Translatio Potestatis,*" in *Emperor of Culture: Alfonso X the Learned of Castile and His Thirteenth-Century Renaissance,* ed. Robert I. Burns (Philadelphia, 1990), 90–108; Peter Linehan, *History and Historians of Medieval Spain,* 463ff.; Francisco Márquez Villanueva, *El Concepto Cultural Alfonsí* (Madrid: Mapfre, 1994). The following work appeared too late to be taken into account: Georges Martin, ed., *La historia alfonsí: El modelo y sus destinos, siglos XIII–XV* (Madrid: Casa de Velázquez, 2000).

35. This is the conclusion of Fraker, "Alfonso X."

36. *Primera crónica general,* prologue (4).

37. "Era mas razón de tener con los romanos, que eran de parte de Europa, que con los de Carthago, que eran de Affrica," *Primera crónica general,* §26. See Americo Castro, *La Realidad historica de España* (Mexico City: Porrua, 1973), 61.

38. See Cárdenas, "Alfonso's Scriptorium"; Márquez Villanueva, *El Concepto cultural,* 100ff.

39. See Alan Deyermond, "The Death and Rebirth of Visigothic Spain in the *Estoria de España,*" *Revista Canadiense de Estudios Hispanicos,* 9 (1985):345–67; Olga Tudorica Impey, "'Del duello de los godos de Espanna': La retorica del llanto y su motivacion," *Romance Quarterly* 33 (1986):295–307.

40. See François Medeiros, *L'Occident et l'Afrique (XIIIème–XVème siècles): Images et représentations* (Paris: Éditions Karthala, 1985); for the image of the black Saracen in the *Chanson de Geste,* see above, chap. 5.

41. *Primera Crónica General,* §559, p. 312; Tudorica Impey, "'Del duello.'"

42. *Primera Crónica General,* §559, p. 313. Here is another passage concerning the conversion of churches into mosques: "E los moros . . . loauan el nombre de Mahomat a altas uozes et ante todos en la eglesia de los cristianos o el nombre de Cristo solie seer loado," §561, p. 316.

43. The description of the "purification" of the mosque of Córdoba is taken from Rodrigo Jiménez de Rada (cited above, chap. 7, n. 30); *Primera Crónica General,* §1046, p.733. On this passage, see Louise Mirrer, *Women, Jews, and Muslims in the Texts of Reconquest Castile* (Ann Arbor: University of Michigan Press, 1996), 51.

44. *Siete partidas,* 1:5:18, see González Jiménez, *Alfonso X,* 237–38. On the place of Muslims and Jews in Alfonso's legal texts, see Dwayne Carpenter, "Minorities in Medieval Spain: The Legal Status of Jews and Muslims in the *Siete partidas,*" *Romance Quarterly* 33 (1986):275–87; Carpenter, *Alfonso X and the Jews: An Edition and Commentary on* Siete Partidas *7.24 "De los judíos," University of California Publications in Modern Philology* 115 (1986); L. Simon, "Jews in the Legal Corpus of Alfonso el Sabio," *Comitatus* 18 (1987): 80–97; Tolan, "Alphonse X le Sage: Roi des trois religions." On Alfonso's legislative works see Jerry Craddock, *The Legislative Works of Alfonso X el Sabio: A Critical Bibliography* (London: Grant and Cutler, 1986); Craddock, "La cronología de las obras legislativas de Alfonso X el Sabio," *Anuario de Historia del Derecho Español* 51 (1981):365–418; Craddock, "The Legislative Works of Alfonso el Sabio," in Burns, ed, *Emperor of Culture,* 182–97; Robert MacDonald, "Law and Politics: Alfonso's Program of Political Reform," in Robert Burns, ed., *The Worlds of Alfonso the Learned and James the Conqueror: Intellect and Force in the Middle* Ages (Princeton: Princeton University Press, 1985), 150–202.

45. *Siete partidas,* 7:25:1.

46. *Siete partidas,* 7:25:9.

47. *Siete partidas,* 4:7:8.

48. *Siete partidas,* 3:16:8. See also 3:11:21: "En qué manera deben jurar los moros."

49. *Siete partidas,* 7:25:2.

50. *Siete partidas,* 7:25:3.

51. *Siete partidas,* 4:6:6. Alfonso here follows the work of earlier legislation, notably that of Pope Clement III; see Kedar, "Muslim Conversion in Canon Law," 321–22.

52. "Contumelia creatoris, que quiere tanto decir como denuesto de Dios et de nuestra fe, es manera de espiritual fornicacion, por que podrie acaescer que serie fecho divorcio entre algunos que estodiesen casados" (*Siete partidas,* 4:10:3). The legal point here is to equate refusal to see Christian truth with fornication, since fornication is traditionally considered legitimate grounds for annulment of a marriage.

53. *Siete partidas,* 7:25:10, 7:24:9.

54. *Siete partidas,* 7:28.

55. *Siete partidas,* 7:28:6. See Simon, "Jews in the Legal Corpus of Alfonso el Sabio."

56. He says of his father:

o mui bon Rei Don Fernando
que senpre Deus e ssa Madre amou e foi de seu bando
por que conquereu de mouros o mais de Andaluzia.

(Alfonso X, o Sabio, *Cantigas de Santa Maria,* ed. Walter Mettmann, 2 vols.

[Coimbra, 1959; reprint Vigo, 1981], §221:11–13)

And in another *Cantiga:*

e quand' algũa cidade de mouros ya gãar
ssa omagen [of the Virgin] na mezquita põya eno portal.

(Cantigas, §292:28–29)

As for his father-in-law:

el Rei d' Aragon, Don James de gran prez,
a eigreja da See da gran mezquita fez.

(Cantigas, §169:34–35)

8. Apocalyptic Fears and Hopes Inspired by the Thirteenth-Century Crusades

1. Innocent III, *Quia major* (PL 216:818). On Innocent's *Quia major,* see Penny Cole, *The Preaching of the Crusades to the Holy Land, 1095–1270* (Cambridge, Mass.: Medieval Academy, 1991), 104–9.

2. On the place of Islam in Joachim's apocalyptic thought, see David Burr, "Antichrist and Islam in Medieval Franciscan Exegesis," in Tolan, ed., *Medieval Christian Perceptions of Islam,* 131–52 (esp. 132–35); Southern, *Western Views,* 40–41; E. R. Daniel, "Apocalyptic Conversion: The Joachite Alternative to the Crusades," *Traditio* 25 (1969):127–54.

3. Giulio Cipollone, *Cristianità-Islam: Cattività e liberazione in nome di dio* (Rome: Editrice Pontificia Università Gregoriana, 1992), 346–47, 429.

4. See Cipollone, "Innocenzo III e i saraceni: Attegiamenti differenziati (1198–1199)," *Acta historica et archaeologica mediaevalia* 9 (1988):167–87; Cipollone, *Cristianità-Islam,* 325–447.

5. For a brief general introduction to the council, see Jane Sayers, *Innocent III: Leader of Europe, 1198–1216* (London: Longman, 1994), 95–101.

6. Canons of Nablus, ed. Benjamin Z. Kedar, "On the Origins of the Earliest Laws of Frankish Jerusalem: The Canons of the Council of Nablus, 1120," *Speculum* 74 (1999), 310–35. See James Brundage, "Prostitution, Miscegenation, and Sexual Purity in the First Crusade," in Edbury, ed., *Crusade and Settlement,* 57–65, reprinted in Brundage, *The Crusades, Holy War, and Canon Law* (Aldershot: Variorum, 1991), see 60–61.

7. Lateran IV, canon 68, in *Concilia oecumenicorum decreta,* p. 266, trans. from H. Rothwell, *English Historical Documents, 1189–1327* (London: Eyre and Spottiswoods, 1975), as reprinted in P. Geary, *Readings in Medieval History* (Peterborough: Broadview, 1989), 460–85. This canon is reiterated in the *Decretals* compiled by Ramon de Penyafort for Gregory IX (henceforth referred to by the standard abbreviation, X), 5.6.15, in A. Richteri, ed., *Corpus iuris canonici,* 2 vols. (Leipzig, 1879; reprint Graz, 1959), 2:776–77. The reference to Moses does not, it appears, refer to any specific biblical passage, but rather to widespread Jewish practice of distinguishing themselves from non-Jews through dress.

8. Powell, "The Papacy and the Muslim Frontier," in Powell, ed., *Muslims Under Latin Rule,* 175–203 (here 190–91).

9. Lateran IV, canon 68. This canon is reiterated in X, 5:6:15, in *Corpus iuris canonici,* 2:776–77.

10. On the Crown of Aragon, see Elena Lourie, "Anatomy of Ambivalence: Muslims

Under the Crown of Aragon in the Late Thirteenth Century," in Lourie, *Crusade and Colonisation* (Aldershot: Variorum, 1990), 52; David Nirenberg, *Communities of Violence: Persecution of Minorities in the Middle Ages* (Princeton: Princeton University Press, 1996). On Castile, see O'Callaghan, "Mudejars of Castile and Portugal," in Powell, ed., *Muslims Under Latin Rule*, 44.

11. Lateran IV, canon 69.

12. "Christianae religionis decorem tali commixtione confudant," Lateran IV, canon 70.

13. Lateran III, canon 26, in *Concilia oecumenicorum decreta*, p. 223. This canon is reiterated in X, 5:6:5, in *Corpus iuris canonici*, 2:773.

14. James Powell, *Anatomy of a Crusade, 1213–1221* (Philadelphia: University of Pennsylvania Press, 1986); Sayers, *Innocent III*, 164–72.

15. On Jacques de Vitry, see Henri Platelle, "Jacques de Vitry," DS 8:60–62; Cole, *Preaching of the Crusades*, 132–38; Carolyn Muessig, "Jacques de Vitry," in John Friedman and Kristen Figg, eds, *Trade, Travel and Exploration in the Middle Ages: An Encyclopedia* (New York: Garland, 2000), 298–99. On his preaching to the Muslims, cf. Kedar, *Crusade and Mission*, 116–29. His sermons are listed and described by Johannes Schneyer, *Repertorium der lateinischen Sermones des Mittelalters*, 9 vols. (Westfalen: Ascendorff, 1969–79), 3:179–221. On Oliver, see Anna-Dorothee von den Brincken, "Islam und Oriens Christianus in den Schriften des Kölner Domscholasters Oliver (+1227)," in Zimmerman and Craemer-Ruegenberg, eds., *Orientalische Kultur und europäisches Mittelalter*, 86–102; J. van Moolenbroek, "Signs in the Heavens in Groningen and Friesland in 1214: Oliver of Cologne and Crusading Propaganda," *Journal of Medieval History* 13 (1987):251–72; Cole, *Preaching of the Crusades*, 128–32.

16. See above, chap. 6.

17. Jacques de Vitry, *Historia orientalis*, ed. F. Moschus (Douai, 1597; reprint Westmead, 1971), §15; *Lettres de Jaques de Vitry 1160/70–1240, évêque de Saint-Jean d'Acre*, ed. R. B. C. Huygens (Leiden: Brill, 1960, 2000), §5:5–43.

18. Jacques de Vitry, *Lettres*, 2:390–94.

19. Jacques de Vitry, *Lettres*, 2:223–29.

20. Jacques de Vitry, *Lettres*, 4:173–77.

21. "Credo autem, sicut multorum relatione didici, quod fere tot sunt chrisitiani inter Sarracenos, quot sunt Sarraceni, qui cotidie cum lacrimis dei expectant auxilium et peregrinorum succursum," Jacques de Vitry, *Lettres* 2:245–49. Later in the same letter, the number of Christians has increased: "Credo autem quod christiani habitantes plures sunt numero quam Sarraceni," (2:397–98). In Egypt, too, he says, there are more Christians than Saracens (4:49).

22. Ps. 106 [Vulgate 107]:16; Ps. 46 [Vulgate 47]:3.

23. Jacques de Vitry, *Lettres* 7:500–504.

24. Oliver of Paderborn, *Historia damiatina*, in *Die Schriften des Kölner Domscholasters, spätern Bischofs von Paderborn und Kardinal-Bischofs von S. Sabina Oliverus*, ed. O. Hoogeweg, *Bibliothek des litterarischen Vereins in Stuttgart* 202 (1894), §35, here quoted from the English translation by John J. Gavigan, *The Capture of Damietta* (Philadelphia: University of Pennsylvania Press, 1948; reprint New York, 1980), 89–90.

25. See Tolan, "Un cadavre mutilé," 66–67.

26. Jacques de Vitry, *Lettres*, 7:534–560; cf. Oliver of Paderborn, *Historia damiatina*, §55–56.

27. Jacques de Vitry, *Lettres*, 7:205–10; cf. Oliver of Paderborn, *Historia damiatina*, §55–56.

28. Jacques de Vitry, *Lettres*, 7:472–82; the text is at 7:218–471; see Jean Richard,"The Mongols and Franks," *Journal of Asian History* 3 (1969):45–57, reprinted in J. Richard, *Orient et Occident au Moyen Age: contacts et relations, XIIe–XVe s.* (London: Variorum, 1976), esp. 45; Richard, "L'Extrême-Orient légendaire au moyen-âge: Roi David et Prêtre Jean," *Annales d'Ethiopie* 2 (1957):225–42, reprinted in J. Richard, *Orient et Occident au Moyen Age*, esp. 228, 230; François de Medeiros *L'Occident et l'Afrique*, 193–203; Charles Beckingham and Bernard Hamilton, eds. *Prester John, the Mongols,and the Ten Lost Tribes* (Aldershot: Variorum, 1996); Powell, *Anatomy*, 178–80.

29. Francis's mission is discussed below, chap. 9.

30. Oliver of Paderborn, *Epistola* 5 (in *Schriften*, 296–307), esp. 296, 300; on this letter, see Brincken, "Islam und Oriens Christianus."

31. Oliver, *Epistola* 5 (p. 297), citing Ps. 66:8 ("Benedicat nos Deus, Deus, Deus noster").

32. Oliver, *Epistola* 5 (p. 298); he later (p. 303) says that some people claim that 'Umar had rebuilt Solomon's temple, while others say it was Saint Helen or Heraclius.

33. Oliver, *Epistola* 6 (*Schriften*, 307–14).

34. Oliver, *Epistola* 5 (pp. 298–99).

35. See Tolan, "Le Baptême du Roi 'Païen' dans les Épopées de la Croisade," *Revue de l'Histoire des Religions* 216 (2000); Tolan, "Mirror of Chivalry: Salâh al-Dîn in the Medieval European Imagination," in *Images of the Other: Europe and the Muslim World before 1700, Cairo Papers on Social Science* 19:2 (summer 1996):7-38.

36. James Muldoon, *Popes, Lawyers, and Infidels: The Church and the Non-Christian World, 1250–1550* (Philadelphia: University of Pennsylvania Press, 1979), 40.

37. These letters are translated by Christopher Dawson, *Mission to Asia* (New York: Harper and Row, 1966; reprint Toronto: University of Toronto Press, 1980), 73–76; see James Muldoon, "The Nature of the Infidel: The Anthropology of the Canon Lawyers," in Scott Westrem, ed., *Discovering New Worlds: Essays on Medieval Exploration and Imagination* (New York: Garland, 1991), 115–24, esp. 117–21.

38. Jean de Joinville, *Vie de Saint Louis*, ed. J. Monfrin (Paris: Garnier, 1995), §133–35, 471–92; trans. (into English) M. Shaw, *Chronicles of the Crusades* (London: Penguin, 1963), 161–353. William of Rubruck's mission is discussed below, chap. 9.

39. Muldoon, *Popes, Lawyers, and Infidels*, 62.

40. Adam Knobler, "Pseudo-Conversions and Patchwork Pedigrees: The Christianization of Muslim Princes and the Diplomacy of Holy War," *Journal of World History* 7 (1996):181–96.

41. See Joachim Lavajo, "The Apologetical Method of Ramon Marti, according to the Problematic of Ramon Lull," *Islamochristiana* 11 (1985):155–76, esp. 172–73.

42. Ronald Messier, "The Christian Community of Tunis at the Time of St. Louis'

Crusade," in Vladimir Goss and Chrsitine V. Bornstein, eds., *The Meeting of Two Worlds: Cultural Exchange between East and West during the Period of the Crusades* (Kalamazoo, 1986), 241–55; Jacques Le Goff, *Saint Louis* (Paris: Gallimard, 1996), 290–96; A. Berthier, "Les écoles de langues orientales fondées au XIIIème siècle par les Dominicains en Espagne et en Afrique," *Revue Africaine* 73 (1932):84–103 (esp. 93ff). Ramon Martí's missionary efforts are discussed below, chap. 9.

43. William of Tripoli, *Notitia de Machometo*, §6.

44. William of Tripoli, *Notitia de Machometo*, §15, p. 260.

45. See Peter Engels's introduction to William of Tripoli, *Notitia de Machometo*, 52–74. On the dating of the text, see 53–54; [pseudo-]William of Tripoli, *De statu Sarracenorum*, §21, in William of Tripoli [Wilhelm von Tripolis], *Notitia de Machometo; De statu Sarracenorum*, p. 328.

46. [pseudo-]William of Tripoli, *De statu Sarracenorum*, §14, pp. 302–4.

47. [pseudo-]William of Tripoli, *De statu Sarracenorum*, §48, p. 360.

48. William of Tripoli, *Notitia de Machometo*, §1, p. 196; [pseudo-]William of Tripoli, *De statu Sarracenorum*, §1, p. 268

49. [pseudo-]William of Tripoli, *De statu Sarracenorum*, §2, p. 270.

50. William of Tripoli, *Notitia de Machometo*, §2, p. 198; [pseudo-]William of Tripoli, *De statu Sarracenorum*, §2, p. 270–72.

51. [pseudo-]William of Tripoli, *De statu Sarracenorum*, §3, p. 274. Muhammad's rise to power is portrayed in a more negative light by William of Tripoli, *Notitia de Machometo*, §2, p. 196–200.

52. William of Tripoli, *Notitia de Machometo*, §3, p. 202; [pseudo-]William of Tripoli, *De statu Sarracenorum*, §3, p. 276.

53. The main historical source for the author of *De statu Sarracenorum* seems to be either the annals of Eutychios or William of Tyre's *Gesta orientalium principum*; see Engels's introduction to William of Tripoli, *Notitia de Machometo*, 89–99.

54. [pseudo-]William of Tripoli, *De statu Sarracenorum*, §9, pp. 288–90.

55. He says that Frederick "dolose et fraudulenter factus est ita eorum amicus, quod ipsum crederent esse Sarracenum potius quam christianum," and goes on to describe how he tricked them into abandoning their strongholds in the Sicilian hills in exchange for the town of Lucera, ([pseudo-]William of Tripoli, *De statu Sarracenorum*, §15, p. 308). Various Christian authors accused Frederick of being more Saracen than Christian, but *De statu* is the only text I know of that accuses him of pretending to be so in order to swindle the Saracens.

56. [pseudo-]William of Tripoli, *De statu Sarracenorum*, §23, pp. 330–34.

57. [pseudo-]William of Tripoli, *De statu Sarracenorum*, §11, p. 296. The author comes back to the capture of Baghdad at §14 (pp. 302–4), where he describes Hülägü's slaughter of the caliph's family before his eyes: "Ante cuius oculos interfici fecit uxores et concubinas, filios et filias et omnes propinquos, de quibus videbatur, quod spes posteriraris posset oriri, ut in radice arboris succisa Machometi in illa civitate non remaneret successor in aeternum."

58. [pseudo-]William of Tripoli, *De statu Sarracenorum*, §17, pp. 314–16.

59. [pseudo-]William of Tripoli, *De statu Sarracenorum,* §18, pp. 318–22.

60. [pseudo-]William of Tripoli, *De statu Sarracenorum,* §22, p. 330.

61. [pseudo-]William of Tripoli, *De statu Sarracenorum,* §55, p. 370.

62. "Machometum dicunt nuncium Dei fuisse et ad se tantum a Deo missum. Hoc legi in Alcorano, qui est liber eorum," Burcardus de Monte Sionis, *Descriptio Terrae sanctae,* §15, ed. C. J. Lauren, in *Peregrinationes medii aevi Quatuor* (Leipzig: Akademie Verlag, 1864). On Burchard, see Aryeh Grabois, "Burchard of Mount Sion," in Friedman and Figg, eds, *Trade, Travel and Exploration,* 82–83; Grabois, "Christian Pilgrims in the Thirteenth Century and the Latin Kingdom of Jerusalem: Burchard of Mount Sion", in B. Kedar et al., eds, *Outremer: Studies in the History of the Crusading Kingdom of Jerusalem Presented to Joshua Prawer* (Jerusalem: Yad Izhak Ben-Zvi Institute, 1982), 285–96.

63. For example, Koran 14:4, "Each apostle We have sent has spoken only in the language of his own people, so that he might make plain to them his message."

64. The contrasting descriptions of Saracens and Latins are at Burcardus de Monte Sion, *Descriptio terrae sanctae,* chap. 33.

65. Fidentius of Padua, *Liber recuperationis terrae sanctae,* in Girolamo Golubovich, ed., *Biblioteca bio-bibliographica della terra santa e dell' oriente francescano,* 5 vols. (Quaracchi: Collegio di S. Bonaventura, 1906–27), 2:1–60.

66. Fidentius of Padua, *Liber Recuperationis Terrae Sanctae,* 13.

67. Fidentius of Padua, *Liber Recuperationis Terrae Sanctae,* 18.

68. Fidentius of Padua, *Liber Recuperationis Terrae Sanctae,* 16–19.

69. Fidentius of Padua, *Liber Recuperationis Terrae Sanctae,* 20–21.

70. William of Tripoli, 595; see above, chap. 7.

71. Fidentius of Padua, *Liber Recuperationis Terrae Sanctae,* 21.

72. Ritualized desecration of crosses and other Christian objects did indeed occur at times; for examples, see Carole Hillenbrand, *The Crusades: Islamic Perspectives* (Edinburgh: University of Edinburgh Press, 1999), 304–10.

73. During the fifth Crusade, a book by the same title was "discovered"; it predicted the events of the fifth Crusade and a similarly optimistic sequel; see above, p. 200.

74. Fidentius of Padua, *Liber Recuperationis Terrae Sanctae,* 26.

9. Franciscan Missionaries Seeking the Martyr's Palm

1. Jacques de Vitry, *Lettres,* 6:255–264b.

2. Jacques de Vitry, *Lettres,* 1:107–35, 6:242–255b.

3. Jacques de Vitry, *Historia occidentalis,* ed. J. F. Hinnesbusch (Fribourg: University Press, 1972), chap. 32.

4. Thomas of Celano, *Vita prima,* §55, Latin edition in *Analecta Francescana,* 10 (Florence, 1926), trans. (into English) Placid Hermann, *St. Francis of Assisi* (Chicago: Franciscan Herald Press, 1963).

5. On Francis's interview with al-Kâmil, see Martiniano Roncaglia, *I Francescani in oriente durante le crociate (sec. 8),* 4:1 of *Biblioteca bio-bibliografica della terra santa e*

dell' oriente francescano (Cairo, 1954), 21–26; Francis De Beer, "Saint François et l'Islam," *Concilium* 169 (1981):23–36; Kajetan Esser, "Das missionarische Anliegen des heiligen Franziskus," *Wissenschaft und Weisheit* 35 (1972):12–18; Giulio Basetti-Sani, *L'Islam Francesco d'Assisi: La missione profetica per il dialogo* (Florence: La Nuova Italia, 1975), 153–93. Different medieval accounts of their interview are printed together in Girolamo Golubovich, *Biblioteca bio-bibliografica della terra santa e dell' oriente francescano,* 5 vols. (Florence, 1906–13), 1:1ff. I am currently writing a book on Francis's encounter with al-Kâmil.

6. *Analecta Franciscana* 3 (Quaracchi, 1897), 21, cited by Esser, "Das missionarische Anliegen," 17.

7. Thomas of Celano, *Vita prima,* §57.

8. Thomas of Celano, *Vita prima,* §106.

9. These texts (along with those concerning the martyrs of 1227) are partially edited in AASS (January 16), 2: 426–35. Various medieval Franciscan chronicles recount the stories of the martyrs, notably the *Chronica Generalium ministrorum ordinis fratrum minorum* (in *Analecta francescana,* 3:15–33, 579–96, 613–16), which is dated to 1374 by G. Golubovich, *Biblioteca bio-bibliografica,* 1:65. See P. Streit and P. Didinger, *Bibliotheca missionum,* 15 (Freiburg, 1951); *Afrikanische Misssionsliteratur, 1053–1599,* 20–25; Aires Nascimento, "Lenda e livro *Dos milagres dos mártires de Marrocos,*" in G. Lanciani, ed., *Dicionário da literatura medieval galega e portuguesa* (Lisbon, 1993), 388–89; Maria Helena da Cruz Coelho, *Ócio e negócio* (Coimbra: Inatel, 1998), 103–10. Thanks to Stéphane Boissellier, Isabelle Heullant-Donat, and Maria Helena da Cruz Coelho for these references. On the fifteenth-century iconography of the martyrs, see Doris Carl, "Franziskanischer Märtyrerkult als Kreuzzugspropaganda an der Kanzel von Benedetto da Maiano in Santa Croce in Florenz," *Mitteilungen des Kunsthistorischen Institutes in Florenz* 39 (1995):69–91. On Franciscan mission in general, see E. R. Daniel, *The Franciscan Concept of Mission in the High Middle Ages* (Lexington: University of Kentucky Press, 1975).

10. Dieter Berg, "Kreuzzugsbewegung und Propagatio Fidei: Das Problem der Franziskanermission im 13. Jahrhundert und das Bild von der islamischen Welt in der zeitgenössischen Ordenshistoriographie," in Zimmerman and Craemer-Ruegenberg, eds., *Orientalische Kultur und europäisches Mittelalter,* 59–76 (esp. 73ff).

11. On the dating of the 1221 *Regula non bullata* and the 1223 *Regula bullata,* see *Fontes francescani,* 15–16.

12. Quotation from Armstrong and Brady, in Francis of Assisi, *Francis and Clare: The Complete Works,* 108n (hereinafter cited as Francis, *Complete Works*).

13. *Regula non bullata,* §16 (*Fontes Francescani,* 198–200); translation in Francis, *Complete Works,* 121; Matt. 10:16.

14. *Regula non bullata,* §16 (*Fontes Francescani,* 198–200). A much shorter version of this is found in the later Franciscan rule, the 1223 *Regula bullata,* §12 (*Fontes Francescani,* 180–81; translation in Francis, *Complete Works,* 144).

15. Honorius III addressed his bull *Vinee Domini custodes* to "dilectis filiis fratribus predicatoribus et minoribus in regno Miramolini," T. Ripoll and A. Bremond, eds.,

Bullarium ordinis fratrum praedicatorum, 8 vols. (Rome, 1729–49), 1:16; see Kedar, *Crusade and Mission,* 143–44.

16. Streit and Didinger, *Bibliotheca missionum,* 15:25–26; Roncaglia, *I Francescani in oriente,* 97. On the martyrs of Valencia, see above, chap. 7; Burns, *Islam Under the Crusaders,* 32–37.

17. Carl, "Franziskanischer Märtyrerkult als Kreuzzugspropaganda."

18. *Bullarium Franciscanum* 1 (Rome, 1759), 26; reedited with corrections by I. Vázquez Janeiro, "Conciencia eclesial e interpretación de la Regla franciscana," *Spicilegium Pontificii Athenaei Antoniani* 24 (Rome, 1983):27–28; see Vázquez Janeiro, "I Francescani e il dialogo con gli ebrei e saraceni nei secoli XIII–XV," *Antonianum* 65 (1990):533–49 (esp. 542–43).

19. Raymond de Penyafort, *Responsiones ad dubitabilia circa communicationem Christianorum cum Sarracenis,* in *Summae,* 3:1025–36; on this text, see Tolan, *Les Relations,* 164–68.

20. *Bullarium Franciscanum* 1:105ff; see Berg, "Kreuzzugsbewegung und Propagatio Fidei," 68.

21. Matthew Paris, *Chronica majora,* 3:343; trans. J. Giles, *English History from the Year 1235 to 1273,* (London, 1852; reprint New York, 1968), 14.

22. For the sources, see this chapter, note 9; AASS (October), 6:384-92. On the martyrs of 1227, see (in addition to the works noted above) A. Piazzoni, "Daniele, Santo," *Dizionario biografico degli Italiani* 32 (1986):588–89.

23. Burns, *Islam Under the Crusaders,* 32–37; Burns, "Almohad Prince and Mudejar Convert."

24. E. R. Daniel, "The Desire for Martyrdom: A *Leitmotiv* of St. Bonaventure," *Franciscan Studies* 32 (1972):74–87.

25. Bonaventure, *Legenda maior,* in *Analecta franciscana,* 10, §9:8.

26. "Contuebatur in pulchris Pulcherrimum et per impressa rebus vestigia posequabatur ubique Dilectum, de ominbus sibi scalam faciens, per quam conscenderet ad apprehendendum eum qui est desiderabilis totus," Bonaventure, *Legenda major,* 9:1.

27. Bonaventure, *Apologia pauperum,* in *Opera omnia,* 10 vols. (Florence, 1882–1902), 8:253, cited by Daniel, "Desire for Martyrdom," 84 n. 36.

28. "Bonaventure recognized that the desire for martyrdom was the primary motivation of the Franciscan missionaries," Daniel, "Desire for Martyrdom," 85.

29. Berg, "Kreuzzugsbewegung und Propagatio Fidei."

30. Messier, "The Christian Community of Tunis," 250.

31. From a sermon in British Library MS Harley 3221, f.197v; thanks to David D'Avray for providing this reference for me. On Servasanto, see C. Schmitt, "Servasanctus de Faenza," DS 14:671–72.

32. John of Piano Carpini, *Historia Mongolorum,* ed. Enrico Menesto, *Giovanni di Pian di Carpini: Storia dei Mongoli* (Spoleto: Centro Italiano de studi sull'alto Medioevo, 1989); English translation in Dawson, *Mission to Asia,* 3–72. On John of Piano Carpini, see Gregory Guzman, "John of Piano Carpini," in Friedman and Figg, eds., *Trade, Travel, and Exploration,* 307–9; Michèle Guéret-Laferté, *Sur les routes de l'Empire*

mongol: Ordre et rhetorique des relations de voyage au XIIIᵉ et XIVᵉ siècles (Paris: Honoré Champion, 1994).

33. William of Rubruck, *Itinerarium,* in A. van den Wyngaert, ed., *Sinica Franciscana 1* (Quaracchi: Collegio de S. Bonaventura, 1929), 164–332; English translation in Dawson, *Mission to Asia,* 89–220; trans. Peter Jackson, *The Mission of Friar William of Rubruck: His Journey to the Court of the Great Khan Möngke, 1253–1255* (London: Hakluyt Society, 1990). See also the sumptuously illustrated French translation with notes and commentary, Guillaume de Rubrouck, *Voyage dans l'Empire Mongol,* ed. and trans. Claude and René Kappler (Paris: Imprimerie Nationale, 1997). On William, see Charles Connell, "William of Rubruck," in Friedman and Figg, eds., *Trade, Travel, and Exploration,* 646–48; Guéret-Laferté, *Sur les routes de l'Empire mongol.*

34. As translated by Muldoon, *Popes, Lawyers, and Infidels,* 36–37.

35. Matthew Paris, *Chronica,* 4:345–46.

36. Guzman, "Reports of Mongol Cannibalism."

37. Joinville, *Vie de Saint Louis,* §133–35, 471–92 (discussed above, chap. 8).

38. William of Rubruck, *Itinerarium,* 293–97; the translations I give are from Dawson, *Mission to Asia,* 190–94 (with slight modifications).

39. On Bacon, see A. Crombie and J. North, "Bacon, Roger," *Dictionary of Scientific Biography 1* (1970), 377–85; Southern, *Western Views,* 52–61. It may well be Bacon's scientific ideas, particularly his astrology, that landed him in jail; see Paul Sidelko, "The Condemnation of Roger Bacon," *Journal of Medieval History* 22 (1996):69–81.

40. Roger Bacon, *Opus maius,* ed. J. Bridges, 3 vols. (London, 1900), 3:122, trans. Southern, *Western Views,* 57.

41. For example: "Christiani principes, qui laborant ad eorum [i.e., of the pagans] conversionem, et maxime fratres de domo teutonica, volunt eos reducere in servitutem, sicut certum est Predicatoribus et Minoribus et aliis viris bonis per totam Alemanniam et Poloniam, et ideo repugnant; unde contra violenciam resistunt, non ratione secte melioris," Bacon, *Opus maius pars septima seu moralis philosophia,* ed. Eugenio Massa (Turin, 1953), 200.

42. Kedar, *Crusade and Mission,* 178–79.

43. Bacon, *Opus maius,* 3:122.

44. Bacon, *Opus maius pars septima seu moralis philosophia,* 195–96; Gregory the Great, *Homilies on the Gospels* 2:26 (PL 76:1197).

45. Bacon, *Opus maius pars septima seu moralis philosophia,* 189.

46. Bacon, *Opus maius pars septima seu moralis philosophia,* 189–90; the astrological explanations are at 193–95.

47. Bacon, *Opus maius pars septima seu moralis philosophia,* 211, 221, 219.

48. Bacon, *Opus maius pars septima seu moralis philosophia,* 198.

49. Bacon, *Opus maius pars septima seu moralis philosophia,* 199–205, 213–14.

50. Bacon, *Opus maius pars septima seu moralis philosophia,* 214.

51. Bacon, *Opus maius pars septima seu moralis philosophia,* 205–11.

52. Bacon, *Opus maius pars septima seu moralis philosophia,* 214, where he refers to *Opus maius,* 1:187ff, 202ff, 222–24, 262ff.

53. Bacon, *Opus maius pars septima seu moralis philosophia,* 215.

54. Bacon, *Opus maius pars septima seu moralis philosophia,* 215–17.

55. Bacon, *Opus maius pars septima seu moralis philosophia,* 22–23, 206–7, 208, 215.

56. Bacon, *Opus maius pars septima seu moralis philosophia,* 208, 22.

57. Bacon, *Opus maius,* 1:266.

58. Golubovich, 2:70.

59. Thomas de Chobham, *Summa de arte praedicandi,* ed. F. Morenzoni, CCCM 82 (1988); on the dating of *Summa de arte praedicandi,* see Morenzoni's introduction (xxxvi–xxxviii). On Thomas and his *Summa,* see Franco Morenzoni, *Des Écoles aux paroisses: Thomas de Chobham et la promotion de la prédication au début du XIIIᵉ siècle* (Paris, 1995); A. Solignac, "Thomas de Chobham," DS 15:794–96.

60. Thomas de Chobham, *Summa de arte praedicandi,* 85–86.

61. Thomas de Chobham, *Summa de arte praedicandi,* 86.

62. Thomas de Chobham, *Summa de arte praedicandi,* 86.

10. The Dominican Missionary Strategy

1. Robles Sierra, "Raymond de Penyafort," DS 86:190; Laureano Robles, *Escritores dominicos de la Corona de Aragon, siglos XIII–XV* (Salamanca: Universidad de Salamanca, 1972), 13–57; José María Coll, "San Raymundo de Peñafort y las misiones del norte africano en la edad media," *Missionalia hispanica* 5 (1948):417–57.

2. See above, chap. 7.

3. Chronicler Pere Marsili asserts that Martí was a "Magnus Rabinus in Hebraeo," which some have taken to mean that he was a convert from Judaism and perhaps a former rabbi, though Jeremy Cohen (*The Friars and the Jews: The Evolution of Medieval Anti-Judaism* [Ithaca: Cornell University Press, 1982], 130n) argues convincingly that this is unlikely, and that "magnus Rabinus" means simply "a great teacher of Hebrew."

4. The document does not say *where* the school was established, though recent scholarship suggests either Mallorca or Tunis. Eusebio Colomer ("La controversia islamo-judeo-cristiana en la obra apologética de Ramón Martí," in Santiago Otero, ed., *Diálogo filosófico-religioso,* 229–57, esp. 233–37) discusses the reasons for this and opts for Tunis as the most probable site. See A. Berthier, "Les Écoles de langues orientales fondées aux XIIIᵉ siècle par les Dominicains en Espagne et en Afrique," *Revue Africaine* 73 (1932):84–103.

5. On Ramon Martí's knowledge and use of Arabic texts of philosophy, see Angel Cortabarría Beitia, "La connaissance de l'Islam chez Raymond Lulle et Raymond Martin O.P.: Parallèle," *Cahiers de Fanjeaux* 22 (1987), *Raymonde Lulle et le Pays d'Oc,* 33–55; Cortabarría, "La connaissance des textes arabes chez Raymond Martin, O.P. et sa position en face de l'Islam," *Cahiers de Fanjeaux* 18 (1983), *Islam et Chrétiens du Midi,* 279–324; Cortabarría, "Fuentes árabes del *Pugio fidei* de Ramón Martí," *Ciencia tomista* 112 (1985):581–98; Angel Rodriguez Bachiller, *Influencia de la filosofia árabe en el Pugio de Raimundo Martí* (Madrid: Casa Hispano-Arabe, 1969). An Arabic-Latin glossary of the thirteenth century was attributed to Martí, though it is unclear if it was in fact his (see

Richard, "L'Enseignement des langues orientales," 164n). On his knowledge of Hebrew and the Talmud, see Cohen, *Friars and the Jews*, 129–69; Robert Chazan, *Daggers of Faith: Thirteenth-Century Christian Missionizing and Jewish Response* (Berkeley: University of California Press, 1989), 115–36. On his polemical works, see Joachim Lavajo, "Cristianismo e Islamismo na peninsula iberica: Raimundo Martí, um precursor do diálogo religioso," doctoral diss., University of Evora, Portugal, 1988; Josep Hernando i Delgado, "De nuevo sobre la obra antiislámica attribuida a Ramón Martí, dominico catalán des siglo XIII," *Sharq-al-Andalus* 8 (1991):97–108; Hernando i Delgado, "Le 'De seta Machometi' du cod. 46 d'Osma, oeuvre de Raymond Martin (Ramón Martí)," *Cahiers de Fanjeaux* 18 (1983):351–71; Tolan, "Rhetoric, Polemics, and the Art of Hostile Biography." A useful introductory survey of Martí's life and works is found in the pious biography by Robles Sierra, *Fray Ramon Martí de Subirats, O.P., y el diálogo misional en el siglo XIII* (Caleruega, 1986). For more bibliography on Martí, see Horacio Santiago Otero and Klaus Reinhardt, *Biblioteca bíblica ibérica medieval* (Madrid: Consejo Superior de Investigacions Cientificas, 1986), 297–302; Robles, *Escritores dominicos de la Corona de Aragon*, 68–77.

6. See Chazan, *Barcelona and Beyond;* Robles, *Escritores dominicos de la Corona de Aragon*, 66–67.

7. Despite the full title often attributed to Martí's work (*Pugio fidei adversus Mauros et Judaeos*) there is very little anti-Islamic argumentation here. The work falls into three parts, the first of which is directed against philosophical objections to revealed monotheistic religion; it seems directed against intellectual opponents in Paris (the so-called Latin Averroists), not against Jews or Muslims. Part 2 attempts to show that the Messiah has come, and part 3 attempts to prove the Trinity; these arguments are directed against Jews. On the *Pugio fidei*, see Cohen, *Friars and the Jews*, 129–69; Chazan, *Daggers of Faith*, 115–36.

8. According to Cohen (*Friars and Jews*, 127), Pablo Cristiá staged at least two or three other debates with prominent Jews.

9. P. Sjoerd van Koningsveld and G. A. Wiegers, "The Polemical Works of Muhammad al-Qaysî (fl. 1309) and their Circulation in Arabic and Aljmiado among the Mudejars in the Fourteenth Century," *Al-Qantara: Revista de estudios árabes* 15 (1994):163–99.

10. Ramon Martí, *De seta machometi o De origine, progressu, et fine Machometi et quadruplici reprobatione prophetiae eius*, ed. and trans. (into Spanish) Josep Hernando i Delgado, *Acta historica et archaeologica medievalia* 4 (1983):9–51. Under the title of *Quadruplex reprobatio* this work has been falsely attributed to John of Wales; it was partially edited in Strasbourg in 1550 by W. Dreschsler as *Galensis de origine et progressu Machometis*. Hernando i Delgado ("Le 'De seta Machometi' du cod. 46 d'Osma") has shown that it is indeed a work of Ramon Martí; see also his "De nuevo sobre la obra antiislámica attribuida a Ramón Martí."

11. Ramon Martí, *De seta Machometi*, 52–54.

12. Ramon Martí cites Ibn Ishâq's *Sira* as "libro qui vocatur *Ciar*, id. est, *Actus Machometi*" (*De seta Machometi*, 18; he cites it several times subsequently), al-Bukhâri as *Bochari* (first time at 20), and Muslim as *Moslim* (20). In the latter two cases, as Her-

nando notes (21n), Martí mistakenly presents the authors' names as the titles of their tracts.

13. Ramon Martí, *De seta Machometi*, 41.

14. Ramon Martí, *De seta Machometi*, 26.

15. Ramon Martí, *De seta Machometi*, 34.

16. Roth, *Jews, Visigoths, and Muslims in Medieval Spain*, 220.

17. Ramon Martí, *De seta Machometi*, 36–38; Koran 17:92–93. This scene is discussed above, chap. 2.

18. Ramon Martí, *De seta Machometi*, 44.

19. Ramon Martí, *De seta Machometi*, 44–48.

20. Ramon Martí, *De seta Machometi*, 48.

21. Ramon Martí, *De seta Machometi*, 52.

22. Thanks to Gretchen Starr-Lebeau for suggesting this contrast.

23. Ramon Martí, *De seta Machometi*, 52–63.

24. Ramon Martí, *De seta Machometi*, 52–62; *Explanatio simboli Apostolorum*, ed. J. March y Battles, "En Ramon Martí y la seva *Explanatio simboli Apostolorum*," in *Annuari de l'Institut d'Estudis Catalans* (1908):443–96 (here 452–55); for a comparison of the two sections, see Hernando, "La *De seta Machometi*," 360–63.

25. Hillgarth, *Ramon Lull*, 21–22; Joachim Lavajo, "The Apologetical Method of Ramon Marti, According to the Problematic of Ramon Lull," *Islamochristiana* 11 (1985): 155–76; the "king" in question is Abû 'Abdallah Muhammad I al-Mustansir.

26. Ramon Martí, *Explanatio symboli Apostolorum*, 491.

27. Ramon Martí, *Explanatio symboli Apostolorum*, 493.

28. Ramon Martí, *Explanatio symboli Apostolorum*, 493; he is citing Ibn Sînâ's *Al-Llâhiyyât*, according to Cortabarría, "La connaissance," 281.

29. Ramon Martí, *Explanatio symboli Apostolorum*, 494; Cortabarría, "La connaissance," 280–84.

30. N. Eymeric in *Raymundiana seu documenta quae pertinent ad S. Raymundi de Pennaforti vitam et scripta*, F. Balme, C. Paban, and J. Collomb, eds., MOFPH 4:1 (1898), and 4:2 (1901) (here 4:2, 82); see Burns, "Journey from Islam," 346.

31. Missionary strategy became a subject of some debate among Franciscans of the mid-thirteenth century, with some of them professing a more intellectual "Dominican" approach to mission. See Berg, "Kreuzzugsbewegung und Propagatio Fidei," 67.

32. Burns, *Muslims, Christians, and Jews*, 94.

33. See Cohen, *Friars and the Jews*, 104–6, 129; Anthony Bonner's comments in Ramon Llull, *Doctor Illuminatus: A Ramon Llull Reader* (Princeton: Princeton University Press, 1993), 75–76.

34. This hypothesis has caused some debate; Burns argues convincingly in its favor (*Muslims, Christians, and Jews*, 100–101).

35. Thomas Aquinas, *Summa contra gentiles*, trans. by English Dominican Friars (London: Burns, Oates, and Washbourne, 1924), 1:6; on this passage, see James Waltz, "Muhammad and the Muslims in St. Thomas Aquinas," *Muslim World* 66 (1976):81–95.

36. Thomas Aquinas, *De rationibus fidei contra Saracenos, Graecos et Armenos ad*

Cantorem Antiochenum: Reasons for the Faith against the Muslims (and one Objection of the Greeks and Armenians) to the Cantor of Antioch, trans. Joseph Kenney, *Islamochristiana* 22 (1996):31–52, §3, 33.

37. Aquinas, *De rationibus fidei,* §2, trans. Kenney, p. 33.

38. For Riccoldo's biography, see Emilio Panella, "Ricerche su Riccoldo da Monte di Croce," *Archivum Fratrum Praedicatorum* 58 (1988):5–85.

39. Riccoldo da Montecroce, *Liber peregrinationis,* in *Pérégrination. en terre sainte et au Proche Orient et lettres sur la chute de Saint-Jean d'Acre,* Latin edition and French translation by René Kappler (Paris: Honoré Champion, 1997) 118–19 (following Kappler's reading of *turgemanum* [interpreter] for the manuscript's *turchimannum*).

40. Riccoldo, *Letter* 3, p. 284; Riccoldo, *Liber peregrinationis,* 160.

41. See Jensen, introduction to Riccoldo, *Libelli ad nationes orientales,* electronic edition of Latin text with introduction by Kurt Jensen (http://www.ou.dk/hum/kvj/riccoldo/).

42. Riccoldo, *Letter* 3, p. 286.

43. "Tolle, lege!" with obvious reference to the well-known passage in Augustine's *Confessions* (8:12).

44. Riccoldo, *Liber peregrinationis,* 154–56.

45. Riccoldo, *Liber peregrinationis,* 172.

46. Riccoldo, *Liber peregrinationis,* 172.

47. Riccoldo, *Liber peregrinationis,* 186–88.

48. Riccoldo, *Liber peregrinationis,* 192.

49. Riccoldo, *Liber peregrinationis,* 192; Riccoldo, *Libellus contra legem Saracenorum,* in J. Mérigoux, ed., *Memorie domenicane,* n.s. 17 (1986):1–144, §11, 112. As Mérigoux notes (112 n. 20), the *Khatîb* sometimes holds a stick or lance while he pronounces the *khutba;* see J. Pedersen, "Khatîb," EI² 4:1141. William of Tripoli says that the Saracens' "Ravi, cum predicant legem, ensem sive gladiium tenent in manibus suis in signum terroris" (William of Tripoli, *Notitia de Machometo,* §14, p. 254; cf. §15, p. 258).

50. Riccoldo, *Liber peregrinationis,* 198–200.

51. On his use of sources, see Mérigoux's introduction to Riccoldo, *Contra legem Sarracenorum,* pp. 27–33.

52. Riccoldo, *Contra legem Sarracenorum,* chap. 1, p. 63.

53. Riccoldo, *Contra legem Sarracenorum,* chap. 2, p. 68.

54. Riccoldo, *Contra legem Sarracenorum,* chap. 2, p. 68.

55. Riccoldo, *Contra legem Sarracenorum,* chap. 2, p. 68.

56. Riccoldo, *Contra legem Sarracenorum,* chap. 4.

57. Riccoldo, *Contra legem Sarracenorum,* chap. 14.

58. Riccoldo, *Contra legem Sarracenorum,* chap. 13, p. 117.

59. Riccoldo, *Contra legem Sarracenorum,* chap. 3, p. 75.

60. Riccoldo, *Contra legem Sarracenorum,* chap. 13, p. 121. The Nizamiyya madrasa was founded by the caliph Nizâm al-Mulk in 1067; the Mustansiriyya madrasa by the caliph al-Mustansir bi'llâh in 1233. Neither of these caliphs prohibited the study of philosophy. See Mérigoux's commentary on p. 121.

61. Riccoldo, *Contra legem Sarracenorum*, chap. 15.

62. Riccoldo, *Contra legem Sarracenorum*, chap. 15, p. 125.

63. On the disillusionment with and abandonment of the Dominican strategy of anti-Jewish missionizing, see Chazan, *Daggers of Faith*, 159–81.

64. Klaus Reinhardt, "Un musulmán y un judío prueban la verdad de la fe cristiana: la disputa entre Abutalib de Ceuta y Samuel de Toledo," in Santiago Otero, ed., *Diálogo filosófico-religioso*, 191–212. On Alfonso Buenhombre, see Robles, *Escritores dominicos de la Corona de Aragon*, 120–35.

65. The hoax was exposed by Reinhardt, "Un musulmán y un judío," who makes a very convincing case for Alfonso's authorship; in contrast J. R. Díez Atoñanzas and J. I. Saranyana in the same volume make a rather weak case for attributing four of the seven letters to the eleventh-century Toledan author Samuel el Marroquí.

66. Ora Limor, "The Epistle of Rabbi Samuel of Morocco: A Best-Seller in the World of Polemics," in Limor and Strousma, eds., *Contra Iudaeos: Ancient and Medieval Polemics between Christians and Jews* (Tübingen: J. C. B. Mohr, 1996), 177–94.

11. From Verdant Grove to Dark Prison: Realms of Mission in Ramon Llull

1. Jocelyn Hillgarth, *Ramon Lull and Lullism in Fourteenth-Century France* (Oxford: Oxford University Press, 1971), 21–22; Lavajo, "The Apologetical Method of Raymond Marti"; Cortabarría, "Connaissance de l'Islam chez Raymond Lulle et Raymond Martin."

2. Lavajo, "The Apologetical Method of Raymond Marti," 159.

3. "Sarraceni bene litterati non credunt vere quod Machometus sit propheta. Nam in alcoranus, in quo est lex eorum, inueniunt multa inconuenientia contra sanctitatem et veram prophetiam," Llull, *De acquisitione Terre Sancte*, quoted by Pamela Drost Beattie, " 'Pro exaltatione sanctae fidei catholicae': Mission and Crusade in the Writings of Ramon Llull," in Simon, ed., *Iberia and the Mediterranean World*, 113–29 (quotation at 119n). "Aquells sarrahins qui han soptil enteniment no creen que Mafumet sia profeta." Llull, *Doctrina pueril, Obres doctrinals* 1 (Palma, 1906), 127.

4. Anthony Bonner gives a translation of the *Vita coaetanea* with detailed notes and commentary filling out the missing gaps in Llull's biography (Llull, *Doctor Illuminatus*). Among the valuable recent analyses of the *Vita coaetanea*, see especially Dominique de Courcelles, *La parole risquée de Raymond Lulle* (Paris: Vrin, 1993), 77–116; Valérie Galent-Fasseur, "Dieu, soi-même et l'autre: L'énergétique de la conversion dans la *Vita coaetanea* de Ramon Llull," *Wodan: Greifswalder Beiträge zum Mittelalter* 74 (1997): 35–45.

5. Llull, *Vita coaetanea, Opera latina* 8 (CCCM 34), 274–76, trans. Bonner, Llull, *Doctor Illuminatus*, 13.

6. Llull, *Vita coaetanea, Opera latina* 8 (CCCM 34), 277, trans. Bonner, Llull, *Doctor Illuminatus*, 14.

7. Llull, *Vita coaetanea, Opera latina* 8 (CCCM 34), 279, trans. Bonner, Llull, *Doctor Illuminatus*, 16–17.

8. Llull, *Vita coaetanea, Opera latina* 8 (CCCM 34), 280, trans. Bonner, Llull, *Doctor Illuminatus*, 17–18.

9. Courcelles, *Parole risquée*, 93–95.

10. Llull, *Vita coaetanea, Opera latina* 8 (CCCM 34), 281, trans. Bonner, Llull, *Doctor Illuminatus*, 18.

11. Llull, *Vita coaetanea, Opera latina* 8 (CCCM 34), 291, trans. Bonner, Llull, *Doctor Illuminatus*, 29.

12. "Et ideo ego, qui sum verus Catholicus, non intendo probare Articulos contra Fidem, sed mediante Fide," *Liber de convenientia fidei et intellectus in objecto,* cited by Thomas Burman, "The Influence of the *Apology of al-Kindî* and *Contrarietas alfolica* on Ramon Lull's Late Religious Polemics, 1305–1313," *Medieval Studies* 53 (1991):197–228 (citation at 216 n. 97).

13. Llull, *Llibre de contemplació en Déu,* trans. in Kedar, *Crusade and Mission,* 190–91.

14. Kedar, *Crusade and Mission,* 191; Mark Johnston, "Ramon Llull and the Compulsory Evangelization of Jews and Muslims," in Simon, ed., *Iberia and the Mediterranean World,* 3–37.

15. Kedar, *Crusade and Mission,* 189–99.

16. For an introduction to Llull's elaboration of the *Art* and to the vast bibliography surrounding it, see Mark Johnston, *The Evangelical Rhetoric of Ramon Llull* (Oxford: Oxford University Press, 1996), esp. chap. 1, "Ramon Llull's Art of Arts" ; Bonner, "Llull's Thought," in Llull, *Doctor Illuminatus,* 45–56; Armand Llinares, "Raymond Lulle à Montpellier: La refonte du 'Grand Art,'" in *Raymond Lulle et le Pays d'Oc, Cahiers de Fanjeaux* 22 (1987):17–32.

17. Vicente Servera, "Utopie et histoire: Les postulats théoriques de la praxis missionnaire," in *Raymond Lulle et le Pays d'Oc, Cahiers de Fanjeaux* 22 (1987):191–229.

18. According to Colomer ("Raimund Lulls Stellung zu den Andersgläubigen," in Lewis and Niewohner, eds., *Religionsgespräche im Mittelalter,* 217–36), Llull composed the tract in 1271–72, first in Arabic, then in Catalan. For Llinares and Bonner, he composed it between 1274 and 1276 (Armand Llinares, introduction to his French translation of Ramon Llull, *Le livre du gentil et des trois sages* [Paris: Cerf, 1993], 7 n. 1; trans. Bonner, Llull, *Doctor Illuminatus,* 81).

19. See above, chap. 3 (for Abû Qurrah) and chap. 5 (for Abelard).

20. Llull, *Libre del gentil e los tres savis,* prologue; trans. Bonner, Llull, *Doctor Illuminatus,* 90.

21. On Llull's use of "necessary reasons," see Sebastián Garcías Palou, "Las rationes necessariae del Bto. Ramón Llull, en los documentos presentados por él mismo, a la Sede Romana," *Estudios Lulianos* 6 (1962):311–25.

22. The only other example I know of a disputation that does not end in the conversion of the adversary is Abelard, *Dialogus philosophi cum Iudeo et Christiano;* on this text, see Von Moos, "Les collations d'Abélard."

23. This is the conclusion reached by J. Cohen in his analysis of book 2 of the *Libre del gentil* (Cohen, *The Friars and the Jews,* 205–14).

24. Llull, *Libre del gentil e los tres savis* book 4; trans. Bonner, Llull, *Doctor Illuminatus*, 160.

25. See Courcelles, *Parole risquée*, 160–65.

26. Llull, *Liber de fine*, CCCM 35:267 (cf. 286–87). He presents the *Libre del gentil* similarly in various other works; see Llinares, introduction to his translation of the *Libre del gentil*, 39–45.

27. See Hillgarth, *Ramon Lull*, 73–74; W. Barthold and J. Boyle, "Ghâzân, Mahmûd," EI² 2:1043.

28. Llull, *Liber de fine*, CCCM 35:272, 279, 290.

29. Llull, *Liber de fine*, CCCM 35:250.

30. Llull, *Liber de fine*, CCCM 35:251.

31. Similarly, in his *Phantasticus*, Llull has his cleric say "uideo complures praedicatores, ut fratres minores et alios religiosos, ad praedicandum saracenis, tartaris et aliis infidelibus se committere, sed paruus eorum adhuc, quem faciant, apparet fructus" (Llull, *Phantasticus*, CCCM 78:29).

32. Llull, *Liber de fine*, CCCM 35:252–55.

33. Llull, *Liber de fine*, CCCM 35:256.

34. Llull, *Liber de fine*, CCCM 35:257.

35. Llull, *Liber de fine*, CCCM 35:266. Llull is in fact describing the scenario of one of his own works, the *Liber de quinque sapientibus*, where a Muslim comes to doubt Islam because of his reading in philosophy and wishes to become Christian; he affirms that many other Muslims will be ready to follow him, if only the Christians could agree among themselves.

36. Llull, *Liber de fine*, CCCM 35:267.

37. Llull, *Liber de fine*, CCCM 35:255. On his use of the same passage from Luke in his *Liber phantasticus*, see below, n. 43.

38. Llull, *Liber de fine*, CCCM 35:272–73.

39. Another candidate at one point was perhaps French king Philippe IV le Bel; see Hillgarth, *Ramon Lull*, 66.

40. Llull, *Liber de fine*, CCCM 35:271. Llull gives a rule for this new order at 273–75. In his *Phantasticus*, Llull also warns that the cardinals, Pope, and other participants of the 1311 Council of Vienne should follow Llull's advice if they fear for judgment day (Llull, *Phantasticus*, CCCM 78:29).

41. Llull, *Liber de fine*, CCCM 35:276–77. In later works, written in Paris and dedicated to Philippe IV le Bel, Llull advocates a two-pronged attack, against Spain and the East; see Hillgarth, *Ramon Lull*, 69–70, 84ff.

42. "Quod si bene uelint auertere, facile multum est ad probandum per unum librum, qui uocatur Alquindi, et per alium, qui Telif nominatur, et per alium, quem fecimus de Gentili," Llull, *Liber de fine*, CCCM 35:283. On this passage and on the identification of these three texts, see Charles Lohr, "Ramon Llull, Liber Alquindi and Liber Telif," and Burman, "The Influence of the *Apology of al-Kindî*."

43. In his *Phantasticus*, Llull specifies that the two swords of Luke 22:38 refer to

preaching and war against infidels. The church is to use the spiritual sword of preaching in priority, "deinde si resisterent, tunc papa contra ipsos procurare deberet gladium saecularem." (Llull, *Phantasticus*, CCCM 78:28).

44. This is convincingly argued by Burman, "The Influence of the *Apology of al-Kindî*."

45. Llull, *Liber de predicatione contra Iudaeos*, 1305, CCCM 38. On this work, see Johnston, *Evangelical Rhetoric*; Burman, "The Influence of the *Apology of al-Kindî*."

46. Johnston, "Compulsory Evangelization," 21–24.

47. The analysis that follows is based largely on Burman, "The Influence of the *Apology of al-Kindî*"; see also Cohen, *The Friars and the Jews*, 214–23.

48. Llull, *Liber de participatione Christianorum et Saracenorum* CCCM 78:246.

49. As A. Oliver and M. Senellart remark (in their introduction to Llull, *Liber de participatione Christianorum et Saracenorum*, CCCM 78:239), Ibn al-Lihiqny, had come to power with the help of Catalan and Sicilian naval power; he had good relations with Frederic III and it was rumored that he might be ready to convert to Christianity. See Hillgarth, *Ramon Lull*, 129–32.

50. Llull, *Liber de participatione*, CCCM 78:260.

51. Hillgarth, *Ramon Lull*, 129–32.

52. Llull, *Liber de fine*, CCCM 35:289.

53. He expounds the three points of his intervention at the council in Llull, *Phantasticus* (also known as *Liber disputationis Petri et Raimundi*), CCCM 78:14.

54. Llull, *Phantasticus*, CCCM 78:14.

55. Llull, *Phantasticus*, CCCM 78:17–18.

Conclusion

1. Martin Luther, letter dated 27 October 1542, published in Karl Hagenbach, "Luther und der Koran vor dem Rate zu Basel," *Beiträge zur vaterländischen Geschichte* 9 (1870): 291–326, cited by Kritzeck, *Peter the Venerable and Islam*, viii n. 3. For a brief discussion with bibliography, see Kritzeck, vii–ix; Mérigoux, introduction to Riccoldo da Montedroce, *Contra legem Sarracenorum*, 56–58.

2. Tolan, *Petrus Alfonsi*, 108–10.

3. Panella, "Ricerche su Riccoldo da Monte di Croce."

4. Ana Echevarria, *The Fortress of Faith: The Attitude towards Muslims in Fifteenth-Century Spain* (Leiden: Brill, 1999); Southern, *Western Views*, 83–103; Darío Cabanelas Rodríguez, *Juan de Segovia y el Problema Islámico* (Madrid, 1952).

5. Nancy Bisaha, " 'New Barbarian' or Worthy Adversary? Humanist Constructs of the Ottoman Turks in Fifteenth-Century Italy," in Frasetto and Blanks, eds., *Western Views*, 185–205.

6. For an introduction to the vast bibliography on the link between law and social interaction, see Powell, ed., *Muslims Under Latin Rule*; Gervers and Bikhazi, eds., *Conversion and Continuity*. On the relationship between violence and social coexistence in

fourteenth-century Catalonia, see Nirenberg, *Communities of Violence: Persecution of Minorities in the Middle Ages* (Princeton: Princeton University Press, 1996).

7. Cohen, *Friars and the Jews;* Cohen, "The Muslim Connection, or the Changing Role of the Jew in High Medieval Theology," in Cohen, ed., *From Witness to Witchcraft: Jews and Judaism in Medieval Christian Thought* (Wiesbaden: Harrassowitz, 1996), 141–62.

8. Moore, *Formation of a Persecuting Society.*

9. Nirenberg, *Communities of Violence,* introduction.

10. See Hillenbrand, *The Crusades: Islamic Perspectives.*

11. The twentieth anniversary of the publication of *Orientalism* was the occasion for two retrospectives: Lucy Pick, ed., "Orientalism and Medieval Studies," *Medieval Encounters* 5 (1999):265–357; "Review Essays: *Orientalism* Twenty Years On," *American Historical Review* 105 (2000):1204–49. The notion of an "adolescent" medieval stage of orientalism comes from the latter issue: Kathleen Biddick, "Coming Out of Exile: Dante on the Orient(alism) Express," 1234–49.

12. Tolan, "Using the Middle Ages to Construct Spanish Identity: *Reconquista, Repoblación,* and *Convivencia* in Nineteenth- and Twentieth-Century Spanish Historiography," in Jan Piskorsky, ed., *Die mittelalterliche Ostsiedlung in der Historiographie und Literatur: Vergleichende Untersuchungen vor dem Hintergrund der anderen europäischen interethnischen Kolonisationsvorgänge des Mittelalters* (Poznań: Poznańskie Towarzystwo Przyjaciół Nauk, 2001).

13. Biddick, "Coming Out of Exile," 1248–49.

14. Among the most important works on medieval colonialism are Robert Bartlett, *The Making of Europe: Conquest, Colonization, and Cultural Change, 950–1350* (London: Penguin, 1993); R. Bartlett and A. McKay, eds., *Medieval Frontier Societies* (Oxford: Oxford University Press, 1989); M. Balard and A. Ducellier, eds., *Coloniser au Moyen Age* (Paris: Armand Colin, 1995); M. Balard and A. Ducellier, eds., *Le Partage du monde: Échanges et colonisation dans la Méditerranée médiévale* (Paris: Publications de la Sorbonne, 1998); Jan Piskorsky, ed., *Die mittelalterliche Ostsiedlung in der Historiographie und Literatur.*

15. Medeiros, *L'Occident et l'Afrique,* chap. 9 (esp. 237–38).

Select Bibliography

༄◦᪲◦༄

The following bibliography is not exhaustive. It is meant to provide suggestions for further reading, indicating the most important and most interesting primary sources and modern studies.

General and Comparative Works

HISTORICAL BACKGROUND

Flori, Jean. *La première croisade*. Bruxelles: Complexe, 1992.
————. *Pierre l'ermite et la première croisade*. Paris: Fayard, 1999.
Gervers, Michael, and Ramzi J. Bikhazi, eds. *Conversion and Continuity: Indigenous Christian Communities in Islamic Lands, Eighth to Eighteenth Centuries*. Toronto: Pontifical Institute of Medieval Studies, 1990.
Hillenbrand, Carole. *The Crusades: Islamic Perspectives*. Edinburgh: University of Edinburgh Press, 1999.
Riley-Smith, Jonathan Simon Christopher. *The First Crusade and the Idea of Crusading*. Philadelphia: University of Pennsylvania Press, 1986.
Schatzmiller, Maya, ed. *Crusaders and Muslims in Twelfth-Century Syria*. Leiden, 1993.
Tolan, John, and Philippe Josserand. *Les relations entre les pays d'Islam et le monde latin du milieu du Xème siècle au milieu du XIIIème siècle*. Paris: Bréal, 2000.

CHRISTIAN PERCEPTIONS OF ISLAM

Caspar, Robert, et al. "Bibliographie du dialogue islamo-chrétien." *Islamochristiana*, 1 (1975):125–81; 2 (1976):187–242; 3 (1977):255–86; 4 (1978):247–67; 5 (1979):299–317; 6 (1980):259–99; 7 (1981):299–307; 10 (1984):273–92.
d'Alverny, Marie-Thérèse. *Connaissance de l'Islam dans l'Occident médiévale*. London: Variorum, 1994.
Daniel, Norman. *Islam and the West: The Making of an Image*, revised edition. Oxford: One World, 1993.
de Medeiros, François. *L'Occident et l'Afrique (XIIIe–XVe siècles)*. Paris: Karthala, 1985.
Frasetto, Michael, and David Blanks, eds. *Western Views of Islam in Medieval and Early Modern Europe: Perception of the Other*. New York: St. Martin's Press, 1999.

Said, Edward W. *Orientalism*. New York: Random House, 1978.

Santiago Otero, Horacio, ed. *Diálogo filosófico-religioso entre cristianismo, judaísmo, e islamismo durante la edad media en la península iberica*. Turnhout: Brepols, 1994.

Simon, Larry, ed. *Iberia and the Mediterranean World of the Middle Ages: Studies in Honor of Robert I. Burns*. 2 vols. Leiden: Brill, 1995.

Southern, Richard. *Western Views of Islam in the Middle Ages*. Cambridge, Mass., 1962.

Tolan, John, ed. *Medieval Christian Perceptions of Islam: A Book of Essays*. New York: Garland, 1996.

Eastern Christian Reactions to Islam

PRIMARY SOURCES

John of Damascus [Jean Damascène]. *Écrits sur l'Islam*. Trans. (into French) Raymond Le Coz. Paris: Cerf, 1992.

———. *John of Damascus on Islam: The "Heresy of the Ishmaelites."* Trans. Daniel Sahas. Leiden: Brill, 1972.

———. *Works* (Die Schriften des Johannes von Damaskos). Ed. P. Bonifatius Kotter. 5 vols. Berlin, 1969–81.

Passion of 'Abd al-Masîh. Ed. and trans. Sidney H. Griffith. "The Arabic Account of 'Abd al-Masîh an-Naǧrânî al-Ghassânî." *Le Muséon* 98 (1985):331–74.

Passion of Anthony Ruwah. Ed. and trans. Ignace Dick. "La passion arabe de S. Antoine Ruwah néo-martyr de Damas (+ 25 déc. 799)." *Le Muséon* 74 (1961):109–33.

Risâlat al-Kindî. Trans. (into French) Georges Tartar. *Dialogue islamo-chrétien sous le Calife al-Ma'mûn (813–834): Les épîtres d'al-Hashimî et d'al-Kindî*. Paris: Nouvelles Éditions Latines, 1985.

The Seventh Century in the West-Syrian Chronicles. Ed. and trans. Andrew Palmer, Sebastian Brock, and Robert Hoyland. Liverpool: Liverpool University Press, 1993.

Theophanes. *The Chronicle of Theophanes the Confessor*. Trans. Cyril Mango and Roger Scott. Oxford: Clarendon Press, 1997.

SECONDARY

Brock, S. "Syriac Views of Emergent Islam." In G. H. A. Juynboll, ed., *Studies on the First Century of Islamic Society*, 9–21. Carbondale, Ill., 1982.

Ducellier, Alain. *Chrétiens d'Orient et Islam au Moyen Age*. Paris: Armand Colin, 1996.

Griffith, Sidney. "Anastasios of Sinai, the *Hodegos*, and the Muslims." *Greek Orthodox Theological Review* 32 (1987):341–58.

———. "Theodore Abû Qurrah's Arabic Tract on the Christian Practice of Venerating Images." *Journal of the American Oriental Society* 105 (1985):66–67.

———. "The View of Islam from the Monasteries of Palestine in the Early 'Abbâsid Period: Theodore Abû Qurrah and the *Summa Theologiae Arabica*." *Islam and Christian-Muslim Relations* 7 (1996):9–28.

Kaegi, Walter. *Byzantium and the Early Islamic Conquests*. Cambridge: Cambridge University Press, 1992.

———. "Initial Byzantine Reactions to the Arab Conquest."*Church History* 38 (1969):139–49.

Khoury, Adel-Théodore. "Apologétique byzantine contre l'Islam (VIIIᵉ–XIIIᵉ siècle)." *Proche-Orient Chrétien* 29 (1979):241–305; 30 (1980):132–74; 32 (1981):14–49.

———. *Les théologiens byzantins et l'Islam* 1: *Textes et auteurs* (*VIIIᵉ–XIIIᵉ s.*). Louvain, 1969.

———. *Les théologiens byzantins et l'Islam* 2: *Polémique byzantine contre l'Islam* (*VIIᵉ–XIIIᵉ s.*). Leiden: Brill, 1972.

Levtzion, Nehemia. "Conversion to Islam in Syria and Palestine and the Survival of Christian Communities." In Gervers and Bikhazi, eds., *Conversion and Continuity*, 289–311.

Martinez, F. J. "Eastern Christian Apocalyptic in the Early Muslim Period: Pseudo-Methodius and Pseudo-Athanasius." Ph.D. diss, Catholic University of America, 1985.

Moorhead, John. "The Earliest Christian Theological Responses to Islam."*Religion* 11 (1981):265–74.

———. "The Monophysite Response to the Arab Invasions."*Byzantion* 51 (1981):579–91.

Reinink, G. J. "Pseudo-Methodius: A Concept of History in Response to the Rise of Islam."In Averil Cameron and Lawrence Conrad, eds., *The Byzantine and Early Islamic Near East*, 1:149–87. Princeton: Darwin Press, 1992.

Samir, Samir Khalil, and Jørgen S. Nielsen, eds. *Christian Arabic Apologetics during the Abbasid Period, 750–1258*. Leiden: Brill, 1994.

Reactions to Islam in the Latin World before 1000

PRIMARY

Aimoin. *Translatio sanctorum martyrum Georgii monachi, Aurelii et Nathaliae*. AASS Iul. 6:459–69; PL 115:939–60.

Bede. *De locis sanctis*. Ed. J. Fraipont. CCSL 175 (1965), 251–80.

———. *Ecclesiastical History of the English People*. Trans. L. Sherley-Price. London: Penguin, 1955, 1990.

———. *Ecclesiastical History of the English People* (Historia ecclesiastica gentis Anglorum). Ed. Carolus Plummer. 2 vols. Oxford: Oxford University Press, 1896, 1975.

Chronicle of Fredegar: The Fourth Book of the Chronicle of Fredegar and Its Continuators. Trans. J. M. Wallace-Hadrill. London, 1960.

Chroniques Asturiennes (*fin IXᵉ siècle*). Ed. and trans. (into French) Yves Bonnaz. Paris: CNRS, 1987.

Crónica mozárabe de 754. Ed. José Eduardo Lopez Pereira. Zaragoza: Anubar, 1980.

La Crónica profética. Universidad de Oviedo, Publicaciones del Departamento de Historia Medieval 11 (1985).

SECONDARY

Collins, Roger. *The Arab Conquest of Spain, 710–797*. Oxford: Oxford University Press, 1989.

Coope, Jessica A. *The Martyrs of Córdoba: Community and Family Conflict in an Age of Mass Conversion.* Lincoln: University of Nebraska Press, 1995.

Millet Gérard, Dominique. *Chrétiens mozarabes et culture islamique dans l'Espagne des VIIIᵉ–IXᵉ siècles.* Paris: Études Augustiniennes, 1984.

Rotter, Ekkehart. *Abendland und Sarazenen: Das okzidentale Araberbild und seine Entstehung im Frühmittelalter.* Berlin: Walter de Gruyter, 1986.

Wallace-Hadrill, J. M. "Bede's Europe." In Wallace-Hadrill, *Early Medieval History,* 60–75. Oxford: Oxford University Press, 1975.

———. "Christian Views of Islam in Early Medieval Spain." In Tolan, ed., *Medieval Christian Perceptions of Islam,* 85–108.

———. *Conquerors and Chroniclers of Medieval Spain.* Liverpool: Liverpool University Press, 1990.

———. "The Earliest Latin Lives of Muhammad." In Gervers and Bikhazi, eds., *Conversion and Continuity,* 89–101.

Saracen Idolatry in European Ideologies

PRIMARY

Chanson d'Antioche. Ed. Suzanne Duparc-Quioc. Paris: Librairie orientaliste Paul Geuthner, 1977.

Chanson de Roland. Ed. Ian Short. Paris: Livre de Poche (Lettres gothiques), 1990.

——— (The song of Roland). Trans. Gerard J. Braut. University Park: Pennsylvania State University Press, 1978.

Die Chronik von Karl dem Grossen und Roland: Der lateinische Pseudo-Turpin in den Handschriften aus Aachen und Andernach. Ed. Hans-Wilhelm Klein. Munich: W. Fink, 1986.

Hrotsvitha of Gandersheim. *Opera.* Ed. H. Homeyer. Munich: MGH, 1970.

Jean Bodel. *Jeu de Saint Nicolas.* Ed. Albert Henry. Geneva: Droz, 1981.

La Chanson de Jérusalem. Ed. Nigel Thorpe. Vol. 6 in *The Old French Crusade Cycle.* Tuscaloosa: University of Alabama Press, 1992.

Passio Thiemonis Archiepiscopi. MGH SS 11:51–62.

Petrus Tudebodus. *Historia de Hierosolymitano itinere.* Ed. J. Hill and L. Hill. Paris: Librairie orientaliste Paul Geuthner, 1977.

———. Trans. (into English) J. Hill and L. Hill. Philadelphia: American Philosophical Society, 1974.

Raymond d'Aguilers. *Liber.* Ed. J. Hill and L. Hill. Paris: Librairie orientaliste Paul Geuthner, 1969.

———. Trans. (into English) J. Hill and L. Hill. Philadelphia: American Philosophical Society, 1968.

SECONDARY

Albert-Llorca, Marlène, and Jean-Pierre Albert. "Mahomet, la Vierge, et la frontière." *Annales* 50 (1995):855–86.

Bancourt, Paul. "Les Musulmans dans les chansons de geste du Cycle du roi." 2 vols. Ph.D. diss., l'Université de Provence, Aix-en-Provence, 1982.

Camille, Michael. *The Gothic Idol: Ideology and Image-Making in Medieval Art*. Cambridge: Cambridge University Press, 1989.

Cole, Penny J. "'O God, the Heathen Have Come into Your Inheritance' (Ps. 78.1): The Theme of Religious Pollution in Crusade Documents, 1095–1188."In Maya Schatzmiller, ed., *Crusaders and Muslims in Twelfth-Century Syria*, 84–111. Leiden: Brill, 1993.

Daniel, Norman. *Heroes and Saracens: An Interpretation of the Chansons de Geste*. Edinburgh, 1984.

Duparc-Quioc, Suzanne. *La Chanson d'Antioche: Étude critique*. Paris: Librairie orientaliste Paul Geuthner, 1978.

Flori, Jean. "La caricature de l'Islam dans l'Occident médiéval: Origine et signification de quelques stéréotypes concernant l'Islam." *Aevum* 2 (1992):245–56.

———. "Oriens horribilis": Tares et défauts de l'Orient dans les sources relatives à la première croisade." *Orient und Okzident in der Kultur des Mittelalters: Monde oriental et monde occidental dans la culture médiévale. Wodan: Greifswalder Beiträge zum Mittelalter* 68 (1997):45–56.

Loutchitskaja, Svetlana. "Barbarae nationes: Les peuples musulmans dans les chroniques de la Première croisade."In Michel Balard, ed., *Autour de la première croisade*, 99–107. Paris, 1996.

———. "L'image des musulmans dans les chroniques des croisades."*Le Moyen Age* 105 (1999):717–35

Paull, Michael R. "The Figure of Mahomet in Middle English Literature." Ph.D. diss., University of North Carolina, 1969.

Muhammad as Heresiarch in the Twelfth Century

PRIMARY

Adelphus. *Vita Machometi*. Ed. B. Bischoff. "Ein Leben Mohammeds (Adelphus?) (Zwölftes Jahrhundert)." *Anecdota Novissima: Texte des vierten bis sechzenten Jahrhundert* (1984):106–22.

Alan of Lille. *Contra paganos* [part 4 of *De fide catholica*]. Ed. Marie-Thérèse d'Alverny. *Cahiers de Fanjeaux* 18 (1983):325–50.

Embrico of Mainz. *Vita Mahumeti*. In Guy Cambier, ed., *Collection Latomus* 52. Brussels: Latomus, 1961.

Gautier de Compiègne. *Otia de Machomete*. In R. B. C. Huygens, ed., *Alexandre du Pont, Roman de Mahomet*. Ed. Y. G. Lepage. Paris: Kliensieck, 1977.

Guibert de Nogent. *The Deeds of God through the Franks*. Trans. Robert Levine. Woodbridge: Boydell, 1997.

———. *Dei gesta per Francos*. Ed. R. B. C. Huygens. CCCM 127A (1996).

Peter of Cluny [Petrus Venerabilis]. *Liber contra secta, sive haeresim Saracenorum* and *Summa totius haeresis Saracenorum*. In Reinhold Glei, ed. and trans. (into German), *Schriften zum Islam*. Corpus Islamo-Christianum, series latina 1. Alternberg: CIS-Verlag, 1985.

Petrus Alfonsi [Pedro Alfonso]. *Diálogo contra los Judíos* (Dialogi contra Iudaeos). Latin edition by Klaus-Peter Mieth; trans. (into Spanish) Esperanza Ducay. Colección Larumbe n°9. Zaragoza: Instituto de Estudios Altoaragoneses, 1996.

SECONDARY

Barkai, Ron. *Cristianos y Musulmanes en la España medieval.* Madrid: Rialp, 1984.

Burman, Thomas E. *Religious Polemic and the Intellectual History of the Mozarabs.* Leiden: Brill, 1994.

———. *"Tafsīr* and Translation: Robert of Ketton, Mark of Toledo, and Traditional Arabic Qur'ān Exegesis."*Speculum* 73 (1998):703–32.

———. *"Tathlîth al-wahdânîyah* and the Twelfth-Century Andalusian-Christian Approach to Islam." In Tolan, ed., *Medieval Christian Perceptions of Islam,* 109–28.

Iogna-Prat, Dominique. *Ordonner et exclure: Cluny et la société chrétienne face à l'hérésie, au judaïsme et à l'islam, 1000–1050.* Paris: Aubier, 1998.

———. *Order and Exclusion.* Ithaca: Cornell University Press, 2001.

Kritzeck, James. *Peter the Venerable and Islam.* Princeton: Princeton University Press, 1964.

Levine, Robert. "Satiric Vulgarity in Guibert de Nogent's *Gesta Dei per Francos."Rhetorica* 7 (1989):261–73.

Moore, Robert I. "Guibert of Nogent and His World." In Henry Mayr Harting, ed., *Studies in Medieval History Presented to R. H. C. Davis.* London, 1985.

Tolan, John. "Anti-Hagiography: Embrico of Mainz's *Vita Mahumeti." Journal of Medieval History* 22 (1996):25–41.

———. "Peter the Venerable on the 'Diabolical Heresy of the Saracens.' "In Alberto Ferreiro, ed., *The Devil, Heresy, and Witchcraft in the Middle Ages: Essays in Honor of Jeffrey B. Russell,* 345–67. Leiden: Brill, 1998.

———. *Petrus Alfonsi and His Medieval Readers.* Gainesville: University Press of Florida, 1993.

Urvoy, Dominique. "La pensée religieuse des Mozarabes face à l'Islam." *Traditio* 39 (1983):419–32.

Muslims in the Ideologies of Christian Spain, 1100–1300

PRIMARY

Alfonso el Sabio. *Las siete partidas.* Madrid: Real Academia de la Historia, 1807, 1972.

———. *Primera crónica general de España* [or *Estoria de España*]. Ed. Ramón Menéndez Pidal. Madrid: Gredos, 1955.

Jaume I. *Llibre dels feyts.* Ed. Ferran Soldevilla. Barcelona: Edicions 62, 1982.

Lucas de Tuy. *Chronicon mundi.* Ed. A. Schott. *Hispaniae illustratae* 4 (1608):1–119.

Rodericus Ximenius de Rada [Rodrigo Jiménez de Rada]. *Historia de rebus Hispanie siue historia gothica.* CCCM 72 (1987).

Vidal mayor. Facsimile edition. Huesca: Diputación Provincial, 1989.

SECONDARY

Boswell, John. *The Royal Treasure: Muslim Communities in the Crown of Aragon in the Fourteenth Century.* New Haven: Yale University Press 1977.

Bramon, D. *Contra moros i jueus: Formació i estratègia d'unes discriminacions al país valencià.* Valencia: Eliseu Climent, 1981.

Burns, Robert I. *Islam Under the Crusaders: Colonial Survival in the Thirteenth-Century Kingdom of Valencia.* Princeton: Princeton University Press, 1973.

——. *Moors and Crusaders in Mediterranean Spain.* London: Variorum, 1978.

——. *Muslims, Christians, and Jews in the Crusader Kingdom of Valencia.* Cambridge: Cambridge University Press, 1984.

Lourie, Elena. *Crusade and Colonisation.* Aldershot: Variorum, 1990.

Nirenberg, David. *Communities of Violence: Persecution of Minorities in the Middle Ages.* Princeton: Princeton University Press, 1996.

O'Callaghan, Joseph. *The Cortes of Castile-León.* Philadelphia: University of Pennsylvania Press, 1989.

Powell, James, ed. *Muslims under Latin Rule, 1100–1300.* Princeton: Princeton University Press, 1990.

The Crusades and the Mongols in Christian Thought, 1187–1291

PRIMARY

Jacques de Vitry. *Historia occidentalis.* Ed. J. F. Hinnesbusch. Fribourg: University Press, 1972.

——. *Lettres de Jaques de Vitry, 1160/70–1240, évêque de Saint-Jean d'Acre.* Ed. R. B. C. Huygens. Leiden: Brill, 1960, 2000.

Jean de Joinville. *Vie de Saint Louis.* Ed. J. Monfrin. Paris: Garnier, 1995.

——. Trans. (into English) and ed. M. Shaw. In *Chronicles of the Crusades,* 161–353. London: Penguin, 1963.

Mission to Asia. Trans. Dawson Christopher. New York: Harper and Row, 1966; reprint Toronto: University of Toronto Press, 1987.

Oliver of Paderborn. *The Capture of Damietta.* Trans (into English) John J. Gavigan. Philadelphia: University of Pennsylvania Press, 1948; reprint New York, 1980.

——. *Epistola* and *Historia damiatina.* In O. Hoogeweg, ed., *Die Schriften des Kölner Domscholasters, spätern Bischofs von Paderborn und Kardinal-Bischofs von S. Sabina Oliverus. Bibliothek des litterarischen Vereins in Stuttgart* 202 (1894).

William of Tripoli [Wilhelm von Tripolis]. *Notitia de Machometo: De statu Sarracenorum.* Ed. Peter Engels. Corpus Islamo-Christianum, Series Latina. Würzburg, 1992.

SECONDARY

Cipollone, Giulio. *Cristianità-Islam: Cattività e liberazione in nome di dio.* Rome: Editrice Pontificia Università Gregoriana, 1992.

Cole, Penny J. *The Preaching of the Crusades to the Holy Land, 1095–1270*. Cambridge, Mass.: Medieval Academy of America, 1991.

Muldoon, J. *Popes, Lawyers, and Infidels: The Church and the Non-Christian World, 1250–1550*. Philadelphia: University of Pennsylvania Press, 1979.

Richard, Jean. *Croisés, missionaires, et voyageurs: Les perspectives orientales du monde latin médiéval.* London: Variorum, 1983.

———. *La Papauté et les missions d'orient au moyen âge (XIIIᵉ–XVᵉ siècles)*. Rome: École Française de Rome, 1977.

———. *Orient et Occident au Moyen Âge: Contacts et relations (XIIᵉ–XVᵉ s.)*. London: Variorum, 1976.

Setton, Kenneth Meyer. *The Papacy and the Levant, 1204–1571*. Philadelphia: American Philosophical Society, 1976.

Siberry, Elizabeth. *Criticism of Crusading, 1095–1274*. Oxford: Oxford University Press, 1985.

Missionaries to Islam, Thirteenth and Fourteenth Centuries

PRIMARY

Bacon, Roger. *Opus maius*. Ed. J. Bridges. 3 vols. London, 1900.

———. *Opus maius pars septima seu moralis philosophia*. Ed. Eugenio Massa. Turin, 1953.

Bonaventure. *Legenda maior. Analecta franciscana* 10 (Florence, 1926).

———. *Opera omnia*. 10 vols. Florence, 1882–1902.

Francis of Assisi. *Francis and Clare: The Complete Works*. Ed. and trans. Regis Armstrong and Ignatius Brady. New York, 1982.

Ramón Llull. *Doctor Illuminatus: A Ramon Llull Reader*. Ed. and trans. A. Bonner. Princeton: Princeton University Press, 1993.

———. *Obres originals del Illuminat Doctor Mestre Ramon Llull*. 21 vols. Mallorca, 1906–50.

———. *Selected Works of Ramon Llull*. Trans. A. Bonner. 2 vols. Princeton: Princeton University Press, 1985.

Ramon de Penyafort. *Summae*. In Xavier Ochoa and Aloysius Diez, eds., *Universa Bibliotheca Iuris*. 3 vols. Rome, 1976–78.

Ramon Martí. *De seta Machometi o de origine, progressu, et fine Machometi et quadruplici reprobatione prophetiae eius*. Ed. and trans. (into Spanish) Josep Hernando i Delgado. *Acta historica et archaeologica medievalia* 4 (1983):9–51.

———. *Explanatio simboli Apostolorum*. Ed. J. March y Battles. "En Ramon Martí y la seva *Explanatio simboli Apostolorum.*" *Annuari de l'Institut d'Esudis Catalans* (1908):443–96.

Riccoldo da Montecroce. *Epistolae V de perditione Acconis, 1291*. Ed. R. Röhricht. *Archives de l'orient latin* 2 (1884):258–96.

———. *Libelli ad nationes orientales*. Electronic edition of Latin text with introduction by Kurt Jensen (http://www.ou.dk/hum/kvj/riccoldo/).

———. *Libellus contra legem Saracenorum*. Ed. J. Mérigoux. *Memorie domenicane,* n.s. 17 (1986):1–144.

———. *Pérégrination: En terre sainte et au Proche Orient et lettres sur la chute de Saint-Jean d'Acre*. Ed. and trans. (into French) René Kappler. Paris: Honoré Champion, 1997.

Thomas Aquinas. *De rationibus fidei contra Saracenos, Graecos et Armenos ad Cantorem Antiochenum: Reasons for the Faith against the Muslims (and One Objection of the Greeks and Armenians) to the Cantor of Antioch.* Trans. Joseph Kenney. *Islamochristiana* 22 (1996):31–52.

———. *Summa contra gentiles.* Trans. English Dominican Friars. London: Burns, Oates, and Washbourne, 1924.

SECONDARY

Altaner, Berthold. *Die Dominikanermissionen des 13. Jahrhunderts: Forschungen zur Geschichte der kirchlichen Unionen und der Mohammedaner und Heidenmission des Mittelalters.* Habelschwerdt, 1924.

Beattie, Pamela Drost. " '*Pro exaltatione sanctae fidei catholicae*': Mission and Crusade in the Writings of Ramon Llull." In Simon, ed., *Iberia and the Mediterranean World,* 113–29.

Burman, Thomas. "The Influence of the *Apology of al-Kindî* and *Contrarietas alfolica* on Ramon Lull's Late Religious Polemics, 1305–1313."*Medieval Studies* 53 (1991): 197–228.

Chazan, Robert. *Barcelona and Beyond: The Disputation of 1263 and Its Aftermath.* Berkeley: University of California Press, 1992.

———. *Daggers of Faith: Thirteenth-Century Christian Missionizing and Jewish Response,* Berkeley: University of California Press, 1989.

Cortabarría Beitia, Angel. "Fuentes árabes del *Pugio fidei* de Ramón Martí."*Ciencia tomista* 112 (1985):581–98.

———. "La connaissance de l'Islam chez Raymond Lulle et Raymond Martin, O.P.: Parallèle."*Cahiers de Fanjeaux* 22 (1987), *Raymond Lulle et le Pays d'Oc,* 33–55.

———. "La connaissance des textes arabes chez Raymond Martin, O.P., et sa position en face de l'Islam."*Cahiers de Fanjeaux* 18 (1983), *Islam et Chrétiens du Midi*: 279–324.

Courcelles, Dominique de. *La parole risquée de Raymond Lulle.* Paris: Vrin, 1993.

Daniel, E. R. *The Franciscan Concept of Mission in the High Middle Ages.* Lexington: University Press of Kentucky, 1975.

Golubovich, G. *Biblioteca bio-bibliografica della terra santa e dell' oriente francescano.* Florence, 1906–13.

Hernando i Delgado, Josep. "De nuevo sobre la obra antiislámica attribuida a Ramón Martí, dominico catalán des siglo XIII."*Sharq-al-Andalus* 8 (1991):97–108.

———. "Le 'De seta Machometi' du cod. 46 d'Osma, oeuvre de Raymond Martin (Ramón Martí)."*Cahiers de Fanjeaux* 18 (1983), *Islam et Chrétiens du Midi,* 351–71.

Hillgarth, J. N. *Ramon Lull and Lullism in Fourteenth-Century France.* Oxford: Oxford University Press, 1971.

Johnston, Mark D. "Ramon Lull and the Compulsory Evangelization of Jews and Muslims." In Simon, ed., *Iberia and the Mediterranean World*, 3–37.

Koningsveld, P. Sjoerd van, and G. A. Wiegers. "The Polemical Works of Muhammad al-Qaysî (fl. 1309) and Their Circulation in Arabic and Aljmiado among the Mudejars in the Fourteenth Century."*Al-Qantara: Revista de estudios árabes* 15 (1994):163–99.

Lavajo, J. C. "The Apologetical Method of Ramon Marti, According to the Problematic of Ramon Lull."*Islamochristiana* 11 (1985):155–76.

Lohr, Charles H. "Christianus arabicus, cuius nomen Raimundus Lullus."*Freiburger Zeitschrift für Philosophie und Theologie* 31 (1984):57–88.

———. "Ramon Lull and Thirteenth-Century Religious Dialogue."In Santiago Otero, ed., *Diálogo filosófico-religioso*, 117–29.

———. "Ramon Llull, Liber Alquindi and Liber Telif."*Estudios Lulianos* 12 (1968): 145–60.

Roncaglia, Martiniano. *I Francescani in oriente durante le crociate (sec. XIII)*. Vol. 4, part 1 of *Biblioteca bio-bibliografica della terra santa e dell' oriente francescano*. Cairo, 1954.

Vázquez Janeiro, Isaac. "I Francescani e il dialogo con gli ebrei e saraceni nei secoli XIII–XV." *Antonianum* 65 (1990):533–49.

Index

❧❦❧